CONTENTS

The ***Michelin maps*** *you will need are no* **989** *- France: main roads, and, with this guide:*

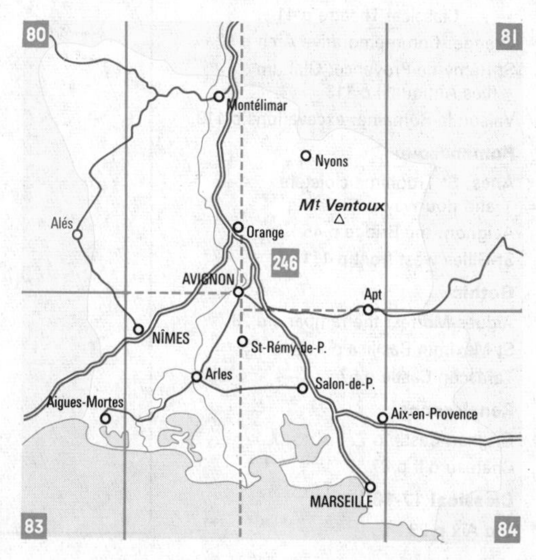

Michelin maps *are kept up to date - never travel with last year's map*

OUTSTANDING SIGHTS

★★★

Ardèche Valley
  and the Haute Corniche pp 35-39
Les Baux-de-Provence p 54
Orgnac Aven p 98
The Vaucluse Fountain p 126

★★

Nesque Georges p 91
Pont-d'Arc p 37
Donzère Defile p 102
Tanargue Massif p 123
Marseilles Old Port p 83
Nîmes, Jardin de la Fontaine p 94
Marzal Aven p 38
Chaussée des Géants near
  Roussillon p 34
Rustrel Colorado p 35
The Concluses p 52

SPLENDID VIEWPOINTS

★★★

Les Baux p 33
Cape Canaille p 67
Croix de Provence p 110
Marseilles: N.-D.-de-la-Garde p 83
Mourre Nègre p 79
St-Pilon p 108
Mount Ventoux Summit p 129

★★

The Caume p 33
Chenavari Peak p 90
Lançon p 59
Marcoule: Belvedere p 106
Meyrand Pass p 123

MAJOR MONUMENTS

★★★

Roman

Pont du Gard p 99
Nîmes: Amphitheatre p 93
  Maison Carrée p 93
Orange: Classical Theatre p 96

Gothic

Avignon: Palace of the Popes pp 45-47

★★

Roman

Arles: Amphitheatre p 41
  Classical Theatre p 41
Orange: Commemorative Arch p 97
St-Rémy-de-Provence: Glanum
  (Les Antiques) p 113
Vaison-la-Romaine: excavations p 119

Romanesque

Arles: St-Trophime cloisters
  and doorway p 42
Avignon: the Bridge p 45
St-Gilles west front p 111

Gothic

Aigues-Mortes: the ramparts p 28
St-Maximin Basilica p 112
Tarascon Castle p 57

Renaissance

Grignan Castle p 77
Château d'If p 87

Classical 17-18C

Old Aix p 29

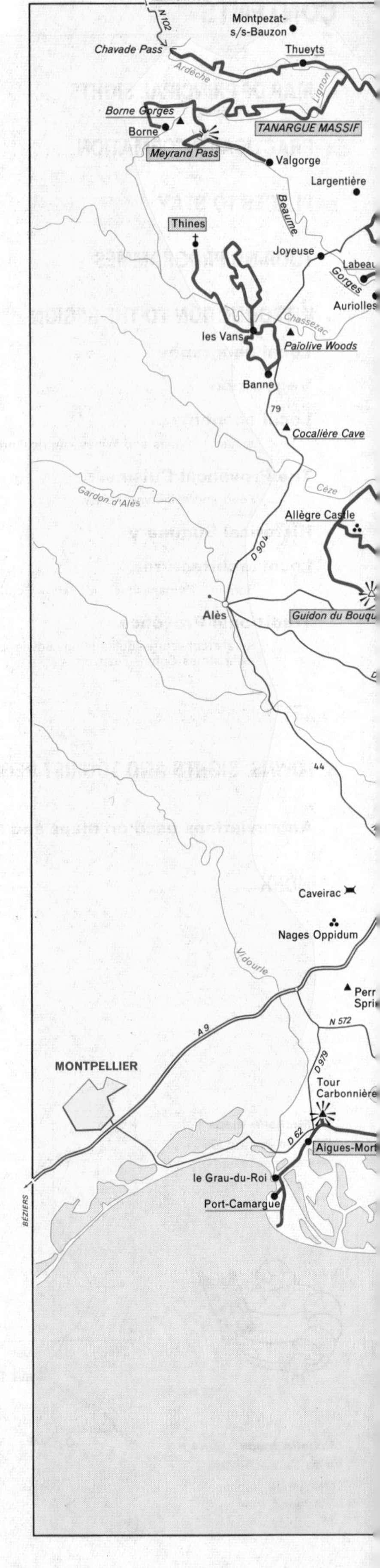

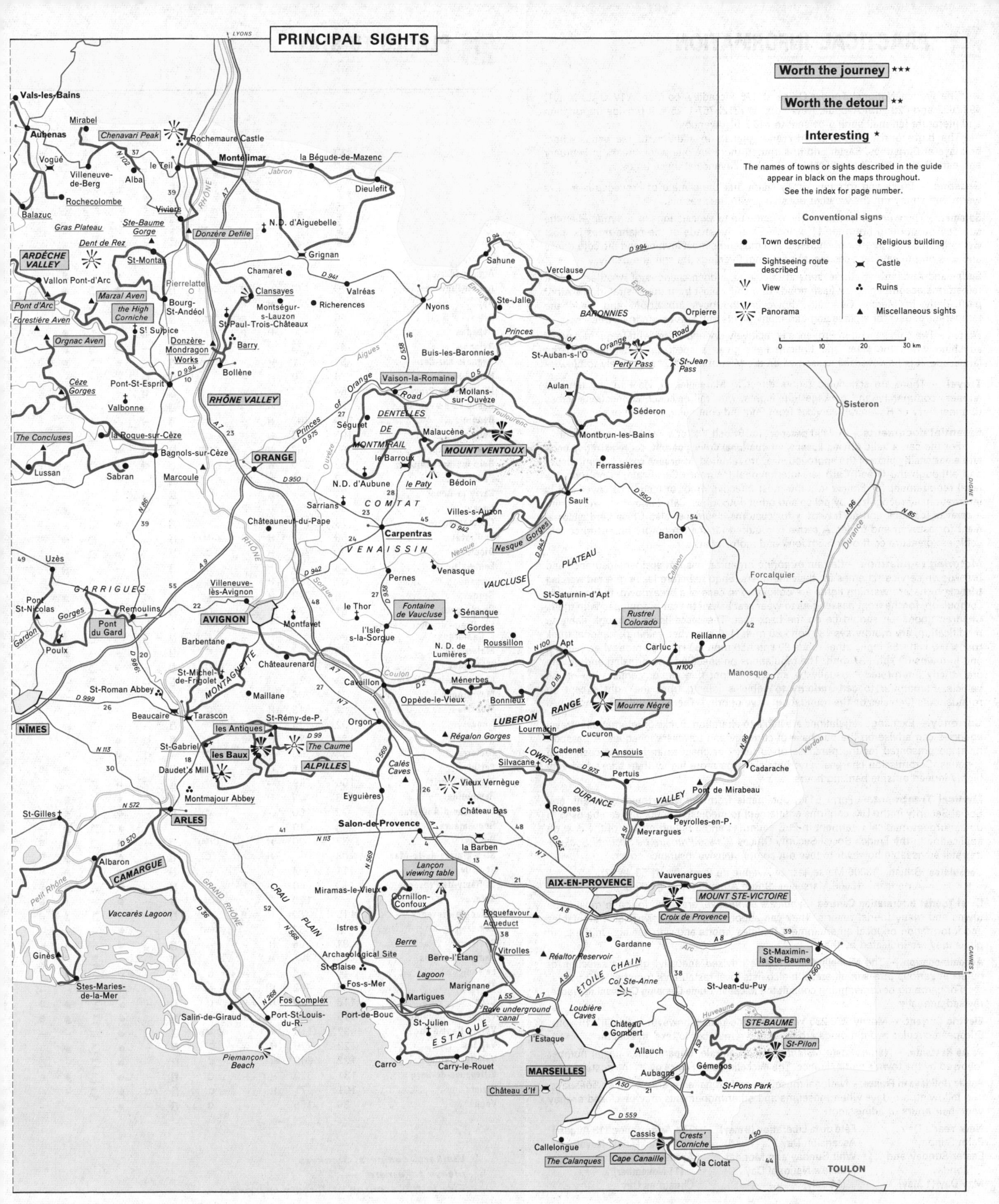

PRINCIPAL SIGHTS
Worth the journey ★★★
Worth the detour ★★
Interesting ★
The names of towns or sights described in the guide appear in black on the maps throughout.
See the index for page number.
Conventional signs
Town described
Sightseeing route described
View
Panorama
Religious building
Castle
Ruins
Miscellaneous sights
0 10 20 30 km
LYONS
Vals-les-Bains
Mirabel
Aubenas
Chenavari Peak
Rochemaure Castle
Vogüé
le Teil
Montélimar
la Bégude-de-Mazenc
Jabron
Villeneuve-de-Berg
Alba
Dieulefit
Rochecolombe
Balazuc
Viviers
RHÔNE
N.D. d'Aiguebelle
Gras Plateau
Ste-Baume Gorge
Donzère Defile
Dent de Rez
ARDÈCHE VALLEY
St-Montan
Grignan
Sahune
Verclause
Vallon Pont-d'Arc
Chamaret
Pierrelatte
Marzal Aven
Clansayes
Valréas
Nyons
Ste-Jalle
Eygues
Pont d'Arc
Bourg-St-Andéol
Montségur-s-Lauzon
Richerences
Ennuye
BARONNIES
Orpierre
Forestière Aven
the High Corniche
St-Paul-Trois-Châteaux
St Sulpice
Orgnac Aven
Donzère-Mondragon Works
Barry
Princes of Orange Road
Buis-les-Baronnies
St-Auban-s-l'O
Perty Pass
St-Jean Pass
Cèze Gorges
Bollène
Aigues
Pont-St-Esprit
Vaison-la-Romaine
Mollans-sur-Ouvèze
Aulan
Sisteron
Valbonne
RHÔNE VALLEY
Séderon
Séguret
DENTELLES DE MONTMIRAIL
Toulourenc
The Concluses
la Roque-sur-Cèze
Malaucène
Montbrun-les-Bains
Bagnols-sur-Cèze
ORANGE
MOUNT VENTOUX
le Barroux
Ferrassières
Lussan
Sabran
Marcoule
N.D. d'Aubune
le Paty
Bédoin
Sault
Ouvèze
COMTAT
Sarrians
Villes-s-Auzon
Châteauneuf-du-Pape
Carpentras
Nesque Gorges
Banon
VENAISSIN
Nesque
VAUCLUSE PLATEAU
Durance
Uzès
Venasque
GARRIGUES
Pernes
Forcalquier
Calavon
Villeneuve-lès-Avignon
Pont St-Nicolas
Gorges
Remoulins
Sorgue
le Thor
Fontaine de Vaucluse
St-Saturnin-d'Apt
Gardon
Pont du Gard
AVIGNON
Montfavet
Sénanque
Rustrel Colorado
Poulx
l'Isle-s-la-Sorgue
Gordes
Barbentane
N.D. de Lumières
Roussillon
Reillanne
Apt
Carluc
St-Michel-de-Frigolet
MONTAGNETTE
Châteaurenard
Coulon
Manosque
St-Roman Abbey
Cavaillon
Ménerbes
Maillane
Oppède-le-Vieux
Bonnieux
NÎMES
Beaucaire
Tarascon
St-Rémy-de-P.
les Antiques
Orgon
LUBERON RANGE
Mourre Nègre
Régalon Gorges
Lourmarin
Cucuron
St-Gabriel
les Baux
The Caume
Cadenet
Ansouis
Verdon
Daudet's Mill
ALPILLES
Calès Caves
Silvacane
LOWER DURANCE VALLEY
Pertuis
Cadarache
Vieux Vernègue
Pont de Mirabeau
Montmajour Abbey
Eyguières
Château Bas
Rognes
St-Gilles
ARLES
Salon-de-Provence
Peyrolles-en-P.
Meyrargues
la Barben
Albaron
CAMARGUE
Lançon viewing table
CRAU PLAIN
Petit Rhône
GRAND RHÔNE
AIX-EN-PROVENCE
Vauvenargues
Miramas-le-Vieux
MOUNT STE-VICTOIRE
Vaccarès Lagoon
Cornillon-Confoux
Roquefavour Aqueduct
Croix de Provence
Arc
Istres
Berre
Gardanne
St-Maximin-la Ste-Baume
Ginès
Archaeological Site
St-Blaise
Berre-l'Etang
Vitrolles
Réaltor Reservoir
ÉTOILE CHAIN
CANNES
Lagoon
Fos-s-Mer
Col Ste-Anne
Stes-Maries-de-la-Mer
Fos Complex
Martigues
Marignane
St-Jean-du-Puy
Salin-de-Giraud
Port-St-Louis-du-R.
Port-de-Bouc
Rove underground canal
Loubière Caves
Huveaune
St-Julien
ESTAQUE
Château Gombert
STE-BAUME
l'Estaque
Allauch
St-Pilon
Piémançon Beach
Carro
Carry-le-Rouet
MARSEILLES
Aubagne
Gémenos
St-Pons Park
Château d'If
Cassis
Crests' Corniche
Callelongue
The Calanques
Cape Canaille
la Ciotat
TOULON
DIGNE

PRACTICAL INFORMATION

The French National Tourist Office at 178 Piccadilly, London W1V OAL, ☎ (01) 499 7622 and 628 Fifth Avenue, New York, ☎ (212) 757-1125 will provide information and literature (all mail should be sent to 610 Fifth Avenue).

The high tourist season is July and August; in addition to the usual school holidays at Christmas, Easter and in summer, there are one week breaks in February and early November; it is advisable to book in advance at these times.

Seasons. – Poets and romantics may claim that the climate of Provence is always warm and sunny but the weather does vary with the seasons.

Summer. – The weather is most likely to come up to expectations in summer when the sun can be burning hot after 11 o'clock. Then the shade of the plane trees is most welcome, the cool interior of churches and museums most inviting and the cold drinks and ices on the cafe terraces most appetizing. Evenings are still and balmy.

Spring and Autumn. – Both seasons are liable to sudden changes of weather; violent rainstorms accompanied by flash floods or a chilly blast from the Mistral (north wind) particularly in March. Generally, however, the days are bright and clear, the temperature ideal for sightseeing and many plants and shrubs are in flower.

Winter. – The cold season in Provence is relatively dry and warm with frequent days of sunshine when the clear and brilliant light gives a spectacular definition to the landscape. It is however the season when the Mistral *(p 101)* is most likely to blow.

Travel. – There are scheduled flights direct to Marseilles or via Paris by national airlines; commercial and package tour flights, with rail or coach connections; cross Channel ferry or Hovercraft services from England continuing by train or car.

Essential documents. – A valid **passport** (or British Visitor's Passport) is required.

For the car, a valid **driving licence, international driving permit, car registration book** and a **nationality plate** of the approved size, are required. **Insurance cover** is compulsory and although the Green Card (an International Insurance Certificate) is no longer a legal requirement for France it is the most effective proof of insurance cover and is internationally recognized by police and other authorities. Caravan owners will require a **caravan log-book** and an **inventory** for customs clearance; also **Green Card endorsement** for caravan and trailer. A **carnet** is required for the temporary import of certain vehicles: pleasure craft over 5.5m long and motor boats.

Motoring regulations. – Certain motoring organizations run accident insurance and breakdown service schemes for their members. Enquire before leaving. A **red warning triangle** or hazard warning lights are obligatory in case of a breakdown. In France it is compulsory for the front passengers to wear **seat belts** if the car is equipped with them. Children under ten should be on the back seat. The **speed limits,** although liable to modification, are motorways 130 kph - 80 mph (110 kph when raining); national trunk roads 110 kph - 68 mph; other roads 90 kph - 56 mph (80 kph - 50 mph when raining) and in towns 60 kph - 37 mph. The regulations on speeding and drinking and driving are strictly interpreted – usually by an on the spot fine and/or confiscation of the vehicle. Remember to cede **priority** to vehicles joining from the right except on roundabouts (vehicles on the roundabout have priority). There are tolls on motorways.

Currency. – Exchange regulations are liable to alteration. Banks or international travel agencies can advise on the purchase of currency and travellers' cheques. A passport must be presented for the purchase of currency or cheques and for the cashing of cheques. Commission charges vary; hotels charge more highly than banks and very highly indeed outside banking hours.

Medical Treatment. – Form E111, obtainable from the Department of Health and Social Security in the UK, confirms entitlement to medical benefits and can be used to obtain urgent medical treatment in EEC countries and a refund of part of the cost on application to the French Social Security Offices *(Caisse Primaire de Sécurité Sociale).* It is still adviseable however to take out comprehensive insurance cover.

Consulates: British - 13006 Marseilles, 24 Avenue du Prado (☎ 91 53 43 32).
American - 13006 Marseilles, 9 Rue Armény (☎ 91 54 92 00).

Local Tourist Information Centres *(Syndicats d'Initiative)* are to be found in most large towns and many tourist resorts. They can supply large scale town plans, timetables and information on local entertainment facilities, sports and sightseeing. On the town plans they are indicated by the ℹ.

Accommodation. – The **Michelin Guide France** (revised annually) gives a selection of hotels at various prices in all areas. It also lists local restaurants together with prices.

For camping or caravanning consult the **Michelin Guide Camping Caravaning France,** revised annually.

Electric Current. – Mostly 220-230 volts; in some places however it is still 110 volts. European circular two pin plugs are the rule – remember to take an adaptor.

Poste Restante. – Name, *Poste restante,* Poste Centrale, Départment's postal number followed by the town's name, France. The **Michelin Guide France** gives the postal codes.

Public Holidays in France. – National museums and art galleries are closed on Tuesdays. The following are days when museums and other monuments may be closed or may vary their hours of admission:

New Year's Day
Palm Sunday
Easter Sunday and Monday
May Day **(1 May)**
Fête de la Libération **(8 may)**
Ascension Day
Whit Sunday and Monday
France's National Day **(14 July)**
The Assumption **(15 August)**
All Saints' Day **(1 November)**
Armistice Day **(11 November)**
Christmas Day

PLACES TO STAY

	Page in this guide or fold of Michelin map 246	Altitude in metres	Guide France Hotels = H	Town Plan = P	Camping sites = C local maps = (M)	Tourist Centre = ℹ	Attractive Setting = ◁	Beside the sea, a lake or river = ●	Swimming pool = 🏊 Supervised bathing = ≋	Horse riding = ♞	Bicycles available for hire = B
Aigues-Mortes	27	–	H	–	–	ℹ	–	●	–	♞	–
Aix-en-Provence	29	177	H	P	C(M)	ℹ	–	●	🏊	♞	B
Apt	34	221	H	P	C	ℹ	–	–	🏊	–	B
Arles	40	9	H	P	C	ℹ	–	●	🏊	♞	B
Aubenas	36	300	H	P	C	ℹ	◁	●	🏊	♞	B
Avignon	44	23	H	P	C	ℹ	–	●	🏊	♞	B
Bagnols-sur-Cèze	51	51	H	–	C(M)	ℹ	–	●	🏊	♞	B
Barbentane	89	50	H	–	–	ℹ	◁	–	–	–	–
Les Baux-de-Provence	54	280	H	–	–	ℹ	◁	–	–	♞	–
Beaumes-de-Venise	70	150	–	–	C	ℹ	◁	●	≋	–	–
Bédoin	129	300	H	–	C	ℹ	–	–	🏊	–	–
Bollène	105	58	H	–	C	ℹ	–	●	🏊	–	–
Bourg-St-Andéol	60	68	H	–	C(M)	ℹ	◁	●	–	–	–
Buis-les-Baronnies	53	370	H	–	C	ℹ	◁	●	🏊	♞	B
Cadenet	72	160	H	–	–	ℹ	–	–	–	♞	–
Carry-le-Rouet	74	–	H	–	–	ℹ	◁	–	≋	–	–
Cassis	66	4	H	P	–	ℹ	◁	–	–	♞	–
Châteaurenard	73	113	H	–	–	ℹ	–	●	🏊	♞	B
La Ciotat	68	–	H	P	C(M)	ℹ	◁	–	🏊	♞	B
Dieulefit	90	386	H	–	C	ℹ	◁	●	🏊	–	B
Fontvieille	33	20	H	–	C	ℹ	–	–	–	♞	–
Gémenos	107	150	H	–	C	–	–	–	🏊	–	–
Gordes	76	373	H	–	–	ℹ	◁	–	–	♞	–
Goudargues	51	70	H	–	C	ℹ	◁	●	–	♞	–
Le Grau-du-Roi - Port-Camargue	64	–	H	–	C	ℹ	–	–	🏊	♞	B
Malaucène	70	377	–	–	C	ℹ	–	–	–	♞	B
Martigues	88	–	H	P	C	ℹ	–	●	🏊	–	–
Maussane-les-Alpilles	㉖	28	H	–	C	ℹ	◁	–	🏊	–	–
Meyrargues	71	206	H	–	–	–	◁	–	–	–	–
Mouriès	㉖⑫	18	H	–	C	–	–	–	–	–	–
Nîmes	92	39	H	P	–	ℹ	–	–	🏊	♞	B
Nyons	121	270	H	P	C	ℹ	◁	●	🏊	–	–
Orpierre	54	700	–	–	C	–	◁	●	🏊	–	–
Pertuis	72	216	H	–	C	ℹ	–	–	🏊	♞	B
Pont-St-Esprit	105	59	–	–	–	ℹ	–	●	🏊	–	–
Remoulins	118	27	H	–	C	ℹ	–	●	–	♞	–
La Roque-d'Anthéron	73	150	–	–	C	ℹ	–	●	🏊	♞	B
Roquemaure	㉔	19	H	–	–	–	–	●	🏊	♞	–
Ruoms	37	120	H	–	C(M)	ℹ	–	●	🏊	♞	B
Stes-Maries-de-la-Mer	108	–	H	–	C	ℹ	–	●	–	♞	B
St-Gilles	111	7	H	–	–	ℹ	–	●	🏊	♞	B
St-Rémy-de-Provence	113	60	H	P	C	ℹ	◁	●	🏊	♞	B
Salavas	㉓	120	–	–	C(M)	ℹ	–	●	≋	♞	B
Salon-de-Provence	115	82	H	P	–	ℹ	–	–	🏊	♞	B
Sampzon	㉓	387	–	–	C(M)	–	–	●	–	–	–
Sault	91	765	H	–	–	ℹ	◁	●	–	♞	–
Sausset-les-Pins	74	–	H	–	–	ℹ	–	–	🏊	–	B
Le Thor	⑪	64	–	–	C	ℹ	–	●	–	♞	–
Thueyts	35	462	H	–	–	ℹ	◁	●	–	–	–
Uzès	116	138	H	P	C	ℹ	–	●	🏊	♞	B
Vaison-la-Romaine	119	200	H	P	C	ℹ	◁	●	🏊	♞	B
Vallon-Pont-d'Arc	37	118	H	–	C(M)	ℹ	–	●	≋	–	–
Valréas	122	270	H	–	C	ℹ	–	●	🏊	♞	B
Vals-les-Bains	122	248	H	P	C	ℹ	–	●	🏊	–	–
Villeneuve-de-Berg	131	320	H	–	C	ℹ	–	●	🏊	♞	B
Viviers	101	71	H	–	C	ℹ	◁	●	🏊	–	–
Vogüé	36	155	–	–	C	ℹ	–	●	–	–	–

Walkers, campers, smokers
please take care
Fire is the scourge of forests everywhere

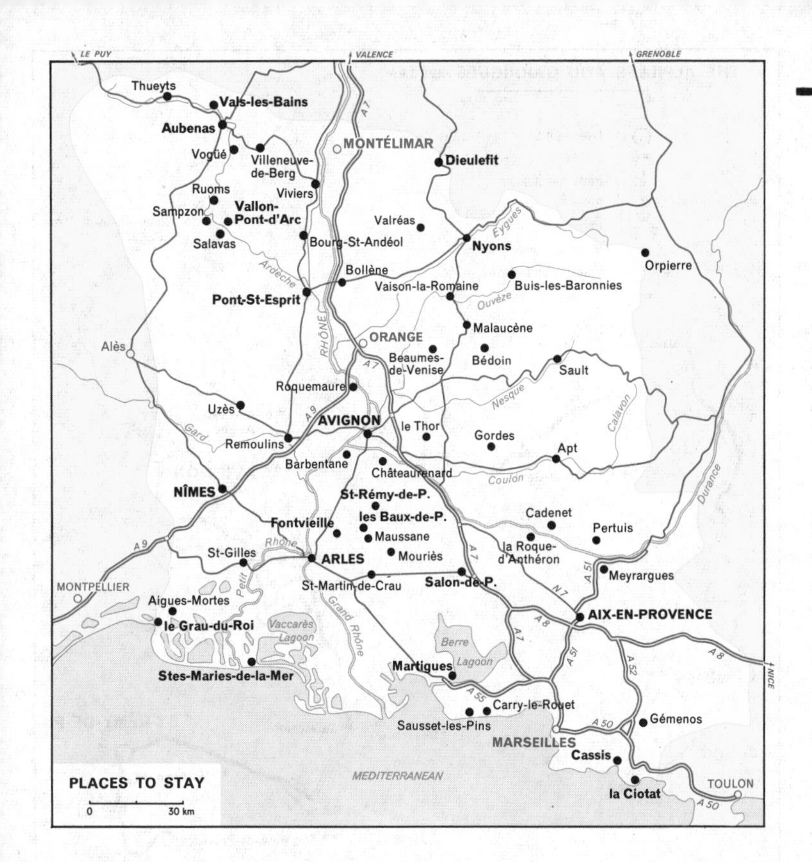

Join us in our never ending task of keeping up to date.
Send us your comments and suggestions, please.
Michelin Tyre Public Limited Company.
Tourism Department.
81 Fulham Road, LONDON SW3 6RD.

TOURING PROGRAMMES

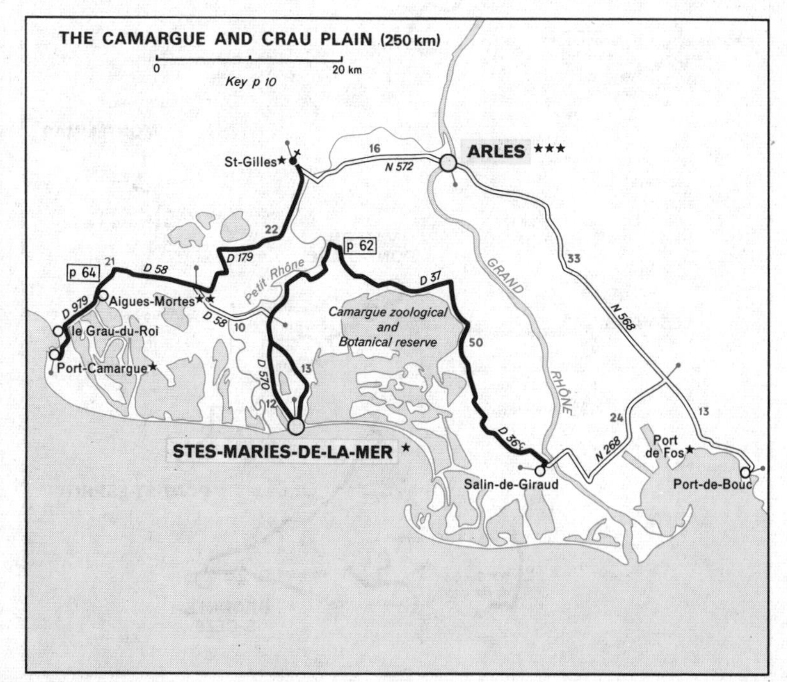

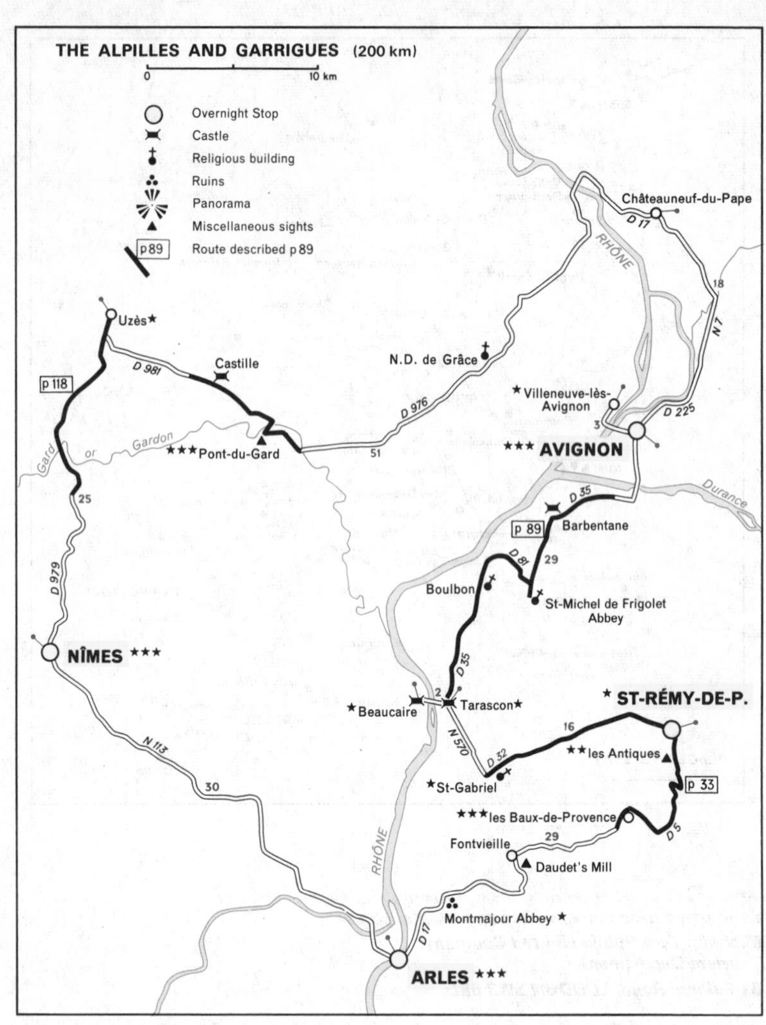
THE ALPILLES AND GARRIGUES (200 km)
0
10 km
Overnight Stop
Castle
Religious building
Ruins
Panorama
Miscellaneous sights
p89
Route described p 89
Châteauneuf-du-Pape
D 17
RHÔNE
18
N 7
Uzès ★
D 981
Castille
p 118
N.D. de Grâce
D 976
★ Villeneuve-lès-Avignon
D 225
3
Gard or Gardon
★★★ Pont-du-Gard
51
★★★ AVIGNON
Durance
D 35
p 89
Barbentane
25
D 81
29
D 979
Boulbon
St-Michel de Frigolet Abbey
NÎMES ★★★
D 35
★ ST-RÉMY-DE-P.
★ Beaucaire
2
Tarascon ★
16
N 570
★★ les Antiques
N 113
D 32
★ St-Gabriel
p 33
30
★★★ les Baux-de-Provence
D 5
RHÔNE
Fontvieille
29
Daudet's Mill
Montmajour Abbey ★
D 17
ARLES ★★★

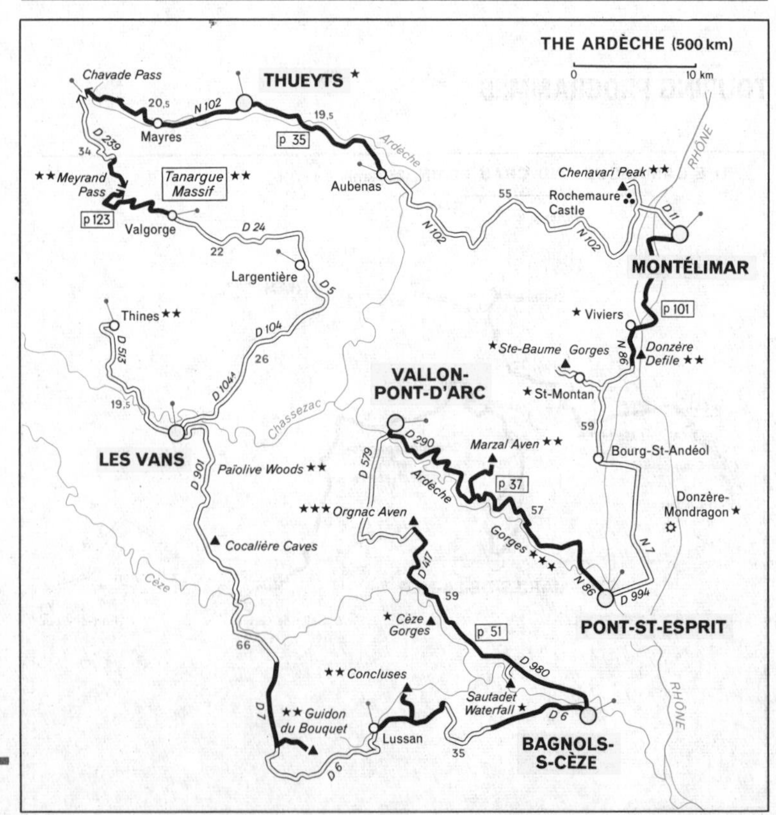
THE ARDÈCHE (500 km)
0
10 km
Chavade Pass
THUEYTS ★
20,5
N 102
19,5
Mayres
p 35
Ardèche
D 239
34
★★ Meyrand Pass
Tanargue Massif ★★
Aubenas
Chenavari Peak ★★
RHÔNE
55
Rochemaure Castle
p 123
Valgorge
D 24
N 102
D 11
22
N 102
MONTÉLIMAR
Largentière
D 5
Thines ★★
★ Viviers
p 101
D 104
D 513
26
★ Ste-Baume Gorges
N 86
Donzère Defile ★★
VALLON-PONT-D'ARC
★ St-Montan
D 104A
19,5
Chassezac
59
LES VANS
D 290
Marzal Aven ★★
Bourg-St-Andéol
D 579
Païolive Woods ★★
p 37
D 901
Ardèche
57
Donzère-Mondragon ★
★★★ Orgnac Aven
Cocalière Caves
N 7
Gorges ★★★
D 417
Cèze
N 86
D 994
59
★ Cèze Gorges
PONT-ST-ESPRIT
p 51
66
D 980
★★ Concluses
RHÔNE
Sautadet Waterfall ★
D 6
D 7
★★ Guidon du Bouquet
Lussan
35
D 6
BAGNOLS-S-CÈZE

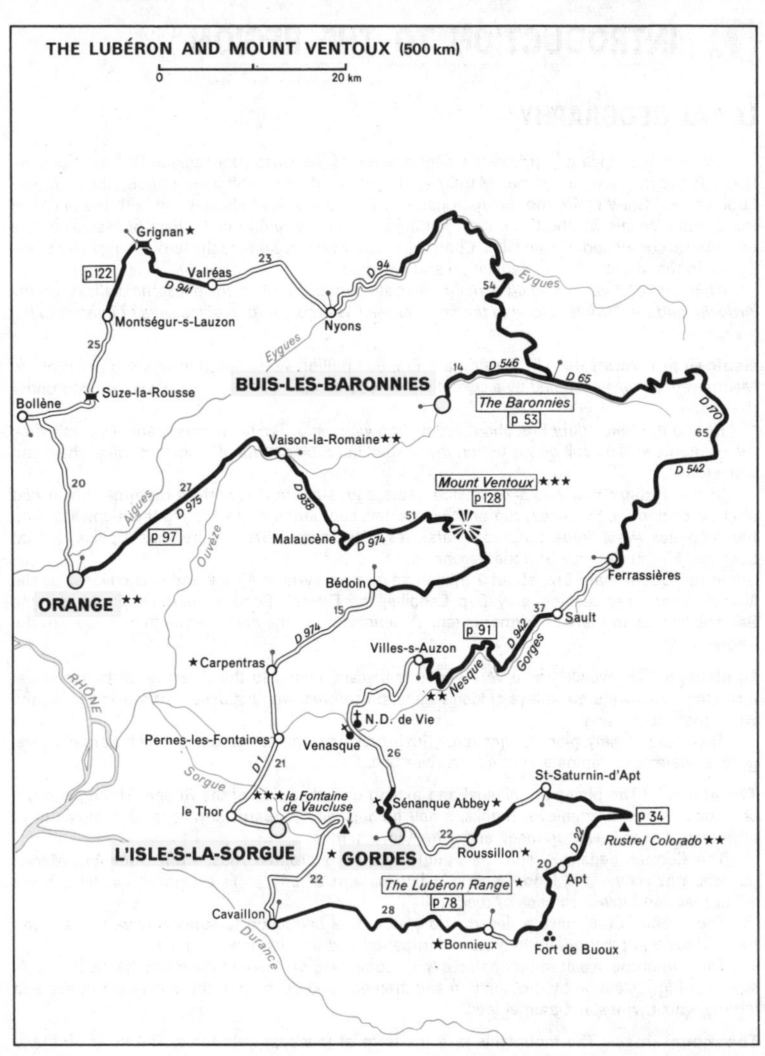
THE LUBÉRON AND MOUNT VENTOUX (500 km)
0
20 km
Grignan ★
p 122
Valréas
23
D 941
Montségur-s-Lauzon
25
Nyons
D 94
54
Eygues
Eygues
Suze-la-Rousse
Bollène
BUIS-LES-BARONNIES
14
D 546
D 65
The Baronnies
p 53
D 170
65
D 542
Vaison-la-Romaine ★★
20
27
D 975
Aigues
D 938
Mount Ventoux ★★★
p 128
51
Malaucène
D 974
p 97
Ouvèze
ORANGE ★★
Bédoin
15
Ferrassières
37
Sault
D 942
D 974
p 91
Gorges
★ Carpentras
Villes-s-Auzon
★★ Nesque
RHÔNE
N.D. de Vie
Venasque
Pernes-les-Fontaines
26
D 1
21
Sorgue
★★★ la Fontaine de Vaucluse
Sénanque Abbey ★
St-Saturnin-d'Apt
p 34
Rustrel Colorado ★★
le Thor
L'ISLE-S-LA-SORGUE
★ GORDES
22
Roussillon ★
D 22
20
22
The Lubéron Range ★
Apt
p 78
Cavaillon
28
★ Bonnieux
Fort de Buoux
Durance

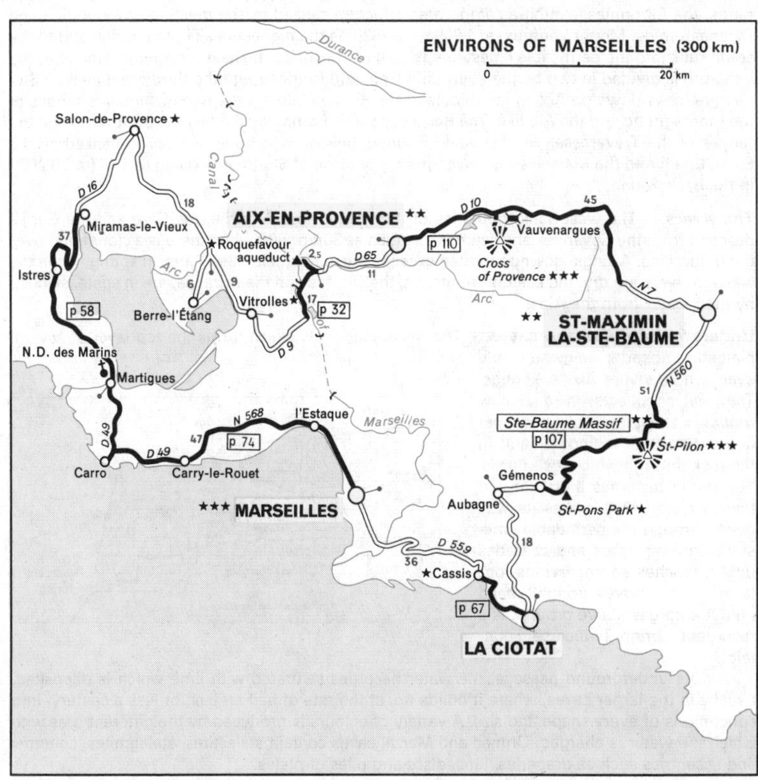
ENVIRONS OF MARSEILLES (300 km)
0
20 km
Durance
Salon-de-Provence ★
D 16
18
Canal
Miramas-le-Vieux
37
AIX-EN-PROVENCE ★★
D 10
45
Vauvenargues
★ Roquefavour aqueduct
p 110
Istres
6
9
Arc
2.5
D 65
11
Cross of Provence ★★★
p 58
Berre-l'Étang
Vitrolles ★
17
p 32
Arc
N 7
★★ ST-MAXIMIN LA-STE-BAUME
D 9
N.D. des Marins
Martigues
N 560
51
N 568
l'Estaque
Marseilles
D 49
47
p 74
Ste-Baume Massif ★★
p 107
St-Pilon ★★★
Carro
D 49
Carry-le-Rouet
Gémenos
Aubagne
St-Pons Park ★
★★★ MARSEILLES
18
D 559
36
★ Cassis
p 67
LA CIOTAT

INTRODUCTION TO THE REGION

LOCAL GEOGRAPHY

Modern Provence comprises the départments of Vaucluse, Bouches-du-Rhône, Alpes-de-Haute-Provence, Var and Alpes-Maritimes. Its physical composition is varied; the Ventoux, Lubéron and Ste-Victoire mountains together with the Alpilles hills contrast with the plains of the Comtat Venaissin, the Crau and the Camargue in the Rhône delta. East of Marseilles the coastline is composed of high cliffs. Common to the whole region are the luminous quality of the light and the Mediterranean vegetation and life-style.

This guide does not keep strictly to these limits but also includes the valleys of the Ardèche and the Middle Rhône to the north as well as other peripheral features of interest to the visitor.

Geological formation. – In the Primary Era, 600 million years ago, the western basin of the Mediterranean was occupied by a crystalline rock continent - Tyrrhenia and Provence was under the sea.

During the Secondary Era, about 200 million years ago, Tyrrhenia was gradually levelled by the elements and its soil deposited on the seabed in regular strata of limestone, clay, shale and sandstone.

In the Tertiary Era, about 60 million years ago, slow but powerful pressures, which had already formed the Pyrenees, compressed the new submarine strata, forcing them upwards into the high east-west folds north of Marseilles: Ste-Baume, Ste-Victoire, the Alpilles, Mount Lubéron, Mount Ventoux and the Baronnies.

In the Quarternary Era, about 2 million years ago, Tyrrhenia sank and was covered by the Mediterranean sea leaving only Cap Canaille, the Esterel, Corsica, Sardinia, Sicily and the Balearic Islands to mark its former extent. A depression to the north began to develop into the Rhône Valley.

Landscape. – Provence has a very varied landscape owing to the diversity of its geological formation; well-watered valleys of lush vegetation contrast with flat deserts, dry hills and jagged white mountain peaks.

There are closely planted vineyards, lush orchards, market gardens, which border rivers, gorges, waterfalls, rapids and dried out river beds.

The plains. – The plains are alluvial and extend on either side of the Rhône. Throughout the centuries, Romans, medieval monks, small holders and modern farming co-operatives have improved the land with drainage and irrigation schemes.

The Comtat Venaissin and the Petite Crau have profited most from irrigation. Market gardens now cover the land creating a fine pattern of tiny plots separated by tall cypress windbreaks and lower screens of reed.

The Grande Crau, once a desert of dry stones, is beginning to support olive and almond trees, vines and pastureland by virtue of irrigation and the clearing of stones.

The Camargue, a salt-impregnated marsh, composed of alluvium deposited by the Rhône, is slowly being reclaimed by desalination and drainage and devoted to the cultivation of rice and latterly wheat, vines and animal feed.

The mountains. – The mountains take the form of low east-west folds. The most northerly range, the Baronnies, exhibit a complicated structure caused by the meeting of the Alpine and Pyrenean folds. Mount Ventoux, at 1 909m - 6 263ft, is the highest peak in the region and to the south runs into the permeable limestone plateau of Vaucluse. The next most important peak, the Lubéron, is divided in two by the Lourmarin Gap, and further south the third great peak of Ste-Victoire looks down on Aix. In the middle of the Rhône Plain are the two picturesque ranges of the Montagnette and the Alpilles. The Berre Lagoon is framed by the heights of St-Mitre and the ranges of the Trévaresse, Vitrolles and l'Estaque, beyond which lies Marseilles flanked by the Étoile Chain and the Marseilleveyre with the rocky mass of Ste-Baume rising to 1 147m - 3 763ft in the background.

The rivers. – The west bank tributaries of the Rhône - the Ardèche, the Cèze and the Gard - descend from the Cévennes and can rise as much as 30ft or 60ft when there is a cloudburst over the mountains. A single downpour often exceeds the annual rainfall of Paris. In spring, when the western rivers are dry, the eastern tributaries, the Ouvèze and the Durance, are in spate, swollen by melt water from the Alps.

Underground rivers and caves. – The calcareous rock, which forms the top layer of several plateaux, absorbs rainwater and even whole rivers like a sponge. The water collects in a hollow *(doline)*, scooping out a deeper depression until it finds a fault in the rock through which it can pass. The trickle becomes a stream and then a river which makes its way down through the permeable limestone forming lakes and cascades until it reaches an impervious rock layer. Then it drives straight ahead until it emerges above ground as a resurgent spring (Vaucluse Fountain).

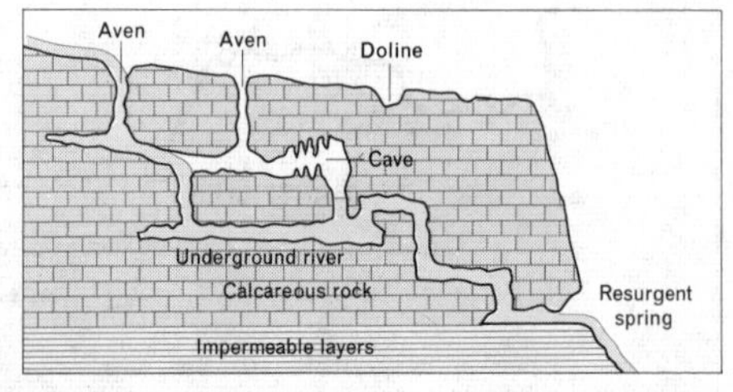

On its underground passage, the water becomes saturated with lime which is deposited, usually in the larger caves, where it builds up, at the rate of half an inch or less a century, into concretions of every shape and size. A variety of colours is produced by the different ores with which the water is charged. Orgnac and Marzal caves contain stalactites, stalagmites, columns and eccentrics such as draperies, fans, discs and piles of plates.

VEGETATION

Provence enjoys two flowering seasons: a short burst of brilliant colour in the spring and a second blossom time in the autumn, which goes on well into the winter. During the great heat of summer the plants are dormant except for those equipped to withstand the heat with long or bulbous roots, glossy leaves or a protective perfumed vapour.

Olives. – The olive, which was introduced into Provence by the Greeks some 2 500 years ago, is called the immortal tree; wild olives or those grafted on to wild stock will continually renew themselves. A tree grown from a cutting dies relatively young at 300 years. The olive, of which there are 60 varieties, will grow on calcareous and siliceous soil up to 600m - 2 000ft. It starts to fruit between 6 and 12 years and reaches maturity between 20 and 25 years. The finest trees flourish on the coast where they attain up to 20m - 65ft in height and 4m - 13ft round the trunk. Their silver green foliage can extend up to 20m - 65ft round, providing protection for early vegetables. Olive groves are sometimes interplanted with fig and almond trees and many are owned by cooperatives.

Olive tree

Oaks. – The two oaks in the region are both evergreens. The **holm** *(quercus ilex)*, which grows on calcareous soil below 800m - 2 500ft and in stunted form is a characteristic element of the *garrigue (p 14)*, has a short grey-black trunk supporting dense foliage. The **kermès** or **scrub oak** of 3-5ft is also a hillside feature.

Pines. – The three regional pines have unmistakable silhouettes.

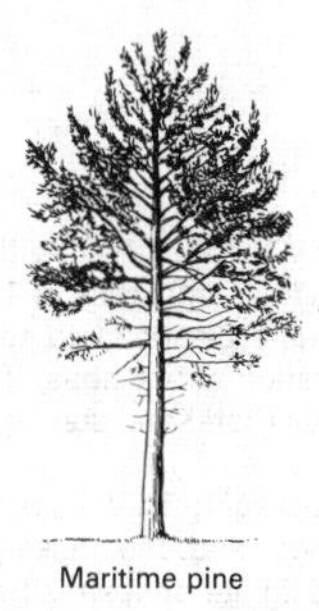

Maritime pine

Parasol pine

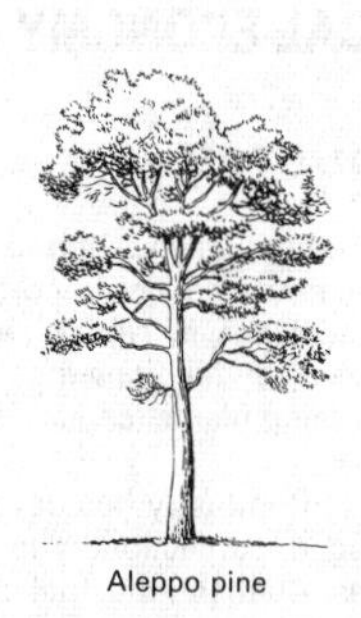

Aleppo pine

Other trees. – Dark green **cypresses** stand sentinel in the churchyards or in serried ranks to screen the early vegetables from the wind (the quicker growing **Lombardy poplar** is now being used to form wind breaks); in early spring the pink blossom of the **almond trees** delights the eye; in towns and villages the streets and squares are shaded by the smooth-barked **plane trees** or the dark green canopy of the branching **lotus tree** *(micocoulier)* which yields a fruit mentioned by Homer in the Odyssey as inducing a state of dreamy forgetfulness and loss of desire to return home – hence lotus-eaters. It has also been identified by some as the jujube tree.

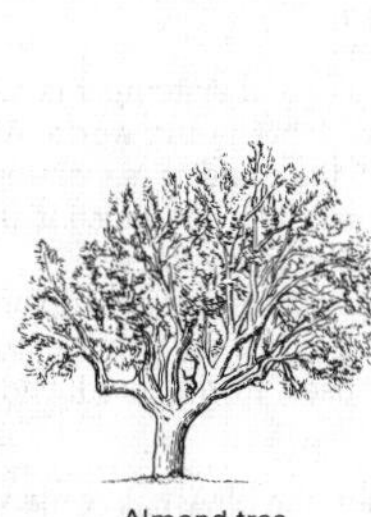

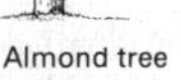

Almond tree

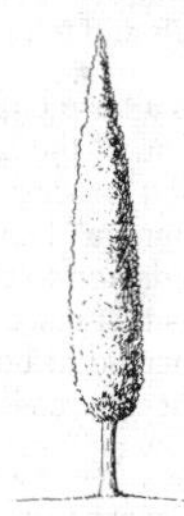

Cypress

Lotus tree

Woodlands. – The rare woodlands of Provence are to be found on the mountain slopes up to 1 600m - 5 000ft. The southern slopes of Mount Ventoux are covered in holm and durmast oaks, together with cedars, beeches and pines, while on the northern face grow pines and larches. The Petit Lubéron boasts a fine cedar forest and clusters of beeches thrive in the shelter of the north face of Ste-Baume.

Myrtle

Cistus

Thyme

Rosemary

The Garrigue. – In Provence this word is used to describe the area to the north of Nîmes around Uzès, a stretch of low limestone hills with minute parcels of land between the outcrops of white calcareous rock from which the soil has been washed down into the valleys. Vegetation is sparse consisting mostly of stunted holm oaks, durmast-oaks, thistles, gorse and cistus, as well as **lavender, thyme** and **rosemary,** interspersed with a short dry grass which provides pasture for flocks of sheep.

The wild aromatic plants together with such herbs as **basil, marjoram, savory** and **sage** which are cultivated commercially are sold in the famous herb markets.

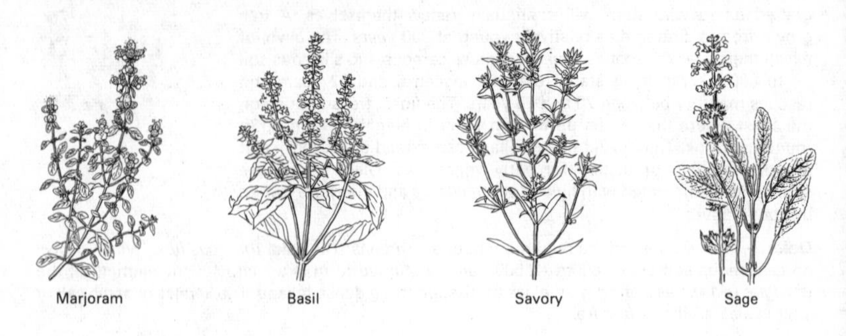
Marjoram Basil Savory Sage

LOCAL ECONOMY

INDUSTRY

Traditionally second to agriculture in Provence, industry has adapted to modern conditions and is now of major importance as a source of local employment. The small industries of 19C - silk stockings in Nîmes and tanning in Marseilles – have almost totally disappeared to be replaced by engineering, shipbuilding and repair, railway and aviation workshops, food processing plants (cereals, sugar, oil) and breweries, with shipyards in La Ciotat and steelworks in Fos.

Light industry has developed around the towns: cardboard and packaging in Valréas and Tarascon, confectionery in Aix, Apt and Nyons, fruit preserving, garment and shoemaking in Nîmes. A small industrial complex has grown up at Gardanne where a lignite deposit is being worked to fuel a power station producing 3.4 milliard kWh a year, and bauxite and cement works have gone into production.

Petroleum and its associated industries. – Berre Lagoon has become over the last 30 years France's major oil refining centre. Dependent petro-chemical factories have developed rapidly on the expanding industrial estates at Lavéra, Mède and Fos-sur-Mer. Even the saltmarshes around Salin have attracted factories which use the salt to produce chemical compounds such as chlorine, sulphuric acid and soda.

Electricity. – The hydro-electric installations on the Lower Rhône at Caderousse, Avignon and Vallabrègues, and on the Lower Durance at Jouques, St-Estève-Janson, Mallemort, Salon and St-Chamas, produce respectively 3 milliard kWh and 2.5 milliard kWh.

Ochre and Bauxite. – **Ochre,** which is used as a base pigment in paint and distemper is mined in the Apt-Roussillon area which produces some of the best quality ochre in the world. About 3 000 tonnes are produced annually by a long process in which the sand is separated by panning from the sandy clay and iron oxyde mineral, leaving the ochre 'flower' which is dried, crushed, refined and even baked to produce a darker colour before it is ready for sale.

Bauxite, named after Les Baux where it was first discovered, is now mined chiefly in the Var and in the Hérault, although resources are expected to be exhausted in the near future. France still supplies 2/3 of her needs from domestic sources which is used in the production of aluminium and its alloys.

Oil and Soap. – Although introduced by the Greeks from Asia Minor, the olive has come to be considered a native of Provence. The quality of the oil obtained depends on the harvest and the method of production. Green and black olives are harvested between November and May and pressed between millstones without the stones being crushed. The resulting mash is placed on coconut mats *(scourtins)* and the oil which filters through is called "virgin oil". Cold water is added to the mash for a second pressing which yields "fine" or "extra fine" oil. Subsequent pressings with the addition of hot water yield low-grade oil which is not for sale and the fourth pressing is used for lamp oil and soap making. The stones and pulp are then separated; the pulp is converted into fertilizer or solid fuel; a fifth oil extracted from the crushed stones is used in industry, while the residue, washed and dried, serves as fuel for bakers' ovens.

Olive oil was the basic ingredient of **Marseilles' soap** until it was replaced in 19C by tropical vegetable oils, such as groundnut, coconut and palm, which were being refined locally. Household soap from Marseilles makes up 45% of French consumption of washing products.

Salt. – In 13C monks were already working the saltmarshes in the Camargue near Aigues-Mortes and Salin-de-Giraud. Each about 40 sq miles in extent, they now produce about 556 000 tonnes of salt annually. Between March and September a shallow flow of seawater (not more than a foot deep) is pumped across large "tables" for about 20 miles until a saturated solution of sodium chloride has been formed. This is then passed into 20 acre crystallising pans, 5 ins deep, divided by dykes *(cairels).* Between late August and early October, when evaporation is complete, the salt crystals are raked to the edge, washed and piled into huge white glistening mounds *(camelles),* some 21m - 70ft high. After further washing, drying and crushing, the salt crystals are ready for use in industry, to feed to animals or for human consumption.

VINES AND WINES

VINEYARDS | ORCHARDS

CÔTES DU RHÔNE Appellation controlée vineyards
Côtes du Ventoux Lesser vineyards
● **Gigondas** Named vintages

Vineyards occupy some 130 500ha - 322 335 acres in the southern Rhône Valley and Provence.

While the vines in the plains produce *vin ordinaire,* those planted on the hillsides and generally described (with those also north of Montélimar) as **Côtes du Rhône,** are individual and enjoyable.

The most celebrated vintage of the area is **Châteauneuf-du-Pape.**

Everything depends on the stock, the soil, the orientation, the weather and the vinification. Generally, the **rosé** wines are fragrant, pleasant and often fruity; the **whites,** usually dry and crisp; the **reds** anything from full-bodied and fruity to light and subtle – more particularly **Châteauneuf** is warm and full-bodied, **Gigondas** are heady, **Rasteau** are usually sweet and best with dessert, **Palette** (produced near Aix) is another dessert wine, **Cassis** reds are full–bodied and fruity, the whites, dry (not to be confused with the black currant liqueur). **Beaumes-de-Venise** is a muscatel.

From the far, right bank of the Rhone come **Tavel,** a bright pink, fragrant rosé, **Lirac,** a red or rosé, and **Listel** (near Aigues-Mortes) a so-called *rosé des sables* or sweet aperitif.

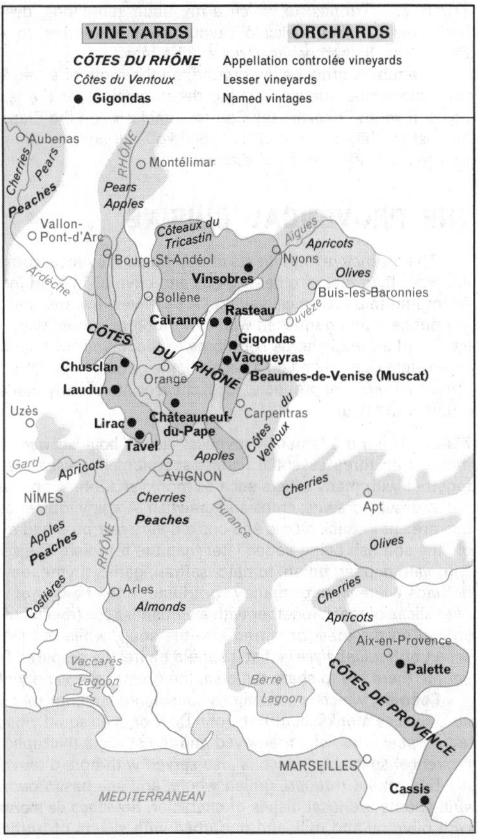

AGRICULTURE

The orchards and market gardens, which produce several crops a year, are concentrated in the Comtat Venaissin and the Petite Crau, formerly devoted to cereal crops and animal husbandry. The whole region is now divided up into little parcels of land protected from the wind by screens of cypress and reeds. Most early produce is sold to a packer or sent to a cooperative where it is sorted and packed before being dispatched to market or put into cold store. The main railheads are Châteaurenard, Cavaillon, Carpentras, Barbentane and Avignon.

Fruit and Vegetables. – Each distributive centre tends to specialize: Carpentras is known for strawberries, tomatoes and melons; Cavaillon for asparagus, melons and new potatoes, Rognonas for cabbages, Le Thor for dessert grapes, Lauris for asparagus, Remoulins for cherries and the Rhône Valley for peaches, pears and apricots.

Cereals. – The area between Arles and Tarascon, hitherto the main centre for growing wheat in Provence, is now producing maize and rape as well, and the windmills so dear to Alphonse Daudet have been replaced by modern milling machinery in the towns. Rice was first planted in the Camargue to facilitate the desalination of the soil and prepare it for other crops. From 250ha – 618 acres in 1942 production rose to 33 000ha – 81 540 acres in 1961 but has since dropped to 4 200ha – 10 378 acres in 1981 as vines or maize or rape have taken over. The rice is sown directly into completely level enclosures of 3ha – 7 acres, surrounded by embankments and flooded from April to September. It is harvested in late September – early October and then husked, blanched and even polished before sale.

Almonds. – Almond trees, which grow all round the shores of the Mediterranean, were first imported into France from the Orient in 1548. The development of later blossoming varieties have led to increased cultivation. The most famous of the local almond confectionery are *calissons* from Aix and Salon, *caladons* from Nîmes and *nougat* from Montélimar.

Olives. – The silver green of the olive groves is a common sight in the country round Nyons, Salon and Buis-les-Baronnies and on the southern slopes of the mountain ranges. The black olives of Nyons, preserved in brine, are a delicacy.

Lavender. – In 19C lavender was gathered on the hillsides where it grew wild but it is now grown as a field crop above 700m - 2 000ft and a more productive but less fragrant hybrid, lavandin, is cultivated on the lower slopes and in the valleys. The most extensive fields are to the north of Nîmes and on the Vaucluse Plateau. Between July and September the flowers are harvested, dried and distilled. About 50 tonnes of flowers are dried annually for sale in lavender bags. Most of the picking is now done by machinery but the inaccessible or closely planted older fields are still picked by hand.

Herbs. – The famous **Herbs of Provence** *(illustrations pp 13-14)* have doubled in popularity in recent years and are sold in the international market in Buis-les-Baronnies. Basil and marjoram are cultivated round St-Rémy, tarragon on the Vaucluse Plateau, while thyme, rosemary and savory are still gathered from the hillsides where they grow wild. Lime trees are now grown in the fields between Buis-les-Baronnies and Carpentras and in June the flowers are picked and dried for **lime tea.**

Truffles. – Truffles, to which a mystique still clings, despite their now being cultivated, are harvested for their delicate savour from November to April and marketed mostly in Apt, Carpentras, Richerenches, Uzès and Valréas.

The tubers grow below ground, on the roots of a tree known in Provence as the white oak, from the whitish down covering the undersides of the leaves. The trees are planted in huge fields in south Tricastin, the Comtat Venaissin, on the Claparèdes Plateau and the Lubéron. The harvest in 1983 amounted to 11 600 kg – all sold by the gramme! It was Brillat-Savarin who referred to truffles as black diamonds.

THE PROVENÇAL CUISINE

The distinctive ingredients of traditional Provençal cookery are **olive oil** and garlic. The garlic is milder than that of other regions and olive oil is used for cooking in preference to other fats. According to a Provençal saying "A fish lives in water and dies in olive oil". Some local dishes are pungent and garnished with raw onion or served with a piquant sauce. Saffron and a great variety of aromatic herbs contribute to the flavour of traditional dishes, which may be wrapped in vine leaves or grilled on a bed of herbs or on an open fire of vine twigs. Butter and milk are not important regional products; local cheeses are usually made from goat's milk and are sharp and crumbly in texture.

Fish. – The most famous Provençal dish is **bouillabaisse,** a cross between a soup and a stew, made from three essential fishes: scorpionfish *(rascasse),* gurnet *(grondin)* and eel *(congre),* together with many others such as monkfish, John Dory, weaver fish, whiting, bass, sea perch, and mussels, prawns, crabs and crawfish. A spiny lobster added makes a very special dish. The fish are cut in thick pieces and cooked very fast on a bed of vegetables in stock emulsified with oil, the soft fish being added later than the firm fish. The seasoning is quite as important as the fish; salt, pepper, onion, tomato, saffran, garlic, thyme, bay leaf, sage, fennel, orange peel with perhaps white wine or brandy contribute to the flavour of the stocks which is served as a soup over slices of toast, together with a piquant sauce **(rouille)** of garlic and red pepper which may be spread on the toast or stirred into the soup, while the fish is served on a separate dish. The secret of *bouillabaisse* is that it should be freshly prepared from the finest ingredients. The more people there are to share the dish, the greater the variety of fish in the pot.

Bourride, which is sometimes considered superior to *bouillabaisse,* is made from firm white fish, such as monkfish, turbot, John Dory or even squid, poached with onion, bay leaf, fennel and lemon peel. The fish is removed and the stock is thickened with **aioli,** a garlic mayonnaise and Provençal speciality, which is also served with hors-d'œuvre and vegetables.

Red mullet *(rouget),* grilled whole, and sea bass *(loup)* grilled on a bed of fennel stalks or vine shoots are local dishes of character. **Brandade de morue,** a rich cream of salt cod pounded with olive oil and milk and perfumed with slivers of truffles and garlic, has come down to us from medieval fast days.

Certain towns have their own fish specialities: the small restaurants around the Old Port in Marseilles serve *bouillabaisse,* clams **(clovisses),** mussels **(moules),** edible sea urchins **(oursins)** and ascidia or seasquirts **(violets)** tasting strongly of iodine; St-Rémy is known for **catigau,** a dish of grilled or smoked Rhône eel in sauce; in the Camargue sand crustaceans **(tellines)** are served with a piquant sauce.

Fruit and vegetables. – The market stalls of Provence are piled high with brightly coloured vegetables and luscious fruit. There are peppers, courgettes and aubergines to be stewed together as ratatouille, cardoons to be served in cream sauce, fennel to be cooked whole or sliced raw into salad to impart a delicate aniseed flavour. Above all there are tomatoes and onions, the basic ingredients of many dishes. Local Charenton, honeydew and water melons provide refreshment. The figs are sweet and juicy. Peaches and apricots, cherries and strawberries and dessert grapes are all grown in the region.

The local olives are small and succulent. Nîmes is the principal market for the green stuffed olives whereas the mature black ones, preserved in brine, come from Nyons and Carpentras.

Ices. – Ices of every taste and colour make a welcome refreshment in the summer heat. As well as the more usual flavours, restaurants and confectioners often produce their own specialities from local fruit, such as apricot, peach, blackcurrant and even medlar.

Specialities. – Other Provençal specialities are: sausages **(saucissons)** from Arles, a kind of tripe **(pieds-paquets)** from Marseilles, preserved melons from Avignon, almond sweets **(calissons)** from Aix, caramels **(berlingots)** from Carpentras, almond cakes **(caladons)** and crisp biscuits **(Villaret)** from Nîmes, special chocolates **(tartarinades)** from Tarascon, **crystallized fruit** from Apt, **nougat** from Montélimar and Sault, **black olives** from Nyons.

FOOD AND DRINK VOCABULARY

addition	bill	**garçon, serveuse**	waiter, waitress
assiette	plate	**glace**	icecream, icecube
beurre	butter	**huile, vinaigre**	oil, vinegar
bière	beer	**lait**	milk
café	black coffee	**moutarde**	mustard
café au lait	white coffee	**œuf**	egg
carte des vins	wine list	**pain**	bread
confiture	jam	**pâtisserie**	pastry
couteau	knife	**petit déjeuner**	breakfast
cuillère	spoon	**poisson**	fish
déjeuner	lunch	**sel, poivre**	salt, pepper
dîner	dinner	**sucre**	sugar
eau	water	**verre**	glass
fourchette	fork	**viande**	meat
fromage	cheese	**vin**	wine

HISTORICAL SUMMARY

BC 600	The Greeks found Massalia (Marseilles).
542	The Carthaginians capture Marseilles and remain for 60 years.
340	The Marseilles navigator, Pytheas, explores the northern seas for amber and tin.
218	Hannibal passes from Spain through Provence to cross the Alps.
125	Marseilles appeals to Rome for aid against the Celts.
122	Aix is founded by the Romans.
102	Marius defeats the Teutons at Aix.
Late BC 10	As direct rule is imposed under Augustus, Roman civilization spreads throughout Provence.
AD 2C	Nîmes reaches its greatest glory.
4C	Arles reaches its greatest glory.
413	Foundation of St-Victor's Abbey in Marseilles.
476	Fall of the Roman Empire.
5-6C	Vandals, Alamans, Visigoths, Ostrogoths, Franks invade Provence in turn.
520	Arles created the provincial administrative centre of Gaul.
574	Saxon invasion.
9C	Four separate Moorish invasions during the century.
859	The Normans land in the Camargue.

THE COUNTS OF PROVENCE

10C	Provence is annexed by the Holy Roman Empire; the Counts of Provence, however, retain their independence; the towns expand and assert their autonomy.
12C	Provence passes to the Counts of Toulouse and then the Counts of Barcelona.
1246	Charles of Anjou, brother of St Louis, marries the Count of Barcelona's daughter and becomes Count of Provence.
1248	St Louis embarks from Aigues-Mortes on 7th Crusade.
1309-1403	The Popes and anti-popes at Avignon. Great Schism of the West: 1378-1417.
1348	Population of Provence decimated by the first great plague.
1409	Foundation of University of Aix.
1434	René of Anjou becomes Count of Provence; dawn of the Golden Age of Good King René.
1481	Charles of Maine, René's nephew, bequeathes Provence to King Louis XI.

PROVENCE WITHIN THE KINGDOM OF FRANCE

1486	Ratification at Aix of the Union by the Three Estates of Provence (representatives of the clergy, nobility and commons).
1501	Inauguration of the Parliament of Aix (Parlement de Provence) as supreme court of justice with limited political authority.
1524-36	Invasion of Provence by Charles V, Holy Roman Emperor.
1539	Edict of Villers-Cotterêts decrees French as the language for all administrative laws in Provence.
1545	Suppression of Vaudois heretics by Francis I;
1555	Nostradamus publishes his astrological predictions, *Centuries* (d 1566).
1560-98	Wars of Religion end with the Edict of Nantes allowing freedom of conscience to Protestants; they construct churches and fortified places in which to live.
1600	Olivier de Serres, father of French agriculture publishes *The Farming Scene and Management of Agricultural Fields.*
1629	The dismantling of forts and castles by Richelieu.
1685	Revocation of the Edict of Nantes; suppression of Protestantism, flight of 3 500 000 Huguenots to Protestant countries.
1713	The Principality of Orange is transferred from the House of Orange Nassau to Louis XIV under the Treaty of Utrecht.
1720	Plague again decimates the population.
1787	Edict of Toleration ends persecution of Protestants.

FROM THE REVOLUTION TO 20C

1791	Avignon and the Comtat Venaissin are annexed to France.
1792	500 Marseilles volunteers march to Paris singing the *Marseillaise.*
1825	Construction at Tournon of the first suspension bridge over the Rhône.
1854	Foundation of the Provençal literary group, the Félibrige.
1859	Publication by Frédéric Mistral of the Provençal poem, *Mireio.*
1880	Phylloxera destroys half the vineyards of the Ardèche; orchards planted on a massive scale in the Rhône and other valleys.
1934	Compagnie Nationale du Rhône founded to harness the river.
1942-4	German forces invade Provence; Lyons becomes the capital of the Resistance Movement; destruction of the bridges in the Rhône Valley.
1944	Allied forces land on the Mediterranean coast.
1948-52	Construction of Donzère-Mondragon Power Station on the Rhône *(p 100)*.
1956	France's first nuclear reactor, at Marcoule, begins operating.
1962	Foreign Legion transferred from Algeria to Aubagne.
1965	Commencement of construction of Fos harbour complex.
1970	A6, A7 motorways link Paris and Marseilles.
1977	Marseilles' underground begins service.

LOCAL ARCHITECTURE

The founding of Marseilles in 6BC by Phoceans from Asia Minor brought Greek civilization to Provence, but the Greeks were interested in trade rather than conquest and their cultural influence was less marked than that of the Romans who succeeded them for five centuries, and established strong links with the Latin and Hispanic peninsulas which persisted into the Middle Ages. After the fall of Rome a slow development in the mountains of Provence, marked by Toulousian and Burgundian features, resulted in the flowering of Provençal Romanesque art in 12C. By 13C, through the crusades to the Holy Land and against the Albigensians, northern French influence began to penetrate the south, a movement consolidated by the union of Provence with the Kingdom of France in 1486, and subsequent architectural trends – Gothic, Renaissance, etc. – were introduced to Provence via northern France.

ROMAN STYLE

The Romans were slow to occupy Provence. Marseilles was a strong and independent presence with its own long history and Greek traditions, but eventually the need to protect the land route to Spain and the trade route up the Rhône from roaming Gallic tribes led to the creation of a province, Gallia Narbonensis, in 120BC. It soon became a most favoured and densely populated province – *the* province, hence its modern name – and a favourite place of exile for men banished from Rome. Some of the finest surviving monuments of the early Roman Empire are to be found in Provence.

The Romans built on a large scale and with great speed, due less to the number of men employed than to good planning and the use of specialized equipment. The architects were usually Greek freedmen from the East as were the artists and sculptors, whereas the technicians and masons tended to be Italian or local.

For building material the Romans used the local limestone which was easy to dress. Originally walls were dry stone blocks held in place by weight but later iron clamps were used. From 1C mortar was used to fill in the cavities and to present a smooth surface as in the Maison Carrée in Nîmes. The Romans also used a form of cement – a core of mortared rubble faced with courses of small squared blocks of stone. The composition was alternated with courses of brick from 2C onwards. A variety of roofing techniques was employed: flat slabs of stone supported on walls or colonnades in the Greek manner, barrel vaulting over temples and galleries, pitched roofs covered with tiles for rectangular constructions and domes to cover circular buildings.

Roman town planning

Although the Roman towns of Provence did not develop from military camps but mostly from Gaulish or Greek settlements, they were built to the usual **grid pattern,** divided into four quarters by two main streets meeting at right angles and leading to the main gates in the town walls. Until 3C AD people were able to live in open cities; **town gates,** as at Arles and Nîmes, were designed to impress. **Circuit walls,** for which permission had to be obtained from Rome, were an expensive burden and took on the irregular shape of the expanding town. The **streets** were not paved but lined by footpaths up to 50cm - 2ft above the roadway and sheltered by arcades. Strategically placed stepping stones enabled horses and carts to pass between them while pedestrians could cross over above the dust and mud.

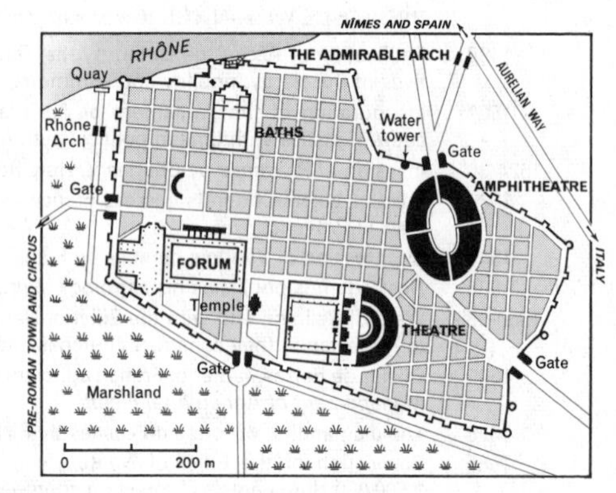

Roman Arles.

Forum. – The forum, a large paved open space surrounded by an arcade, was the centre of public and commercial life in a Roman town. People congregated there to read notices, exchange news and listen to political speeches. Shops occupied the ground floor premises and stalls were set up in the arcades. In the immediate neighbourhood stood the public buildings: temples, baths, local government offices, treasury, commercial centre and granary, election halls and orators' platform, law courts and prison.

Temples. – Apart from the official cults of the Capitoline triad, Jupiter, Juno and Minerva, and later of the Emperor, the Romans were tolerant of the local Gallic gods to whom they gave Roman names and attributes.

Roman temples (maison carrée at Nîmes, for example) were closely derived from Greek models and consist of a podium with steps leading up to an open porch before an inner sanctuary. The whole was surrounded by a free-standing or engaged colonnade. Temples dedicated to a healing spirit often formed the centre of a group of buildings with baths and dormitories for the reception of pilgrims.

Commemorative Arches. – The arches in Orange, Glanum, Carpentras and Cavaillon resemble the triumphal arches of Rome, raised in honour of victorious generals, but were built to commemorate the founding of the cities in which they stand and the exploits of the veterans who settled there.

Early constructions tend to be single-arched but later ones, as at Orange, have a central arch flanked by two smaller arches. The general theme of the decorations was Roman military superiority over the barbarian.

Amphitheatres. – Amphitheatres consisted of tiers of seats surrounding an arena in which a variety of human and/or animal contests, as well as public executions, took place. Early structures were of wood but soon after 50AD Nîmes and Arles had stone amphitheatres designed by T. Crispius Reburrus. The tiers of seats were supported by two storeys of arcades above which was the attic storey shaded by a retractable sun awning. The first rows were reserved for consuls, senators and magistrates and members of local guilds who arrived in litters. In another section sat priests, knights and Roman citizens while freedmen and slaves sat in the attic.

The spectators could reach their seats quickly by an extensive system of corridors, staircases and separate entrances. In the interval refreshments were sold under the arcades; during the performances incense was burned to neutralise the smell of the animals, and important people were attended by slaves operating sweet-smelling sprays.

Gladiators were generally slaves or captives, although there were teams of professionals trained by managers who hired them out to rich patrons or to candidates at public elections. They were matched against one another or against animals using a variety of weapons and techniques. In theory a gladiatorial duel ended in the death of the loser but he could raise a finger to beg for mercy, and the thumbs up or down given by the president sealed his fate. Victory was rewarded with a cash prize, with freedom for a slave or a ribbon discharging the gladiator from fighting again.

Exotic animals such as lions, tigers, panthers, elephants and rhinos performed only in Rome or in the presence of the Emperor. In the provinces bulls, bears, boars and mastiffs were matched in contests, and even sealions and crocodiles where the arena could be flooded as at Nîmes. Then the gladiators fought in the water or from galleys. The major events were interspersed with minor diversions: dogs were set on deer or to worry hedgehogs, birds of prey were released against hares, rabbits and pigeons.

Slaves with iron-tipped whips kept the contests going and red powder was sprinkled on the ground to hide the blood.

Theatres. – The Roman theatres of Provence in Arles, Orange and Vaison-la-Romaine derive from the Greek plan and have a semi-circle of tiered seats facing the stage across an orchestra. The stage backdrop consisted of three tiers of columns, niches and statues faced with marble and mosaic in bright colours. Doors, originally one and later three, led backstage. Scene changes slid in through the wings, descended from above, rose through trap doors or were mounted on three-sided vertical prisms which pivoted between the columns. At the beginning and end of a performance a curtain, some 3m - 13ft high, was lowered and raised from a slot in the ground between the stage and orchestra by means of lead weights. Above the stage, a roof sloping out and up, acted as a sounding board as did the hollow doors on stage and the curved wings of the auditorium. Large empty vases strategically placed among the seats also acted as amplifiers. Stage effects included thunder and lightning, smoke and apparitions. The audience expressed its disapproval with rotten apples.

Behind the stage were the dressing rooms – Roman actors wore elaborate headdresses of mask and wig, elaborate costumes and high-soled shoes. A portico leads to a garden and shops. Here political, musical and literary societies met, lotteries were held, bread and money distributed; people were also entertained here by cock fighting, conjurors, bear tamers, tight rope walkers, sword swallowers, jugglers, acrobats, mime artistes and puppeteers.

To begin with the Romans borrowed from Greek drama – Greek comedy probably survived longest in Marseilles – but gradually Roman adaptations developed their own form and the art of mime became important. Satire and comedy remained popular but humour became so licentious that in 5AD under Christian influence play going was suppressed.

Baths. – A distinctive feature of Roman cities were the baths which, from a suite of bathrooms grouped round an exercise ground, developed into a social and recreational centre with gardens and club rooms for lectures and poetry readings.

The bather left his clothes in a locker in the changing rooms *(apodyterium)* and, after taking exercise, went through a series of rooms: warm room *(tepidarium),* hot room *(caldarium),* steam room (*laconicum* or *sudatorium*) and a cold room *(frigidarium);* other features were the swimming pool *(natatio)* and a cold plunge *(piscina).* After massage the bather emerged refreshed to enjoy walking and chatting in the gardens or readings in the club rooms.

Hadrian decreed that men and women should bathe separately. Sometimes two sets of baths were built or the sexes used one set of facilities at different times. Bath buildings developed into complex structures and were sumptuously decorated with mosaic and marble; some were lit from above through clerestory windows under domed roofs.

The heating system consisted of several small rooms like bakers' ovens in which fires were maintained. Hot air circulated under the floors *(hypocaust)* between the brick supports and through the wall cavities before escaping through chimneys. The hottest room which faced south or west had high picture windows of glass, creating a solarium. Hot, tepid and cold water circulated automatically by thermosiphon. The Romans also made use of natural spring waters as at Aix.

Aqueducts. – Large quantities of water were required to supply the public baths, civic fountains and private houses of a Roman town. For preference the water was collected at source from a north facing slope to ensure its purity and stored away from direct sunlight to keep it fresh and cool. To carry the water to the towns, the Romans built aqueducts, sinking the water channel in a trench or tunnel below ground whenever possible. Little remains of the Arles aqueduct at Barbégal, but the Pont du Gard which carried an aqueduct from Uzès to Nîmes across the valley of the River Gard, is an impressive example of Roman engineering. Sometimes water was carried across a valley in sealed lead piping. In Nîmes there is a large circular basin and settling tank with a series of outlets through which the water was allocated to the municipal water system.

Houses. – The excavations at Glanum and Vaison-la-Romaine, two modest country towns, reveal a picture of middle class life in the Early Roman Empire. Houses of various types have been uncovered: a trader's dwelling over a shop, a two-storeyed house, and a grand mansion. The houses under shallow tiled roofs were built facing inwards and presented a blank exterior, but inside there was painted plaster on the walls decorated in red, yellow, green, blue, black and white and even orange and pink. There was glass in the windows, and floors were of concrete or mosaic.

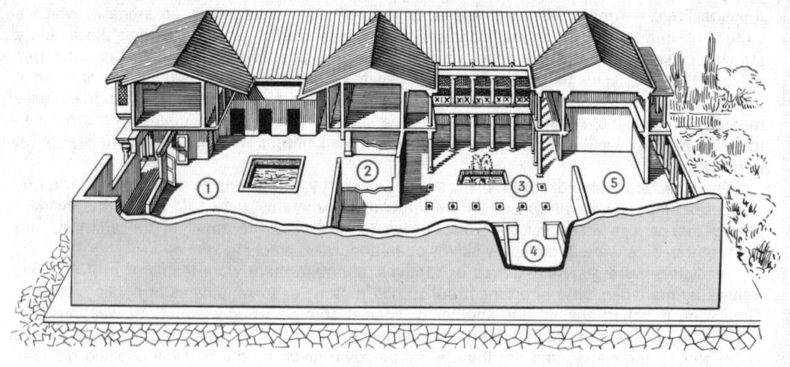

Roman House.

From the street a door, guarded by a porter or a sign saying « Beware of the dog », opened into a short corridor leading to a large hall *(atrium,* 1), open to the sky in the centre to allow rainwater to collect in a basin *(impluvium)*.

The rooms opening off the hall included the owner's study (*tablinum,* 2) where books and accounts were kept. A narrow passage *(fauces)* led to another court (*peristyle,* 3) with a central pool or fountain and surrounded by a covered gallery with the family rooms opening off it. As well as bedrooms, simply furnished, there would be a dining room (*triclinum,* 4) where the diners reclined on couches before tables set round three sides of a square so that the meal could be served from the open side. Food was cut small and eaten with the fingers or with spoons. Wine goblets were of clay, metal or glass. Then there was the main saloon (*oecus,* 5). Beyond the living rooms were the baths, kitchen and ovens, slaves rooms, stores and stables. There was running water and main drainage from the kitchen and latrine.

The PROVENÇAL ROMANESQUE STYLE

The brilliant Gallo-Roman civilization disappeared beneath a flood of Barbarian invasions; a dark age followed from 5-11C when few buildings were erected of which only isolated specimens now remain such as the small baptistry at Aix and at Venasque.

In 12C Provence embarked on one of the most brilliant periods in its history, accompanied by the equally splendid architectural flowering still visible in the multitude of churches, large and small, erected in towns, on distant hillsides and in the valleys. They were Romanesque in style with the special characteristics developed in the school which evolved in the area between the Rhône, the Drôme, the Alps and the Mediterranean and which, more conservative than creative, combined features from antiquity, the Languedoc, the Auvergne and Lombardy.

The style's principal traits, outlined below, are best exemplified in churches in the Rhône Valley; the Old Major Cathedral, Marseilles; St-Trophime, Arles; St-Gilles, N.-D.-des-Domes Cathedral, Avignon, and the Old Cathedral, Orange.

Exterior features: stonework. – The limestone blocks are always regular and finely dressed, with only the thinnest bed of mortar between the stones. Material was taken from abandoned Roman buildings and re-used, or the buildings themselves were adapted to become, in the case of the Arles amphitheatre, an entire village.

(After photo by Arch. Phot., Paris)

The amphitheatre village, Arles.

Plan. – Provençal Romanesque churches are directly descended from the Roman basilica and Carolingian church. Their general appearance is of a solid mass. Transepts are rare and shallow. Often there is a single nave with side chapels hollowed out of the thickness of the walls. Massive buttresses, between which were set the lancet windows of the nave, relieve the austere monotony of the exterior. The east end takes the form of an apse with two flanking apsidal chapels, where there are side aisles. Only the great pilgrimage churches of St-Gilles and St-Trophime, Arles, have ambulatories.

Towers. – Solid square towers, decorated with blind Lombardy arcading, beneath a pyramidal roof, are to be found either over the most easterly bay of the choir or more usually supported by a dome over the crossing.

West front. – The west front was often plain or the decoration was confined to a large carved tympanum above a horizontal lintel but the 12C produced the finely sculptured façades of St-Trophime in Arles and St-Gilles, which have some of the best figure sculpture in France for the period. The columns and entablatures, as well as the arched porch of St-Trophime, reflect Roman influence.

Interior. – The gloom of the austere and cavernous interior is penetrated by narrow shafts of light through the lancet windows of the nave.

Chancel and apse. – An oven vaulting usually covers the apse which is joined to the crossing by a high barrel vault.

Transept and dome. – The problem of the nave and transept vaulting meeting and supporting the weight of a tower was solved by placing a dome on squinches over the crossing, in the style of the Auvergne school.

Nave. – Broken barrel vaulting, which exerts more downward and less outward thrust than tunnel vaulting – both types were known to the Romans – came to replace the wooden roofing of 5-11C which was vulnerable to fire. The majority of churches comprised a single nave, the downward thrust of the high vault being absorbed in the thickness of the walls, but a few had side aisles, which acted as buttresses and had tunnel and broken barrel vaulting. Owing to the height of the side aisles there were no tribunes but a decorative band of blind arcading with three arches to each bay, the central arch being pierced by a lancet window.

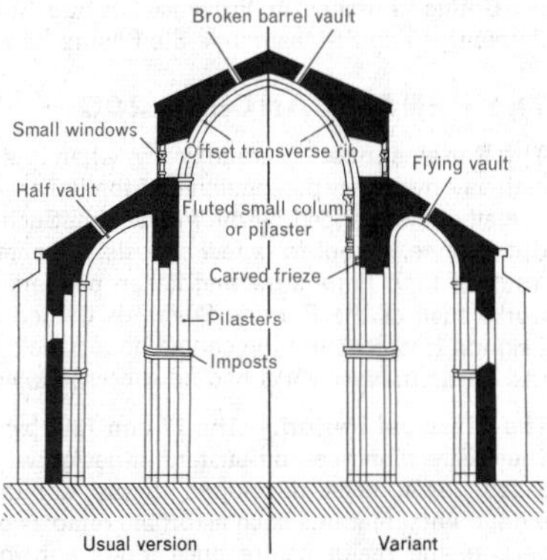

Vertical section
of a Provençal Romanesque Church.

Decoration. – With the exception of the west fronts of St-Trophime in Arles *(p 41)* and St-Gilles *(p 111)*, the Romanesque churches in Provence were externally plain and sober; internal decoration was confined to carved altar fronts, to fluting, rope moulding and foliage and to sculpted capitals.

The widening of the head of a column to form a capital, on to which several structural arches could descend, provided the stonemason with an architectural feature where he could give his individual talent free rein. Themes were taken from the Old and New Testaments and from local tradition.

Some of the best examples of this decorative art are to be found in the apse of Stes-Maries-de-la-Mer and the cloisters of St-Trophime, Montmajour and St-Paul-de-Mausole (fantastic animals).

MILITARY ARCHITECTURE

Medieval fortifications, against roving mercenaries and pirates, are well illustrated by Aigues-Mortes where the circuit wall encloses a Roman style grid plan, Villeneuve-lès-Avignon which has a fine gatehouse with two heavily machicolated round towers, the church of Stes-Maries-de-la-Mer, as well as the town walls of Avignon and the castles of Beaucaire and Tarascon.

On either side of the Rhône Valley the hilltops are crowned by ruins where a natural strongpoint has been fortified as at Châteauneuf-du-Pape, Mornas, Mondragon, Chamaret, Thouzon (Le Thor), Oppède-le-Vieux and Les Baux.

Many villages were built in a ring round a hilltop or clinging to a steep slope beneath the walls of the local feudal castle out of the way of marauding bands. The houses, built of local stone, lean against one another for support and are hardly visible against the natural rock. The streets are narrow and twisting with steps on the steepest gradients. A communal fountain stands in a picturesque cobbled square.

Many of these **hill villages** are now deserted as the inhabitants have built modern houses on their land in the valleys below.

GOTHIC STYLE

The Gothic style is marked by the systematic use of rib vaulting, pointed arches and flying buttresses which revolutionized construction by reducing the outward thrust on the supporting walls enabling a lighter structure to be built to a greater height. The custom of making pilgrimages and the veneration of relics led to the chevet – an ambulatory with radiating chapels at the east end, as in St-Trophime in Arles.

Rib vaulting appeared early in Provence; the Gothic arches in the crypt of St-Gilles and the porch of St-Victor in Marseilles are pre-1150 although systematic use of rib vaulting did not occur until 13C.

In 14C a Papal Gothic style developed in Avignon; across the river in Villeneuve the cardinals built churches, cloisters and palaces. Under Dominican influence single nave preaching churches were erected.

Romanesque

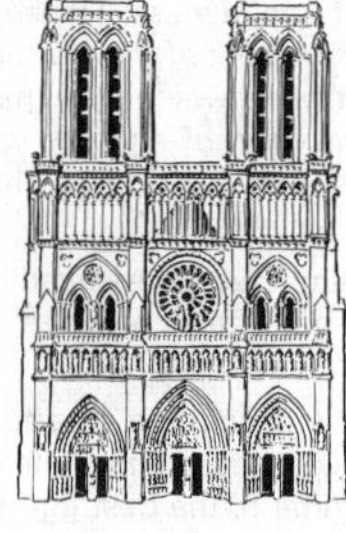
Gothic

Renaissance

Classic

The interiors of Gothic churches in Provence may seem austere; carving was confined to ceiling bosses, keystones, shallow capitals and funerary effigies, while painted murals became the principal form of decoration.

The popes attracted artists from France, Germany, Flanders and Italy to Avignon which held first place in Provençal painting for three centuries. Italians decorated the Papal Palace with frescoes and there is Siennese influence in the Villeneuve Charterhouse. With the popes' departure Italian influence declined and the Avignon school turned to panel painting instead of frescoes.

Gothic churches in Provence include St-Pierre in Avignon, Old St-Siffrein Cathedral in Carpentras and St-Maximin-la-Ste-Baume Basilica.

The RENAISSANCE to 20C

The Renaissance. – Paradoxically, when it is recalled that the Rhône Valley was the principal highway by which personalities of the Italian Renaissance entered France, Provence remained virtually uninfluenced by the movement. Such buildings as were erected in 16C were after the Gothic style, except for a few chapels and chateaux. But in painting there was a response as a result of King René attracting Italian painters and sculptors whose influence produced native works such as the *Burning Bush* (Aix Cathedral), the *Coronation of the Virgin* (Villeneuve-lès-Avignon Hospice) and the carved door panels at St-Pierre, Avignon, and St-Sauveur Cathedral, Aix. These master works had no successors, however, in Provence or even in France.

The Classical Period. – The 17 and 18C, by contrast, produced a large number of buildings. They were dignified and austere in design without distinctive regional characteristics. The so-called Jesuit style developed in the Comtat Venaissin churches, bringing with it Italian monumental features such as ornate retables or altarpieces, panelling and baldachins. Avignon became the major centre once more with local artists such as the **Mignards** and **Parrocels** producing religious pictures and **Bernus de Mazan,** carving, for churches throughout the region.

An entirely novel element was the building of town houses by the old and new moneyed nobility, the magistracy and others: a few remain in Avignon but the finest line the streets of Aix. These well proportioned, dignified stone houses are distinguished by doorways coroneted with ironwork balconies often supported by robust caryatids or muscular atlantes, the work of Rambot, Toro and above all **Puget** (1620-94), an artist and architect from Marseilles, who became one of the great sculptors of 17C France. He began as a carver of ships' prows, was promoted by Colbert but soon fell into disgrace through intrigue and devoted himself to urban decoration in his native south. In his wake followed the sculptors, **Houdon** (1741-1828) and **Chastel** (1726-1793) and portrait painters, **Rigaud** (1649-1743), **Nattier** (1685-1766), **Latour** (1704-88) and Joseph **Vernet** (1714-89).

Contemporary with the new domestic architecture is the work of local furniture and cabinet-makers, fine china ware, pottery from the works in Moustiers and Marseilles and the delicate wrought iron work preserved in the Calvet Museum, Avignon.

19 and 20C. – The 19C was an era of contrasts in which **Espérandieu** (1829-74) erected the Major Cathedral and N.-D.-de-la-Garde Basilica in Marseilles in the Roman Byzantine style, and the Longchamp Palace water tower in the Neo-Classical style. Civil engineers constructed the Roquefavour aqueduct, the underground Rove Canal and bridges across the Rhône in a clean limbed utilitarian manner.

Of the vast amount of building which has taken place in 20C the most original and outstanding is **Le Corbusier's** (1887-1965) Cité Radieuse in Marseilles, a modern housing project comprising six blocks of dwellings. Only one block *(unité d'habitation)* was completed, the forerunner of many subsequent tower blocks.

It was in 19C that Provence again made its mark in art history when Ziem, Courbet, Bracassat, Cézanne and Van Gogh tried to capture its clear Mediterranean light and brilliant colours on their canvases.

Romanesque belfry

Romanesque spire

Gothic spire

Renaissance belfry

Classical dome

TRADITIONAL PROVENCE

RURAL ARCHITECTURE

The Provençal house in the country, whether a **mas,** a **bastide** or an **oustau,** will have the following characteristics:

– a shallow sloping roof of Roman style curved terracotta tiles, with a decorative frill under the eaves, composed of a double or triple row of tiles embedded end-on in the wall and known as a **génoise;**

– stone walls, more or less smoothly rendered, with no windows on the north side and those on the other three sides just large enough to let in light but keep out the summer heat;

– a north-south orientation, with sometimes a slight turn to the east to avoid the direct blast of the *mistral* and a serried row of cypresses to serve as a windbreak to the north, while plane and lotus trees provide shade to the south.

(After photo by Ed. Vincent, Fréal Cie, 1970)

A 'mas'.

A *mas* is a large farm where farmhouse and outbuildings are grouped beneath a single shallow roof; an *oustau* is a smallholder's version of a *mas* and a *bastide* a small, usually square, house beneath a shallow pyramid roof.

(After photo by Combier, Mâcon)

A gardian's 'cabane'.

The **cabanes** are scattered about the Camargue so that the **gardians** (herdsmen) live near their animals. The two room house has white walls curving round into an apse at the north end against the wind and is covered in deep rush thatch. Modern versions for tourists are being built near holiday resorts.

BULLFIGHTING

Although Spanish style bullfights – to the death – for which the men and animals come from Spain, are held in the big cities such as Arles and Nîmes, Provence has its own distinctive version of the sport *(course à la cocarde)* in which the bulls are not killed. A rosette *(cocarde)* is attached to the bull's horns and young men dressed in white *(razeteurs)* compete to remove the rosette with a sort of metal claw held in the hand. The *razeteurs* take their name from the *razet,* the half circle round the bull's head into which they must dash to snatch the rosette. The winner receives a money prize. Sometimes, when hard pressed, the *razeteurs* leap the barrier into the stands, a feat known as the *coup de barrière.* The bull has been known to make the leap too. The animals used are the local strain – black and agile – and bred in the Camargue for the ring *(p 62).*

Two rooms in the Museum of Old Nîmes *(p 95)* are devoted to bullfighting – one for the Spanish style and one for Provençal.

BOWLS

The popular local game of *boules* is played with iron clad balls on any piece of more or less level ground by teams of 3 or 4 players.

The attackers *(pointeurs)* land their balls as close as possible to the jack *(cochonnet)* while the defenders *(tireurs)* try to knock out their opponent's ball leaving their own in its place. Over short distances a player throws with his feet together *(à la pétanque)* but over long distances (10m - 30ft) the player may take two or three steps before delivering the ball *(à la longue).* A game always attracts a group of spectators and gives rise to animated discussions about technique and lively disputes as to who has won.

LANGUAGE and LITERATURE

Provençal language. – Provençal or (more correctly) the Occitanian or Oc language is the dialect now spoken in several areas of southern France, particularly the Comtat Venaissin and the area round Nîmes and Uzès. It developed in southern Gaul from the low Latin spoken during the later days of the Roman Empire. In northern Gaul the Oïl language developed and became French. « Oc » and « Oïl » were the words used for Yes in the south and north respectively. Political and social differences added to the linguistic differences between the two regions; in the north the Germanic influence was much stronger than in the south. By 12C the two languages were distinct. The boundary between them ran from the mouth of the Loire through the southern Vosges but later from the Gironde estuary via the northern edge of the Massif Central to the Alps.

Provençal flourished in 12C and 13C and was known outside its area, in Germany, in England at the court of Richard the Lion Heart and in Italy where Dante hesitated between Provençal and Tuscan for his Divine Comedy. The troubadours, several of whom are named by Dante, made the language and literature famous through their poetry, written for the courts of southern France where women enjoyed consid-

folquet de marseilla

(After photo by Bibliothèque Nationale)

13C manuscript : Folquet de Marseille.

erable freedom. The lyrics were inspired by the stylized etiquette of courtly or chivalrous love. A poet paid homage to his lady in highly sophisticated and obscure language and set his verses to music. By 13C the art was in decline, although Provençal was still spoken by the papal court in Avignon in 14C. The increasing influence of northern France through the Albigensian Crusade hastened the end which came in 1539 with the Edict of Villers-Cotterêts, imposing the Oïl language of the north for administrative purposes.

For the next three centuries Provençal fragmented into local dialects, although its literary expression was kept alive by Petrarch, by the sonnets of Bellaud-de-la-Bellaudière (16C) and by the religious verses of Nicolas Saboly (17C).

The Félibrige. – In May 1854, Frédéric **Mistral,** Roumanille his schoolmaster, **Aubanel** printer and publisher and four other poets founded a society near Avignon which they named the Félibrige, after an old song. The aim of the society was the revival of the Provençal language and the rationalization of its spelling. In 1859 Mistral, who was the leader of the group, published his verse romance, **Mireio,** later set to music by Gounod, which by its evocation of Provençal life soon won recognition in Paris for the author and the Félibrige; epic and short poems and plays followed and then the **Trésor du Félibrige** (1879-86), a vast dictionary of the words and proverbs of the Provençal language.

Revival of the language was only a part of the concept; Mistral determined that the ancient customs and spiritual values must also be renewed if Provence were to come truly alive again; he travelled the region making his views known and when, in 1905, he won the Nobel Prize for Literature, he used the money to enlarge and enrich the **Museon Arlaten** in Arles.

Today numerous museums display local costumes and crafts; many festivals and even pilgrimages recall local history and traditions.

Under the influence of radio and television spoken Provençal may be dying, but recent government policy is to encourage local dialects in the schools, and the Institute of Occitanian Studies aims to re-establish a common language.

CHRISTMAS CRIBS

Christmas cribs have a long tradition in Provence although it was not until the late 18C that they became at all common and developed a typically local character – a few 18C groups, often highly original and beautifully modelled, may still be seen in churches but most are now in museums (Aix, Marseilles and Arles).

Church Cribs. – Christmas was not an important festival in the early church nor did cribs form part of the medieval celebrations except for rare low reliefs of the adoration of the shepherds or the kings as in the St-Maximin crypt.

In 1545 the Council of Trent sought to advance the Counter Reformation through the encouragement of popular piety. The practice of setting up a crib in church arrived in Provence from Italy in 17C. There is a particularly beautiful crib from this period in the church of St-Maximin; the carved figures, about 50cm - 20ins high, are of gilded wood. In 18C bejewelled wax figures were introduced with glass eyes and wigs. Only the head, arms and legs were carved and attached to a richly dressed articulated frame. The 19C saw the employment of printed or painted cardboard cut-outs with gaily coloured clothing, or figures made from spun glass, cork or a resin-and-bread-crumb compound.

Live Cribs. – At midnight mass in many churches today – Séguret, Allauch, Isle-sur-la-Sorgue and Marseilles – there is a virtual nativity mask. In Gémenos, children in costume place the Infant Jesus in a straw-filled manger. In Les Baux, a little cart, decorated with greenery and bearing a new-born lamb, is drawn into church by a ram and accompanied by shepherds. The procession is headed by angels and fife and drum players while the congregation sing old Provençal carols. The lamb is offered to the church and the cart stands to one side in the aisle throughout the year.

Talking Cribs. – 18C passion for marionettes was adapted to produce talking cribs in which mechanical figures enacted the Nativity to a commentary and carols. Characters were added to the already numerous cast and, as imagination ran wild, historical accuracy and relevance vanished: reindeer, giraffes and hippopotami joined the other animals, the pope arrived in a carriage to bless the Holy Family...

In 19C, Napoleon, accompanied by his soldiers and a man of war firing salvoes brought the scene up to date! Another new idea came to those presenting a crib close to Marseilles station : the Three Kings travelled to the scene in a steam train!

Santon cribs. – The *santon* cribs are the most typically Provençal. They first appeared in 1789 at the time of the Revolution when the churches were closed and cribs, therefore, inaccessible. Jean-Louis Lagnel, a church statue maker from Marseilles, had the idea of making small figures which families could buy at little cost. Known in Provençal as **santouns,** little saints, the figurines had an immediate and wide appeal. They were modelled in clay, fired and naïvely painted in bright colours. Limited at first to Biblical personnages, they were soon joined by men and women from all walks of life, dressed, of course, in the local costume; the Holy Family, the shepherds and their sheep, the Three Kings, occupied the stage together with the knifegrinder, the pipe and tabor player, the smith, the blind man and his guide, the fishwife, wetnurse, milkmaid, the huntsman, fisherman and even the mayor!

So great was the figurines' success, as virtually every family began to build up a collection, that a **Santons Fair** was inaugurated in Marseilles which is still held on the Canebière from the last Sunday in November to Epiphany. *Santon* makers established workshops in towns throughout Provence while in the country men and women made figures in the long winter evenings. The craft reached its peak in 1820-30s which is why so many of the characters, now mass-produced, appear in the dress of that period.

The drum and fife player.

PRINCIPAL FESTIVALS

PLACE AND DATE		CELEBRATION
Aix-en-Provence	mid-July to early August	International Music Festival
Allauch	Sunday following 24 June	Provençal Festival of St-John-the-Baptist; blessing of the animals
	24 December	Provençal Midnight Mass
Apt	Whitsun	Grand artistic procession; music festival
Arles	Easter Saturday, Sunday, Monday	Easter festival. Spanish style (to the death) bullfights
	Last Sunday in April	Cowboy *(gardian)* festival. Mass, blessing of the horses. Bullfights
	Late June to late July	Open-air performances in the Roman theatre
	First Monday in July	Golden cocade bullfight
	July to September	Spanish style (to the death) and Provençal style bullfights *(course à la cocarde – p 23).*
	Early December to early January	International Santon-makers Show
Avignon	Mid-July to mid-August	Dance and Drama Festival
Les Baux	24 December	Shepherds' Festival★★. Midnight Mass
Beaucet 246 fold 11	May and September	Pilgrimage to St-Gens' Church
Boulbon	1 June	Bottle procession. Canticles in praise of St Marcellinus and blessing of the wine
Carpentras	Mid-July	Festival of Our Lady of Good Health (evening procession)
Châteaurenard	First Sunday in July	St Eligius' chariot decorated and drawn by 40 horses in Saracen harness; Provençal style bullfights *(course à la cocarde p 23)*
Courthézon 246 folds 10 and 24	First or second Sunday in June	Vine stock festival. A vine stock is carried to church. Sermon in Provençal. Dancing and singing of 1493 Hymn of Grace
Fontvielle	24 December	Christmas Eve Provençal mass
Graveson	Last Sunday in July	St Eligius' festival similar to the one at Châteaurenard
Marseilles	Last Sunday in November to Epiphany	Santons Fair
Martigues	First Saturday in July	Venetian Evening. Procession of decorated boats
Monteux 246 fold 10	Sunday and Monday following 15 May	St Gens' festival; procession in local costume marked by shotgun fire, sermon in Provençal
	Tuesday following fourth Sunday in August	St John's Fireworks (the firework makers of Monteux are famous)
Nîmes	Whitsun	Whitsun Festival. Bullfights and contests
	Whitsun to September	Bullfights and contests
	June to September	Spanish style (to the death) bullfights and contests
Nyons	Easter Sunday and Monday	Spring Flower Festival
	First fortnight in July	Olive and folklore festival
Orange	Mid-July to early August	Arts Festival in Roman Theatre: drama, opera, ballet and symphony concerts
Roussillon	Ascension and following two days	"Ochre" Festival
Ste-Baume	21 and 22 July	Mary Magdalen festival with midnight mass
Stes-Maries-de la-Mer	24 and 25 May	Gipsy pilgrimage★★
	Sunday nearest to 22 October	Procession to and blessing of the sea
Séguret	Third week in August	Provençal festival
	24 December	Mystery play. Provençal vigil
Tarascon	Last Sunday in June	Tarasque festival: folk procession, with Daudet's character, Tartarin
	14 July	Arrival of the bulls
Uzès	July	Musical evenings
Vaison-la-Romaine	Early July to mid-August or mid-July to end August	International Folklore Festival and Classical Theatre Festival
Valréas	23 June	St John the Baptist's Day
Ventabren	24 December	Nativity Play or Live Crib
Villeneuve-lès-Avignon	Late April	Feast of St Mark: procession of beribboned vine stock through the streets

KEY

★★★ Worth a journey

★★ Worth a detour

★ Interesting

Sightseeing route with departure point and direction indicated

on the road — in town

The following symbols, when accompanied by a name or a letter in heavy type, locate the sights described in this guide

Mainly on local maps

- Castle – Ruins
- Chapel – Cross or calvary
- Panorama – View
- Lighthouse – Mill (wind or water)
- Dam – Factory or power station
- Fort – Quarry
- Miscellaneous sights

Mainly on town plans

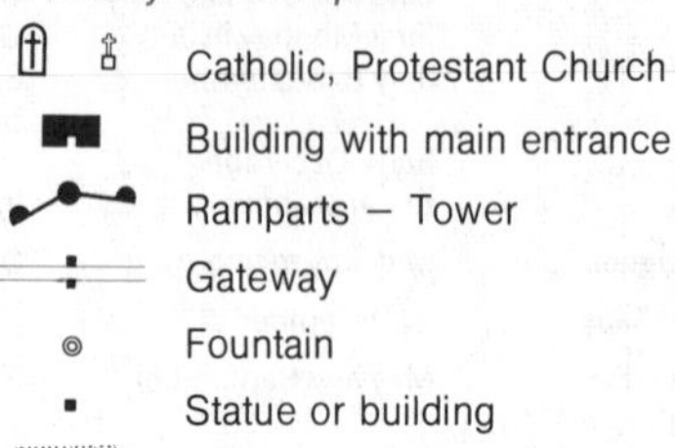

- Catholic, Protestant Church
- Building with main entrance
- Ramparts – Tower
- Gateway
- Fountain
- Statue or building
- Gardens, park, woods
- Letter locating a sight

Conventional signs

- Motorway (unclassified)
- Dual carriageway
- Major through road
- Tree-lined street
- Stepped street
- Pedestrian street
- Impassable or under construction
- Footpath
- Trolleybus, tram
- Station
- A | B Reference grid letters for town plans
- ③ Reference number common to town plans and MICHELIN maps
- 12 Distance in kilometres
- 1429 Pass – Altitude
- Public building
- Hospital
- Covered market
- Barracks
- Cemetery
- Racecourse – Golf course
- Outdoor or indoor swimming pool
- Skating rink – Viewing table
- Telecommunications tower or mast
- Stadium – Water tower
- Airport – Airfield
- Coach station
- Main post office (with poste restante)
- Tourist information centre
- Car park

In all MICHELIN guides, plans and maps are always orientated with north at the top.
Main shopping streets are printed in a different colour at the beginning of the list of streets.

Abbreviations

- *A* Motorway (Autoroute)
- A Local agricultural office (Chambre d'Agriculture)
- C Chamber of Commerce (Chambre de Commerce)
- *D* Secondary road (Route Départementale)
- G Police station (Gendarmerie)
- *GR* Long distance footpath (Sentier de Grande Randonnée)
- H Town Hall (Hôtel de Ville)
- J Law Courts (Palais de Justice)
- M Museum
- *N* Trunk road (Route Nationale)
- P Préfecture Sous-préfecture
- POL. Police
- *R.F.* Forest Road (Route Forestière)
- T Theatre
- U University

Additional signs

Ferry services
- Passengers and cars
- Passengers only

The towns and sights described in this guide are shown in black on the maps.

TOWNS, SIGHTS AND TOURIST REGIONS

AIGUES-MORTES ★★

Michelin map 83 fold 8 – *Local map p 62* – Pop 4 475 – *Facilities p 8*

Aigues-Mortes, which has hardly grown in 700 years, still shelters behind its towering 13C golden stone ramparts and so, fortified and solitary, retains much of its medieval appearance. Originally it was entirely surrounded by a moat and accessible only by a narrow causeway across the sea marshes.

Local industries are salt production (dating from 8C) and vine growing.

Crusader port to small inland township. – The town was developed in 1240 by Louis IX, St Louis, who was preparing to set out on a crusade to liberate Jerusalem. Although nominally King of France, Louis possessed no Mediterranean seaport as the country was not yet unified. A local monastery hearing of his intended voyage, presented him with the small fishing village at the end of an isthmus, known from its isolated and somewhat mournful situation as Dead or Still Waters – Aigues-Mortes.

The king constructed the Constance Tower to defend the harbour and began the ramparts which were completed together with the full complement of towers and gateways, by his son, Philip the Bold.

In 1248 St Louis set sail with a fleet of 38 ships on the Seventh Crusade. A long campaign in Egypt, where the king was captured and ransomed, and a second in Palastine were both unsuccessful and in 1254 he returned to France. In 1270, with unabated devotion, he set out on the Eighth Crusade, again sailing from Aigues-Mortes, this time bound first for Tunis where he died of the plague. In mid–14C the population of this privileged town – Louis had granted special rights and exemptions to attract inhabitants – numbered 15 000 or three times its present population: decline has come through the silting up of the shore until now Aigues-Mortes stands some 5 miles from the sea, surrounded only by marshes, saltflats and lagoons.

First sight★★. – At first sight the mediaeval walls rise from the marshes like a mirage against the flat horizon. The best approach is at sunset along D 979 from Le Grau-du-Roi, while the road from the north passes the outpost of the Carbonnière Tower.

Crusaders embarking from Aigues-Mortes as illustrated in a medieval chronicle.

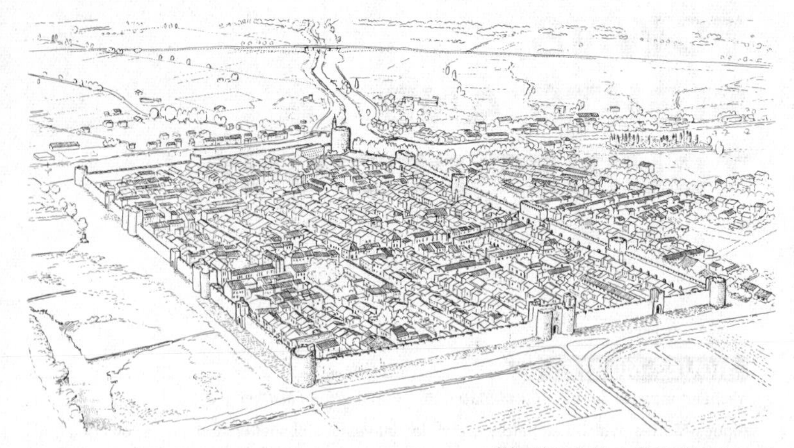

(After photo by Vu du Ciel by Alain Perceval)

The fortified town of Aigues-Mortes from the south.

Constance Tower★★. – *Open 1 April to 30 September, 9am to noon and 2 to 6pm; 1 October to 31 March, 10am to noon and 2 to 5pm; closed Easter, 1 May, 25 December; 8F, 4F Sundays and holidays.* The tower, erected as the harbour and city keep, and originally reinforced by a moat, was connected to the ramparts in 16C. Of the many defences there remain the portcullis and the embrasures through which missiles were hurled on attackers. Inside may be seen the garrison bread oven (in the guardroom) and, on upper floors approached by a spiral staircase, St Louis' Oratory, a minute chapel built into the thickness of the wall, and the Knights' Hall. This served principally as quarters for well known prisoners among whom, over a period of 500 years, were political detainees, Templar barons and Huguenots. Two Protestants held in the tower were **Abraham Mazel,** a leading Calvinist who escaped down knotted bedclothes with 16 co-religionists in 1705, and **Marie Durand** whose indomitable courage finally secured her release together with ten of her companions from the cell in which she had been incarcerated for 38 years (1730-68) – note her graffito: Resister.

Climb to the watch tower summit *(53 steps)* for an immense **panorama★★** embracing the rectilinearly laid out town, the surrounding plain punctuated by the Cévennes (N), the Grande Motte « pyramids » (W), Mount Sète (SW) and the Midi and Camargue salt marshes.

Ramparts★★. – *Start a tour at NW corner, the La Gardette Gate: 3/4 hour.*

The ramparts were built in one style between 1272 and 1300 to enclose a formal rectangular grid pattern of street. The walls were protected by a sea-water moat, since filled in, with five towers to guard the five gates and posterns. A broad way ran round inside the walls allowing the garrison swift access to any point. The landward side had only two gateways, the Gardette and St-Antoine; the west, a postern, the Ballast Loaders' Wicket (Porte des Remblais); the east, a postern and a gate, the Shoemakers' Wicket (Porte des Cordeliers) and the Queen's Gate (Porte de la Reine). The seaward wall, to afford easy passage for men and cargo between the town and the ships in the harbour, was pierced in five places respectively by the Arsenal Postern, the Maritime Gate, a ceremonial entrance, the Galleons' Postern (Porte des Galions), the Mill Gate (Porte des Moulins) close by the mill which ground grain for the garrison, and the Organeau Postern (Porte de l'Organeau), an organeau being the great iron ring to which the ships were moored.

The towers, in order of approach, are the Salt (Sel), the Wick Tower (Tour de la Mèche) where a light was kept constantly burning to ignite cannon fuses, the Villeneuve, the Magazine (Poudrière) and the Burgundians' Tower (Tour des Bourguignons). This last got its name during the Hundred Years War, when the defending Burgundians were surprised and slaughtered by the Armagnacs (1418) who stacked their victims' bodies in the tower, salting the corpses liberally to prevent putrefaction, until they could bury them.

EXCURSIONS

The Midi Salt Marshes (Les Salins du Midi). – *3 km – 2 miles S of Aigues-Mortes. Visits are organised 1 July to 31 August; Wednesday and Friday afternoons by the tourist information centre, ☎ 66 51 95 00, and Tuesdays and Thursdays at 2pm by the Grau-du-Roi tourist information centre, ☎ 66 51 67 70. For more on saltmarshes see p 14.*

Teillan Castle. – *13 km – 8 miles N by D 979, D34 on the left and D 265 at the main crossroads in Marsillargues. Immediately beyond the bridge, turn right into a dirt road. Local map p 62. Guided tour 15 June to 15 September 2 to 6pm; closed Mondays (and Tuesdays if Monday is a holiday); 15F, park only 10F.*

The castle, which was transformed in the early Middle Ages into a priory and in 17C into a private mansion, retains a defensive appearance in the ancient keep which overtops the residential wings. There is a view from the terrace which embraces the Cévennes, the Languedoc Plain, Aigues-Mortes and the Camargue. The outbuildings reconstructed in 17C include a pigeon loft containing 1 500 nests and a revolving ladder. In the park a chain pump can be seen in a small vaulted outhouse.

With this guide use the Michelin Maps (scale 1:200 000) shown on p 3.

AIX-EN-PROVENCE ★★

Michelin map 84 fold 3 – *Local map p 110* – Pop 124 550 – *Facilities p 8* – *For additional plan of Aix-en-Provence see the current Michelin Red Guide France*

Aix is a delightful town: large enough to have a prosperous and bustling life, small enough to be explored on foot between pauses at the cafés in the Cours Mirabeau watching the world go by the dappled shade of the plane trees: cars trundle in the central thoroughfare, young folk gather, women and children shop and stop to eat ice-cream, tourists wander and, at lunchtime and in the evening, student buskers may appear to put on their clown make-up in public, juggle, sing, fire-eat and parade on stilts.

The town is the old capital of Provence and is graced with 17-18C town houses, narrow streets, quiet squares, arcades and fountains – the massive thermal fountain spouting warm water half-way along the Cours Mirabeau, the magnificent fountains at either end, the endearing Dolphin Fountain in Rue Cardinale and small anonymous fountains in every square. The cathedral, with architectural and artistic treasures from every period, complements the museums displaying archaeological finds, painting (but not Cézanne) and tapestry.

Around old Aix a new town has developed which is both a spa and an industrial complex – it is the biggest centre in Europe for prepared almonds, part of the production being used to make confectionery including the local Aix speciality, a small iced diamond of almond paste, the *calisson.*

HISTORICAL NOTES

The Romans. – In 4C BC the Salluvians, a Celtic-Ligurian tribe, who occupied the territory around their capital of Entremont on the plateau some two miles north of Aix, blocked the expansion of the traders of Marseilles who turned to Rome for assistance. Under Consul Caius Sextius, the Romans destroyed Entremont *(since excavated)* and to consolidate their victory they founded Aquae Sextiae (future Aix) in 122BC near the already famous warm springs.

Twenty years later, Barbarians from eastern Europe, travelling with their families in covered wagons, met the Romans under General Marius near Aix; 100 000 Teutons were slain and 100 000 were taken prisoner. Hence the name of Mount Ste-Victoire *(east).*

Good King René. – The court of the Counts of Provence which was centred on Aix from the 12C and reputed for its poetry, music, troubadours' songs and romances, knew a golden age in the 15C under King René. The King, Duke of Anjou, Count of Provence, titular King of Sicily, was one of the most civilized men of his age: a rare and gifted character, he was versed in Greek, Latin, Hebrew, Catalan and Italian, had studied mathematics, geology and law, was a musician, poet and painter; he enjoyed equally the company of courtier and peasant, organized popular festivals, revived chivalric contests and worked in his own vineyards where he introduced the muscatel grape from Sicily.

René was twice married, first when he was 12, to Isabelle of Lorraine who brought him as dowry the Duchy of Lorraine, the second time (two years after Isabelle's death) to a young bride of 21, Jeanne de Laval – the popular Queen Jeanne. At the end of his reign, René, never a martial figure, philosophically accepted his territorial loss, when Louis XI annexed Anjou to the Kingdom of France, and thenceforward spent all his time in the Provençal countryside and town of Aix where he died in 1480 at the age of 72.

Provençal capital to festival town. – The union of Provence to the crown brought a viceroy to the city which since the dawn of Christianity had been a metropolitan see, and since 1409 a university town; in 1501 it became the seat of a newly created parliament where the states met, most often the local people felt, only to impose tax increases – hence the couplet:

Parliament, mistral and Durance
Are the scourges of Provence.

In 17 and 18C, Aix became a fashionable provincial town: boulevards and squares were laid out, the stately houses for which the town is still known were built. Among the most prominent citizens at the end of this period was **Mirabeau,** soon to be the most eminent orator of the French Revolution. His behaviour was already notorious when, ugly and penniless, he set his cap at Aix's richest heiress and won her, after first compromising her and then boasting of his exploit. On the couple being disinherited, this scion of a noble family ran up debts locally to the order of £1 million before being imprisoned in the Château d'If; in 1783 he was summoned for divorce, defended himself brilliantly but lost on appeal. Nevertheless, scandal apart, when elections were called to the States General in 1789, Count Mirabeau, disdained and rebuffed by his peers, was triumphantly elected to represent the Third Estate for both Aix and Marseilles – he sat for Aix.

In 19C as Marseilles developed, Aix declined: the provincial capital became a subprefecture, the parliament a court of appeal, the university with the faculties of law and letters only. The archbishop's palace alone remained, to become the focal point of the now internationally famous **Summer Music Festival** (July, August).

■ OLD AIX★★ *time: 4 hours*

The circle of boulevards and squares which ring the town mark the line of the ancient ramparts. The Cours Mirabeau forms an approximate east west axis with, to the north, the Old Town, (Vieil Aix) containing the Cathedral and Archbishop's Palace, and, to the south, the 17-18C Quartier Mazarin, named after the man who founded it, Michel Mazarin, archbishop of Aix and brother of the Cardinal.

Cours Mirabeau★★ (BY). – The wide avenue between four rows of plain trees has been the focal point of the town since it was planted in 17C. The ends are marked by 19C fountains, the one to the east by David d'Angers, portraying King René holding a bunch of muscatel grapes (**CY E**). Midway, at the junction with the Rue Joseph-Cabassol, is a 1691 fountain (**BY B**) and at the junction with the Rue Clemenceau, is another, in appearance a weed covered pile of rocks, running with water from the hot springs known to the Romans 2 000 years ago (**BY D**)).

The north of the avenue, today, is lined with pavement cafés and shops: to the south there remain a few houses with dignified doorways and wrought iron balconies supported on caryatides: no 10 dates from *c* 1710, no 19 from 1700, no 20 and no 38 from mid-17C.

Turn left out of the Cours Mirabeau up the Rue Clemenceau to the Place St-Honoré; turn left again out of the square along the Rue Espariat.

(After photo by Ed. de France, Marseille)

Aix-en-Provence. — Cours Mirabeau.

Hôtel Boyer d'Eguilles. – *No 6.* The mansion dates from 1675 and contains fine interior panelling and doorways. It houses the **Natural History Museum** *(open 10am to noon and 2 to 6pm; closed Sundays and holidays and 2 January; 3.50F)* which has interesting collections of mineralogy and palaeontology.

Continue to the Place de l'Hôtel de Ville, noting no 10 Rue Espariat, the **Hôtel d'Albertas** of 1707 and the **Place d'Albertas,** a cobbled square lined by three storey terraced houses, rusticated and round arched below regular upper windows decorated with ironwork balconies and finished with a plain cornice. At the square's centre is a circular fountain.

Turn right up the Rues Aude (note no 13) and Maréchal Foch (no 7).

Place de l'Hôtel-de-Ville (BY 37). – Overlooking the square, where a flower market is held, is the old grain market (now the post office), decorated with carvings by the 18C sculptor, Chastel, a native of Aix, and 17C **Town Hall** (BY H) with its fine contemporary ironwork balcony, it's gateway and paved **courtyard★**. On the first floor are the Méjanes Library and the **Saint-John Perse Collection** *(open Mondays to Fridays 9am to noon and 2 to 5pm; Saturdays 11am to 5pm; closed Sundays and holidays; 5F)* which contains MSS and photographs illustrating the life and work of this diplomat and poet who won the Nobel Prize for literature in 1960.

The **Clock Tower** (BY F) in the corner of the square is 16C. Built of the local golden stone, it is pierced at ground level by an arch through to the street beyond; half-way up is an ornately decorated niche with jacquemarts; above are a circular ironwork balcony, the clock, a second iron trim and the typical Provençal wrought iron bell cage.

Museum of Old Aix (BX M). – *17 Rue Gaston-de-Saporta. Open 1 April to 30 September 10am to noon and 2.30 to 6pm; the rest of the year 10am to noon and 2 to 5pm; closed Mondays, 1 January, Easter Sunday, 14 July, 25 December and October; 10F.*

The museum, in Hôtel d'Estienne de St-Jean (wrought iron banisters), displays a collection of marionettes evoking the talking cribs *(p 24)* and the local Corpus Christi procession. In the same street, no 19 *(open 8am to 4pm; closed weekends and holidays)* is 17C with false perspective murals decorating the inside staircase; no 23 is 15C (altered in 18C).

Tapestry Museum★ (Musée des Tapisseries) (BX M[1]). – *The Archbishop's Palace, Place des Martyrs de la Résistance. Open 1 February to 22 December by appointment only; closed Tuesdays, 1 and 11 November; 6.50F; 10F during exhibitions; ☏ 42 21 05 78. Take the left hand staircase through the gateway.*

Note the entrance decorated with a cardinal's hat.

The interior is atmospheric, although there is little furniture. Among the Beauvais tapestries, which were mostly assembled in 17-18C when the archbishops were in residence, is a series inspired by the Natoire cartoons of the *Life of Don Quixote.*

St-Sauveur Cloister★ (BX N). – The Romanesque cloister is a delight with small, paired columns, supporting a lightweight roof.

St-Sauveur Cathedral (BX R). – The cathedral is a mixture of styles. The belfry is 14-15C Gothic. The 16C Flamboyant Gothic nave was added to the earlier 11C Romanesque south aisle which opens into 5C **baptistry★;** the pool for total immersion is surrounded by eight Roman columns supporting a Renaissance cupola. Two of the cathedral treasures, which are kept shuttered *(ask sacristan, except during church services, to unlock them),* are the **west door panels★,** carved in walnut by Jean Guiramand of Toulon in 1504, depicting the four major prophets of Israel and twelve pagan Sybils in 16C court dress and, hanging in the nave, a 15C triptych of the **Burning Bush★★,** symbolizing the Virginity of Mary, by Nicolas Froment, painter to King René, who is shown kneeling in prayer with his Queen Jeanne in the side panels; the castles in the background are Beaucaire and Tarascon.

Return to the Cours Mirabeau by the Place de l'Hôtel-de-Ville, the Rues Vauvenargues, Méjanes, des Bagniers and Clemenceau.

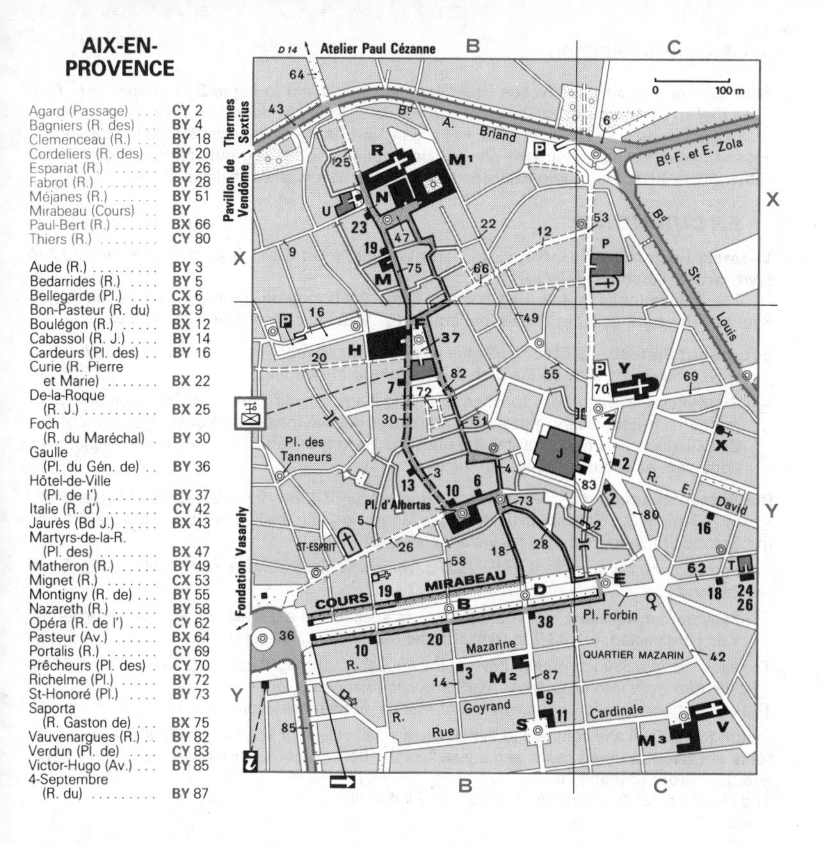

■ ADDITIONAL SIGHTS

Paul-Arbaud Museum (BY M²). – *2a Rue du 4-Septembre. Open 2 to 5pm; closed Sundays and holidays and in October; 10F.*

The museum comprises a library on Provence, local ceramics, pictures and sculpture.

In the same street are two more noteworthy houses, at no 9, the early 18C balconied and bossaged **Hôtel de Villeneuve d'Ansouis** and at no 11, the **Hôtel de Boisgelin,** a vast residence of 1650 with remarkable carved decoration. Along the neighbouring Rue Mazarine (at the junction with Joseph Cabassol), behind an imposing entrance, stands the **Hôtel de Caumont** (no 3), an elegant 1720 mansion ornamented with balconies and pediments.

The Four Dolphin Fountain★ (BY S). – The dolphins have been spouting water into the basin since 1667.

St-Jean-de-Malte (CY V). – The chapel of the former priory of the Knights of Malta, which dates from the late 13C and was Aix's first Gothic building, is known for the purity of its **nave★**.

Granet Museum★ (Fine Arts and Archaeology) (CY M³). – *Open 10am to noon and 2 to 6pm; closed Tuesday, 1 May, 14 July, 15 August, 1 and 11 November and 23 December to 1 February; 10F.*

The 17C former priory is hung with pictures of the classical 16-19C schools: note the portrait of **Sir Thomas More** with spectacles well down his nose; attributed to Mabuse, the Bronzino study of Dante... One gallery is entirely devoted to Cézanne.

The archaeology galleries contain an effective display of finds from the Entremont excavations *(p 32)*: heroes' torsos, death masks...

Rue de l'Opéra (CY 62). – In this street houses of interest include: no 18 built in *c* 1650, remodelled in 1830, no 24 18C and no 26 dating from 1680 after drawings attributed to Puget.

In the Rue Émeric-David (CY) no 16 built in 1739 includes wrought iron balconies on consoles decorated with fantastically carved masks. In the Rue Lacépède the ornate façade, relieved by five recesses, is of a former 17C **Jesuit Chapel** (CY X).

Ste-Marie-Madeleine (CY Y). – *Closed 11.30am to 3pm and Sunday afternoons.*

The west front is modern although the church is 17C. Inside is a marble **Virgin★** by 18C sculptor, Chastel (south aisle), a massive picture attributed to Rubens (north transept) and the central panel of a 15C **triptych of the Annunciation★** (north aisle).

Outside in the square, is the 18C **Preachers' Fountain** (CY Z) again by Chastel and, at no 2, a house of 1676 decorated with two ships figureheads; just south is an early 17C mansion at no 2 Rue Thiers.

Sextius' Baths (Thermes Sextius). – 18C spa complex stands close to the site of the Roman baths (hot springs, 34° C - 93° F). Still in the park is a tower from the 14C city wall.

Vendôme Pavilion. – *34 Rue Célony. Open 10am to noon and 2 to 6.30pm (5pm in winter); closed Tuesdays and 1 May; 6.50F.*

The mansion, built in 1667 as the provincial residence of the Cardinal de Vendôme, might be a classical English country house set in well kept formal gardens. The biscuit coloured stone façade, unfortunately heightened in 18C, is dignified by three classical orders and an ironwork balcony supported on robust atlantes, as original as the banister of the miniature horseshoe staircase inside.

Paul Cézanne Studio. – *Avenue Paul-Cézanne. Open 10am to noon, 2.30 to 6pm (2 to 5pm 1 October to 31 May); closed Tuesdays and holidays; 5.50F, 8F during exhibitions.*

Cézanne was born in Aix in 1839. In Paris in 1861 he was influenced by the Impressionists but soon departed from their style and working alone, outside the group, returned finally to his native Aix in 1870. The studio has been reconstituted as it was at his death in 1906.

EXCURSIONS

Vasarely Foundation★. – *4km - 2 1/2 miles W out of town. Open 9.30am to 12.30pm and 2 to 6pm; closed Tuesdays, 1 January; 15F.*

The foundation is in a striking building 87m - 285ft long on the hill known as the Jas de Bouffan. The eight galleries display the artist's (b 1908) typically geometrical style work.

Entremont Plateau. – *2.5km - 1 1/2 mile then 1/4 hour on foot Rtn. Leave Aix by the uphill D 14 going N; after 2.5km walk up the path on the right to the plateau.*

Excavations. – *Open 9am to noon and 2 to 6pm; closed Tuesdays.* The foundations of ramparts, round towers, a gateway and houses give an idea of the considerable size of this Celtic-Ligurian town. All the statuary unearthed is in the Granet Museum. From the plateau's edge one looks out to Mount Ste-Victoire.

Roquefavour Aqueduct★; Ventabren. – *Round tour of 43km - 27 miles – allow 2 hours. Leave Aix by D 9 going S.* To the south lie the Étoile Mountains with the Pilon du Roi (670m - 220ft) and the Grande Étoile, topped by a television relay mast.

Turn right, along the west bank of the Réaltor Reservoir (D 65^D) and across the Marseilles Canal; just beyond La Mérindole turn left into the D 65.

Roquefavour Aqueduct★. – The aqueduct, a spectacular example of 19C civil engineering, was constructed in 1843-7 to transport the Marseilles Canal across the Arc Valley.

To reach the top, 330 yds - 300m beyond the aqueduct, turn right uphill into D 64. After 1 1/2km - 1 mile turn right into unsurfaced road; proceed to keeper's lodge.

The excavations passed on the way are of Marius' Roman encampment.

Return to the D 64 and continue to **Ventabren,** a small village of 1 537 inhabitants, alleyways, the ruins of Queen Jeanne's castle and a **view★** of the Berre Lagoon, Martigues, the Caronte Canal and the Vitrolles Mountains.

The D 64^A and D 10 (going right) bring you back to Aix.

The ALPILLES★★

Michelin map 246 folds 12 and 26

The Alpilles, geologically a limestone extension of the Lubéron Range, rise in a series of sharp 300-400m – 985-1 310ft crests between Avignon and Arles. The bare white stone peaks stand out against the blue sky while below are the typical intersecting dry valleys, clad on their lower slopes with olive and almond trees, and occasional lines of cypresses.

The BAUX ALPILLES★★

Round tour starting from St-Rémy-de-Provence

40km - 25 miles – about 1/2 day

Leave St-Rémy-de-Provence (p 117) going SW, by the Chemin de la Combette; turn right into the Vieux Chemin d'Arles.

Tour du Cardinal. – The Cardinal's Tower is, in fact, a 16C country house with an attractive Renaissance balcony and ornamental windows and friezes.

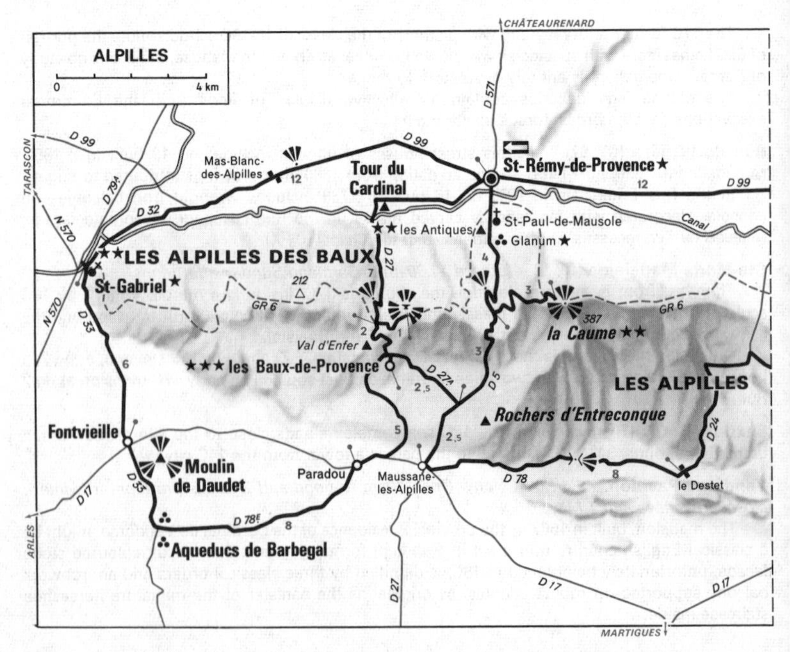

Turn left into D 27. The road winds between cypress enclosed fields before rising through a rock landscape to the heart of the Alpilles – look back over the Comtat Venaissin.
Just before the top of the hill bear left into a corniche *road; after 1km - 1/2 mile park the car.*

Les Baux Viewing Table. – *Description p 56.*

Return to D 27 and turn left. The road makes its way through Hell Valley (Val d'Enfer).

Les Baux-de-Provence★★★. – *Description p 54.*

Continue along D 27 through Paradou to D 78^E^. The road winds through olive groves.

Barbegal Aqueducts. – *1/4 hour on foot Rtn.* Note the impressive ruins (on the left in particular) of a pair of Gallo-Roman aqueducts. The western one supplied Arles with water while the other served a huge flour mill on the south slope of the hill; the ruined mill is a rare example of Gallo-Roman mechanical engineering.

Bear right on the D 33. You will pass by **Alphonse Daudet's Mill** (Moulin de Daudet: millstones etc and 19C author's museum: *open 9am to noon and 2 to 7pm (6pm 1 October to 31 May); 5F)* to an avenue of umbrella pines which leads to Fontvieille.

Fontvieille. – Pop 3 432. *Facilities p 8.* Tradition lives long in the small town where the chief industry for centuries has been quarrying Arles limestone and where Alphonse Daudet is recalled for his letters addressed as from the Mill *(see above)* and where also, in the 18C parish church, the old ceremony of the shepherds' offering is celebrated each Christmas Eve.

Continue again along D 33. The road runs through a countryside of olive groves, pinewoods and fields of early vegetables, bisected at intervals by long files of poplars.

St Gabriel★. – *To visit apply at the Auberge du Carrefour.* The small, late 12C chapel, has a west doorway framed within a rounded arch by antique style columns and a pediment. This last and the tympanum are richly, if somewhat naively, carved with the Annunciation, the Visitation, Adam and Eve and Daniel in the lions' den. The interior, by contrast, is plain comprising a single aisle covered by broken barrel vaulting and an oven vaulted apse. Note the funerary column of Augustus' time.

Return by D 32 and D 99.

The EYGALIÈRES ALPILLES★★

Round tour from St-Rémy-de-Provence.

73km - 45 miles – about 5 hours local map below.

Leave St-Rémy-de-Provence (p 113) by ③, D 5.

Old Monastery of St-Paul-de-Mausole. – *Description p 114.*

Les Antiques★★ and Glanum★. – *Description p 113.*

The road continues deep into the mountains where one sees the regular lines of the rock strata; a bend opens up a view of the Montagnette and the Durance Valley. *After 4km - 2 miles turn left into the road up the Caume. The road may be closed in summer.*

The Caume Panorama★★. – Alt 387m - 1 270ft. Beyond the television relay mast, there opens out a vast panorama of the surrounding countryside, including the Alpilles in the foreground, and beyond, the Crau, Camargue and Rhône Plains, the Guidon du Bouquet with its characteristic, beak-like outline, Mount Ventoux and the Durance Valley.

Return to D 5 and turn left. The road traverses a pinewood and several small gorges.

Rochers d'Entreconque. – The « rocks » lie to the left of the road and are, in fact, worked out bauxite quarries as can be seen from their characteristic dark red colour. Suddenly, briefly, the road runs through olive, apricot and cherry orchard country.

Turn right into D 27^A^ for Les Baux.

Les Baux-de-Provence★★★. – *Description p 54.*

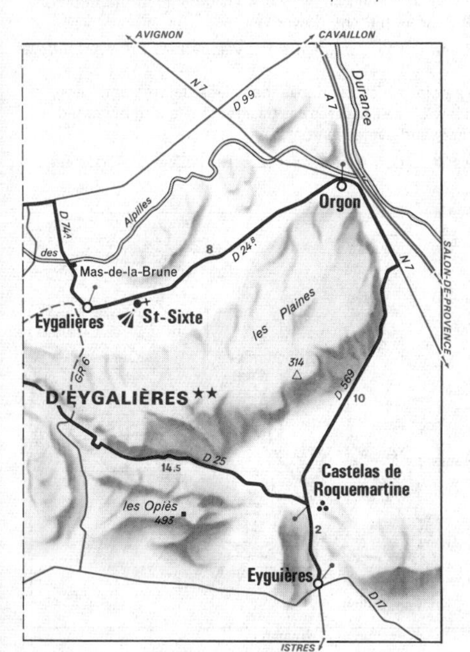

Turn round and by way of D 5 make for Maussane-les-Alpilles (facilities p 8). At the town entrance bear left and left again into D 78. The road runs through olive groves at the feet of the Alpilles before rising gently to a low pass from which there is a view of Les Opiès, a hillock crowned by a tower. At Le Destet, turn left into D 24 which, as it rises, reveals the Caume. After 5km - 3 miles bear right into D 25 which circles the Plaines Massif.

Castelas de Roquemartine. – Castelas comprises a group of ruins of various ages perched on the hillside.

Eyguières. – Pop 4 171. *2km - 1 mile south of Castelas de Roquemartine by D 569.* The typical small town is made even more delightful by its many splashing fountains.

Take D 569 north through the olive groves to N 7 which leads to Orgon.

Orgon. – Pop 2 341. The small town beside the Durance possesses a 14C church in which the choir and nave are slightly out of alignment. 14C painted panels decorate the north side of the aisle. The chapels were added in 17C. Crowning the hill overlooking the town and commanding a view of the Durance Valley, the Lubéron and the hills, is the modern chapel, N.-D.-de-Beauregard *(road subject to restrictions).*

Take D 24^{B} along the north flank of the Plaines Massif.

St Sixtus. (St-Sixte) – The 12C chapel, crowning a stony hill, stands on the site of a pagan temple erected to the spirit of the local spring *(see Eygalières below).* The arch between the nave and the oven-vaulted apse rests on boar's head consoles. Outside note the 16C hermitage and the view of Eygalières and the Alpilles.

Eygalières. – Pop 1 427. The small town of narrow winding streets rises in tiers up the hill to an ancient castle keep. Once a neolithic settlement, it was later occupied by a Roman legion sent to divert the local spring waters to Arles. Park the car in the square and walk through the Auro Gate and up to the church tower for a view of the Caume, Alpilles and Durance.

Take D 74^{A}, which near Mas de la Brune (elegant 16C mansion) crosses the Alpilles Canal, a waterway bordered by market gardens. *Bear left at D 99 for St-Rémy-de-Provence.*

APT

Michelin map 81 fold 14 – *Local maps pp 81 and 127* – Pop 11 560 – *Facilities p 8* – *See town plan in the current Michelin Red Guide France*

Apt, a small bustling town in the Calavon Valley, is known for crystallized fruit and preserves, lavender essence and truffles; it is the centre of the rare enterprise of ochre mining and refining *(p 14)*; in the Catholic tradition, it is famous as the seat of the major cathedral church dedicated to St Anne (annual pilgrimage: last Sunday in July). It is a good excursion centre; drives through the Lubéron Range *(p 78)* and the Vaucluse Plateau *(p 126)* can easily be done.

Old St Anne's Cathedral (Ancienne cathédrale Ste-Anne). – *Closed Mondays and Saturday and Sunday afternoons.* The main structure dates from 11 or 12C, the north aisle from 14C. At the back of the apse a 14C stained glass window given by Pope Urban V, depicts St Anne holding the Virgin and Child Jesus in her arms.

Interest in the cathedral centres in **St Anne's** or the **Royal Chapel,** (first off the north aisle) built in 1660, the year Anne of Austria came in pilgrimage, and in the **treasury** in the chapel sacristy *(guided tour 10 July to 10 September 11am to 5pm; closed Sunday afternoons, Mondays and holidays).* The chapel contains a gilded wood reliquary bust of the saint, an Italian marble group of St Anne and the Virgin, and the family tomb of the Dukes of Sabran *(pp 52 and 79)*; the treasury, 11-12C liturgical MSS, shrines decorated with 12-13C Limoges enamels, 14C Florentine gilded wood caskets and « St Anne's Shroud », an 11C Arabian standard brought back from the First Crusade (1096-9). Also noteworthy are a Byzantine-style picture of St John the Baptist (2nd north chapel) and a 12C Romanesque-Byzantine altar (Corpus Domini Chapel, chancel south side). Of the two superimposed **crypts,** one pre-Romanesque the other Romanesque, the latter contains 13C sarcophagi and a Roman capital as an altar pedestal.

Archaeological Museum. – *Open 1 April to 30 September, 10am to noon and 2.30 to 5pm (2.30 to 4.30pm the rest of the year); closed Saturday afternoons, Tuesdays, Sundays and holidays; 3.40F.* The museum, in an 18C mansion, comprises local archaeological finds as well as 17-19C Apt, Moustiers, Allemagne-en-Provence and Castellet pottery.

EXCURSION

The Ochre Drive★★. – *52 km - 32 miles – about 3 1/2 hours. Leave Apt by N 100.*

Julien Bridge (Pont Julien) – The bridge, named after a colony established locally by Caesar, spans the Coulon River by three arches mounted on piers of considerable girth but pierced to allow flood-waters to pass swiftly through them, downriver.

Make for Roussillon by way of D 108 and D 149. Just before the village turn off, right, into a surfaced road.

Park the car and walk *(3/4 hour Rtn)* to a point which overlooks the village before continuing, left of the cemetery, to the cliff edge for a view of the **Chaussée des Géants**★★ a length of jagged rust red cliffs, relieved by a scattering of pines and evergreen oaks.

Roussillon★. – Pop 1 313. *Facilities p 8. Ochre Festival p 25.* The **village**★ stands on an unusual **site**★ on the highest of the hills between the Coulon Valley and the Vaucluse Plateau. These hills are composed of ochre rock of 16 or 17 different shades, all reflected in the local houses. Walk along the narrow, stepped, **Rue de l'Arcade,** to the *castrum* on the cliff top from where there is a view *(viewing table)* of the Vaucluse Plateau (N) and, beyond, the crest of Mount Ventoux, and of the Coulon Valley and the Grand Lubéron (S). From the Porte Aurouse at the opposite end of the village can be seen the **Needle Rocks** (Aiguilles du Val des Fées).

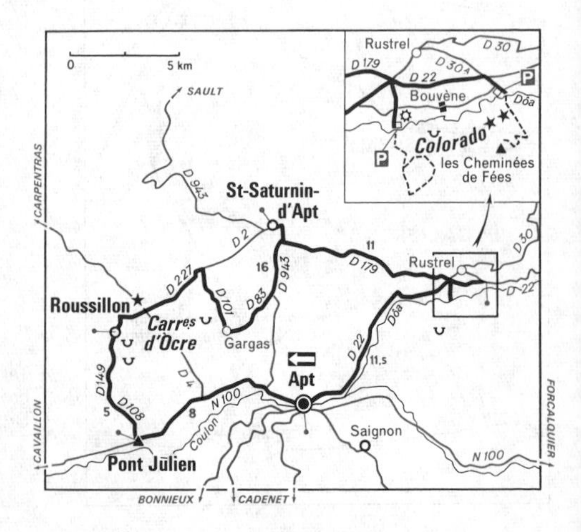

Take D 227 out of Roussillon; cross D 4, turn right into D 2 and right again almost immediately into D 101, going towards Gargas.

Ochre Quarries (Carrières d'Ocre). – The quarries lie in a spot known as Les Deverlons. The first sight is of a vast field in which some twenty settling tanks have been sunk. Take the dirt road *(open to the public, drive with care)* to the washing area from where one continues on foot *(1/2 hour Rtn)* to the opencast drilling section.

At the entrance to Gargas turn left into D 83, then left again into D 943.

St-Saturnin-d'Apt. – Pop 1 741. The village, perched on the first foothills of the Vaucluse Plateau, is overlooked by old castle ruins and a Romanesque chapel. Take the alley left of the village church and climb to the chapel for a view of the Apt countryside and Lubéron Range. The upper, Ayguier Gate, is a relic of 15C defences.

Return south along D 943 and turn left, along D 179. On the way, if the season is right, you will see the many cherry orchards which cover the plain in full flower.

Rustrel Colorado★★. – *2 hours on foot Rtn.* The gigantic ochre quarry is a rare sight and can be explored in two walks.

– The canyon: *at the D 179, 22, 30^A crossroads, take the road opposite to Bouvène (surfaced at the start); park the car beside the Dôa River, ford the Dôa and walk first between the settling tanks before bearing left immediately and following the stream to the floor of the quarry cirque. Climb gently to the left towards a ridge where there is a well defined path to several natural viewpoints.* Among the sights is a second quarry with entrances half-way up the cliff face to old underground workings. *Retrace your path to the first cirque and return, bearing left all the way.*

– The belvederes: *at the D 179, 22, 30^A crossroads, turn left into D 22; after 1.5km - 2/3 mile bear right, downhill, to a car park beside the Dôa. Ford the river and follow the yellow arrows.* After a short rise and a curve to the right, the path cuts through a pinewood to come out at a viewpoint overlooking the old quarry workings, an ochre coloured landscape of cliff faces, clay capped earth pillars (Cheminées de fées), saw toothed ridges...

Return by the way you came.

Take D 22 back to Apt.

The ARDÈCHE Valley★★★

Michelin maps 76 south of folds 17 to 19 and 80 folds 8 to 10

The Ardèche, as it descends the 119km - 74 miles from its source to its outflow on the Rhône, above Pont-St-Esprit, passes through a landscape of vertical cliff walls, basalt strata, sunlit basins carpeted with orchards and vineyards. Ruined feudal castles overlooking perched villages, ravines, spectacular gorges... suddenly give way to Mediterranean scenery. A part of the valley is now a nature reserve.

The river flow. – Where the other rivers in the region have been controlled, the Ardèche is unpredictable: autumn spates are followed by a shallow rivulet in winter, spring torrents rush swiftly as the snows melt and then subside to a comparative trickle throughout the summer; the flood-waters, when they come, advance as a wall of water at 10 to 15mph.

THE UPPER VALLEY★

The Chavade Pass to Aubenas – *43km - 27 miles – about 5 hours - local map p 36*

Chavade Pass (Col de la Chavade). – Alt 1 266m - 4 154ft. The pass marks the Atlantic-Mediterranean watershed.

The road, N 102, descends from the col and, after 800m - 875 yds, crosses the nascent Ardèche which can be seen falling in a cascade upstream. The harshness of the valley, which is dominated from the south by the dome of the Croix de Bauzon and the razor-edged Rock of Abraham, is softened by orchards surrounding the self-contained villages, where every house has a vine or creeper on its front wall; the old approach road was carried over a hump-backed bridge. From the cliff tops medieval ruins command the road: Montlaur Castle (upstream from Mayres), Chadenac Keep and **Ventadour Castle** (at the entrance to Pont-de-Labeaume).

Mayres. – Pop 366. The village's low built houses appear to be almost all decorated with iron balconies and gay plant and vine covered trellises.

500m - 457 yds downstream, carrying the road to Malbos, is a typical medieval hump-backed bridge (pont) paved with its original large flagstones and a good valley **viewpoint**★.

Thueyts★. – Pop 1 013. *Facilities p 8.* The small town, which lives by fruit farming and quarrying, is perched on a dense flow of rock which originally poured out of the now extinct volcano behind it, the Gravenne de Montpezat. The early quaternary rock flow spread south blocking the bed of the river which, in the million or more years since the eruption, has cut a new course, revealing a thick basalt stratum.

A **walk**★ *(1 1/2 hours Rtn)* starting from the belvedere beside N 102 at the east end of the village, brings you to the **gorge floor**★ where you can inspect the basalt at close quarters. Cross the bridge over the Médéric and take a path on the right beneath the bridge which continues between the rock and the so-called Hell's Mouth (Gueule d'Enfer) Waterfall. *Follow the red arrows, left at the intersection, to the Devil's Bridge (Pont du Diable), spanning the Ardèche. Go a few hundred yards up the far bank to see the view of the cleft before returning to the intersection. Take the other path, skirting the cliff face to a viewpoint and a fissure in the rock.* This cleft which is known as the **King's Ladder** (Échelle du Roi), is paved with rough and slippery steps of black, prismatic, basalt. *Return through the fruit gardens.*

As you come out of Thueyts glance at the **view** dominated by Mount Ste-Marguerite (NE).

Neyrac-les-Bains. – The modest sulphur water spa on the flank of the Soulhiol Volcano was known to the Romans, and in the Middle Ages was thought to cure leprosy.

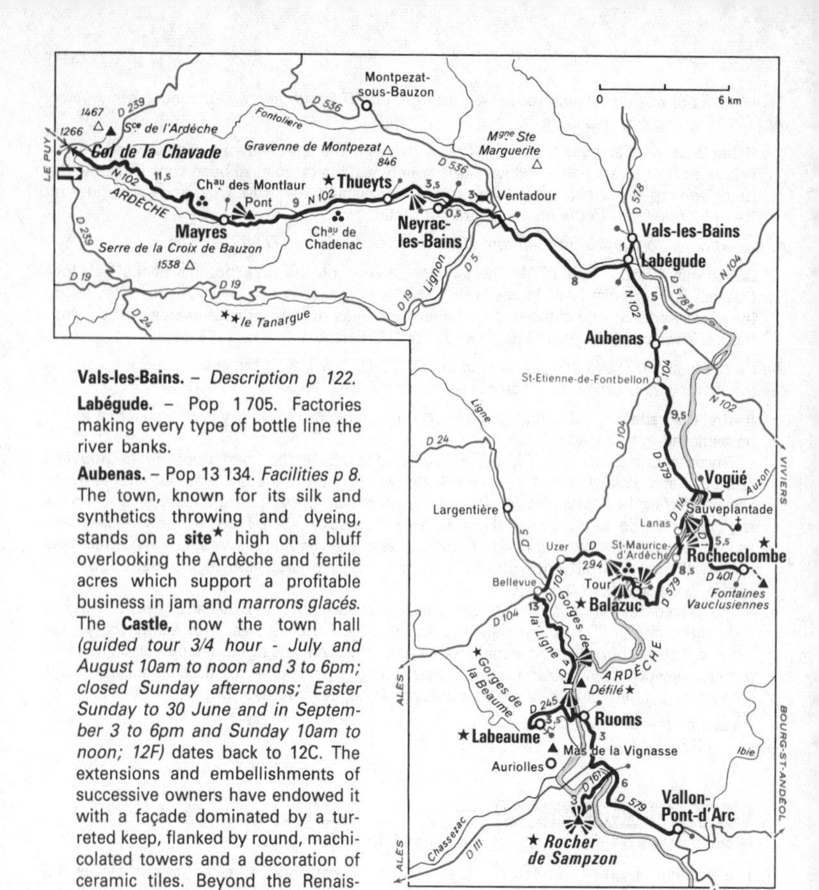

Vals-les-Bains. – *Description p 122.*

Labégude. – Pop 1 705. Factories making every type of bottle line the river banks.

Aubenas. – Pop 13 134. *Facilities p 8.* The town, known for its silk and synthetics throwing and dyeing, stands on a **site**★ high on a bluff overlooking the Ardèche and fertile acres which support a profitable business in jam and *marrons glacés.* The **Castle,** now the town hall *(guided tour 3/4 hour - July and August 10am to noon and 3 to 6pm; closed Sunday afternoons; Easter Sunday to 30 June and in September 3 to 6pm and Sunday 10am to noon; 12F)* dates back to 12C. The extensions and embellishments of successive owners have endowed it with a façade dominated by a turreted keep, flanked by round, machicolated towers and a decoration of ceramic tiles. Beyond the Renaissance courtyard is an 18C grand staircase and panelled apartments. Opposite is 16C **Gargoyle House,** named after the beasts grinning on the polygonal turret. The churches present, in **St-Laurent,** a Baroque ensemble of carved wood altarpieces and 17C pulpit and, in **St-Benoît,** *(same times as castle, 4F),* a hexagonal plan.

THE MIDDLE VALLEY★★

Aubenas to Vallon-Pont-d'Arc – *40km - 25 miles - about 2 1/2 hours*

The luminous Ardèche Valley widens out into a succession of fertile basins while the river describes a hugh loop to the west, its green waters making a vivid contrast with its banks of clear grey gravel and golden sand.

Leave Aubenas by D 104; bear left into D 579 at St-Étienne-de-Fontbellon.

Vogüé. – Pop 570. *Facilities p 8.* A 16C château, built on the site of the original medieval fortress, still dominates the network of centuries old, arch straddled streets built, against the cliff face which rises vertically above the river.
(Château open July and August 3 to 6pm ; the rest of the year only Sunday afternoons; closed 1 October to Easter, 14 July and 15 August; 10F).

Rochecolombe★. – *5.5 km - 3 1/2 miles from Vogüé Description p 61.*
Cross back to the west bank by Vogüé Bridge and continue along D 114. The peak on the horizon is the Dent de Rès (alt 719m - 2 360ft). At Lanas the road recrosses the river by a narrow bridge from which there is a view upstream of the Auzon/Ardèche confluence.

At St-Maurice-d'Ardèche bear right into D 579; 300m beyond Balazuc station turn right into D 294. As the road climbs, the basin just crossed comes into **view**★ again with the Coiron Plateau as a backcloth (NE).

Balazuc★. – Pop 275. The limestone village, perched against the cliffside and once fortified, stands in a quiet and peaceful defile although, in 8 and 9C it was sufficiently « on the map » to be occupied by a colony of Saracens. The best view of the village is from the far bank *(after the bridge, leave the car in a path to the left)* when the small belfry which surmounts the Romanesque parish church and the old ruined towers stand out to full advantage.

The bridge below the village is the starting point *(take the road on the right which climbs)* for a pretty walk downstream between the cliff walls – the isolated keep on the right is known as Queen Jeanne's Tower. Beyond Balazuc the road climbs to the arid, rock strewn plateau only to descend into the Uzer Depression; the uphill road is marked by a **view**★ which extends both up and down the defile, and that downhill by the vista, straight ahead, of the tall buildings of Largentière, one of Montréal's ruined towers.

Continue along D 104 through Uzer and D 4 from Bellevue towards Ruoms. A narrow road bordered by rock outcrops, marks the approach to the Ligne Gorge; from the southern end there is a good **view** upstream to where the Ligne flows into the Ardèche, the confluence is framed by 100m - 300ft high cliffs striped by the rock strata. The Ligne Gorge is followed by the **Ruoms Defile**★ with dramatic views now appearing at the far end of a tunnel now plunging to swift green water below. The Sampzon Rock *(p 37)* is silhouetted at the end of the valley.

Don't cross the Ruoms Bridge but continue straight on and turn right into D 245.

Labeaume★. – *3.5km - 2 miles from the bridge.* Pop 405. The aged village with narrow uphill streets situated on the flank of the Beaume Gorges, merges almost totally into the rock face, the picturesque, balconied houses being built of the natural stone. The low level bridge with no parapet walls but stout piers, which spans the river at the village's foot, is the perfect artifact in such surroundings. The river is the Beaume which rises 1 250m - 4 100ft up on the Tanargue Massif *(p 123)* and hollows out a 40km - 25 miles course before flowing into the Ardèche downstream. Walk up the north (left) bank to see the eroded walls of the limestone **gorges★**. For a slightly longer walk *(1/2 hour Rtn)*, cross the bridge and continue along an uphill path which ends at an acacia grove; turn left and 500m - 1/3 mile further on, right, which brings you to a crossroads.

Continue for 800m - 1/2 mile. The **Mas de la Vignasse** *(guided tour 1 May to 30 September 9am to noon and 2 to 6pm; closed Tuesdays; 15F)*, a farmhouse on the outskirts of the village of **Auriolles** (pop 166) and once the property of the 19C novelist, Alphonse Daudet's mother's family who were prosperous silk merchants, has been restored and transformed into two museums: Alphonse Daudet Museum and in the former silkworm farm a Museum of Popular Art and Traditions.

Ruoms. – Pop 1 839. *Facilities p 8.* The old walled centre of the small commercial town is unexpected – a quadrilateral of ramparts flanked by seven towers. At the heart of the old streets is a small Romanesque church with an unusual arcaded belfry faced with motifs worked in volcanic rock.

Leave Ruoms by D 579 going S towards Vallon - Pont-d'Arc.

Sampzon Rock★ (Rocher de Sampzon) – *3 km - 2 miles along D 579 turn right over the Ardèche into a narrow road which climbs steeply through many bends. Park below Sampzon Church and walk to the top (3/4 hour Rtn) first by the tarmac path and then by the path level with the turning place.* From the top (television relay mast) there is a **panorama★★** including the Vallon Basin, the Orgnac Plateau and the serpentines of the Ardèche.

After skirting the river the road veers away into the vineyards and orchards which carpet the Vallon Basin. Just before Vallon-Pont-d'Arc there is an appetizing view of the Ardèche Gorges.

THE ARDÈCHE GORGES★★★

Vallon-Pont-d'Arc to Pont-St-Esprit – *58 km - 36 miles – allow 1/2 day*

On leaving the Vallon basin, the Ardèche reaches the lower Vivarais limestone plateau which it divides, by its deep course, into two extensive plateaux, the Gras *(p 60)* to the north and the Orgnac *(p 98)* to the south. The calcareous rock, which supports only evergreen oak and scrub, is hollowed everywhere into caves, such as the Grotte des Tunnels which once had an underground stream.

A **panoramic road,** D 290, has been so constructed along the edge of the Gras Plateau, that it overlooks the gorge throughout the major part of its length.

Vallon-Pont-d'Arc. – Pop 1 907. *Facilities p 8.* Vallon is the nominal starting point for the descent of the gorges both by road and by boat *(p 39)*. In its own right it possesses two rare sights: in the town hall are seven **17C Aubusson tapestries,** six illustrating scenes in the deliverance of Jerusalem and a seventh, the ancient art of grafting a fruit tree.

The second sight is a **silkworm farm** (Magnanerie) *(3km - 2 miles along D 579 going to Ruoms, then down a turning to the left)*. The farm is in the village of **Les Mazes.** Between May and September the worms may be seen in all stages up to silk enveloped cocoon.

Leave Vallon by D 290. The road makes for the Ardèche, past the ruins of feudal Vallon built high on the plateau and across the River Ibie.

Pont-d'Arc★★. – *Park the car. To reach the river level, walk 150m back towards Vallon where a path leads down to the bank.* The river originally skirted the area now taken by the road but later adopted the bed of a small semi-subterranean stream which flowed beneath the then scarcely hollowed rock. The autumn and spring floodwaters which made the river alter course have, over thousands of years, worn away the rock until the arch now measures 59m across and 39m high - 195 × 128ft.

The scenic splendour begins immediately you leave Pont-d'Arc: the river flows in wide curves punctuated by rapids all in the framework of a 30 km - 20 miles gorge enclosed by rock walls 300m - 1 000ft high in some places, dramatically coloured in tones of white, dark and light grey and overgrown with scrub oak and vegetation; the river is jade green. The road generally keeps close to the cliff edge; there are parking places at each viewpoint so that you can appreciate each aspect from a variety of angles.

Just beyond Chames, the road goes up and affords a view of a rock **cirque★**.

Serre de Tourre Belvedere★★. – The viewpoint poised almost vertically 200m - 750ft above the Ardèche, offers a superb **picture** of the river winding round the Pas de Mousse rock on which stand the few remaining ruins of 16C Ebbo Castle. Also to be seen are the Saleyron Cliffs. Mount Lozère and the wide expanse of the Orgnac Plateau.

Gaud Belvederes★★. – The **view** is upstream towards the river bend and the turrets of the small 19C château of the same name.

Autridge Belvederes★. – The Morsanne Needle (Aiguille de Morsanne) appears from both viewpoints in the road's curve like the prow of a ship advancing upstream.

500m - 546 yds beyond the Agrimont Coomb, new **vistas★★** open up of the great bend in the river with the Morsanne now the focal point in the foreground.

Gournier Belvederes★★. – The viewpoints enable one to look down on the stream winding its way through the Gournier Toupine Rocks.

The Madeleine Cave★. – *Access 500m - 546 yds from D 290; guided tours 1 April to 30 June, in September and Sundays in October, 9.30am to noon and 2 to 6pm; 1 July to 31 August 9.30am to 6pm; time: 1 hour; 18.50F.* The cave was hollowed out by a now vanished underground stream which drained the Gras Plateau.

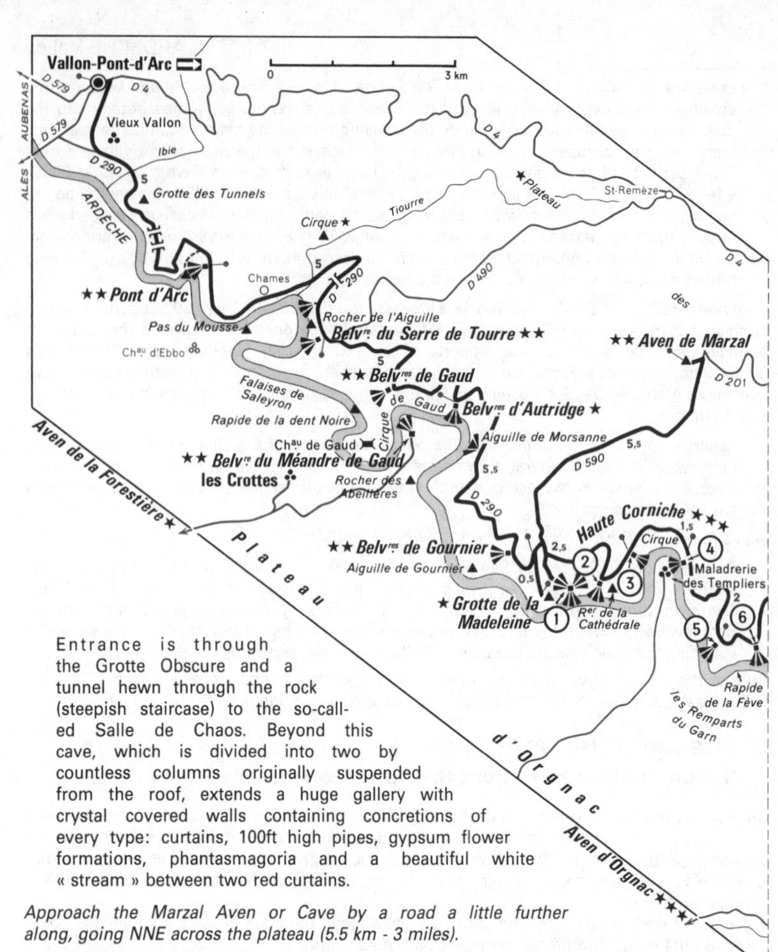

Entrance is through the Grotte Obscure and a tunnel hewn through the rock (steepish staircase) to the so-called Salle de Chaos. Beyond this cave, which is divided into two by countless columns originally suspended from the roof, extends a huge gallery with crystal covered walls containing concretions of every type: curtains, 100ft high pipes, gypsum flower formations, phantasmagoria and a beautiful white « stream » between two red curtains.

Approach the Marzal Aven or Cave by a road a little further along, going NNE across the plateau (5.5 km - 3 miles).

Marzal Aven★★. – *Guided tour 16 April to 30 September, 9am to 6pm; 1 March to 15 April and 1 October to 30 November, only weekends and holidays at 11am, 3.30 and 5pm; time: 1 hour; 24F; temperature: 14 °C - 57 °F.* The cave is outstanding for the variety of its calcite formations which range in their oxide colouring from brown ochre to snow white. Entrance is by way of a staircase (743 steps) from the cave mouth (discovered in 1892; lost; rediscovered 1949) to the high Tomb Cave where regular columns give way to almost transparent curtains and xylophone-like resounding formations. Close by are the bones of bears, stags and bison which must have fallen into the cave and died. The Dog Cave (white curtains, phantasmagoria, richly coloured pipes, bunches of grapes), the Pine Cone Cave, notable for its variety of colour, and the Pillar Cave, through which an underground river used to flow, lead finally to the equally large Diamond Cave where the concretions' fairylike colours are reflected in the glinting crystals which line the walls. A museum, **France Underground** (Musée du Monde Souterrain), displays the discoveries of 19 and 20C speleologists, Martel, Joly, Casteret, Lavaur.

In the **Préhistoric Zoo** *(open 1 April to 31 October, 10am to 6pm; in March and November 2 to 6pm only weekends and holidays; 19F),* follow the pleasantly shaded itinerary (800 m - 875 yds long) to discover the fauna of prehistoric times. The life-size reproductions include the dimetrodon and moschops of the Primary Era, the stegosaurus and tyrannosaurus of the Secondary Era and the more familiar mammoth of the Quaternary. The latter was a contemporary of prehistoric man, who is also represented by several family groups.

Return to the Madeleine crossroads on D 209.

The High (Haute) Corniche★★★. – Six viewpoints in close succession afford unrivalled views of the most outstanding section of the drive.

Madeleine Belvedere (1) – *1/4 hour on foot Rtn.* Rock spikes rising in the foreground resemble the spires of a ruined cathedral (as the rock is known), while downstream the Madeleine Ramparts, at 300m - 1 000ft the tallest cliffs in the gorge, appear to bar the defile.

Cathedral Belvedere (2). – The point commands the Madeleine Cirque and the Cathedral Rock.

Templars' Belvedere (3). – The belvedere affords views of a tight loop in the river flanked by the high walls of a rock cirque. This and the next point are named after the Templars' Leper Hospital (Maladrerie) whose ruins still crown the small spur within the bend.

Maladrerie Belvedere (4). – View of the cathedral upstream.

Rouvière Belvedere (5). – Facing the Garn Ramparts.

Coutelle Belvedere (6). – The vertiginous viewpoint overlooks the river from a height of 180m - 600ft. To the right are the last Garn Ramparts; to the left the Castelviel Rocks, and directly in the river's course, up and downstream, the swift Fève and Cadière Rapids.

Grand Belvedere★. – View of the end of the gorges and the Ardèche's final bend.

Colombier Belvedere★. – View of the bend enclosed by rock strewn banks.

St-Marcel Caves. – *1 km - 1/2 mile off D 290 by a poor downhill road on the right. Open for scientific and archaeological research only.* The caves are like gigantic passageways, decked with massive stalagmites and crystallizations. From the first gallery a ladder leads to an upper passage and platform. On a third level are chambers with glinting crystal covered roofs, concretions, « cauliflowers » and phantasmagoria. In the last immense cavity, known as the Dining Hall (Salle du Repas), the roof looks like an inverted ship's keel.

The road describes a loop along the Fond Ponchon, (a dry valley), skirts the Dona Vierna promontory and makes a wide detour around the Louby Valley to reach the next viewpoint.

Ranc-Pointu Belvedere★★. – The belvedere, perched on the end of the southern slope above the juncture of the Louby and the mainstream, overlooks the Ardèche's last enclosed bend.

As you come away from the gorge the countryside changes completely: the bare defile is replaced by a cultivated valley opening ever more widely as it approaches the Rhône. On the far bank stands the old fortified village of Aiguèze *(p 98)*, commanding the river from its high perch on a rock crest.

St-Martin-d'Ardèche. – Pop 380. The first village on the north bank since Vallon.

St-Sulpice. – *4 km - 3 miles N of St-Martin-d'Ardèche (p 61).*

Cross the Ardèche by the St-Martin suspension bridge. Turn left into D 901 and N 86 which skirt the river to its juncture with the Rhône just above Pont-St-Esprit (p 105).
For the south or right bank of the Ardèche (no road) see p 98, the Orgnac Plateau.

DESCENT OF THE GORGES BY BOAT★★★

Pont-d'Arc to St-Martin-d'Ardèche – *Local map pp 38-39*

The descent, which can be made any time between March late November, is best in May-June.

Practical information. – *Apply in advance to (1) M. J. L. Tourre at the farm in the Tiourre Valley, beyond the Pont-d'Arc, Route des Gorges 07150 Vallon Pont d'Arc, ☎ 75 88 02 95, who, from March to November organises trips in 4 man boats to Sauze – price 560F per boat, return included, or (2) Locacano-Sports 07150 Vallon Pont d'Arc, ☎ 75 88 04 36 who hire out boats by the day or more: April to late September canoes and kayaks at 200F per day for 2 people, 120F for one (return included).*
According to the season and the water level plan allow 6-9 hours to descend. There are several difficult stretches due to rapids.

The shooting of the natural rock Pont-d'Arc, is followed by a long calm stretch, before the river bends sharply and one enters the gorge. To the right are the Pas de Mousse Rock then the Ebbo Cave; the rock on the north, left, bank is the Aiguille Rock. The first rapids, the Dent Noire, occur just below the immensely tall Saleyron Cliffs and are followed by the wide Gaud loop which circles a small 19C château of the same name.

Rapids and smooth flowing stretches, overlooked by canyon-high cliffs, alternate as you pass landmarks such as the Morsanne Needle rock on the left bank and the Abeillères on the right.

After approximately 4 hours you should have negotiated the Toupine de Gournier rocks which lie strewn in the river's course and be in sight of the Cathedral Rock. Before you actually reach the Cathedral you pass the mouth of the Madeleine Cave *(left)*. Just after, the river flows below the enormous Cathedral Rocks. Picnic spots have been set up along the bank (bring your own picnic lunch).

The so-called Madeleine Ramparts are amongst the most spectacular on the trip when seen from water level. Straits, rapids and smooth iridescent passages follow one another as the river continues downwards between sheer cliff walls, bare of all but occasional evergreen oaks. Below the Castelviel Rocks, the opening of the St-Marcel Caves can be seen on the left, and rounding the bend, the Dona Vierna Promontory and Ranc-Pointu Belvedere. The cliffs melt away, the valley widens out, the Aiguèze Tower can be seen on the edge of the rock escarpment on the right.

(After photo by Feher)

The Pont d'Arc.

ARLES ★★★

Michelin map 246 fold 26 – *Local map p 63* – Pop 50 772 – *Facilities p 8. For plan of built up area see the current Michelin Red Guide France.*

Set in the countryside which entranced Van Gogh, Arles contrasts her new found prosperity as a market for the rice crop of the Camargue with her past glories as a Roman capital and medieval religious centre.

HISTORICAL NOTES

Port and market. – Arles' fortunes have always depended on its success as a port and market: in 6C BC the Greeks of Marseilles established the village as a Provençal trading post; in 2C BC the Consul Marius improved it by the construction of a major shipping canal linking the Rhône and the Fos Gulf (Canal de Marseille au Rhône); finally, in 49BC, when Julius Caesar defeated Marseilles, he transferred some of her possessions to Arles, where he founded a colony for his Sixth Legion and the town began to flourish.

In addition to being a maritime and river port, it was situated on the Roman Aurelian Way, the highway between Italy and Spain and, from the time of Constantine in 4C, possessed a bridge across the Rhône; it had road connections with northern and western Gaul. First Roman and later medieval ramparts pierced by four, twin towered gates were erected round the administrative and military quarter on the east bank. The west bank (the actual Trinquetaille quarter) was an open residential area with villas and gardens.

The city on the east bank was divided like a chessboard, the two principal intersecting streets being approximately 12 and 7m - 40 and 22ft wide, the others less than 4m - 13ft. All roads were paved, many had pedestrian sidewalks.

Water brought by an aqueduct 75 km - 47 miles long was distributed from a central cistern to local fountains, the public baths and, on a metred system, to private houses. The town was equipped with main drainage, the master pipe being 3.50m - 11 1/2ft in diameter *(p 42);* the public lavatories were built of white marble and flushed with running water.

The most conspicuous monuments of the Roman period are the amphitheatre, theatre, forum, temples, baths and necropolis.

Trade was such that in 5C it was written that « All that the Orient, unguent Araby, luxuriant Assyria, fertile Africa, Spain and fecund Gaul produce, is to be found in Arles and in as great quantity as in their countries of origin ». But the city was not just a market; it was also a Roman imperial mint, a manufacturing centre for textiles, gold and silverwork and arms, and, as it remains to this day, a town noted for its pork butchers' meats, olive oil, and Rhône wines which then were dark and resinous, unlike today's full-bodied but limpid vintages.

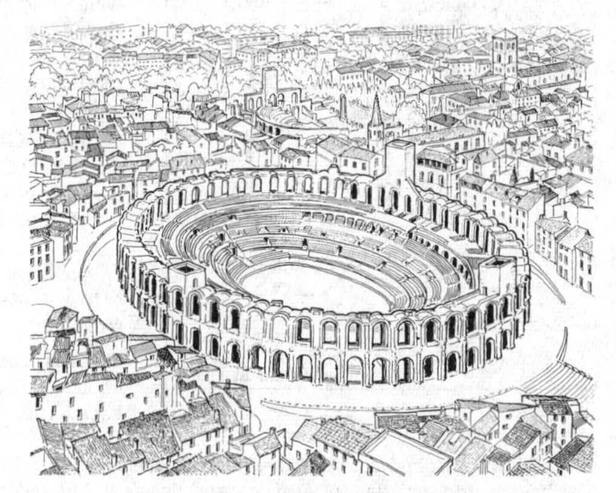

(After photo by Vu du Ciel by Alain Perceval)

The Amphitheatre at Arles.

Prosperity brought political importance. Constantine built himself a palace and held the first Council of Christian bishops in 314; the town became the capital of Gaul and an archiepiscopal see; in 597 in St-Trophime St Augustine was consecrated first bishop of England by St Virgil, Bishop of Arles; in 9C it became the capital of the Kingdom of Arles which included Burgundy and part of Provence. A long period of loss of identity followed, during which the town was incorporated first in the Holy Roman Empire, then, in 13C, in the County of Provence with which in 1482, it was annexed into the Kingdom of France. Political status passed to Aix, commercial prosperity to Marseilles; building, however, continued unabated, most notably in the cathedral and cloister, within the amphitheatre, where a town grew up *(illustration p 20),* and in the streets between the cathedral and the river.

The arrival of the railway in 19C made river traffic obsolete and dealt a severe blow to trade.

Revival has occurred since the war, brought about by the cultivation of the Camargue and the Crau and by the development of tourism.

Van Gogh in Arles. – **Van Gogh** (1853-90), a painter of Dutch origin, came to Arles from Paris in February 1888.

During the fifteen months that he spent there he painted more than 300 canvases, some in several versions, including his own house, *Sunflowers, the Arlésienne, the Alyscamps,* cornfields and market gardens, as well as the famous Langlois drawbridge, which was pulled down in 1926 and recently re-erected on the Arles Canal at Port-de-Bouc.

At the end of the year he was joined by **Paul Gauguin,** a French painter of the Post-Impressionist period, but after a few weeks the artists quarrelled bitterly and in the crisis which followed, Van Gogh cut off his right ear – and then painted the famous *Self-Portrait* (Courtauld Gallery, London). At his own request he entered the asylum at St Rémy-de-Provence *(p 113)* in May 1889 where he remained for another year before shooting himself in July 1890. During that final period he did more paintings than ever, some 300 canvases, plus innumerable drawings and watercolours.

The most extensive collections of the artist's pictures are to be seen not in the region but in major museums such as the National and Tate Galleries and Courtauld Collection in London, Metropolitan and Guggenheim Museums in New York, the Jeu de Paume in Paris and the Vincent Van Gogh Museum in Amsterdam.

ARLES

Antonelle (Pl.) .... Z 5
Cavalerie (R. de la) .... Y 14
Forum (Pl. du) .... Z 16
Hôtel-de-Ville (R.) .... Z 17
Jaurès (R. Jean) .... Z 19
Lices (Bd des) .... Z
République
(R. de la) .... Z 40
4-Septembre (R. du) ..... Y 47
Alyscamps (Av. des) ...... Z 2
Amphithéâtre
(Pl. de l') .... Y 3
Arènes (Rd-Pt-des) ...... YZ 7
Balze (R.) .... Z 8
Blum (R. Léon) .... Y 10
Calade (R. de la) .... Z 12
Camargue (R. de) .... Y 13
Cloître (R. du) .... Z 15
Maïsto (R. D.) .... Y 27
Major (Pl. de la) .... Y 29
Mistral (R. Frédéric) ...... Z 30
Place (R. de la) .... Y 32
Plan-de-la-Cour .... Z 33
Portagnel (R.) .... Y 35
Porte-de-Laure (R.) .... Z 36
Président-Wilson (R. du) ... Z 37
République (Pl. de la) ..... Z 39
Stalingrad (Av. de) .... Y 42
Vauban (Montée) .... Z 43
Victor-Hugo (Av.) .... Z 44
Voltaire (R.) .... Y 45

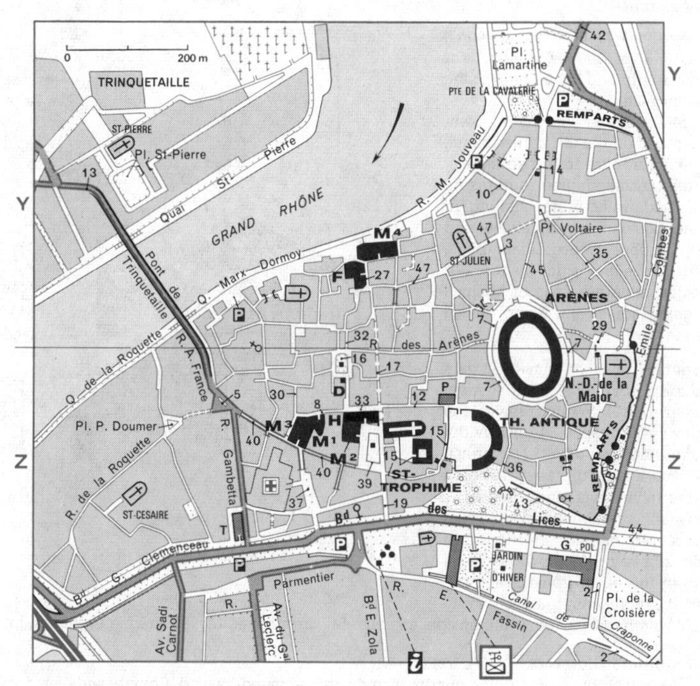

■ MAIN SIGHTS *time: 1/2 day*

Admission to the Amphitheatre, Classical Theatre, Constantine's Palace, St-Trophime Cloisters, Museums of Pagan and Christian Art, Réattu Museum, the Alyscamps – 8.30am to 12.20pm and 2 to 7pm, 1 June to 14 September; to 6.30pm 15 September to 31 October, to 5pm in November, to 4.30pm in December; 9 to 11.50am and 2 to 4.30pm, January and February, to 5.30pm in March; 8.30 to 11.50am and 2 to 6.30pm in April; to 7pm in May; closed 1 January, 1 May and 25 December. All-inclusive ticket (including Museon Arlaten) 17F (available at any monument), 19F during exhibitions.

Amphitheatre★★ **(Arènes)** (YZ). – The arena, which probably succeeded an earlier wooden structure in 1C AD, is slightly larger and later than the one at Nîmes and by the same architect, T. Crispius Reburrus; it measures 136 × 107m - 446 × 351ft and could seat some 26 000 spectators. There are 20 larger arenas out of the 70 known in the Roman world.

The seating is supported on two rows of sixty arches, the lower framed with Doric half columns and the upper with Corinthian. The attic storey has disappeared as have most of the internal stairways and galleries, but the remaining galleries are roofed in Greek style with flat stone slabs.

The amphitheatre owes its preservation to its conversion in the Middle Ages to a fortress *(p 20)* with 200 houses and a church. When the arena was excavated in 1825 the 12C towers were left. The bullfights now held in the arena recall the spectacles of long ago.

Roman Theatre★★ **(Théâtre Antique)** (Z). – The theatre was built during the Augustan Age (1C BC) and could hold 7 000 spectators; the stage measures 102m - 335ft across. All that remains are some seating, the orchestra, the curtain trench and two marble columns from the stage wall. The site, which is still used for concerts, is now enclosed in a walled garden.

The **Roland Tower** dates from the time the theatre became a part of the fortifications.

When a well was being sunk in 17C, the excavations unearthed Greek inspired statues, including the so-called **Venus of Arles** now in the Louvre Museum in Paris (casts in the Museum of Pagan Art and on the Town Hall stairs).

St-Trophime★(Z). – The church is dedicated to a Greek apostle who is supposed to have evangelized Provence. Starting in the Carolingian period, characterized by small stones in the lower courses, the building has been altered in 11, 12 and 15C to produce a harmony of styles.

Dominating not only the cathedral and its precincts but also visible from many quarters of the town, is the three stage square belfry in golden stone, pierced by single or pairs of rounded arches beneath a decorative cornice and shallow pyramidal roof.

The **doorway**★★ on the west front is a masterpiece of Provençal Romanesque style recalling the west front of St-Gilles *(p 111)* and echoing a Roman arch. Among the multitude of carved figures are:

on the tympanum: the Last Judgment with Christ in glory in a mandorla, surrounded by the attributes of the four Evangelists – the winged man (St Matthew), the eagle (St John), the ox (St Luke) and the lion (St Mark);

on the frieze: left – the elect, clothed, advance to have their souls received by an angel; on the lintel – the 12 Apostles; right – the damned are refused admission to paradise and march off, naked and in chains, to hell;

on the doorway capitals: Joseph's vision and the Annunciation; Christ's birth and the bathing of the newborn child.

St-Trophime appears in bishop's robes on the left corner panel, receiving a mitre from two angels. In the corresponding embrasure is a medievally brutal stoning of St Stephen with two angels bearing off his soul (represented by a child). On either side, by the 17C classical style doors, is St Michael weighing souls, and some hellish demons.

Interior. – The church inside is dark and lofty – over 60ft – with a wide, broken barrel vaulted nave, the highest in Provence, lit only by upper rounded windows. The principal decorations are tapestries high on the nave walls, and three early Christian sarcophagi with relief decoration, namely in the north aisle, 2nd bay – 4C, now used as a font, in the north transept – probably 4C, representing a lively *Passage of the Red Sea* and in the apsidal chapel – 5C surmounted by 16C marble Entombment.

(After photo by carte postale Iris)

St Trophime: the west front.

St-Trophime Cloisters★★ (Cloître) (Z).

The cloisters, open in the warm climate, have round-headed Romanesque arches on coupled columns but their distinction lies in the rich medieval carving of the pillars and capitals.

You enter by the west gallery constructed in 14C with Gothic rib vaulting, as is the south gallery; the north and east galleries are earlier, 12C, with Romanesque and barrel vaulting.

The best work is to be found in the north gallery, particularly on the corner pillars. The capitals are decorated with foliage or scenes from the Old and New Testaments or, in the Gothic galleries, from Provençal legends. The pillars are embellished with statues and low reliefs.

From the south gallery glance up at the solid bell tower above the nave and cloister.

(After photo by Zodiaque)

St Trophime Cloisters: north and east galleries.

Museum of Pagan Art★ (Z M[2]). – *Admission: p 41.* The museum, housed in a deconsecrated church, 17C St Anne's, comprises mosaics, statues – the **Venus of Arles** (cast – the original was given to Louis XIV) discovered in the Classical Theatre *(p 41)* and Phaedra and Hyppolytus reclining on a white marble sarcophagus.

In Place de la République stands an **obelisk** (found on the site of the Roman Circus) which indicated the finishing line for chariot races.

Walk through the 17C **Town Hall** (Z H) vestibule, a columned, flat vaulted hallway. The tower dominating the building outside, but invisible from within, is an older, 16C, clock tower.

On the far side is the **Plan de la Cour,** a small, typically medieval square, with narrow streets leading off it and, on the left against the wall, a stone **judgment bench** from which justices once pronounced sentence.

Museum of Christian Art★★ (Z M[1]). – *Admission: p 41.* The museum, in the former 17C Jesuit Chapel, is rich in early Christian sarcophagi – note especially: the passage of the Red Sea, Jonah and the whale, the resurrection of Lazarus, the parable of the loaves and fishes. In the middle of the nave are three 4C sarcophagi discovered during the 1974 excavations of the Trinquetaille quarter, note especially the one of the Trinity or couple with three carved tiers.

Cryptoporticus★. – Beneath the museum is a horseshoe-shaped **underground gallery** *(cryptoporticus)* of 1C BC, 90m-295ft long, 60m-200ft wide. Once part of the forum, it was used from imperial times as a granary; the north arm, cut by the foundations of the temple whose columns stand in Forum Square, has been parallelled by a more modern corridor through which passes the 1C Roman main town drain *(see above)*. Lighting is by the ancient air shafts.

Make for the Museon Arlaten in the delighful old **Rue de la République** with its shops and houses and small fountain at the centre.

(After photo by Museon Arlaten, Arles)

Local bread cupboard.

Museon Arlaten★ (Z M³). – *Open 1 July to 30 September 10am to noon and 2 to 7pm; the rest of the year 9am to noon and 2 to 6pm; closed Mondays between 1 October and 30 June and 1 May and 25 December; 5F.*

The unique museum of Provençal Life, housed in the 16C Gothic style, Castellane-Laval mansion, was created (in 1896) by the passionate advocate and poet of the Provençal language, **Frédéric Mistral** who further enriched it with the money he received in 1904 when he was awarded the Nobel Prize for Literature *(p 24)*.

The first floor galleries present a rich profusion of local tradition – pottery, prints, programmes, poetry and prose MSS, portraits and, above all, furniture – note the bread cupboards high up on the walls – and costumes – the museum attendant wears traditional costume. Further on are excellent furnished and peopled rooms – a seamstress' sewing room, a bedroom, a kitchen, which give a vivid idea of 18C Arles' life.

Take the Rue du Palais on the left.

Place du Forum. – The square is shaded with plane trees and lined with cafés and is, as ever, a place to meet and talk. **Relics** (**Z D**) of the Roman forum which extended from the Place de la République, are evident in the giant Corinthian columns which frame the nameplate at the south end, beyond the masterful statue of **Frédéric Mistral.**

Turn south, away from the river, along Rue du Président Wilson; bear left into **Boulevard des Lices** (**Z**), a broad avenue lined with cafes, their terraces extending out on to the pavements beneath the plane trees. Bordering the Boulevard des Lices, near the tourist information centre, are the Esplanade excavations which have uncovered Gallo-Roman houses and baths. Also discovered is the southern continuation of the ancient road which follows the present day Rue Hôtel de Ville and Rue de la République. *Turn right into Avenue des Alyscamps.*

The Alyscamps★. – The **Sarcophagus Avenue** (Allée des Sarcophages), bordered by tall trees interspersed with flat, low-lying tombs and ending at the ruined remains of the once large Romanesque **Church of St-Honoratus,** is all that now exists of the necropolis which, from Roman times to the Middle Ages, was among the most famous in the western world. Excavations near St-Honorat would seem to indicate that a Christian cemetery developed around the tomb of St Genesius, writer and clerk, patron saint of Arles, who gave his life when, according to legend, he refused to take down a decree against the local Christians. The cemetery not only covered a wide area but contained graves on three superimposed levels, 4-5C, 9-10C, and 12-13C, so numbering many thousands within the one burial ground.

(After photo by B. Martin)

The Alyscamps, Arles.

From the time of the Renaissance, the city councillors took to offering their guests the better carved sarcophagi as presents; monks in charge of the necropolis took funerary stones to build churches and enclose monastery grounds. Some of the sarcophagi are now in the Museum of Christian Art *(p 42)*.

Finally the remaining tombs – empty and artistically null – were assembled into an avenue but even this has not survived unscathed; the railway cuts through the approach and new houses and workshops overlook the site.

Van Gogh painted it several times in colours more brilliant, perhaps, than those seen by the average eye; to walk where 80 generations have been buried over 2 000 years is a rare experience.

■ ADDITIONAL SIGHTS

The town, besides the stout **medieval ramparts** (**YZ**) at the southeast corner and a Romanesque church, **N.-D.-de-la-Major** (**Z**), built on the site of a Roman temple, possesses two other sights of unique interest.

Constantine's Palace★ **(Thermes de la Trouille)** (**Y F**). *Admission: p 41. In winter ask at Réattu Museum.*

The baths *(p 19)* of which only a small area is extant, date from 4C and were the largest in Provence (overall measurements 98 × 45m - 320 × 148ft). Alternate courses of stone and brick were used in the construction.

Réattu Museum★ (Y M4). – *Admission: p 41.*

The museum on the banks of the Rhône, in the 15C Grand Priory of the Knights of St John of Jerusalem, belonged to the painter Réattu (1760-1833). Three of the museum's galleries exhibit his work. There are also works from the Italian (16 and 17C), French (17C) and Dutch (18C) schools as well as the Provençal school (18C).

An important modern and contemporary art collection consisting of watercolours, prints, paintings (Brayer, Léger, Manguin, Vlaminck, Rousseau), tapestries (Lurçat, Prassinos) and sculpture (Bourdelle, G. Richier, Zadkine) can be admired.

Worth noting are the 57 drawings from the Picasso Donation.

On the 2nd floor is a photographic display – photography not as a technique but as an image of the present – exhibiting the most important photographers of today.

EXCURSIONS

Montmajour Abbey★. – *7 km - 4 miles by ①, N 570 and D 17 on the right. Open 9 am to noon and 2 to 6pm; closed Tuesdays, part of November, 1 January, 1 May, 1 and 11 November and 25 December; 10F, 5F Sundays. Guided tour Sundays at 4.30pm and in season at 10am and 3pm.*

The abbey dates back to 10C when Benedictine monks, guardians of a burial ground established on the hill, founded a monastery and began to reclaim the surrounding marshland. By 17C the monastery had declined in size, power, riches and discipline; reforming monks arrived to displace the old, self-indulgent brothers who sacked the building before they departed. In 18C crisis brought action: where roofs had fallen in and walls crumbled, fine new constructions arose in replacement, only for everything to collapse once more when the commandary abbot, Cardinal de Rohan, was compromised in the affair of Marie Antoinette's necklace and Louis XVI suppressed the abbey (1786).

Purchase in 1790s by antique and property dealers resulted in the removal of furniture, furnishings, panelling and finally even masonry from 18C buildings. In the 19C the abbey was slowly bought back by the town, in 1872 restoration of the medieval buildings began, the 18C buildings remain in ruins.

The Abbey★. – The abbey feature dominating the region is its menacing medieval tower, almost devoid of loopholes, machicolated and apparently impregnable. It commands *(124 steps)* a **panorama★** of the Alpilles, Crau Plain, Cévennes, Arles, Beaucaire and Tarascon.

Below is the late 12C **cloister★**, its barrel vaulting supported on paired columns with carved capitals forming groups of three small Romanesque arches beneath shallow relieving arches. The remaining cloister buildings include the barrel-vaulted chapter house and interesting surbased vaulting in the refectory.

Notre-Dame★. – 12C building comprises an upper church which was never completed (chancel, transept and two bays of the nave) and a **crypt★** *(access: southwest corner of the nave)* which is built into the sloping rock of the hillside. Its cruciform plan is completed by terminal transept chapels and five radiating apsidal chapels.

St-Pierre★ *(may be visited during guided tours)* is the original 10C abbey chapel, half hollowed out of the rock and extended at one end by natural caves which once served as a hermitage.

Ste-Croix★. – *200m on the road to Fontvieille, on the right. Not open.* The Chapel of the Holy Cross, marked by a small dome and a belfry, was erected in 12C outside the abbey precincts as the burial ground chapel.

AVIGNON ★★★

Michelin map 246 fold 25 – Local map pp 72 and 102 – Pop 91 474

Plan of built up area in the current Michelin Red Guide France

Avignon, city of the popes, city of the nursery rhyme of everyone dancing in a ring on the bridge, city, as described by Lawrence Durrell, of « honey-coloured, rose-faded walls and machicolated towers rising steeply from a country dusted silver with olive ».

It thrives today as the metropolis of the prosperous Vaucluse region; it is gay, intimate, produces an annual drama festival *(p 25)*, rejoices in cafés and restaurants along the main street and square, the Rue de la République and Place de l'Horloge.

On the far bank of the Rhône, beyond the celebrated bridge, more towers point to the sky – the square keep of Philip the Fair, the round bastion of St André's Fort, protectors of the old cardinals' city, Villeneuve-lès-Avignon *(p 132)*.

The popes at Avignon. – The town had existed uneventfully until, in 1309 Pope Clement V (elected Pope in 1305) took up residence there. Wearied of the local wars of medieval Italy and at the invitation of his King, Philip the Fair (Pope Clement was French), Clement had established himself on the lower Rhône in the Comtat Venaissin *(p 69)*, an enclave ceded to the papacy at the close of the Albigensian Crusade in 1274. The pontifical court, on transferring from Rome, entered upon what came to be known as the "second Babylonian captivity of the church". John XXII succeeded him (in 1316) and established himself in the episcopal palace. In 1348 Pope Clement VI (1342-1352) purchased Avignon from Queen Joan I of Sicily, Countess of Provence.

Six French popes reigned before Gregory XI, the last in the French line, took the papacy back to Rome in 1377. A year later he was succeeded by an Italian whose reforms so displeased the College of Cardinals that they elected an alternate pope who returned to Avignon thus initiating the long dispute known as the Great Schism of the West (1378-1449).

The last alternate or anti-pope left Avignon in 1403. The city returned to the quiet life, increased in status and prosperity, and distinguished, as a memorial to its century as the papal seat, by that unique edifice, the Palace of the Popes.

The satellite citizenry. – Penitent brotherhoods multiplied during the residence of the popes and may still be seen walking in feast day processions in grey, white, blue, black, purple and red hoods. The town, as a papal enclave, became a sanctuary: Jews, on payment of a small indemnity, were safe, so were escaped prisoners and adventurers fleeing litigation; smuggling, forgery and counterfeiting were rife; brothels and bawdy houses flourished, providing pleasure for the citizens of Avignon and visitors to the medieval fair in nearby Beaucaire *(p 56)*.

The town was occasionally ravaged by plagues (the most devastating in 1721 killed 3/4 of the population) or by bands of unemployed mercenaries *(routiers)* who lived by marauding – in 1358 the Pope gave them his blessing and 40 000 ducats to go away; in 1365 the price was 200 000 golden florins.

Until the Revolution the city of 80 000 inhabitants continued in prosperity, splendour and license; fine houses were built, a few of which may still be seen; trade flourished.

St-Bénézet Bridge** **and St-Nicolas Chapel** (ABY). – *Open 9am to noon and 2 to 7pm in July and August, 6pm April, May, June and September, 5pm (closed Tuesdays) in March and 1 October to 14 January; closed 15 January to 28 February and 1 January, 14 July and 25 December; 6F.*

The bridge of the song, which spanned the river by way of the island, was 900m-975yds long when completed in 1190 and was, for years, the only crossing so far down the Rhône. The twenty-two arches have been reduced with the passage of time, by storm and floodwater, to four. On one of the piers stands **St-Nicolas Chapel** (BY), with two storeys, one Romanesque, one Gothic.

The bridge at Avignon.

Legend has it that in 1177, a young shepherd boy, Bénézet, was commanded by voices from heaven to build a bridge across the river at a spot indicated by an angel. Everyone thought him crazy until he « proved » that he was inspired by miraculously lifting a huge block of stone. Bishops gave money, funds flowed in, volunteers appeared and formed themselves into a **Bridge Brotherhood** (Frères Pontifes) and in less than eight years construction was complete. By 15C it had been fortified: the Philippe-le-Bel Tower still stands in Villeneuve but the defences at the southern end have disappeared beneath more modern constructions.

St Bénézet's Bridge was a narrow bridge – a bridge for people on foot or on horseback; it was never one on which one could dance in a ring – the dancing took place on the island in midstream, possibly around one of the bridge piers, in other words, not

Sur le pont d'Avignon

but *Sous le pont d'Avignon/On y danse, tous en rond.*

■ The PALACE OF THE POPES*** (Le Palais des Papes) (BY) *time: 1 hour*

Open 1 July to 30 September 9am to 6pm; guided tour Easter to 30 June 9 to 11.30am and 2 to 5.30pm and 1 October to Easter 9 to 11am and 2 to 4pm; closed 1 January, 1 May and 25 December; 17F (fee increased if there is an exhibition).

To visit the section of the palace occupied by the Archives Départementales (Benedict XII Chapel) apply in advance to the curator.

The great white, stone palace, so impressive from outside and such a medieval maze of galleries, chambers, chapels and passages inside, is disappointingly bare of furnishing – the edifice was damaged during the Revolution, the contents looted, the statuary disfigured and broken; from 1810 the buildings served as barracks or prisons; some wall paintings survived but mouldings and frescoes were cut up and sold by the piece to dealers and antiquaries. Finally, this century, it was rescued by the city.

Construction. – The enclave which covers 15 000sq m–2.6 acres is, in fact, two fortresses built as a symbol of the absolute power of the Church and as a defence against the feuding lords and marauding brigands of the time by successive popes, Benedict XII, 1334-42 and Clement VI, 1342-52. Both palaces have a central courtyard; the Old Palace reflects the austerity of Benedict XII; a Cistercian, the New, the artistic taste and patronage of a great prince of the church, Clement VI, a Benedictine.

Exterior. – The size, the stone, the rock base on which it stands, which make it invulnerable to sapping and battering, the lack of windows, the loopholes, battlements and machicolated square towers, some over 50m - 150ft tall, produce an impression of massive impregnability. Walk round the southwest side, via the narrow and picturesque Rue Peyrollerie to get an idea of its lowering menace.

(After photo by Arch. Phot., Paris)

The Palace of the Popes, Avignon.

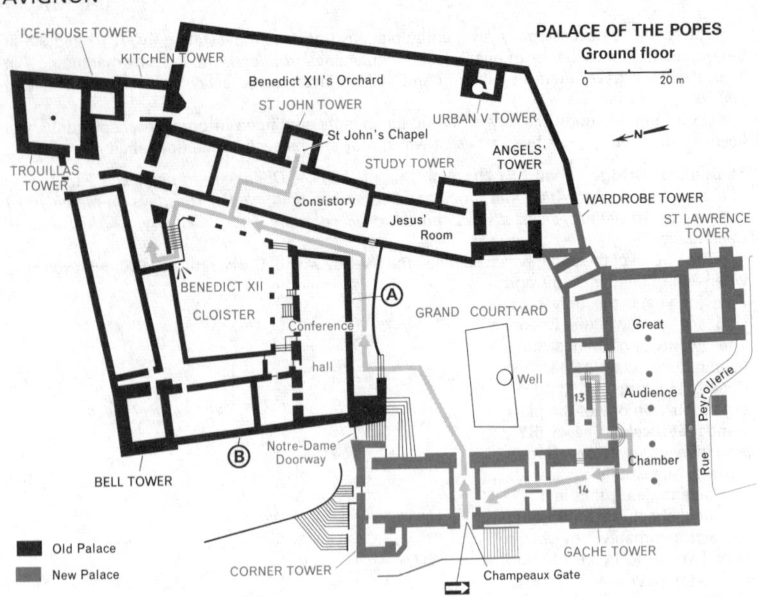

Ground Floor (Old Palace)

Enter the Champeaux (Main) Gate.

Grand Courtyard. – The spacious court is the meeting point of the two palaces, the Old including the Conclave Wing (**A**), being to the left and ahead, the New to the right and rear. Displayed are frescoes by the 14C Siennese, Simone Martini, which were painted originally for the cathedral porch of N.-D. des Doms *(p 48).*

Consistory or Grand Council Chamber. – This chamber is where sovereigns and ambassadors were received and new cardinals proclaimed.

St John's or the Consistory Chapel. – The chapel is named after the frescoes of the two Saints John – the Baptist and the Apostle – painted from 1346-8 by Matteo Giovanetti da Viterbo, painter to Clement VI *(to visit apply in advance for permission).* Adjacent to the Consistory is the Jesus Room under which was located the Treasury (*Closed;* as are the Library and Wardrobe).

Benedict XII Cloister. – The court is overlooked by the papal household lodgings (**B**) *(west)* and at the first floor level *(plan above)* by the Grand Tinel *(east)* – there is a fine view of the lodgings from the stairs leading up to the Grand Tinel – and of St Benedict's Chapel *(north).*

First Floor (Old and New Palace)

Grand Tinel or Banqueting Hall. – In this vast hall (48m long × 10.25m wide - 158ft × 35ft) is hung a lovely series of 18C Gobelins **tapestries.** The immense panelled ceiling, in the form of a ship's keel, has been restored.

St Martial's Chapel. – The oratory abutting the hall is named after the **frescoes** of the saint painted in 1344-45 by Matteo Giovanetti. The tour continues via the kitchen (3) on the top floor of the Kitchen Tower, which was also used to store food. The adjoining tower (Latrine Tower later called Ice House Tower) had a drain in common with the kitchen and latrines on each floor, the waste being washed into a ditch 22m - 72ft deep.

Robing Room. – The antechamber, which also served as a small audience chamber, is hung with two 18C Gobelins tapestries.

The Study Tower which includes Benedict's cabinet (4) with magnificent floor tiles *(restored)* is now closed. The private dining room (5) and kitchen (6) were pulled down in 1810.

Papal Bedchamber (7). – The walls and ceiling of the small room are gaily painted with hundreds of birds perched on trailing vines against a blue blackground; in the window embrasures are designs of exotic birdcages with open doors. The floor tiles of medieval inspiration have been recently restored.

The Stag Room (8). – Here too the **wall paintings** (1343) depict a stag in a wood and scenes of fishing, falconry and ferretting.

The ceiling in larch wood is wonderfully ornate.

(After photo by Arch. Phot., Paris)

Wall painting in the Stag Room.

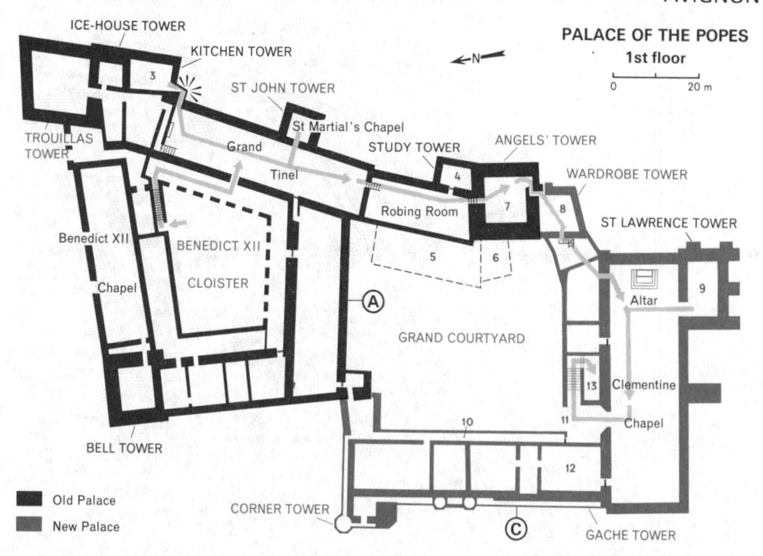

The Clementine, Grand or Clement VI Chapel. – The chapel, which is vast and echoing although comparatively low (19m - 62ft), since it stands above the Great Audience Chamber and on the palace-fortress perimeter, which prevented the roof exceeding the height of the ramparts, was built in 18 months.

South of the pontifical altar (largely restored), the St Lawrence Tower contains the south Sacristy (**9**) or Re-Vestry where the pope changed vestments when officiating at high mass.

A loggia at the chapel's northwest end led to the Grand Dignitaries' wing (**C**) which included the treasurer's and chamberlain's lodging (**12**) and **Indulgence Window** (**11**) from which the pope would give his blessing to crowds in the court below.

It was in the Clementine Chapel that the Conclave of Cardinals would assemble ten days after the death of the pope to hear mass, before walking beneath the elegant ceiling of the Conclave Gallery (**10**) to elect a successor in the Conclave Wing (**A**). To isolate the prelates, doors and windows were bricked up to a height of 8m - 26ft, a practice which went back to 13C when the people of Rome, after waiting three years for a successor to Clement IV, finally put the Cardinals under lock and key (in conclave) to force a decision.

Ground Floor (New Palace)

Descend the Grand Staircase (**13**) *to the ground floor.*

Great Audience Chamber. – The great hall, magnificent despite its emptiness, is divided down the centre by a line of clustered columns on to which the vaulting, once vivid with frescoes, descends.

Here papal pronouncements were made and plaintiffs came to plead their cause before the ecclesiastical tribunal.

On the vaulting, note the Prophets' Fresco painted in 1532 by Matteo Giovanetti.

Lesser Audience Chamber (**14**). – The small chamber, also a court, was presided over by a single judge who heard appeals against decisions made by the other court. In the 17C the vaulting was decorated with paintings in grisaille representing trophies.

Cross the guardroom (**15**) where the wall paintings are also 17C and leave the palace by the Champeaux Gate.

■ The PALACE SQUARE (La Place du Palais) (BY)

The Petit Palais Museum of Medieval Painting and Sculpture★★. – *Open 1 April to 30 September 9.30 to 11.50am and 2 to 6.15pm; the rest of the year 9.15 to 11.50am and 2 to 6pm; closed Tuesdays and public holidays; 12F (free Sundays 1 October to 1 March).*

First a cardinals palace, the Petit Palais then became an episcopal palace, before finally becoming an archiepiscopal palace in 1475.

The façade, with its large windows, was remodelled in the late 15C by Cardinal della Rovere, who later became Pope Julius II, the great art patron - friend of Michelangelo and patron of Bramante and Raphael.

Among the famous who have stayed at the palace were Cesare Borgia in 1498, François I in 1533 and Anne of Austria and the Duke of Orleans in 1660.

The rooms house remarkable 13-15C art, representing the Avignon school, Italian (Florentine, Venetian and Siennese) schools and local Avignon sculpture.

The majority of Italian paintings, some 300 canvases were once part of the collection of the 19C Italian, Gian Pietro, Marquess **Campana di Cavelli,** whose interest became an aquisitive obsession to which he sacrificed his personal fortune; he then drew on the funds of Rome's official pawnbrokers, an institution of which he was the director, which was also a bank and the repository of Vatican funds. Campana's reputation among learned societies and collectors was international but when the bank deficit was found to be one million Roman ducats he was tried, convicted of embezzlement and sentenced to 20 years in the galleys. Napoleon III came to his rescue by buying the entire collection amounting to some 15 000 objects to form the nucleus of a museum he was planning in Paris on the model of the newly founded Victoria and Albert Museum in London.

Nothing came of the idea; the collection was split up and only now have the early paintings been reunited. Campana lived out the rest of his life in exile from Italy (d 1880).

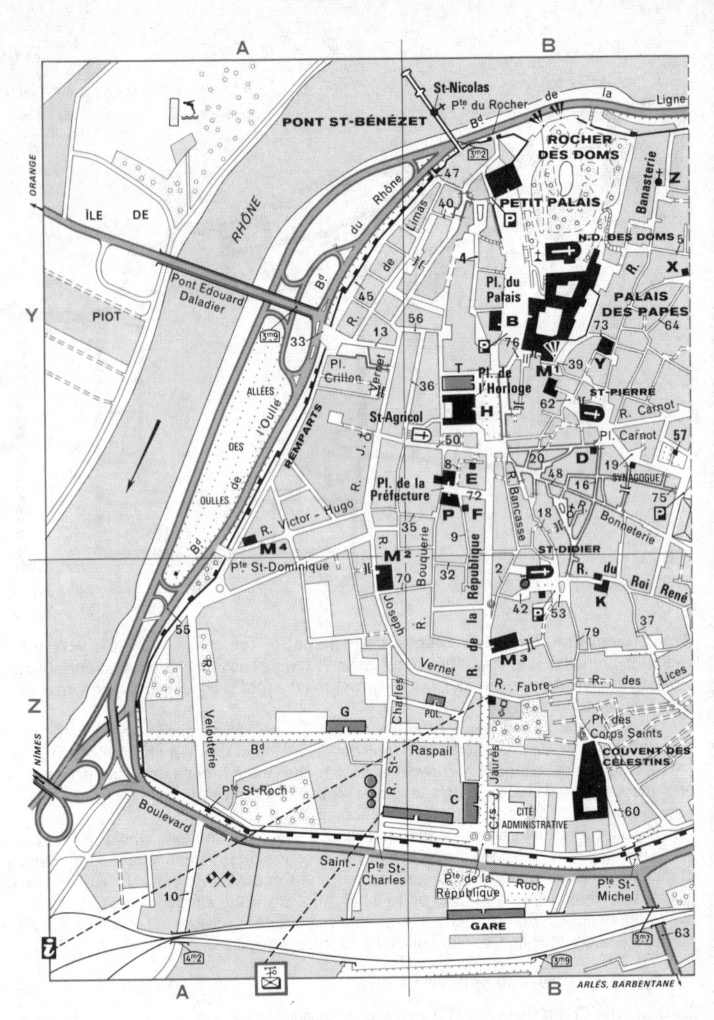

First influenced by the Byzantine tradition as were the other Italian schools, the Venetian school emerged adopting firm linear drawing with sumptuous detailed ornamentation: exemplified in the *Virgin and Child* by **Paolo Veneziano** and the *Holy Conversation* by **Vittore Carpaccio.**

The Siennese school represented by **Taddeo di Bartolo** *(Virgin and Child)* and **Liberale da Verona** *(Abduction of Helen of Troy)* developed its own style as of the 15C: an expression of nobleness, beauty and tenderness is found in its figures and an intensity of colour in the picture itself.

The Florentine school characterized by the search for beauty of form and the desire to present an idealized picture of nature, together with balanced composition and perspective, is represented by the artists **Bartolomeo della Gatta** *(The Annunciation)* and **Botticelli** *(Virgin and Child).* **Carlo Crivelli** (four figuries of Saints) and **Antonio Alberti** *(Virgin and Child)* although respectively from Padua and Ferrara were both influenced by the Paduan school characterized by subtle choice of colours, firm drawing, elegance of ornamentation and realistic observation balanced by absence of idealization and imagination.

The Avignon school – represented by the works of **Enguerrand Quarton** (Requin altarpiece) and **Josse Lieferinxe** (shutters of the altarpiece to the Virgin) – because of its monumental simplicity of composition and the importance light played in these compositions, can be placed mid-way between the realism of the Flemish school and the abstract more intellectual stylization of the Italian schools.

Note also the 12-15C sculpture (tombs of popes and cardinals) from the Avignon school.

N.-D.-des-Doms Cathedral. – The core of the edifice dates back to 12C; the interior was remodelled in the 14 and 17C and the side chapels added. The belfry, the dominant feature from most angles, was erected in 15C after an earlier Romanesque tower had been reduced to its first stage to serve as a plinth for the new construction which, in 1859, was crowned by a very tall statue of the Virgin. The porch is antique in style. The two tympana were magnificiently decorated with frescoes by Simone Martini which have been transferred to the Palace of the Popes *(p 46)*. Inside, an overhang above the crossing supports a small Romanesque **dome**★ and pillared lantern; below are two monuments of interest: 12C white marble episcopal throne at the entrance to the chancel and the Flamboyant Gothic tomb of Pope John XXII in the chapel contiguous to the sacristy.

Dom Rock★★ **(Rocher des Doms).** – The great bluff overlooking the Rhône is now a terraced garden, planted with trees and roses, around a lake where ducks and moorhens swim. From vantage points there are **views**★★ of the Rhône, St-Bénézet Bridge, Villeneuve-lès-Avignon, Mount Ventoux (NE), the Vaucluse Plateau (E) and the Lubéron (SE) *(viewing table).*

The Old Mint (Hôtel des Monnaies) (B). – The massive 17C mansion has a crowning balustrade and a **façade**★ richly decorated with dragons, eagles, cherubs and swags of fruit.

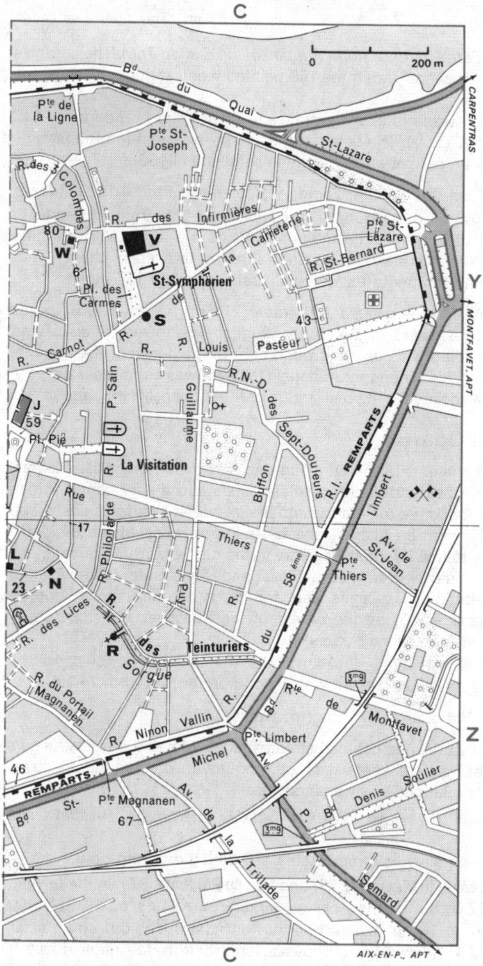

AVIGNON

Fourbisseurs (R. des) .... BY 16
Jaurès (Cours J.) ... BZ
Marchands (R. des) BY 20
République (R.) .. BYZ
St-Agricol (R. et Egl.) ...... BY 50
Vernet (R. J.) ..... AY
Vieux-Sextier (R. du) BY 75

Aubanel (R. Théodore) ... BZ 2
Balance (R. de la) . BY 4
Bertrand (R.) ..... BY 5
Campane (R.) .... CY 6
Collège-du-Roure (R. du) .... BY 8
Dorée (R.) .... BY 9
Eisenhower (Av.) AZ 10
Folco-de-Baroncelli (R.) .. AY 13
Four-de-la-Terre (R. du) .... CZ 17
Galante (R.) ...... BY 18
Jérusalem (Pl.) ... BY 19
Masse (R. de la) ... CZ 23
N.-D.-des-Doms (Egl.) .... BY
Ortolans (R. des) ... BZ 32
Oulle (Pte de l') ... AY 33
Petite-Calade (R. de la) ..... BY 35
Petite-Fusterie (R. de la) ...... AY 36
Pétramale (R.) ..... BZ 37
Peyrollerie (R.) ... BY 39
Pont (R. du) ...... BY 40
Prévot (R.) .... BZ 42
Rascas (R. de) .... CY 43
Rempart-du-Rhône (R. du) .... AY 45
Rempart-St-Michel (R. du) .... CZ 46
Rhône (Pte du) ... BY 47
Rouge (R.) .... BY 48
St-Didier (R. et Egl.) BYZ 53
St-Dominique (Bd) AZ 55
St-Etienne (R.) ... ABY 56
St-Jean-le-Vieux (Pl.) ... BY 57
St-Jean-le-Vieux (R.) .... CY 59
St-Michel (R.) ..... BZ 60
St-Pierre (Pl. et Egl.) BY 62
St-Ruf (Av.) .... BZ 63
St-Symphorien (Egl.) CY
Ste-Catherine (R.) BY 64
Sources (Av. des) .. CZ 67
Vernet (R. Horace) ABZ 70
Viala (R. Jean) .... BY 72
Vice-Légat (R. du) . BY 73
Vilar (R. Jean) .... BY 76
Visitation (Egl.) ... CY
3-Faucons (R. des) . BZ 79
3-Pilats (R. des) ... CY 80

■ ADDITIONAL SIGHTS

Apart from its unique sights, Avignon has a number of characteristic old buildings. These, by quarters, taking the Cour Jaurès – Rue de la République as north-south axis, include:

Northwest – Balance Quarter and part of the Préfecture

Place de l'Horloge (Clock Tower Square) (BY). – The large square – the Roman town's forum –, shaded by plane trees and lively with open air cafés, is overlooked by the theatre and the **Town Hall** (BY H), both built in 19C, the latter around the old 14-15C **clock tower** on which Jacks still mark the hour.

St-Agricol (BY). – *Closed Sunday afternoons.* Broad steps lead up to the west front carved in 15C, the middle of the three centuries during which the church was being built. At the pier is a contemporary Virgin, on the tympanum one of the church's two representations of the Annunciation, the second is on a retable by Boachon (south aisle). Mid-15C marble stoup.

Rue de la Balance (BY 4). – The street is lined on one side by town houses; on the other are modern buildings with small flower-decked patios. Glass blowers may be seen in the Cristallerie des Papes in the Rue de Limas (BY).

Continue in the same direction to come out by the bridge and a view of the ramparts.

The Ramparts* (ACYZ). – The gold coloured walls were erected in 14C by the popes not as an ultimate defence but as a preliminary obstacle against attack which, in the last resort, would be resisted from the palace-fortress. The battlemented ramparts, flanked by towers open to the town and surrounded by a deep moat, were nevertheless highly impressive. (When the perimeter was restored in 19C by Viollet-le-Duc the moat could not be excavated and the walls, therefore, appear much lower than in the Middle Ages).

Northeast – St Pierre – Ste Marthe Quarter

Rue Banasterie (BY). – The street is named after the Provençal word *banastiers,* meaning basket weavers whose medieval corporation was in the street. No 13, Madon de Châteaublanc House (Y), is 17C with a decorated façade of fruit, eagles and masks.

Black Penitents' Chapel (Pénitents Noirs) (BY Z). – *Closed for restoration.* The façade, remodelled in 18C, shows cherubs around a glory on which two angels bear a dish with John the Baptist's head (the brotherhood's emblem is the beheading). Baroque interior.

Go along the Rue Ste-Catherine. No 17, Font Secca House (BY X), built in 1600 has an inner courtyard with an old well overlooked by mullioned windows.

No 16 (CY W) Rue des 3-Pilats, with a triangular pediment, is 17C.

St-Symphorien (CY). – *Open 8 to 9am (10am to noon Sundays) and 6.30 to 7pm.* The church's façade is 15C. Inside, in the first north chapel, are three 16C painted wood statues of Jesus, the Virgin and St John.

A wrought iron gate by the north wall marks the entrance to the cloister of the former 14C monastery of the Barefoot Carmelites (**CY V**). The belfry at the end of the street (on the far side of the Rue de la Carreterie (**CY S**)), is a relic of an Augustinian convent (14-16C).

St-Pierre (BY). – *Open Saturdays 10am to noon and Sundays 8.30am to noon.* 14-15C church is entered by double doors, enriched by 15C Renaissance carved **panels*** : the Virgin, the Angel of the Annunciation, St Michael and St Jerome. The interior contains 17C woodwork framing painted **panels** (chancel), a 16C carved altarpiece by Boachon (first north chancel chapel), 14C dalmatic (third chapel), 15C stone Entombment (first south chapel) and a late 15C pulpit.

Théodore Aubanel Museum (BY M[1]). – *Guided tour (time: 1 hour) 9 to 11am; closed Saturdays, Sundays, holidays and, last week in December, August.* The museum, displaying print, presses, documents and rare editions, is on the ground floor of the house of the Aubanel family, printers and publishers since 1744. Théodore Aubanel (1829-86) was co-founder with the poet Mistral *(p 89)* of the **Félibrige,** a society for the restoration of the Provençal language *(p 24)*.

Southeast – Clothdyers Quarter

This quarter, Quartier des Teinturiers, is bordered along one side by the **Cours Jean Jaurès,** the wide avenue, shaded by plane trees and lined by cafés, hôtels and luxury shops, which extends from the rampart gateway *(opposite the station and major tourist excursion coach and bus station)* and runs into the partly commercial and traffic beset **Rue de la République** (BYZ). On the right, in the Cours Jaurès is the **tourist information centre** in the old St Martial Convent.

Behind the wide main street is a quarter of former medieval trades and crafts still evinced in the street names, small shops with hanging signs and, for the most part, oldish houses including 15C corbelled **Rascas House** (**BY D**) on the corner of the Rues des Marchands and Fourbisseurs (Merchants' and Sword Furbishers' Streets).

Place St-Jean-le-Vieux (**BY 57**) is marked at the corner by the tall square tower of the Commandery of the Knights of St John of Jerusalem which stood on the site from 14-19C.

Church of the Visitation (CY). – *Not open.* 17C former conventual chapel.

Rue des Teinturiers (CZ). – The picturesque, cobbled street, shaded with plane trees, follows the course of the River Sorgue whose waters were used by the clothdyers after whom the street is named. No 26 still has its 15C crenelations and watchtowers.

Grey Penitents Chapel (Pénitents Gris) (**R**). – *No 8. Closed Sunday afternoons, Tuesdays and holidays.*

Inside 16C chapel at the end of an alley, is a remarkable 17C gold glory from Peru.

Go back up the street and follow **Rue de la Masse** (**CZ 23**) and **Rue du Roi René** (BZ). In the former, no 36, 17C Salvan Isoard House (**CZ N**) has ornately carved window surrounds, no 19, Salvador House (**CZ L**), is an impressive square 18C mansion. Rue du Roi René opens out into a **small square** overlooked by a **group*** (**BZ K**) of four 17-18C houses: no 7 Berton de Crillon House is emblasoned with portrait medallions, masks, flower garlands and adorned with a wrought iron balcony; in the inner courtyard is a grand staircase with a stone balustrade; no 8, Fortia de Montréal House, less ornate, has triangular and circular pediments over grotesques; nos 10 and 12, the Honorati and Jonquerettes Houses, are pédimented but bare of decoration.

St-Didier (BYZ). – *Closed Sunday afternoons.* 14C church, in purest Provençal style, has a pentagonal apse and a single aisle lined with chapels. In the first chapel on the south side is a 15C **altarpiece*** by a Dalmatian artist, François Laurana, depicting the Carrying of the Cross but known locally as Our Lady of the Spasm owing to the anguished faces *(electric switch on right pillar)*. The baptistry chapel *(northeast end)* is decorated with late 14C **frescoes*** *(electric switch on right pillar)*.

Livrée Ceccano. – South of St-Didier rises the powerful tower built by the Cardinal of Ceccano in 14C and later incorporated into the Jesuit College. It now houses the public library.

Lapidary Museum* (BZ M[3]). – *Open 10am to noon and 2 to 6pm; closed Tuesdays, 1 January, 1 May, 14 July, 15 August, 1 and 11 November, 25 December.*

The museum is housed in the former Jesuit College, built in 17C after the Gesù Church in Rome. Its exhibits of sculpture and stone carving represent the different civilizations which have left their mark on the region.

Celestine Convent (BZ). – 15C northern Gothic style church with cloisters.

Southwest – southern part of the Préfecture Quarter

Calvet Museum* (AZ M[2]). – *Open 10am to noon and 2 to 6pm. Closed Tuesdays, 1 January, 1 May, 14 July, 15 August, 1 and 11 November; 11F.*

The museum, the product of Esprit Calvet, a doctor, who bequeathed his collections and library to his native town, is in an 18C mansion. The rooms have preserved their decoration (panelling and stucco) as well as furnishings.

The **art collection** includes works from the German Spanish, Flemish, Dutch and Italian schools and yet it is most complete in 16-19C French, particularly Avignon art. Among the artists represented are Nicolas Mignard, Le Nain, David, Géricault, Corot, Manet, Toulouse-Lautrec, Utrillo, Dufy, Soutine, Modigliani and Vasarely...

On the left is a **wrought-iron collection.** Some of the pieces (14-15C) displayed once belonged to houses in Avignon.

In the room next-door is a remarkable **collection of antiquities** (Greek, Etruscan, Roman).

The first floor houses the **collection of local prehistory** which has been grouped by sites.

Requien Museum. – *Access to the library and study area Monday to Friday 9am to noon and 2 to 6pm; the rooms open to the public can be visited Tuesdays to Saturdays 9am to noon and 2 to 6pm.*

Natural history library, herbarium and geological, zoological and local botanical collections.

Louis Vouland Museum (AY M[4]). – *Open 1 July to 30 September 10am to 1pm and 3 to 6pm (8pm Fridays); the rest of the year 2 to 5pm; closed Saturdays, Sundays, Mondays and holidays.*

The museum contains a decorative arts collection concerned in particular with 18C French **furnishings:** a commode signed by Migeon, an inlaid backgammon table, a money changer's desk, and an amusing travelling table service stamped with the Countess Du Barry's coat of arms.

A good collection of porcelain and **faience**★ (Moustiers, Marseilles) can be seen in two rooms. A number of tapestries from the Flemish or Gobelins **(Pastoral Scene)** factories adorn the walls. The small canvas **Child Eating Cherries** by Jan Gossaert called Mabuse is worth noticing.

The Far Eastern collection includes a number of vases and chinese plates as well as a series of ivory polychrome statues.

Hôtel de Sade (BY F). – *No 5 Rue Dorée.* The 16C mansion, with mullioned windows overlooking the street, has an inner courtyard adorned by a pentagonal staircase turret.

Place de la Préfecture (BY). – The quiet square is overlooked from either side by two dignified 18C mansions, both built in a lovely golden-cream stone; the one on the south side, the former Roure College, now houses the Préfecture (**P**).

Roure Palace (BY E). – *No 3 Rue du Collège-du-Roure.* The onetime residence of Baroncelli-Javon has a fine porch decorated with mulberries.

EXCURSIONS

Avignon is an excellent centre both for touring by private car and for organized excursions *(apply to the tourist information centre, Cours Jaurès).*

Pont du Gard★★★. – *20 km - 12 miles W along N 100. Description p 99.* The drive could be extended by the Garrigues tour *(p 118)* and a visit to Uzès *(p 116).*

Villeneuve-lès-Avignon★. – The town faces Avignon across the Rhône. *Description p 132.*

Montfavet. – *6 km - 4 miles on the N 100* (CY) *and N 7^F on the right.*

The church, impressively large for so small a town, was originally part of a 14C monastery of which only two battlemented towers remain. Note the church belfry, the massive flying buttresses, the carvings on the lintel, the Gothic vaulted nave.

Lower Durance Valley. – *113 km - 70 miles by ⑤, N 570. See p 72 reverse direction.*

Le Thor; Thouzon Cave (Grotte de Thouzon) – *20 km - 13 miles E along N 100 – Local map p 72 – Facilities p 8.*

The small town of Le Thor, which is known today for the locally grown Chasselas white dessert grapes dispatched by the ton to markets in northern France, dates back to the Middle Ages. From these early times are still to be seen a bridge over the Sorgue River, a belfry, fragments of ramparts and in particular the **church**★.

This early 13C building is Romanesque, except for the Gothic vaulting in the single aisle which is among the earliest in Provence. The high nave massive buttresses, blind Lombard arcading on the apse and the incomplete square belfry are noteworthy. The exterior is impressive: the doorways, revealing Classical influence, the dome on squinches and the Lamb of God with five eagles carved on the keystone of the four sided apse.

Take D 16 N from Le Thor; after 3 km - 2 miles the track to the cave branches off to the left. Guided tour (time: 1/2 hour) 1 April to 31 October 9am to noon and 1.30 to 7pm; March and November Sundays 2 to 6pm; 14F. The **cave** at the foot of a hill, on which stand the ruins of Thouzon Castle and a monastery (small Romanesque chapel), comprises a 230m - 250 yds passage leading to a shallow hole containing delicate stalactites and curiously shaped and coloured concretions.

BAGNOLS-SUR-CÈZE

Michelin map fold 24 – Pop 17 777. *Facilities p 8*

Bagnols, an old town ringed by shady boulevards on the site of former ramparts, now serves as a dormitory for workers at the Marcoule Atomic Works *(p 106)* and as an excursion centre for tourists. The **modern art museum**★ *(open 15 June to 15 November 10 am to noon and 3 to 7pm; the rest of the year 10am to noon and 2 to 6pm; closed Tuesdays, 1 January, 1 May, 14 July, 1 November, 25 December and February; 5.50F; free on Wednesdays; combined ticket with archaeological museum on Thursdays, Fridays and Saturdays: 8F)* shares the same building as the town hall, a fine 17C mansion exhibiting contemporary works collected by the painter Albert André with the help of Renoir. In addition there are works by the 19C Lyonnais school, faience from Moustiers and Marseilles, commemorative portrait medals of painters and sculptors and a former private collection of artists' signed works – oils, watercolours, drawings, sculpture. (Renoir, Valadon, Bonnard, Matisse, Marquet, Van Dongen).

In Rue Crémieux *(left of museum)* are such 17C **town houses** as nos 10, 25, 29 with fine doorways and no 15 with its ornate façade.

EXCURSION

Orgnac Caves★★★**; Guidon du Bouquet**★★**; The Concluses**★★. – *Round tour of 153 km - 95 miles – allow 1 day. Leave Bagnols-sur-Cèze by N 86 going N and turn left into D 980. Turn left again into D 166 for La Roque-sur-Cèze.*

La Roque-sur-Cèze★. – Pop 133. The village appears grouped around its Romanesque chapel on a hilltop darkly plumed by cypresses; in the foreground, completing the **setting**★ is an old bridge, its several arches reaching down into the stream on sharply pointed piers. The river *(follow the path on the left without crossing the bridge)* soon plunges over the **Sautadet Fall**★ (Cascade du Sautadet) where, in forcing a passage through the limestone, the stream has hollowed out rifts and potholes so that the waters swirl and divide as they fall.

If you continue beyond the abandoned mill-race you will come to the deeper ravines plumbed by the River Cèze. From the southern end lovely view.

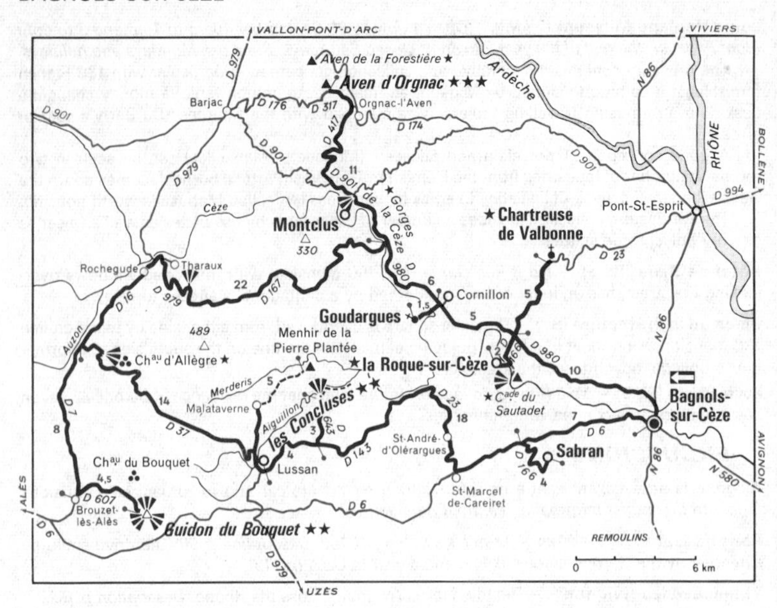

Chartreuse de Valbonne★. – *5 km - 3 miles S by D 23, then a small road on the left. Open 8am to noon (except Sundays and holidays) and 2 to 6pm; closed 16 November to 14 March; ring at the entrance; 6F, guided tour: 8F.* The charterhouse, founded in 1203, rebuilt in 17 and 18C, is now a hospital for tropical diseases.

The main gateway stands at the centre of a long wing, flanked by turrets; a second, 17C, gate opens into the central courtyard opposite the Baroque **church** in which the rich **interior decoration**★ centres on the high altar under a baldachin on twisted columns, in the stucco encrusted chancel. The white stone rose pattern vaulting is of rare workmanship.

A passage from the church *(south side)* leads to the glazed **large cloister;** each gallery is over 100m long. A monk's cell *(guided tours only)* has been reconstructed and furnished.

Return to D 980.

Gourdargues. – Pop 680. *Facilities p 8.* The village, ringed by massive plane trees, is dominated by its church. Originally attached to an abbey in 12C, it was partially reconstructed in 17 and 19C. The tall Romanesque apse is decorated inside with two tiers of arcading.

Continue along D 980. The perched village on the right is Cornillon.

Montclus. – Pop 139. The old village – the best **view**★ is from the junction of D 980 and D 901 – stands guarded by a single tower.

Bear left into D 901 then right into D 712 and D 417.

Orgnac Caves★★★ (Aven d'Orgnac). – *Description p 98.*

Return to D 901 and D 980; turn right into D 167. The road meanders across a harsh plateau. Turn right into D 979. As the road descends, good views appear of the **Cèze Gorges**★.

Continue to Rochegude; take D 16 and D 7 to Brouzet-lès-Alès.

Guidon-du-Bouquet★★. – The highest point of the Serre-du-Bouquet Range is a beak shaped rock. From the steep approach road the ruins of Bouquet Castle are visible to the north. The **panorama**★★ from the summit (alt 629m - 2 065ft) extends from the River Gard or Gardon (SW) to the Ardèche (NE) and includes Cévenne Causses and irregular crests of Lower Vivarais (NW), Mount Ventoux and the Alpilles (E). From the statue of the Virgin there is a vertiginous view of the *garrigue* surrounding Uzès *(p 116)* and, to the rear of the television mast, a view of the Bouquet Range itself.

Return via Brouzet along D 7; turn right into D 37. The road rises revealing an attractive view of the **ruins**★ of Allègre Castle. *Turn left into D 787 just before Lussan.* NE of Malataverne *(10 km - 6 miles Rtn on foot)* stands the so-called **Menhir de la Pierre Plantée,** an evenly shaped stone 5.60m - 17ft high.

Return to D 37. **Lussan** village is perched high on a rock, overlooking the rolling *garrigue.*

At Lussan turn left into D 143 and left again into D 643.

The Concluses★★. – The half mile long Concluses or Aiguillon Gorge was hollowed out of the calcareous grey-white rock by the Aiguillon, a swift running torrent which dries up in summer. It is possible, therefore, in summer, to take a **walk** along the stream bed, examine the pitted rock walls and go through the spectacular Gateway (Portail).

1 hour Rtn. Leave the car at the road's end, preferably in the second of the two parking places, a lay-by halfway down. From here there is a **view**★ upstream of the giant holes in the riverbed. *Take the path on the right signposted: Portail.*

As you descend you see the caves, most notably the Baume de Biou or Bulls' Cave, and come to the promontory and Beauquier Pool, a widening of the stream fringed by trees at the feet of majestic rock escarpments. The path ends at the Portail where the rock overhang finally meets above the river's course. On the return, experienced walkers may enjoy climbing back to the car park by way of a path which starts beside the Bulls' Cave *(allow an extra 1/4 hour).*

Return to D 143 and turn left towards St-André-d'Olérargues and Bagnols.

Sabran. – Pop 1 243. If you enter the old town, perched on a rock spike, and walk up to the foot of the statue of the Virgin in the castle ruins, like the warriors of the Middle Ages, you will command an all-embracing **panorama**★.

The BARONNIES

Michelin map 81 folds 3 to 5

The Baronnies Massif, which forms part of the outer foothills of the Alps, is of low altitude – the Duffre at 1 757m - 5 760ft is the highest point. The row of peaks runs from east to west following the folds of the Pyrenees, broken only by the Upper Eygues and the Ouvèze Valleys. The rock formation includes limestone, black marl, slate and sand and so offers little resistance to the streams and rivers which hollow out the bare ravines and deep defiles which characterize the area. The valley floors are carpeted with vineyards, olive groves and fruit orchards; the slopes with lavender and the hybrid, lavendin *(p 15)*, both distilled locally into lavender water.

ROUND TOUR OVER THE EY PASS*

80 km - 50 miles starting from Buis-les-Baronnies – about 3 hours - Local map below

Buis-les-Baronnies. – Pop 1 957. *Facilities p 8.* The town, lying on the banks of the Ouvèze on the Princes of Orange Road *(p 97)*, is surrounded by olives, apricots, cherries and lavender, – almonds are scattered about – but its claim to fame is as an international **herb market** and on the first Wednesday in July the town becomes the principal European Lime Blossom Market; 85 % of France's herb harvest changes hands in the streets and squares of this old town. The arcades lining the triangular **Market Square** (Place du Marché) where much of the selling goes on date back to 15C; even older is the **Saffre Tower,** relic of 12C ramparts. The town's other features are the dominant **St Julien Rock** 767m - 2 515ft high on the far bank, and the attractive quayside.

Leave Buis by D 546 going NE. The road skirts the Ouvèze before crossing the Ubrieux Gorge. *Turn left into D 108.*

Ey Pass (Col d'Ey) – Alt 718m - 2 355ft. The pass, flanked to east and west by the Montlaud and Linceuil Mountains, overlooks the Ennuye Valley; on the horizon stands the Buisseron.

Ste-Jalle. – Pop 251. The village's character appears from the moment you enter through a postern in the walls to discover old houses, a ruined castle, stout towers...

D 64 continues along the Ennuye Valley. *Turn right into D 94.* The road climbs up the Eygues Valley where minute parcels of land support peach, cherry and olive trees and vines.

Sahune. – Pop 275. The village has given its name to a crossbreed of sheep.

As the road descends to the bottom of the gorge, the regular lines of different stone strata on the cliff face can be seen, also a bubbling waterfall (left). *Turn right into D 162.* The road passes through fields and orchards, with occasional glimpses of the Eygues Valley, before climbing to the pinewood which covers the **Soubeyrand Pass** (alt 994m - 3 260ft). *Turn left after St-Sauveur-Gouvernet into D 64.* The road drops into the Ennuye Valley, rich in apricots and lavender, then climbs to the **Peyruergue Pass** (alt 820m - 2 690ft) before finally descending to the Ouvèze Valley.

D 546 on the right leads to Buis-les-Baronnies.

ROUND TOUR OVER THE PERTY PASS*

147 km - 90 miles starting from Séderon – about 5 hours - Local map below

Séderon. – Pop 298. This village of the Upper Méouge Valley, lies in the shadow of 1 367m - 4 485ft Bergiès Mountain.

Leave Séderon by D 542 going N; turn left into D 170. The road passes near the Eygalayes Cemetery where 35 members of the French Resistance are buried, then begins to climb, bringing into view Mount Lure (alt 1 826m - 5 990ft) to the east. Two glacially cold springs (Sources), the Bruis and the Guilliny, cascade beside the road.

St-Jean Pass (Col St-Jean). – Alt 1 157m - 3 800ft. The pass looks down on the Céans Valley; to the northeast is the Chabre Mountain and in the background Mount Aujour (alt 1 834m - 5 015ft); on its right the Durance Valley runs northeast-southwest.

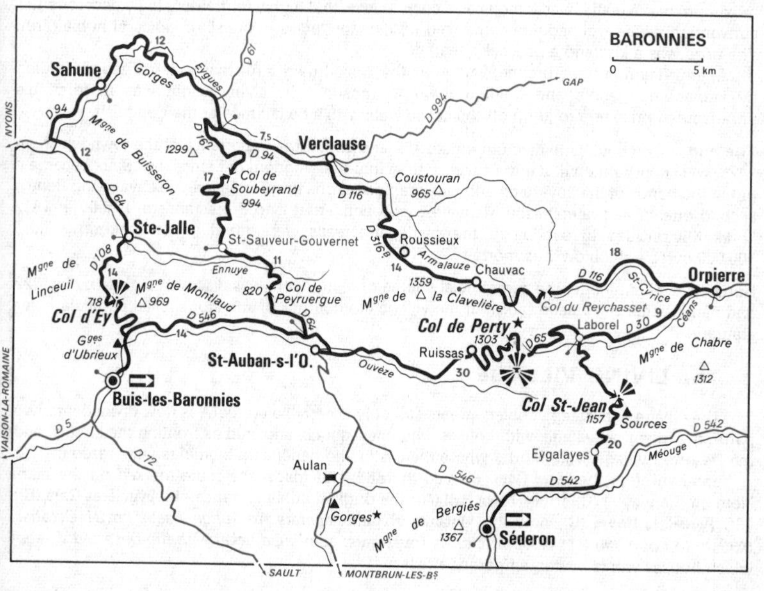

At Laborel turn left into D 65 up the Céans Valley.

Perty Pass★ (Col de Perty). – Alt 1 303m - 4 275ft. A footpath on the south side of the pass leads to viewing tables *(1/4 hour on foot Rtn)* affording a **panorama**★ of the Durance Valley and first Alpine foothills (E), the Ouvèze Valley and Mount Ventoux (W).

The downhill road overlooks the Baronnies and Ruissas, a village of charming small houses. *Turn left for St-Auban.*

St-Auban-sur-l'Ouvèze. – Pop 213. The village, as can be seen from the surviving medieval towers, part of the ramparts and two gates, was built as a military outpost on a rock spur commanding the confluence of the Ouvèze and Chauris; Mount Clavelière rises to the northwest.

Return to D 546 and continue westwards to D 64 on the right. The crossing of the Peyrergue and Soubeyrand Passes is described on p 53 in the opposite direction.

Turn right into D 94, up the Eygues Valley.

Verclause. – Pop 68. The village, built as a fortified outpost on a bluff, commands a **view**★ of the Eygues Valley and Mount Clavelière. There remain from its medieval heyday a massive chapel belfry and a castle keep built between the double perimeter wall.

Double back and take D 116 on the left towards Orpierre. The pyramid mountain straight ahead is the 965m - 3 165ft Coustouran. *Turn right into D 316^B^.* The road rises and passes through the hamlets of Roussieux and Chauvac, before returning to D 116. *Turn right.*

The road follows the Armalauze Valley, crosses the Reychasset Pass and skirts the St-Cyrice, a mountain stream.

Turn left into D 30 which brings you to the Céans Defile.

Orpierre. – Pop 318. *Facilities p 8.* The mountain village lying well back in a cleft formed by the Céans, is dominated to north and south by the 1 324m - 4 340ft Seuillet and 1 077m - 3 510ft Grand Puy. At the centre of a network of alleys stands the church with an apse decorated, in typical Provençal style, with a three tier tile frieze.

Turn round. D 30 goes up the Céans Valley to Laborel; bear left for Séderon.

The companion guides in English in this series on France are Brittany, Châteaux of the Loire, Dordogne, French Riviera, Normandy, Paris.

Les BAUX-DE-PROVENCE ★★★

Michelin map 246 fold 26 – *Local map p 32* – Pop 433 – *Facilities p 8*

The best approach, because it brings you directly into the heart of the village, is D 27. *Park the car (7F) at the village entrance.*

The sight of Les Baux rising from a bare rock spur, a 200m - 656ft wide, half mile long promontory of the Alpilles with vertical ravines on either side, is outstanding by day and magical by moonlight. The **site**★★★ was, of course, chosen for military rather than aesthetic reasons in medieval times and there remain from those days the ruins of a stout fortress, churches, chapels, minute squares and winding streets.

A warrior line. – The lords of Baux were greatly renowned in the Middle Ages, and as Mistral described them were « warriors all – vassals never »; vaingloriously they traced their genealogy back to the Magi King, Balthazar and implanted the Star of Bethlehem on their arms!

From 11C the seigneurs were among the strongest in the south of France, having in their control some 80 towns and villages. They won titles: members of different branches became variously Princes of Orange, Viscounts of Marseilles, Counts of Avellino and Dukes of Andria; one married Mary of Anjou, sister of Joan I, Queen of Sicily and Countess of Provence. Throughout this glittering period, when Les Baux was a town numbering several thousand (its maximum was 6 000) it was famous as a **court of love,** that highly formalized, higly decorous 13C convention where troubadours composed passionate verses in praise of ladies of noble birth. The prize was a kiss and a peacock's feather.

In 14C Raymond de Turenne, known as the « scourge of Provence », terrorized the region by kidnapping people and holding them to ransom. His chief delight was to force his unransomed prisoners to jump off the castle walls while he laughed at their anguish.

The end. – The Baux Line died out in late 14C and with it the importance of the town which, in 1426, was incorporated first into Provence then into the Kingdom of France. Les Baux became a gift in the hands of the sovereign and was granted, at one time, to Jeanne de Laval, King René's second queen, and later to the Manvilles, who converted it to Protestantism. Finally in 1632 Louis XIII decided to subdue it: the castle and walls were razed and the citizenry fined 100 000 livres – the blow was mortal.

Bauxite. – The mineral, the commercial source of aluminium, was discovered close by in 1822 and named after the village; north of the village are quarries of soft stone, used particularly for statuary.

■ The LIVING VILLAGE

The village – its steep cobbled streets still only accessible on foot – is now divided into two parts: the inhabited village, with houses, churches, shops, and studios fronting the streets, and the Deserted Village (Ville Morte) where the castle and dependant buildings were razed in 17C.

Enter through the **Magi Gate,** pierced in 1866, and follow the route marked on the plan. Note on the way: 17C former **Town Hall** (**A**); the original uphill entrance, the **Eyguières Gate** (**B**); 16C **Porcelets House** (**C**), now the **Museum of Contemporary Art** *(open Easter to 31 October, 9.30am to noon and 2 to 6.30pm; closed Thursdays; combined ticket with the Deserted Village)* which houses works by contemporary artists.

St-Vincent Square★ cramped beneath elms and lotus trees, is open on the west side with a view over the valley.

Overlooking the square is **St Vincent's Church (E)**, 12C building flanked on its north side by a campanile. The interior is small, dark and asymmetrical. Beneath the broken barrel vaulting are a 15C knight's tomb, a font carved out of the living rock, windows by Max Ingrand, and the lamb's cart, the centrepiece of the **Shepherds' Festival★★**, celebrated at Christmas midnight mass *(p 25)*.

The shepherds, dressed in their long capes, lead to the altar a newborn lamb in a small cart drawn by a ram.

By the cliff edge is the **White Penitents' Chapel (D)**, with a gable belfry, occulus, blason and rusticated square door. Built in the 17C the chapel was restored in 1936; inside the bare white walls have been painted with naive pastoral frescoes by the Provençal painter, **Yves Brayer** *(p 44)*.

Manville House (H) and the adjoining, now ruined, **Protestant Chapel (F)** are both 16C – with mullioned Renaissance windows between fluted pilasters and, on the chapel's window lintel, the Calvinist watchword and date: *Post tenebras lux 1571.*

The house, now the town hall, has a small inner courtyard. It was given to the town by Prince Bianchi de Medici of Manville. Painting exhibitions occur here.

Continue along the rock walled **Rue du Trencat★** and past the former manorial bread ovens **(J)** to 14C Maison de la Tour-de-Brau.

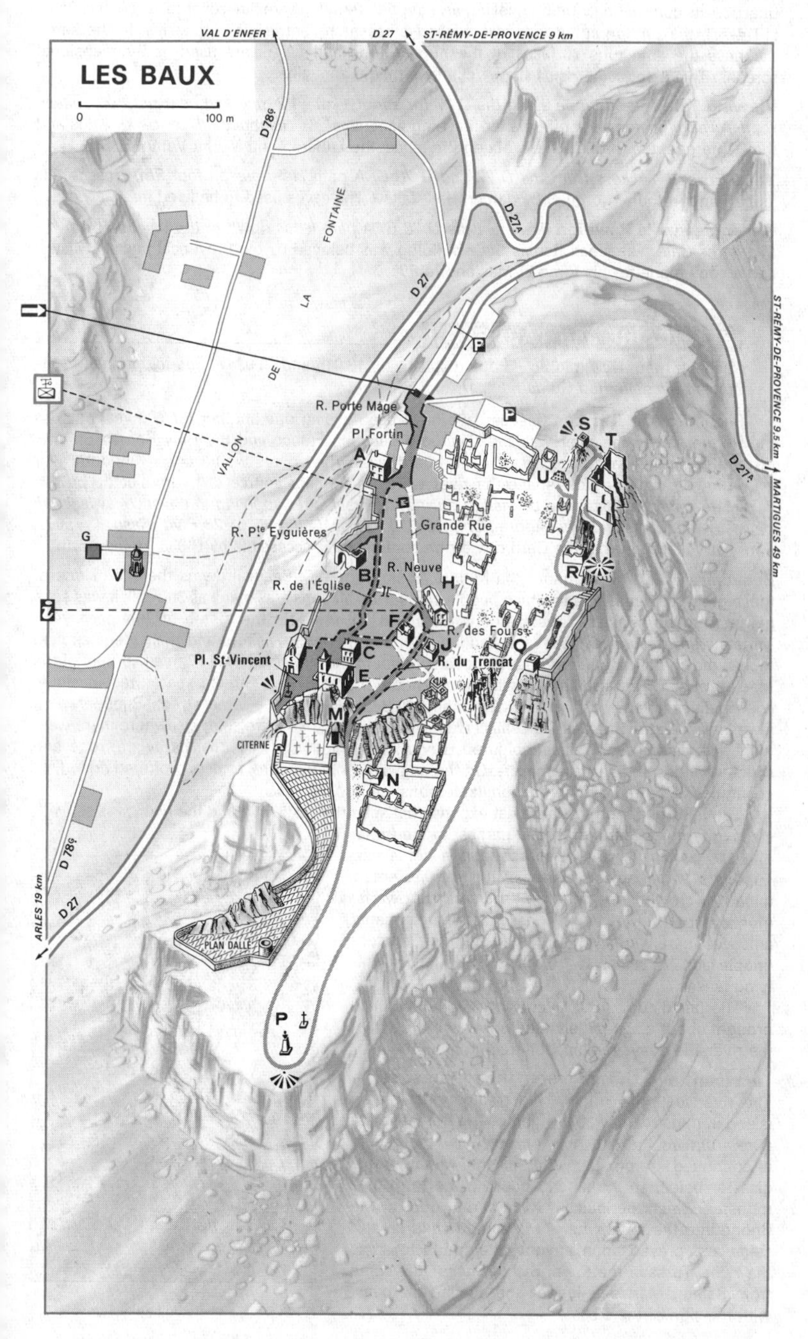

The DESERTED VILLAGE

A fee (10F) to the Deserted Village, the castle and the Museum of Contemporary Art is collected at the Lapidary Museum.

The village, the natural barbican to the medieval stronghold and long since ruined, is a superb place from which to view the surrounding countryside.

Lapidary Museum (M). – Beneath the vaulted ceilings of the former Maison de la Tour-de-Brau the museum displays articles excavated in the village's surrounding area.

Pass 14C ruins of St-Claude and St-Blaise Chapel (**N**) and the pavement, once a rainwater catchment for the underground cistern, to reach the **viewpoint**** beyond the monument to the Provençal poet Charloun Rieu (**P**).

Return past the perched Saracen Tower (**Q**), St Catherine's Chapel (**R**) and the Paravelle Tower (**S**) for a good **view*** of the 13C castle keep (**T**) standing high on its rock commanding a **panorama**** which includes Montmajour Abbey, Arles, the Crau and Camargue Plains.

After the old stone pigeon house (**U**) return to the Lapidary Museum.

ADDITIONAL SIGHTS

Picture Palace* (Cathédrale d'Images). – *Beside the D 27, 500m - 1/3 mile N of the village. Open 15 March to 30 September 10am to 7pm; 1 October to 4 November 11am to 6pm; closed Tuesdays in October; 25F, children 12F. Dress warmly.* The remarkable site of the Bauxite quarries, its colossal decoration evoking an Egyptian temple, were "discovered" by Albert Plécy (1914-77), the photographer who established a research centre in the quarries. In the semi-darkness the limestone surfaces of the huge rooms and pillars are used as 3-dimensional screens. This giant **audio-visual show*** changes theme annually.

Viewing Table. – *Continue along the D 27 for about 1 km - 1/2 mile and bear right on a steep road.* A rocky promontory offers a far-reaching **panorama***** *(signposted, car park):* Arles and the Camargue, the Rhône Valley, Aix-en Provence, the Lubéron and Mount Ventoux.

Val d'Enfer. – *Access from the D 27 and D 78 G.* A path *(1/4 hour on foot Rtn)* crosses this jagged and irregular gorge aptly named Hell Valley. The caves used to be lived in.

Queen Jeanne's Pavillion (V). – *On the D 78 G. A path leads down to the pavilion from the Eyguières Gate.* The small Renaissance building was beloved by the Provençal poets – Mistral had a copy made for his tomb at Maillane *(p 89).*

BEAUCAIRE and TARASCON *

Michelin map 246 fold 26 – Pops respectively 13 015 and 11 024 – *See town plans in the current Michelin Red Guide France*

Beaucaire and Tarascon Castles have have been eyeing one another for 700 years across the Rhone. When the river was the boundary between France and the Holy Roman Empire, instead of singing out « port » or « starboard » the river pilots would cry « Kingdom » or « Empire ». A bridge now spans the river which is a major source of hydro-electric power. **Beaucaire power station** *(may be visited during the week after applying in advance, at least 15 days, to the: C.N.R., 2 Rue André-Bonin, 69316 - Lyon Cedex 4, or 28 Blvd. Raspail, 75007, Paris)* at Vallabrègues at the Gard or Gardon confluence is accessible by D 986^{L} going north.

Beaucaire Fair. – Throughout the Middle Ages, from 13C, Beaucaire was the site of one of those great medieval fairs to which people came from all parts – as many as 300 000, it was said, gathered to do business, roister and celebrate in the town for the month of July each year. Streets were decorated, houses beflagged and crammed with visitors and their merchandise; those who could not get a room on land, slept aboard the ships gathered from all corners of the Mediterranean, Brittany and Gascony and moored in the river. Streets specialized in single commodities after which many were named: Beaujolais was a wine street, Bijoutiers – a jewellers' row; the Rue des Marseillais was where oil and soap were sold; elsewhere there were wool, silk, linen, cotton, lace, coloured woven cloth, clothing, weapons, hardware, rope and saddlery shops and harness makers. On the quayside and on board, traders proffered dried fish, sugar, cocoa, coffee, cinnamon, vanilla, lemons, oranges, dates...

The fairground, on the large flat expanse between the castle cliff and the river, was set with stalls offering everything from games to perfume, pipes to pottery. It was of course, also a horse fair. Tumblers and jugglers, acrobats and clowns entertained the crowds; bearded women, giants and dwarfs, monkeys, performing dogs, lions, bears and elephants amazed. There were even dioramas of Paris, Constantinople and Versailles to be viewed through magnifying lenses.

The fair died in 19C, killed by the railway which brought about a completely different way of life. Only the riverside quays remain, still trading in wine.

Tarascon and its monster, the Tarasque. – The riverside port, originally a trading post on an island in midstream, was fortified by the Romans with a *castrum* on the site now occupied by the castle. It continued to prosper until in the Middle Ages disaster befell, so the legend goes, in the form of a monster which periodically clambered out of the Rhône into the town where it devoured children and cattle and preyed upon anyone attempting to cross the river. To save the town, St Martha *(p 108)* came from Saintes-Maries-de-la-Mer and quelled the beast with the sign of the cross.

St Martha overcoming the Tarasque.

In 1474, in celebration of the miracle, **Good King René** *(p 29)* organized stupendous festivities which are still modestly recalled in an annual fête and procession *(last Sunday in June)* when a huge model of the Tarasque with champing jaws and swinging tail is paraded through the streets. Models of the Tarasque inhabit many local museums.

The two castles. – **Beaucaire:** *guided tour (time: 1 hour) 1 April to 30 September, 10am to noon and 2.15 to 6.30pm; the rest of the year 10.15am to noon and 2 to 5.30pm; closed Tuesdays.* **Tarascon:** *guided tour (time: 1 hour) all year round 9, 10 and 11am and 2, 3 and 4; also 5pm 1 April to 31 May and 5 and 6pm 1 June to 30 September; closed Tuesdays, 1 January, 1 May, 1 and 11 November and 25 December; 7F Sundays and holidays 3.50F.*

Beaucaire Castle*. – Take the steps out of the **Place du Château** to the pine and cypress walk, flowered with irises and broom *(absolutely no smoking).*

Only a shell remains; the castle itself which stood on the crown of the hill surrounded by 11C perimeter wall was almost entirely dismantled in 17C on the orders of Cardinal Richelieu. *To enter the precinct apply to the porter in the courtyard or chapel.*

There remain the **Romanesque chapel** with a twin bayed belfry and carved tympanum, the **Triangle Tower** (in fact polygonal), and a massive round tower flanking the curtain walls which dominate the cliff face and, with the outer barbican, defended the landward approach.

Go into the Triangle Tower with its inexpertly early pointed vaulting and climb the staircase *(104 steps)* in the thickness of the wall to the platform from which there is a **panorama**** of Tarascon, the Rhône Valley, the Montagnette and the Alpilles.

The **museum** has an essentially local collection (costumes, furniture, coins and medals), an interesting section on the Beaucaire Fair *(p 56)* and finds from local archaeological sites.

Also well worth looking at in the town are the domed church of **Our Lady of the Apple Trees** (N.-D.-des-Pommiers) and the **Town Hall.** The church *(closed in the afternoon),* which is in late 18C Jesuit style, incorporates *(exterior east)* the frieze of an earlier Romanesque church on the same site – depicting *the Last Supper, Kiss in the Garden, Flagellation, Carrying of the Cross and Resurrection;* the town hall, (Rue de l'Hôtel de Ville) is a late 17C mansion by Mansard with a central block flanked by wings outlined by a high, balustraded wall; carved flower garlands surround the windows and the grand staircase (courtyard) rises behind a double portico of Ionic columns. Also 17C is no 23, Rue de la République, known from the figures flanking the porch as the **House of the Caryatids.**

Tarascon Castle.** – The majestic, golden stone castle was begun in 12C on the foundations of an earlier Romanesque fort, continued by **King René** *(p 29),* who divided his time in Provence between Aix and Tarascon, and was finally completed in 15C. After long service as a prison, it was restored in 1926 to its medieval appearance, the moat being filled with water.

The castle is in two parts – a courtyard surrounded by a wall flanked by square towers, and a seigneurial lodging, defended by solid corner towers.

(After photo by Ed. S. L., Villeurbanne)

Tarascon Castle.

The **seigneurial apartments,** with finely carved fronts and mullioned windows, overlook the great court; a graceful polygonal staircase turret serves all storeys. Inside are coffered and vaulted ceilings and two superimposed chapels, the upper one being for the royal couple.

From the terrace there is a **panorama**** of Beaucaire and Tarascon on either side of the river, the Rhône Valley and dam at the Beaucaire power station at Vallabrègues, the Montagnette, the Alpilles, Fontvieille, Montmajour Abbey, Arles and the St-Gilles Plain.

The **Church of Ste-Marthe*** close to the castle entrance was consecrated in 10C and rebuilt in 12C when the body of the saint, the sister of Mary Magdalene, was said to have been found; it has been remodelled several times since. The south doorway is Romanesque though lacking its carved decoration; inside are paintings by Provençal artists and 15C triptych (final north chapel), reliquary bust and recumbent figure in marble from the 17C mausoleum (in St Marthe Chapel); the crypt contains St Martha's sarcophagus (3-4C).

The **Town Hall** *(on the corner of Rue du Château and Rue des Halles)* is 17C with a good stone balcony giving the finishing touch to its carved street front. The **Rue des Halles** still contains a few arcaded houses from 15C.

EXCURSION

St-Roman Abbey. – *4.5 km - 2 miles W from Beaucaire by D 999 and the road to the right, then 1/2 hour on foot Rtn. Park the car and take the path which winds through the guarrigue of cistus and kermès oaks. Open 1 July to 15 October (closed Thursdays) 10am to 7pm; the rest of the year and Saturdays and Sundays 3 to 6pm; time: 1/2 hour.*

The 12C abbey building, which is now being excavated, was abandoned by the monks in 16C, gradually transformed into a fortress and then enlarged by the construction of a castle on the upper terrace; stone for both fortress and castle was quarried from the abbey and disappeared from the castle in turn when this was dismantled in 1850.

The chapel, built into the rock, contains the tomb of St Romanus, an 11C abbots' chair and, over tombs sunk into the floor, a lantern to the dead with recesses for oil watching lights.

The **view*** from the terrace extends to the Rhône and the Vallabrègues Dam, Avignon, Mount Ventoux, the Lubéron, the Alpilles and, in the foreground, Tarascon and its castle. Note the graves hollowed out of the rock, the basin from which rainwater was channelled to a collecting tank, the monks' cells and a vast hall.

The BERRE Lagoon★ (Étang de BERRE)

Michelin map 246 folds 13 and 14

The Berre Lagoon, 15 530ha - 60sq miles in extent and nowhere more than 9m - 30ft deep, has been France's principal **petroleum port** for the last 60 years. The Caronte Canal, dredged out where there was once a lagoon of the same name, provides a passage to the Mediterranean. Formerly the underground Rove section of the Marseilles-Rhône Canal afforded access for barges but since a roof-fall in 1963 the waterway has not been clear for any type of boat.

The lagoon is fed with fresh water by the Rivers Arc (from NE) and Touloubre (from N) and the EDF Canal (Électricité de France) and is ringed around its 50 miles perimeter by limestone hills: the Lançon Chain (alt 195m - 640ft), the Vitrolles (alt 271m - 890ft), the Estaque (alt 201m - 660ft), and the St-Mitre (alt 142m - 465ft).

The modern installations are but the latest of man's constructions in the area: buildings still above ground and excavations reveal the presence of earlier inhabitants at St-Blaise, Flavian's Bridge, Miramas-le-Vieux *(see below)* and Port-de-Bouc *(p 88)*. The region, nevertheless, was still largely uninhabited when in 1920, under the San Remo Agreement, France obtained the right to purchase the major part of Iraq's annual crude oil production. The lagoon was transformed into an ideal **port for shallow draft oil tankers;** at the same time harbours also began to be developed on the Gulf of Fos – the French BP company at Lavéra in 1922-4, Shell-Berre at the Pointe de Berre in 1928, the Compagnie Française de Raffinage at La Mède in 1934...

The growth in demand for oil, apparent even in 1938, brought about the transformation soon after the war of **Lavéra,** to enable 80 000 ton tankers to dock and pump their cargoes directly into onshore installations. Finally in 1960s a completely new port was constructed at **Martigues.**

The lagoon complex is also the terminal of **the South European Oil Pipeline.** This line, inaugurated in 1962, supplies four refineries around the lagoon and eleven in regions as distant as Feyzin, Cressier in Switzerland, Baden and Bavaria in Germany; the total amount of oil piped a year is 65.2 million tons.

Dependant on the docks and refineries which ring the lagoon shore and coast around the Gulf of Fos are petro-chemical factory complexes extending far inland, so that from the air or one of the heights overlooking the bay, one sees an irregular mass of silver aluminium storage tanks, tall factory chimneys belching smoke, petroleum gas flares, vast metal warehouses and concrete works and office blocks.

Aviation centre. – At the turn of the century the peaceful lagoons and deserted Crau Plain were an ideal testing ground for pioneer aviators. At **Istres** before the First World War, a military aerodrome was established which exists today; when a civil airport was required for Marseilles it was sited at the east end of the Berre Lagoon at **Marignane.**

Round tour starting from Martigues

113 km - 78 miles – allow 1 day - Local map p 59

Leave Martigues (p 88) by D 5. The road undulates through vineyards, orchards and pinewoods.

St-Mitre-des-Ramparts. – Pop 4 299. The old town, encircled by 15C ramparts still pierced by only two gateways, stands just off the road. A network of small streets and alleys leads to the church where there is a view of the Engrenier Lagoon (SW).

Leave St-Mitre by D 51. The road crosses D 5 and skirts the small Citis Lagoon before passing the foot of the hill on which St-Blaise Chapel is just visible among the pine trees.

St-Blaise archaeological site. – *1/4 hour on foot Rtn. Park the car and walk left, uphill.* The path leads to the town wall of 1231 which surrounds the earlier site. To the left is the small 12C Chapel of St Blaise and abutting it a 17C hermitage. The nearer structure is a relic of an even older church, St Peter's.

Open daily 1 June to 14 September 9am to noon and 3 to 7pm; the rest of the year 2 to 5pm (6pm April and May) and in addition 9am to noon Thursdays, Saturdays and Sundays; closed Tuesdays and 1 May; 5F.

Man's presence on the naturally defensive site, surrounded by lagoons on all but the south side, has been revealed in excavations which show that it was inhabited continuously from 7C BC to 49 BC, then apparently abandoned, before being reinhabited from 5-11C AD. A **Greek rampart★** has been uncovered slightly to the rear of a Palaeochristian wall, also a lower town with houses aligned along a Greek street, a 5C basilica (St Vincent's) and an upper town.

Next to the keeper's house, in the car park, museum displaying pottery, money, etc. from the excavations.

The road, D 51, continues between the Lavalduc and Citis Lagoons.

Istres. – Pop 30 360. The town beside the Olivier Lagoon is a military airport base. The small museum *(open 1 May to 30 September 2.30 to 7pm; closed Tuesdays; 5F)*, is devoted to local history, and folklore. To the north lies the Greco-Ligurian town of Castellan on the edge of the Olivier Lagoon.

Circle the Olivier Lagoon by way of D 53 and then turn left into D 16, which brings you back to the Berre Lagoon.

Miramas-le-Vieux. – The small town on a flat ledge of rock, is characterized by medieval ramparts, the ruins of 13C castle and 15C parish church which replaced the even smaller 12C church still standing in the churchyard.

Continue along D 10 before turning left into D 16, then D 70^{D} straight ahead. Turn right into D 70^{A} at Pont-du-Raud. The road ascends a height overlooking the Touloubre.

Cornillon-Confoux. – Pop 980. At the centre of the perched village stands a small Romanesque church with a gable wall belfry and modern stained glass windows by **Frédérique Duran** *(p 76)*.

There are good local **views★** from the walk which starts at the church and circles the village.

Take D 70 and a tourist road on the right to St-Chamas.

St-Chamas. – Pop 5 045. The town is unique in being dominated by a small, triple arched, aqueduct. The church, which is 17C with a Baroque west front, contains a marble high altar and 16C altarpiece to St Anne (third south chapel).

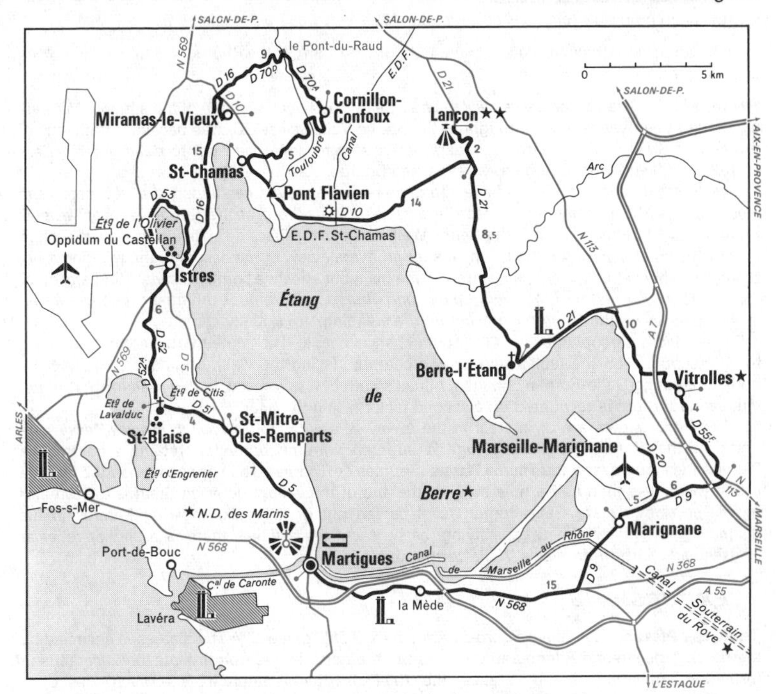

Pont Flavien. – Flavian's Bridge is named after the patrician who in 1C ordered its construction at what is now the south approach to St-Chamas. It crosses the Touloubre in a single span and celebrates the feat in triumphal arches at either end, surmounted by small lions.

Continue along D 10 which passes **St-Chamas power station.**

Turn left into D 21 and left again after 1.7 km - 1 mile into an unsurfaced road. Park the car.

Lançon viewing table. – *1/4 hour on foot Rtn.* Steps *(48)* lead to the top of a rock from which there is a **view**★★ over the lagoon to the surrounding hills.

Turn round and once on D 21 continue to Berre-L'Étang.

Berre-L'Étang. – Pop 12 562. The town lives by fishing and its chemical factories. The chapel, N.-D.-de-Caderot displays at the altar, a 16C painted wood retable and, in a recess opposite the door, a crystal vessel known as the Caderot Vase, said to have contained a lock of the Virgin's hair.

Continue first along D 21, then N 113 on the right; finally turn left for Vitrolles.

Vitrolles★. – Pop 22 739. The original village is now enveloped in an industrial town remarkable for the warm ochre colour of its houses both old and new. An unusual rock, crowned by 11C Saracen Tower and a chapel dedicated to N.-D.-de-Vie, the aviators' guardian, dominates the town site and affords a **panorama**★ southwest over the Berre Lagoon, the Estaque Chain and the St-Mitre heights, between which the Caronte Depression leads to the port and oil installations of Lavéra. In the foreground are the outflow of the Marseilles-Rhône Canal, La Mède and its refinery, Marignane and the airport, and Berre amidst its factories; southeast the Étoile Range with the Pilon du Roi and east, Mount Ste-Victoire *(1/4 hour on foot Rtn from the main cemetery gate; 75 steps).*

Leave Vitrolles by D 55F. At N 113 crossroads, cross into D 9 then right into D 20.

Marseille-Marignane Airport. – The airport, France's second after Paris, is equipped with two runways. Some 4 million passengers and 25 000 tons of freight are handled annually.

Marignane. – Pop 31 213. The town possesses two interesting buildings – the château, known as Mirabeau's Castle, and the church.
One wing of the castle is now the town hall: *(façade interior courtyard side under restoration).* The registry office in the marquess' bedroom and the mayor's parlour in the marchioness' boudoir are rare in their period decoration including painted ceilings *(open during office hours, ask for permission).*
The church nave, which is late 11C, has broken barrel vaulting but is entirely lacking in windows; the aisles and high altar are 16C.

Follow D 9 to N 568 where you turn right. The road to Martigues crosses the Rove *(p 74)* or Marseilles-Rhône Canal and passes through acres of market gardens; glance over the lagoon to the site of **La Mède** marked by two peculiar rocks at the harbour entrance.

BOURG-ST-ANDÉOL

Michelin map 246 fold 23 – *Local map p 102* – Pop 7 665 – *Facilities p 8*

The town, so attractively sited on the right or west bank of the Rhône, is characterized by its church spire.

St-Andéol★. – The church dates back to late 11 early 12C when worship of the sungod, Mithras, which had been widespread throughout the Rhône Valley since 2C, was declining in favour of the cult of St Andéol, an early Christian martyr said to have been put to death near Viviers *(p 102)* in 208 and whose remains had reached Bourg.

Owing to its age many parts have had to be rebuilt or have been added at a later date – the west front is 18C but behind it rises the original, gabled, roof of the Romanesque nave surmounted by 15C Flamboyant Gothic belfry. Walk round to the Place de la République on the south side or the small square on the north side for an overall view of the east end, the two tiered octagonal tower exalted by its stone spire and the plain but effective Lombard style, blind arcading.

Inside *(under restoration; open Sunday and Thursday mornings)*, ornament is concentrated in the apse where the columns, making up the arcading, are skilfully carved.

St-Andéol's sarcophagus is in the south chancel chapel. The white marble coffin, according to an inscription on the tablet held by two cherubs (facing the wall), originally contained the body of a young Gallo-Roman, a pagan, but as so often, was re-used, in this case for St Andéol, whose martyrdom is recounted on a second tablet facing the altar.

Two other sights are of interest in the town – the early 16C mansion, **Nicolay House,** just north of the church, which, although it suffered wartime bombing, retains an attractive Renaissance loggia, and the **Tourne Waters** (Sources de Tourne). The springs rise on the far side of the town, less than half a mile away at the end of the valley; between them is a worn and mossy six foot square Gallo-Roman relief carved out of the rock, showing Mithras in his distinctive Phrygian helmet, cape flying, as he sacrifices a bull – there is a similar relief at Housesteads Fort on Hadrian's Wall, Northumberland.

EXCURSIONS

The Gras Plateau★. – *Leave Bourg-St-Andéol by D 358, going SW.* The plateau is encircled by the rivers Ardèche and Rhône and is blocked to the north by the Coiron Plateau. Calcareous in formation, grey-white in appearance, the 700-800m thick stratum (2 000-2 500ft) has been permeated through the millenia by rain which has drained into the natural and earthquake formed fissures and tunnelled out passages, until now the whole area is riddled by a subterranean system of caves, rivers and lakes.

On the surface the upper levels are clad in deep evergreen oak, with yellow broom in springtime; lower down, where the white rock gives way to more richly coloured ochre, yellow-gold and rust-red marls, there are old almond orchards, fields of lavender and mulberry trees. The roads are lined by box hedges and vineyards where the stock is pruned close to the ground to avoid the wind.

Dent de Rez★. – The 719m - 2 360ft mountain, a double summit divided by the Eyrole Pass, affords a sure bearing wherever you are on the plateau.

Access and ascent are by way of a path (1 1/2 hour on foot Rtn) from the hamlet of Gogne, 4.5 km - 2 miles – NW of Gras. The **panorama★** from the top is wide-ranging. **Gras** itself is a village of 250 people living in old houses; the interior vaulting of the church *(to visit apply to Mme Ferber or Mr Feytel)* is decorated with unusual medallions in vivid colours; perched on a rock spur above the village is a 11C chapel (restored) with a gable wall belfry and oven vaulted apse.

Eastern edge of the Gras Plateau★. – *Round tour of 34 km - 21 miles – about 2 hours. Leave Bourg-St-Andéol by D 4 going towards St-Remèze.*

Laoul Wood viewing table. – From the table (alt 340m - 1 115ft) beside the road the **view★** extends along the Rhône and over the Pierrelatte Plain, the Donzère-Mondragon works (SE), the Tricastin Hills (SE) and Mount Ventoux (ESE).

Continue climbing, past the television mast and across the scrub covered plateau to D 462 on the right, which you take. The road affords alternating glimpses of the Rhône and Lower Vivarais before plunging into the stoney Rimouren Valley at the heart of which lies a small hamlet of the same name *(p 61)* surrounded by old almond trees, small fields of lavender and short stemmed vines. As you continue up the valley, there appears, quite close, the divided peak of the **Dent de Rez.**

Turn right at the Mas du Gras, into D 262. (To ascend the Dent, see above.)

Larnas Church.

Larnas. – Pop 83. The Romanesque church stands to the left of the road; its square north and south ends, curved bays and squat octagonal cupola on a square base make a pleasant contrast with the tall cypresses in the neighbouring old cemetery.

Ste-Baume Gorge★. – On leaving Larnas, the road enters a stoney, calcined gorge, where the heat is so intense in summer that it is known as the **Hot Valley.** As you round the hairpin bends down the cinder coloured rock slopes you will get glimpses of Mount Ventoux (SE) and, in the middle distance of the Pierrelatte Plain. At the ravine's end, as you come abreast of 11-14C **Chapel of San Samonta,** St-Montan appears on its ridge.

St-Montan★. – The village is crowded close with old houses, winding alleys, steps, covered ways and a small church, grouped at the foot of the ancient citadel.

St-André-de-Mitroys. – The Romanesque church is beautifully enhanced by the cypresses in the adjoining cemetery.

Return to Bourg-St-Andéol by D 262 and N 86.

Other villages on the plateau. – The villages, of modest character but attractive appearance, with warm terracotta roofs clustered round a small, well kept Romanesque church, are interesting as variations on a local theme.

Bidon. – Pop 59. An old village with particularly attractive rose coloured roofs.

Rimouren. – Hamlet in a valley hollow.

Rochecolombe★. – Pop 167. The secluded medieval village overlooks a green, translucent, stream flowing through a rock circus. The **site★** is very isolated. The « new » village, grouped around the church, looks up to the ruins of the « old » or medieval village still guarded by the outer walls of a square keep and the belfry of its former Romanesque chapel. From the floor of the circus *1/2 hour on foot Rtn)* you can see the old village in its setting, the stream and two emergent underground springs.

St-Andéol-de-Berg. – Pop 85. Notable for its old houses.

St-Maurice-d'Ibie. – Pop 183. The apse of the village's sober Romanesque church was decorated in 17-18C with unusual and brilliantly coloured medallions.

St-Sulpice. – The dazzling white Romanesque chapel (12-17C) stands on a slight rise in the plateau amid a sea of vines. The south wall is built of re-used stones carved with strapwork designs.

St-Thomé. – Pop 257. The old belfry stands out high above the Escoutay Valley.

Les Salelles. – The village is remarkable for the number of houses with different styles of outside staircase **(couradou).** These lead to the stone or terracotta tiled kitchen and other living rooms on the first floor, the ground floor or semi-basement serving as wine cellar, store, stable or garage.

Sauveplantade. – A Romanesque church, dating back to 10C, marks the village centre.

Walkers, campers, smokers
please take care.
Fire is the scourge of forests everywhere.

The CAMARGUE ★★

Michelin map 83 folds 8 to 10 and 18 to 20

The Camargue, the most original and romantic region of Provence and possibly of France, has been largely preserved in its natural state through its designation in 1928 and 1970 as a botanical and zoological nature reserve. Roads traverse the marshland, affording wide views *(take fieldglasses if you have them).* Late spring or early autumn are the best times for a visit: horses and bulls are easily seen and birds abound, the sun shines (but not overpoweringly) and there are the famous pilgrimages to Stes-Maries-de-la-Mer *(p 108).*

GEOGRAPHICAL NOTES

The Rhône Delta. – The 56 000ha of marshland - nearly 220sq miles – which lie between the two arms of the Rhône, the Grand Rhône to the east, the Petit to the west, have been reclaimed from the sea over the centuries by the gradual accumulation, at the river-mouth, of alluvium brought down by the river from the hinterland. Every year the Grand Rhône, which comprises 9/10 of the flow, hollows out from its banks and sweeps towards the sea 20 million cubic yards of gravel, sand and mud – enough to cover Paris in a silt blanket 25cm or 10 1/2in thick. A part of the deposit is moved on by currents to the Languedoc coast; some used to form sandbanks across the Gulf of Fos until the currents were diverted and the way left clear for shipping to approach the oil ports and the Berre Lagoon (the sand is now rounding out the Sablon Point). The bulk of the alluvium, nevertheless, remains at the rivermouth extending the delta 10-15m a year.

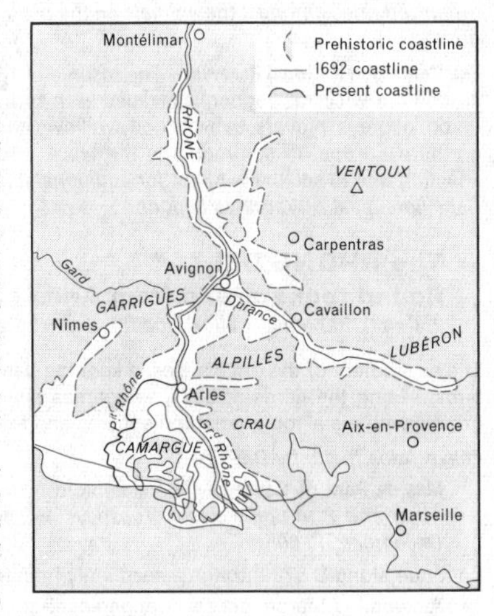

Elsewhere, owing to continental subsidence, the sea is invading the shore: the Vieux Rhône and Petit Rhône promontories have been swept away by southeasterly storms; **Faraman Lighthouse,** 700m inland in 1840 was swallowed by the sea in 1917 so that a new one had to be built; Stes-Maries-de-la-Mer once an inland town, is now protected by breakwaters...

The country of the Camargue. – Although the Camargue is one vast plain, it is divided into three distinct regions.

The cultivated region. – This lies in the upper areas bordering the old and present courses of the Rhône. The soil is impregnated with salt and waterlogged and, therefore, has to be drained, washed free of salt and then irrigated with fresh water from the Rhône. Exhausting as the system is, rice *(p 15),* wheat, vines, fruit trees, forage and rape seed are now grown extensively and there are even trees to relieve the flatness of the landscape – durmast oak, ash, elm, poplar, robinia and willow standing singly, in clumps or planted in long files to act as wind breaks.

The CAMARGUE★★

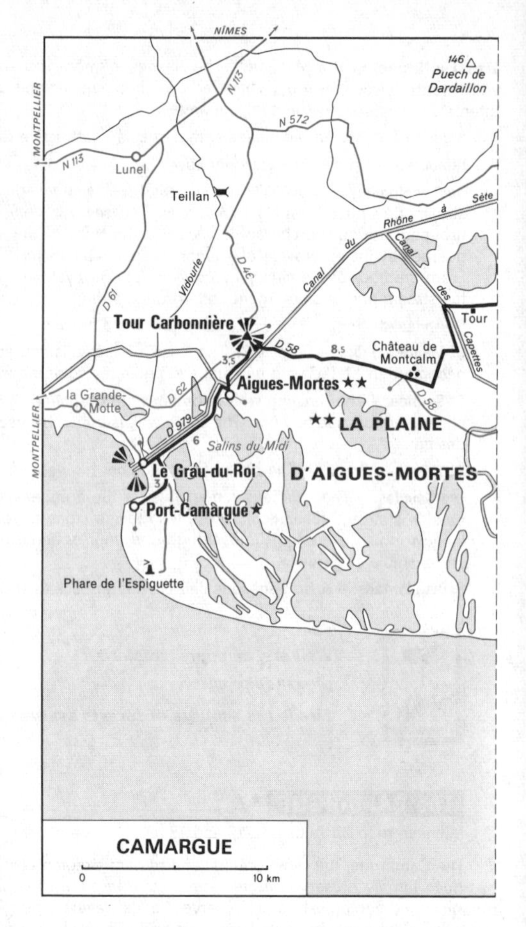

The saltmarshes. – The marshes extend in a chequerboard of saltpans, gleaming pyramids and rounded heaps, around Salin-le-Giraud and along the west bank of the Petit Rhône *(p 14)*.

Traditional Camargue. – The wild southern delta comprises a sterile plain dappled by lagoons and smaller pools – a flat desert of sand and marsh, divided from the sea by low dunes, where since 1928 all fauna and flora have been protected. Plants which thrive in this salt-impregnated landscape are green in springtime, grey in summer and red in winter. Roads have now penetrated but it remains isolated, unchanging and with a desolate appeal.

The Rièges Islands. – The islands which lie at the south end of the **Vaccarès Lagoon,** have a lush vegetation of blue thistles, tamarisk, wild daisies and zinerarias, junipers, wild daffodils and narcissi.

The « Manades » – the sheep, the horses and the bulls. – Bulls and horses wander freely, watched by Camargue cowboys in large felt hats carrying long, three pronged sticks. The bulls, black, lithe and agile, with horns aloft, are the heroes of the Provençal, or **cocarde,** bullfights when the bull lives to see another day; the horses with creamy white coats – the foals are born brown and turn white only in their fourth year – are said to be descendants of the prehistoric beasts whose skeletons were discovered in a vast horse cemetery at Solutré (in the Rhône Valley, NNW of Lyons). They possess stamina, sureness of foot and quick intelligence, qualities well displayed also at *ferrades* when the cowboys use them as mounts to cut out year old steers for branding.

Sheep play an important part in the local economy but they summer in the Alps.

There are a large number of owners who hire out horses for cowboy accompanied, organized rides amongst the animals on the plain, in the marshes or on the beach: 45-50F for an hour.

The Camargue National Reserve. – The reserve of 13 500ha – more than 50sq miles which extends around the Vaccarès Lagoon is invaded each spring and autumn by migrants such as the purple heron, ospreys, plovers, avocets and swallows and affords winter quarters to duck and teal from northern Europe. In summer it is the place to see pink flamingoes. Roads skirt the reserve enabling one to see the wildlife; *for additional information apply to the information centre at La Capellière, east of Vaccarès Lagoon.*

The RHÔNE DELTA★★

Round tour starting from Arles

160 km - 100 miles – allow one full day – Local map above

The excitement of the drive arises in spotting flamingoes wading or on the wing, naming other birds, seeing the herds of bulls, sometimes quite close, and the horses standing singly or in groups with a stallion guarding his mares and foals.

Leave Arles (p 40) by D 570.

Mas du Pont de Rousty. – The sheepfold now houses the **Camargue Museum.** *Open 9am to noon and 2 to 6pm; closed Tuesdays 1 October to 31 March, 1 January, 1 May and 25 December; 10.50F.*

Continue along D 570 through a seemingly infinite cultivated area.

Albaron. – Albaron, once a stronghold, as can be seen from its fine 13-16C tower, is now an important pumping and desalination station.

Continue again along N 570 through Les Bruns and Pioch-Badet.

Ginès. – Information centre on the Camargue, past and present, and vantage point over the lagoon *(open 9am to noon and 2 to 6pm; closed Fridays 1 October to 31 March and 1 January, 1 May and 25 December).*

Pont de Gau Bird Sanctuary (Parc Ornithologique). – *Open 8am to sunset; 15F.*

Boumian Museum. – *Open 1 April to 1 November 10am to noon and 2 to 7pm; 10F.* Camargue life is depicted in 18 tableaux peopled by wax figures: included are a duck shoot, a rodeo **(ferrade),** a cowboy's cabin, a gypsy encampment. There is also an ornithological collection and a display of shot guns.

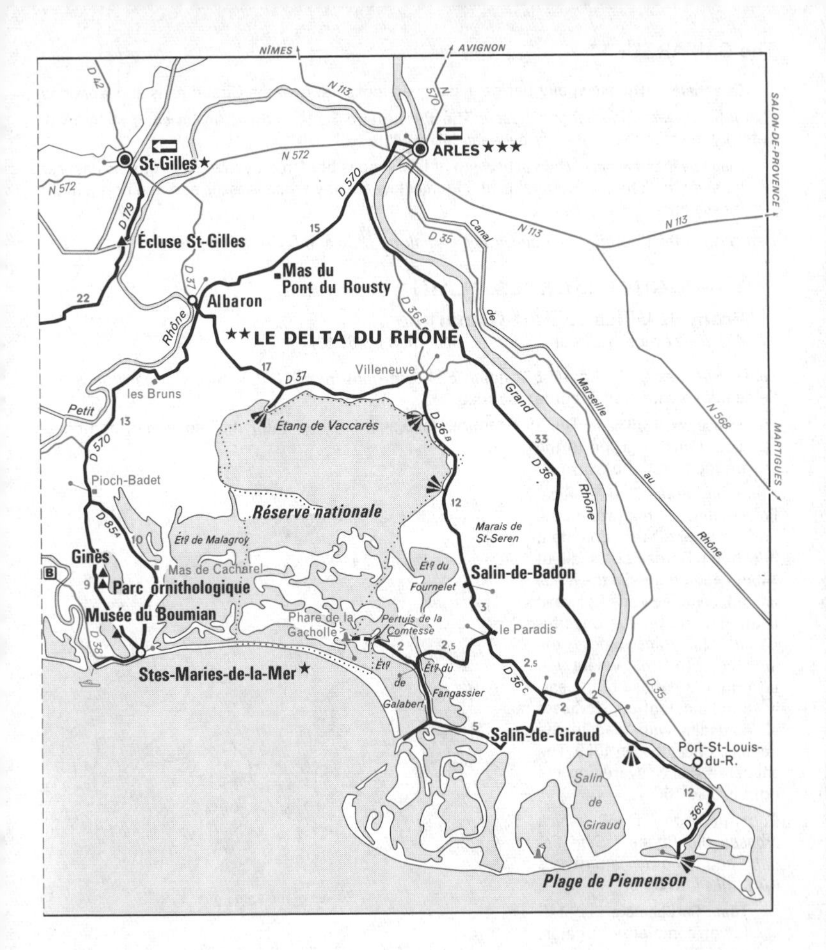

Stes-Maries-de-la-Mer★. – *Description p 108.*

Leave by D 38 and after 1 km - 1/2 mile, turn left into a surfaced road.
On the left is the tomb of Folco de Baroncelli-Javon *(p 109);* it was set up in 1951 on the site of the Mas de Simbeu which was his property. *Park the car just beyond the tomb on the left hand side of the road.*

Boat trip on the Petit Rhône★. – *Regular service between Easter and 2 November; departures daily at 4.15pm Easter to end September; additional trips at 10am, 2.30 and 6pm July and August; 3.15pm October and November; 40F (children 20F); 1 1/4 hour.* The trip, which goes upstream to the Petit Sauvage Ferry, takes you to the grazing pastures on the plain where you may see the wild horses and bulls, and, fishing from the river banks, osprey, grey héron, duck and occasionally flamingoes.

Return to Stes-Maries-de-la-Mer and take D 85^A^. The road crosses the Couvin Marsh, a saltwater landscape of stunted plants and swamp. Cacherel Farm stands out as landmark to the right, Stes-Maries to the rear.

At Pioch-Badet, turn right into D 570; at the entrance to Albaron, turn right again into D 37 which winds through rice-fields; 4.5 km - 2 miles further on bear right.

Méjanes. – The amusement centre on the farm includes a bullring and an electric railway *(10F)* which runs *3.5 km - 2 1/2 miles* along the banks of the Vaccarès. *Pony trekking: 50F per hour; horse-drawn carriages: 20F.*

Continue along D 37. The road crosses an expanse relieved by the occasional clump of trees.

Viewpoint over the Vaccarès Lagoon. – *3/4 hour on foot Rtn. Turn right into an unsurfaced road and park the car.* The footpath, which skirts an irrigation canal, ends at a small belvedere which looks out over the lagoon towards the Rièges Islands *(p 62).*

Return to D 37 where you bear right; in Villeneuve turn right into D 36^B^. To the right is the lagoon, to the left, on St-Seren Marsh, a typical herdsman's cabin *(p 23).* The road skirts the Fournelet Pool.

Salin-de-Badon. – Zoological and Botanical Reserve offices.
From Le Paradis two excursions can be undertaken *(to be done in dry weather)* enabling the tourist to discover the birds of the Camargue and particularly pink flamingoes.
– one goes to the Gacholle Lighthouse where there is a telescope in a hide *(traffic prohibited from Perthuis de la Comtesse, do the last half-mile on foot.*
– the other is along the causeway between the **Fangassier** and **Galabert Pools.**

D 36^C^ and D 36 on the right, bring you to Salin-de-Giraud.

Salin-de-Giraud. – The small town on the west bank of the Rhône with its grid pattern of streets shaded by plane trees, acacias and catalpas, is a chemical manufacturing centre – note how each quarter is named after a firm (Péchiney, Solvay).

Follow the road which skirts the Grand Rhône.

Belvedere. – The viewpoint beside a salt heap looks out over the Giraud pans and workings.

Continue towards Piemançon Beach. The Rhône and Port-St-Louis can be seen at intervals before you cross the causeway between lakes white with salt.

Plage de Piemenson. – The vast sweep of fine sand is bordered by low dunes; to the east can be seen the Estaque Mountains, the Marseilleveyre and Étoile Massifs and due north, in the far distance, the Alpilles.

Return to Arles through Salin-de-Giraud and along D 36 and D 570 on the right.

The AIGUES-MORTES PLAIN★★

From St-Gilles to Port-Camargue

43 km - 27 miles – about 4 hours – Local map pp 62-63.

Leave St-Gilles (p 111) by N 572 going SE; turn right into D 179. Vineyards, pinewoods and fields edged with rushes border the road.

Écluse de St-Gilles. – The lock controls the canal between the Petit Rhône and the Rhône-Sète Canal – go on to the bridge to see the works.

Continue along D 179. Rice-fields extend to the hills on the horizon where the dominant Puech de Dardaillon is all of 146m - 450ft high! On the left is an old watch-tower. *The road bears left to skirt the Capettes Canal.* The ruins before the junction with D 58, where you turn right, are those of the early 18C château of the **Marquess of Montcalm** who died in the defence of Quebec in 1759. The chapel in the vineyards on the right is also 18C.

Continue along D 58, which crosses the Rhône - Sète Canal, and shortly afterwards turn right into D 46.

Horses of the Camargue.

Tour Carbonnière. – 14C tower, complete with gates, portcullisses and battlements, was the advanced barbican of Aigues-Mortes on the old salt road. A small garrison was quartered in the first floor room which is equipped with a big fireplace and a bread oven.
The platform *(66 steps)* commands a **panorama**★ of Aigues-Mortes and the saltmarshes (S), the Cévennes foothills (NW) and the Lesser Camargue (E).

Return to D 58 and turn right.

Aigues-Mortes★★. – *Description p 27.*

Take D 979 SW. The road passes between the Grande Roubine and Midi Saltmarshes.

Le Grau-du-Roi. – Pop 4 204. *Facilities p 8.* The small fishing village at the mouth of the channel connecting the saltmarshes and the sea, has developed into a picturesque resort.

Return to the entrance to Le Grau-du-Roi, to take D 62^{B} on the right.

Port-Camargue★. – The resort, symbol of the development of the Languedoc-Roussillon coast, dates from 1969. Covering 150 ha - 370 acres, it provides mooring for 3 000 pleasure craft, and low-rise accommodation – the smooth stepped façades interspersed with gardens reaching out into the port on crooked finger-like promontories.

As you come out of Port-Camarque, turn right into the surfaced road to the Espiguette Point. In a Camargue landscape of thistles, tamarisk and sea-rockets clinging to wind swept dunes stands a small lighthouse **l'Espiguette Lighthouse** (Phare) commanding the Languedoc coast.

CARPENTRAS ★

Michelin map 246 fold 10 – Pop 25 886

Carpentras is famous for its special caramel sweets, *berlingots.* It is a bustling commercial town with an ancient cathedral and museum set against a backdrop of mountain peaks. In recent times the construction of the Carpentras Irrigation Canal has turned the surrounding plain into a fertile area of market gardens.

To make a circular tour of the town by car before visiting individual buildings on foot, follow the **boulevards,** laid on the site of the old ramparts, starting at Pl. A. Briand, on the south side, and driving clockwise along Bd. Albin-Durand, Bd. Gambetta, Bd. Mal. Leclerc – the 14C **Orange Gate** (Y) to the right is the only remaining part of the city wall – Bd. du Nord. From Pl. du 8 Mai, on the north side, there is a **view** of the Dentelles de Montmirail and Mount Ventoux – before returning via Bd. A. Rogier and Av. Jean Jaurès.

Old St-Siffrein Cathedral★ (Z B). – Enter the cathedral, which dates from 1404, by the Flamboyant Gothic south door (late 15C), known as the Jewish Door after the Jewish converts who passed through it to be baptized. Inside, note the balcony on the end wall of the nave which connects the bishops' apartments to the church, and the oriel above the first bay from which he could follow services. There are pictures in the north chapels by Mignard and Parrocel and sculptures, including a gilded wood glory, by the Provencal, Bernus *(p 66)* in the chancel; to the left is a 15C painting of the Virgin supported by St-Siffrein and St Michael.

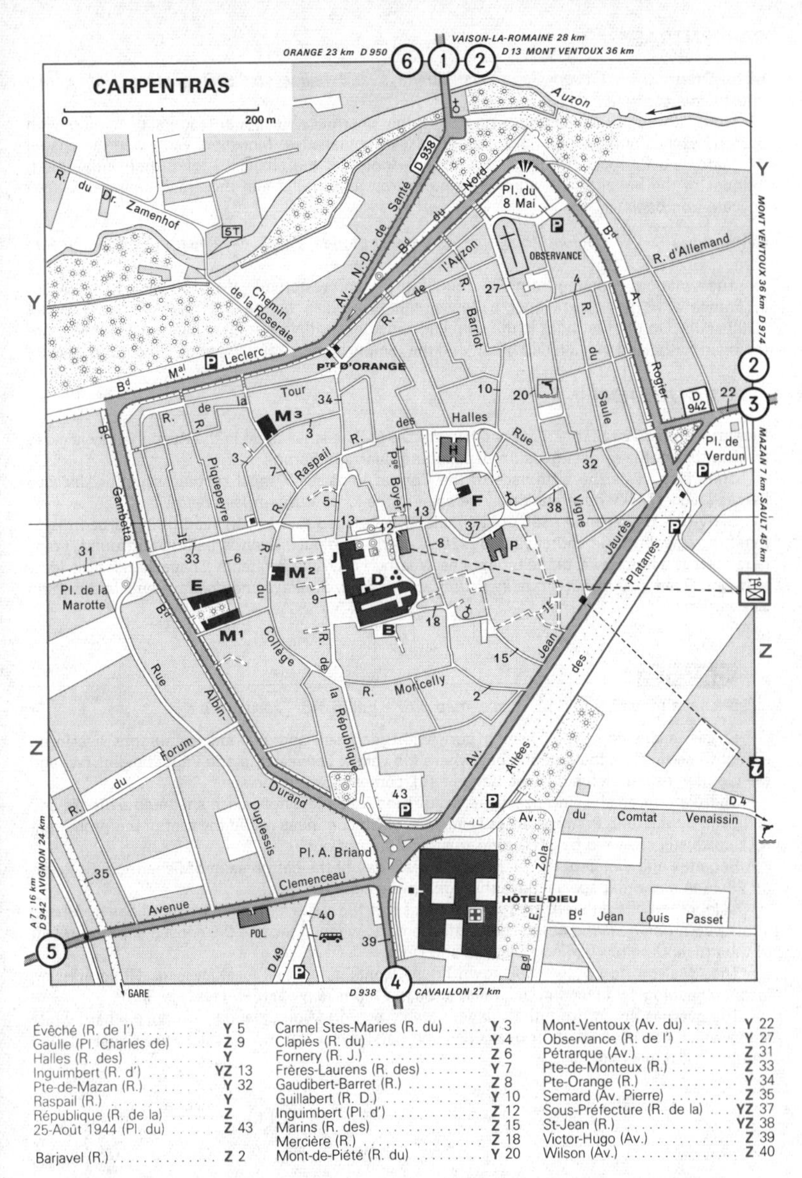

Évêché (R. de l') . . . . Y 5
Gaulle (Pl. Charles de) . . . . . Z 9
Halles (R. des) . . . . Y
Inguimbert (R. d') . . . . YZ 13
Pte-de-Mazan (R.) . . . . Y 32
Raspail (R.) . . . . Y
République (R. de la) . . . . . Z
25-Août 1944 (Pl. du) . . . . . Z 43

Barjavel (R.) . . . . Z 2
Carmel Stes-Maries (R. du) . . . . . Y 3
Clapiès (R. du) . . . . Y 4
Fornery (R. J.) . . . . Z 6
Frères-Laurens (R. des) . . . . . . Y 7
Gaudibert-Barret (R.) . . . . Z 8
Guillabert (R. D.) . . . . Y 10
Inguimbert (Pl. d') . . . . Z 12
Marins (R. des) . . . . Z 15
Mercière (R.) . . . . Z 18
Mont-de-Piété (R. du) . . . . Y 20
Mont-Ventoux (Av. du) . . . . . . Y 22
Observance (R. de l') . . . . Y 27
Pétrarque (Av.) . . . . Z 31
Pte-de-Monteux (R.) . . . . Z 33
Pte-Orange (R.) . . . . Y 34
Semard (Av. Pierre) . . . . Z 35
Sous-Préfecture (R. de la) . . . YZ 37
St-Jean (R.) . . . . YZ 38
Victor-Hugo (Av.) . . . . Z 39
Wilson (Av.) . . . . Z 40

Treasury★. – *Apply to the porter of the Comtat Museum (see below).* Among the exhibits are 14-18C wooden statues (14C Virgin and child, sacerdotal ornaments, 15C Prophet Daniel), a Limoges enamel cross and plate.

Law Courts (Z J). – *Open Monday to Friday; apply to the tourist information centre for times.* The interior of 17C building is decorated with paintings from the same period.

Commemorative Arch (Z D). – The Roman municipal arch behind the Law Courts was built most likely during the same period as the arch in Orange *(p 96);* on the east face two prisoners, one in a tunic, the other in an animal skin, are chained to a tree hung with military trophies.

Inguimbertine Library (Z E). – *Open 9.30am to 6.30pm; closed Monday mornings, Saturday afternoons and Sundays and holidays all day. Rare exhibits available on request.*

The library and two of the town's museums are housed in the 18C mansion, **Allemand House.** The library which was founded in 1745 and named after its donor, a bishop of Carpentras, comprises some 230 000 volumes including 5 000 MSS, 200 incunabula (mostly Italian) and 100 000 early works; there are, besides, remarkable 14-16C books of hours, musical scores and more recent legacies of 19C prints and drawings.

Museums (Z M1). – *Guided tour 10am to noon and 2 to 6pm (4pm 1 October to 31 March); closed Tuesdays and holidays; 2F – common ticket for all four museums and cathedral treasury.*

Comtat Venaissin (Comtadin) Museum. – *Ground floor.* Carpentras was the capital of the Comtat Venaissin *(p 69)* from 1320 to the Revolution: regional mementoes include coins and seals, local head-dresses and bells for cattle and sheep driven through the town to summer and winter pastures.

Duplessis Museum. – *First floor.* Paintings by local primitive artists, Parrocel, Rigaud and the Carpentras artist, Duplessis (1725-1802) and J. Laurens.

Sobirats Museum (Z M2). – 18C house with contemporary interior.

Lapidary Museum (Y M3). – *Apply to Comtadin Museum porter.* The building was formerly the Chapel of the Grey Penitents, consecrated in 1717.

Hôtel-Dieu (Z). – *Closed Saturdays, Sundays and holidays; 2.50F; apply to the tourist information centre for times.*

Going through 18C building one sees the pharmacy, (cupboard doors decorated with pastoral scenes and cartoons including monkey apothecaries; Moustiers ware jars) the chapel (Mignard and Parrocel paintings; the tomb – north of the chancel – of Bishop Inguimbert, founder of the hospital and library; wrought iron altar grille) and the grand staircase with a delicate iron banister.

Synagogue (Y F). – *Guided tour (time: 3/4 hour) Mondays to Fridays 10am to noon and 3 to 5pm.*

The synagogue, dating from 15C, rebuilt in 18C and restored in 1929 and 1958, is the oldest in France and the last relic of a Jewish ghetto, which before the Revolution numbered 1 200 souls. On the first floor is the panelled sanctuary with lamps and candlesticks; below are the oven for baking unleavened bread and the temple annexes and in the basement the piscina.

EXCURSION

Mazan. – Pop 3 729. *7 km - 3 miles by ③, the D 942.* The small town in the Auzon Valley is close to Mormoiron, the largest gypsum deposit and quarry in Europe.

The village was the birthplace of the Comtat Venaissin's most reputed sculptor, **Jacques Bernus** (1650-1728) whose work may be seen in the local museum *(see below).*

Sixty-two Gallo-Roman sarcophagi, which once lined the Roman road from Carpentras to Sault, now wall in the churchyard of 12C N.-D.-de-Pareloup which is half-underground. From here there is a fine **view**★ of the mountains. Nearby 17C White Penitents' Chapel houses the local **museum.** *Open 3.30 to 6.30pm daily in July and August, Sundays and holidays only in June and September.*

CASSIS★

Michelin map 246 fold M – *Local map p 67* – Pop 6 318 – *Facilities p 8*

Cassis, a bustling, small fishing port, with good fish and seafood restaurants, lies in an attractive **setting**★ at the end of a bay where the valley, between the arid Puget heights (W) and the wooded escarpments of Cape Canaille (E), comes down to the sea.

There are three shelving beaches, two of sand, one of shingle, each sheltered by rocks and all linked by the long **Promenade des Lombards** which continues round the foot of the prominent rock spike still crowned by 14C castle *(restored but not open).*

Regattas and watersports celebrate the feast day of the patron saint of fishermen, St Peter, on 29 June and other special days throughout the summer.

Celebration of a different kind came to Cassis in 1867 with a mention of the village by **Mistral** in his poem *Calendal* and at the turn of the century, when it became the chosen summer resort of the artists Derain, Vlaminck, Matisse and Dufy.

The "Maison de Cassis", 18C town house, contains a small **local museum** (**H**) comprising local archaeological finds and documents *(open Wednesdays and Fridays 3 to 5pm).*

The **quarries** not far from the village, notably by Port-Miou Calanque, produce a hard white stone which has been used for quaysides and gateways as far away as the Suez Canal and the Campo Santo in Genoa.

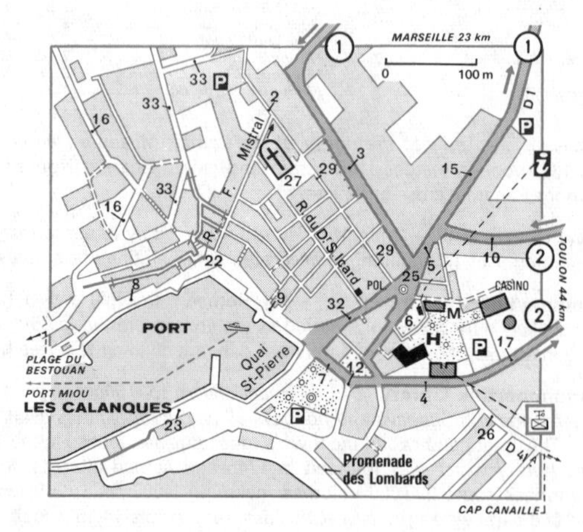

The CALANQUES★★

The valleys of the Marseilleveyre and Puget limestone ranges west of Cassis continue under the sea, forming as they dip below the water, a shoreline of deep **inlets** *(calanques),* between high ridges.

The scenic attraction lies in the brilliant limpidity of the deep blue or, sometimes, blue-green, water below tall, rough white cliffs.

Port-Miou; Port-Pin★; En-Vau★★ Calanques. – *Boat trips: 3/4 hour Rtn; embark from Quai St-Pierre, Cassis. Boats also sail from Marseilles Old Port.*

Access: *take the car to the inland end of Port-Miou inlet (1.5 km-1 mile), park at the top of the slope and do the last 1/2 mile to the harbour on foot; continue on foot along the marked paths – Port-Pin (1 hour Rtn), En-Vau (2 1/2 hours Rtn); or take D 559 (6.5 km-4 miles from Cassis,*

17 km - 10 miles from Marseilles) and turn off south down a narrow road along a gorge, then through a wood, to the Gardiole Pass (Col de la Gardiole 3.2 km - 2 miles). Park the car and continue on foot: En-Vau, 2 hours Rtn; Port-Pin, 3 hours Rtn.*

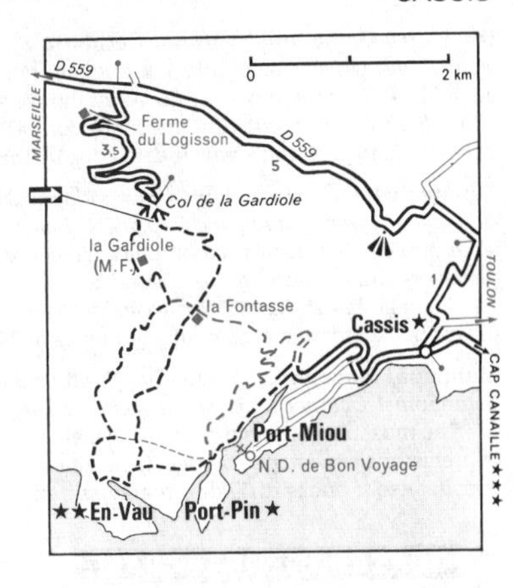

Port-Miou Calanque. – The half mile long inlet shelters a small village of the same name.

Port-Pin Calanque★. – Tucked away at the end of the inlet, with its high rock walls plumed by occasional pines, is a small, shady, beach.

En-Vau Calanque★★. – The best known and prettiest inlet has high white cliffs and tall needle rocks rising out of the sea with a beach of fine sand at the end.

Sormiou and Sugiton Calanques. – The walk from Marseilles to either inlet (access to Sormiou by way of Beaumettes, Sugiton through the University Centre, Domaine de Luminy, SE of the city) makes a magnificent excursion for experienced walkers and climbers, who should beware of the summer heat and lack of drinking water en route.

In summer there are boat trips from Marseilles and Cassis.

EXCURSION

The Crests' Corniche★★. – *19 km - 11 1/2 miles – about 1 1/2 hours. Leave Cassis by ② the Toulon road. At a signpost bear right and at Pas de la Colle turn right.* The stretch of coast road between Cassis and La Ciotat skirts the Canaille, a short limestone range which rises from the sea in towering white cliffs which are among the tallest in France – 362m - 1 190ft at Cape Canaille, 399m - 1 310ft at the Grande Tête. The viewpoints combine to present the full grandeur of the scene.

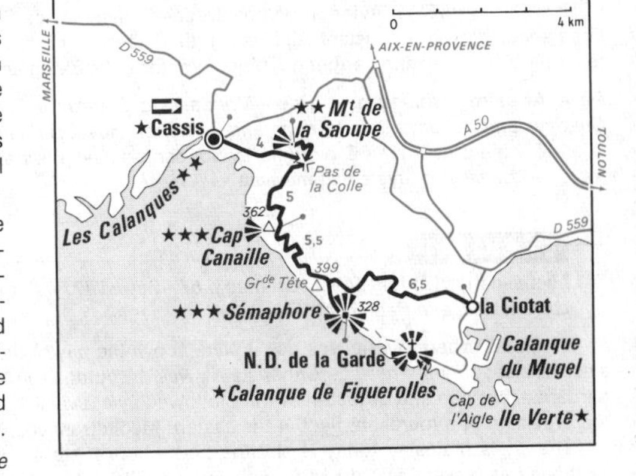

Saoupe Mountain. – The **panorama★★** from the television mast includes Cassis, Riou Island, the Marseilleveyre Massif and St-Cyr-Chain (W), the Étoile Chain and Ste-Baume Massif (N), La Ciotat and Capes Aigle and Sicié (SE).

Return to the Pas de la Colle and continue uphill. Bends and belvederes reveal an ever wider view of Cassis and La Ciotat.

Cape Canaille★★★. – From the guard rail there is an outstanding **view★★★** of the cliff face, the Puget Massif and inlets, Marseilleveyre Massif and islets.

Beyond the Grande Tête, turn right to the semaphore.

Semaphore. – The **view★★★** embraces La Ciotat and its shipyards, the eagle rock at Cape Aigle, the Embiez Islands, and Capes Sicié and Canaille *(telescope).*

Return to the hillside road; bear right for La Ciotat (p 68). The descent into town passes quarries, pinewoods and a « natural » arch of limestone standing on a puddingstone base.

CAVAILLON

Michelin map 246 fold 11 – *Local maps pp 72 and 80* – Pop 20 830 – *See town plan in the current Michelin Red Guide France*

The name Cavaillon, to the French, conjures up fragrant melons and the sweet vegetables of early spring. The melons, about which one could wax lyrical, are sweet and rose pink inside – the harvest begins in May; the vegetables come from the mile upon mile of market gardens which surround the town and make it France's largest designated « national market » with an annual turnover of nearly 200 000 tons.

Panorama. – From the Place François-Tourel on the west side of the town, walk left round the small **Roman arch** re-erected in the square in 1880, and climb the stepped zig-zag path up to the **Calvary** (note the inscription to **Mistral,** the poet, carved into the rock at the second bend – on the right). The **view★** *(viewing table)* embraces the Cavaillon Plain, Mount Ventoux (far NE), the Vaucluse Plateau (NE), the Coulon Valley (NE foreground), the Lubéron (E), the Durance Valley (SE) and the Alpilles (SW).

St-Jacques. – *3/4 hour on foot Rtn from the Place François-Toure.* 12C chapel, remodelled in 16 and 17C, stands among cypresses, pines and almond trees, near a small hermitage occupied from 14C to the beginning of this century.

Accessible also by car (5.5 km - 3 miles) by way of D 938 going N; 50m beyond the crossroad turn left uphill (views of the Montagnette and the Rhône).

Old Notre-Dame and St-Véran Cathedral. – *Open mornings only.* The pentagonal apse and small south cloister belong to the original Romanesque structure, to which a side chapel was added in 14C and another in 18C when the west front was remodelled.
Cross the cloister to enter by the south door. Despite the darkness one can glimpse gilded 17C panelling and choirstalls which date back to 1585.

Synagogue. – *Rue Hébraïque. Open 1 May to 30 September 9am to noon and 2 to 6pm; the rest of the year 10am to noon and 2 to 5pm; closed Tuesdays; 4F.* The synagogue, built in 1772 on a small scale – the Jewish community never exceeded 200 – is decorated with Louis XV style panelling and wrought iron balustrades.

A small **Jewish Comtat Venaissin Museum** includes the oven for baking unleavened bread, prayer books, torahic ornaments and relics of 14C synagogue on the same site.

Municipal Museum. – *Grand' Rue (N end). Guided tour (time: 1 hour) 10am to noon and 2 to 6pm (5pm 1 October to 31 March); closed Tuesdays and 1 May; 4F.*

The museum in the old hospital chapel and outhouses, includes an **archaeological collection**★ of prehistoric cup-shaped stones, table altar, pottery, utensils and coins - and mementoes of the hospital itself: books of 17-18C remedies, ledgers and Moustiers pharmacy jars.

CHÂTEAUNEUF-DU-PAPE

Michelin map 246 fold 24 – Pop 2 060

The town is the source of the most heady of all the Rhône wines. The original vineyard was planted in 14C on land belonging to the Avignon popes and the wine was consumed locally until mid-18C when its renown began to spread.

In 1923 the winegrowers' association laid down strict rules defining the area, the management of the vineyards, harvest dates, the selection of grapes, the thirteen acceptable wine types, vinification and vintage labelling. The strict control has brought about a highly refined and often superb product: a wine known for its finesse and nose – Châteauneuf-du-Pape.

The Popes' Castle. – All that remains of the fortress built by the Avignon popes in 14C and burned down during the Wars of Religion, is one tall tower and stretch of wall. The ruins, however, still command a splendid **view**★★: the Valley of the Rhône, Roquemaure and the ruins of Hers Castle (WSW), Avignon with N.-D.-des-Doms and the Palace of the Popes clearly outlined against the more distant Alpilles (S), the Lubéron and the Vaucluse Plateau (E), the Dentelles de Montmirail and, farther off, Mount Ventoux, the Baronnies and the Lance Mountain (NE).

Père Anselme Museum. – *Open Mondays to Saturdays 8am to noon and 1.30 to 6pm; Sundays and holidays 9am to noon and 2 to 6pm; closed 1 January and 25 December.*

16C wine-press, 17-18C ploughs, a wooden ratchet press and coopers' and vinedressers' tools can be seen in this small **museum**.

La CIOTAT

Michelin map 84 fold 14 – *Local map p 67* – Pop 31 727 – *Facilities p 8* – *See town plan in the current Michelin Red Guide France*

La Ciotat, where the houses rise in tiers above the bay of the same name, has been a port since ancient times when, as Citharista, it was an outpost of Marseilles. Roman occupation, barbarian invasion and devastation were followed by a revival in the Middle Ages, and from 16C the provision of a merchant fleet in the eastern Mediterranean.

The city's mainstay today is still the port where there are shipyards which build oil and methane gas tankers, and docks for ships up to 300 000 tonnes.

■ SIGHTS *time: 1 1/2 hour*

Old Harbour (Vieux Port). – The harbour swarms with fishing boats and pleasure craft.

N.-D.-de-l'Assomption. – *Open Mondays to Fridays 10am to noon and 2 to 6pm (7.30pm July to September); Saturdays 10am to noon only.*

17C church overlooking the harbour is notable for a *Descent from the Cross* by André Gaudion painted in 1616 and a modern frieze by Gilbert Ganteaume of scenes from the Gospels.

La Ciotat-Plage. – The quarter has been created just north of the harbour as a resort with hotels and seaside villas lining the beach. Marking one of the squares open to the sea is a monument to the Lumière brothers, cinema and photographic inventors.

Ile Verte★. – *1/2 hour Rtn. Boats on the quay; 8F per person in season.* The rock at the headland, so clearly a bird of prey when seen from the small fort on the island, is what gave Cape Aigle its name.

The Crests' Corniche★★. – *16 km - 10 miles. Leave La Ciotat by the Avenue Louis-Grozet, D 40, going N, then Avenue Marcel-Camusso on the left. See p 67 for the reverse direction.*

Mugel and Figuerolles★ **Calanques.** – *1.5 km - 1 mile. Leave La Ciotat via Quai Stalingrad and Avenue des Calanques and bear left into Avenue du Mugel.*

Mugel Calanque. – The inlet is dominated by the eagle rock of Cape Aigle. Good view of Ile Verte. *Take Avenue des Calanques and bear left into Avenue de Figuerolles.*

Figuerolles Calanques★. – *1/4 hour on foot Rtn.* A short green valley leads to the small, clear water inlet marked by strangely eroded rocks – the "Capucin Friar" to the right – and cliffs pitted with shallow holes, separated by sharp ribs.

N.-D.-de-la-Garde Chapel – *2.5 km - 1 1/2 miles – plus 1/4 hour on foot Rtn. Leave La Ciotat by the Boulevards Bertolucci, and Narvik, Rue du Cardinal-Maurin and the Chemin-de-la-Garde, on the right; after 500m turn left towards a built up area and park the car. At the chapel, bear right into a path which leads to a terrace above the chapel (85 steps cut out of the rock).* The **view**★★ embraces the full extent of La Ciotat Bay.

The COMTAT VENAISSIN

Michelin map 83 folds 10 and 11

The area between the Rhône, the Durance and Mount Ventoux took the name Comtat Venaissin on its presentation by the crown to the Holy See in 1274 when Philip III, the Bold, persuaded Gregory X to leave Rome and come to France *(p 44)*. The region was only repossessed in 1791 at the Revolution. The first local capital, Pernes-les-Fontaines, was superseded in 1320 by Carpentras.

The Comtat Venaissin comprising the Vaucluse Plain, the largest basin in the Rhône Valley, is renowned for its market gardens. The early fruit and vegetables, grown in the irrigated, calcareous soil, are distributed nationwide from Orange, Avignon, Cavaillon and Carpentras *(pp 96, 44, 67, 64)*.

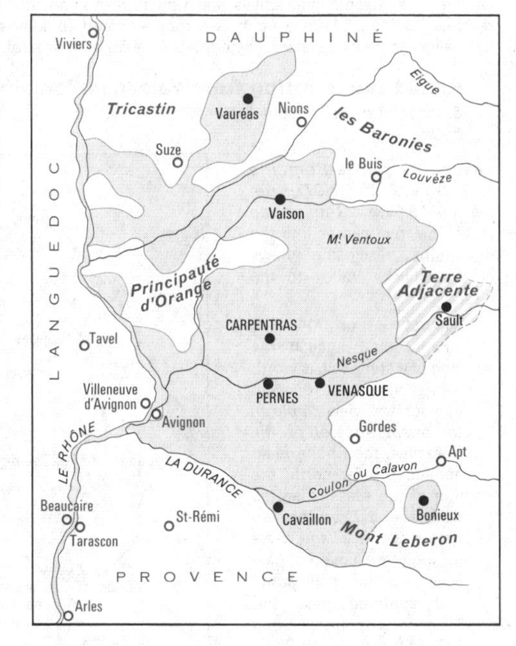

TOUR

Carpentras★. – *p 64.*
Cavaillon. – *p 67.*
Châteauneuf-du-Pape. – *p 68.*
Fontaine-de-Vaucluse. – *p 126.*
Oppède-le-Vieux★. – *p 81.*
Pernes-les-Fontaines. – *p 127.*
Le Thor. – *p 51.*
Vaison-la-Romaine★★. – *p 119.*
Valréas. – *p 122.*
Venasque. – *p 127.*

The CRAU Plain

Michelin map 246 folds 12 and 13 and 26 and 27

The Crau Plain, which extends for 50 000ha - 200sq miles between the Rhône, the Alpilles, the St-Mitre Hills and the sea, is a grey white desert of shingle and gravel which, in places, reaches a depth of 15m - 50ft. For centuries the only signs of man's existence were the roads going north up the Rhône Valley towards Lyons. Since the construction of the Craponne Canal in 1554 to bring the waters of the Durance to their original delta on the Berre Lagoon, and the subsequent development of a network of irrigation channels, the cultivation of the **Petite Crau** in the north has steadily extended until it now covers half the plain. From Arles in the west to Salon in the east, windbreaks of poplar and cypress shelter fields of fruit and vegetables. There are four crops a year of the famous Crau hay – the last of which is grazed in the fields by sheep which winter in the plain.

The **Grande Crau,** to the south, remains the symbolic Provençal desert, a region which fires the imagination and inspired a legendary origin: Hercules, the tale goes, finding his way to Spain barred by the Ligurians, against whom he exhausted his stock of arrows, called on Jupiter for help; the god sent down a hail of stones and rocks which became the plain. More prosaically, geologists attribute the presence of the stones to the Durance, which originally flowed directly into the sea through the **Lamanon Gap.** The rocks and stones brought down by the stream accumulated into a vast delta which eventually dried out when the river changed course and became a tributary of the Rhône.

Starting from St-Hippolyte and driving southeast along N 568 one gets a good idea of the special atmosphere of the Grande Crau as the green countryside gives way to a progressively more barren landscape, devoid of artefacts, of man and beast, except for the very occasional sheepfold and cabin near a well, the staging post on the spring and autumn migratory journeys to and from the mountains.

In addition to the encroachment of agriculture from the north, the continued expansion of the Fos Complex *(p 75)* implies incursion from the south for industrial development, but for the moment the heart of one of France's most fertile regions remains a semi-desert, the Crau Plain.

The DENTELLES DE MONTMIRAIL ★

Michelin map 246 folds 9 and 10

The pine and oak clad heights, some times blanketed with vines, the final foothills of the Ventoux Range overlooking the Rhône, owe their lace point name to the unique sharpness of the peaks. The geological cause of this special outline lies in the upper strata of Jurassic limestone having been forced upright by the folding of the earth's crust and then eroded by wind and weather into needle thin spikes and ridges. St-Amand, the highest of the Dentelles peaks, reaches 734m - 2410ft. The hills, broom-covered in May and June, attract painters and naturalists as well as walkers, who may come for a short stroll or a long hike.

Round tour starting from Vaison-la-Romaine

63 km - 39 miles – about 2 1/2 hours.

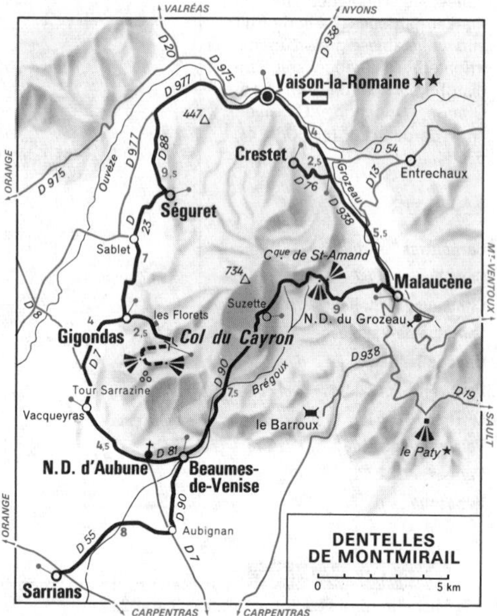

Leave Vaison-la-Romaine *(p 119)* *by ③, the D 977; turn left after 5.5 km - 3 miles into D 88.* The road climbs into the mountains, disclosing views of the Ouvèze Valley to the west.

Séguret. – Pop 714. The village, built against the side of a steep hill, is worth a brief visit both for itself and for the **view** *(table in the main square)* of the Dentelles, the Rhône Plain and, to the far north, the line of the Massif Central. *Park the car at the entrance to the village.* Walk through the covered passage into the main street and continue past 15C Mascarons Fountain and 14C belfry to 12C St-Denis Church for another view. A ruined castle and network of steep streets all add character.

On leaving Séguret turn left into D 23 for Sablet and then the D 7 and D 79 for Gigondas.

Gigondas. – Pop 648. The village is known for the locally produced red Grenache wine, to which it has given its name.

By way of Les Florets, where there is a Club Alpin hut, drive to the Cayron Pass.

Cayron Pass (Col du Cayron). – Alt 396m - 1 300ft. The pass is at the centre of the Dentelles' principal peaks which, with faces rearing nearly 100m - 300ft high, offer all the complexity of feature relished by rock climbers.

Park the car and bear right *(1 hour on foot Rtn)* on the unsurfaced road which winds through the Dentelles. There are splendid **views**★ of the Rhone Plain blocked by the Cevennes, Vaucluse Plateau and Mount Ventoux. The road passes below a ruined Saracen tower. Return to the car and take D 7, then turn left towards Vacqueyras.

N.-D.-d'Aubune. – *Near the Fontenouilles Farm.* The Romanesque chapel at the mountain's foot is surmounted by an elegant **belfry**★ ornamented on each of its four sides by tall, antique style pilasters and rounded bays between larger and smaller pillars – note the decoration of columns and capitals.

Continue left along D 81. The road winds through vineyards and olive groves.

Beaumes-de-Venise. – Pop 1 721. *Facilities p 8.* A terraced village on the southernmost foothills of the Dentelles.

Sarrians. – Pop 5 030. *8 km - 5 miles SW by D 90 and D 55 from Beaumes-de-Venise.* The church, of this small Venaissin town on a rock bluff is a former Benedictine priory. The interior *(entrance through the door overlooking the Place de la Mairie)* has an unusually attractive chancel and is remarkable for the great age of its squinch supported dome.

D 90 climbs the verdant Brégoux Valley to Suzette and then enters the vertical walled St-Amand rock circus from which the lofty outline of Barroux Castle is visible to the south *(p 129)*. The road continues to a pass from which there is a **view**★ on one side of the Dentelles and on the other of Mount Ventoux, the Ouvèze Valley and the Baronnies.

Malaucène. – Pop 2 096. *Facilities p 8.* The church, complete with west front machicolations, was built in early 14C by Pope Clement V when he was residing in the village. Inside, the Provencal Romanesque nave is covered by broken barrel vaulting, the south chapels by ogive vaulting and the apse by a round dome with flat ribs. Note the 18C organ and pulpit. A path along the north wall leads to a Calvary from which there is a view of the Drôme Mountains and Mount Ventoux (E).

D 938 goes northwest up the fertile Grozeau Valley. *Turn left into D 76.*

Crestet. – Pop 326. *Leave the car in the castle car park.* The village is one of the most typical of the Vaucluse, with the church standing in a minute square lined by an arcade and decorated at the centre with a fountain. Narrow streets between Renaissance houses, climb the hill crowned by a 12C castle *(under restoration)* from which there is a good view of the village, the Ouvèze, Mount Ventoux and the Baronnies.

Return to D 938 and turn left for Vaison-la-Romaine.

The Lower DURANCE Valley

Michelin map 84 folds 1 to 4 or 246 folds 25, 11 and 12

The Durance, the great fluctuating river of the south Alps, known for its bursting, unheralded floodwaters and long periods of low ebb, has, at last, been harnessed to serve the local economy: it supplies hydraulic power – 12 400 million kWh a year – and a constant flow of water for irrigation for most of the fruit and vegetable growing area.

The river rises close to the Italian border, pours through a wide gap which it has cut in the mountains and continues on an irregular 324 km - 201 miles course to join the Rhône as its final east tributary, at Avignon. The flow is increased on its way by numerous small mountain streams and the River Verdon, which also rises in the southern Alps and is also liable to spring flooding when the snows begin to melt.

HYDRAULIC UNDERTAKINGS

Above Sisteron. – The Serre-Ponçon reservoir, with a capacity of 1 030 million cubic m - 264 200 million gallons collected when the river is in spate, maintains regular irrigation when the river is low.

Sisteron to Cadarache. – Below Sisteron the river enters the Mediterranean Basin; its course lies between broad banks of stone which absorb and delay the water when the river is in spate; the bed drops steeply, losing height in a 1: 700 gradient (the Rhône 1: 1 900) – ideal for hydro-electric power stations.

Below Cadarache. – The river runs approximately parallel to the coast until it enters the Rhône, but once, when the ice cap melted at the end of the last ice age, the swollen waters burst through the Lamanon Gap on a more direct route to the sea, depositing a huge mass of rock and stone over the wide expanse of what is now the Crau Plain *(p 69)*.

■ The CANAL NETWORK

It is rare for any one region to be so well served by canals, as is Provence between the Durance and the sea. Each was constructed for one of three purposes: **irrigation,** the provision of **town water,** the production of **electricity.**

Craponne Canal. – The 16C course, one of the oldest in Provence, which is now decaying in its upper reaches, has contributed most, through irrigation, to the transformation of the Crau Plain.

Marseilles and Verdon Canals. – Each in its time – both date from 19C – has increased the fertility of the countryside around Aix and Marseilles, but with the immense development in market gardening neither is now sufficient. The Marseilles, 90 km - 60 miles long, begins at St-Estève-Janson and on its course serves the St-Christophe and Réaltor Reservoirs and crosses the Arc Valley by means of the Roquefavour Aqueduct *(p 32)*. To supplement supplies it is to be paralleled by the Provence Canal, when its final course will be diverted to serve the industrial zone of the Berre Lagoon *(p 58)*.

The Verdon, which starts at the industrial canal at Vinon, waters the area around Aix and, augmented by the spring floodwaters of the Verdon, flows through the underground Campane Canal to supply the Bimont Dam Reservoir. It is being rebuilt in part, the better to complement the new Provence Canal.

The EDF (Electricité de France) Canal. – The drop in water level between Cadarache and the Rhône was utilized to supply an 85 km - 53 miles long canal, beginning at the Cadarache Dam and running parallel to the Durance before following the river's original course through the Lamanon Gap to the Berre Lagoon. Five major power stations (Jouques, St-Estève-Janson, Mallemort, Salon and St-Chamas) are served by the canal which goes on to supplement the Craponne, supplying fifteen other channels which irrigate some 75 000ha - 185 000 acres of Lower Provence including the Crau Plain *(p 69)*.

Provence Canal. – The completion of the Serre-Ponçon Dam and the construction of the EDF Canal have removed the need for the Verdon Canal to act as a regulator of the Durance; its waters have, therefore, been diverted into the new Provence Canal which, with an annual flow of 700 million cubic m - 154 000 million gallons drawn from a 3 000 km - 1 865 miles catchment network, supplies town water to Aix, Marseilles and Toulon, irrigates some 60 000ha - 148 000 acres and tops up the Bimont Dam.

Manosque to Avignon – *145 km - 85 miles – allow 1/2 day – Local map pp 72-73*

Leave Manosque (see Michelin Green Guide, French Riviera) by N 207 going SE then N 554. The road follows the river course south.

Cadarache. – Cadarache is known for its dam and nuclear centre *(group visits only, apply in writing at least 3 weeks in advance)* which produces experimental prototype reactors for power stations and naval propulsion.

Mirabeau Defile. – The river bends sharply to the west and emerges from Upper (Haute) Provence through a dramatic narrow channel, cut out by the action of the water, before flowing on downstream under the **Mirabeau Bridge.**

Jouques Power Station (EDF Jouques). – The station was built against the cliff face on the EDF Canal which runs underground right up to the entrance. Annual production: 400 million kWh.

Follow N 96 which skirts the EDF Canal.

Peyrolles-en-Provence. – Pop 2 561. The small town retains from medieval times a tower crowned with a wrought iron belfry, a round tower once part of the ramparts and now in ruins, a church, St Peter's, with a Romanesque nave, and a small 15C chapel, St Sepulchre's, distinguished by a minute belfry gable. Finally the town hall is a grand 17C château, preceded by a great iron gateway and courtyard.

Meyrargues. – Pop 2 406. *Facilities p 8.* The town is dominated, as it has been since 17C, by its château (now a hotel). Below are the remains of a Roman aqueduct.

On leaving, take D 561 and, after 3 km - 2 miles, D 556, on the right.

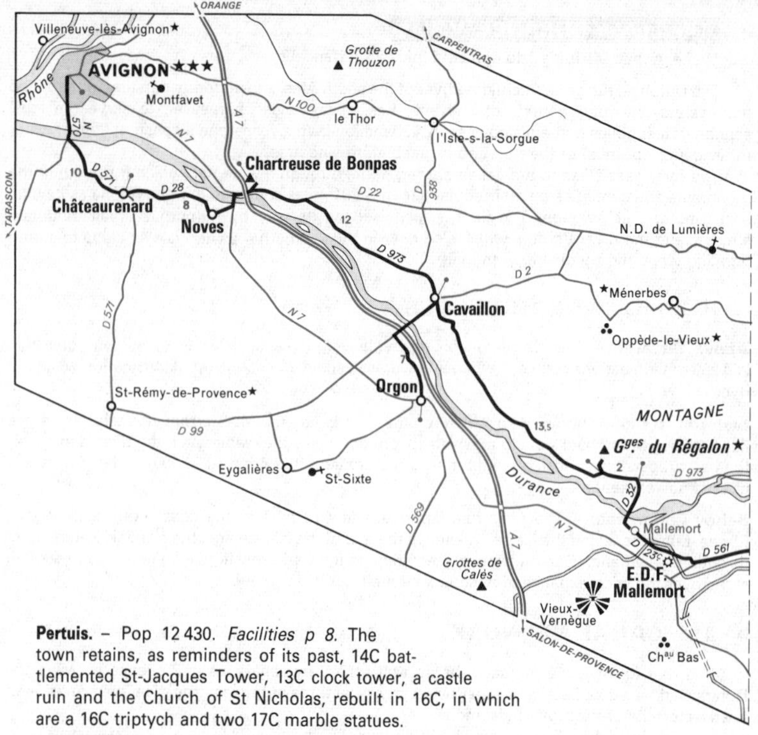

Pertuis. – Pop 12 430. *Facilities p 8.* The town retains, as reminders of its past, 14C battlemented St-Jacques Tower, 13C clock tower, a castle ruin and the Church of St Nicholas, rebuilt in 16C, in which are a 16C triptych and two 17C marble statues.

La Tour-d'Aigues. – Pop 2 479. *6 km - 4 miles from Pertuis by D 956.* At the village centre still stands the gateway portico, in the style of a triumphal arch with Corinthian decoration and a frieze of the attributes of war, which served as the entrance to 16C style castle, built on a medieval site and burned down in 18C. The terrace commands a good view of the surrounding countryside.

Take D 973 W out of Pertuis beside the canal.

Cadenet. – Pop 2 640. *Facilities p 8.* The small town is perched on a spur below the ruins of 11C castle now half hidden by pine trees. Before the 14-17C square towered church (3C sarcophagus **font**★) in the main square, is a statue of the town's famous **drummer boy.** It was he who served in Napoleon's north Italy campaign of 1796, and in the midst of the battle against the Austrians and Italians for the Arcole Bridge, swam the river and beat such a tattoo that the Austrians mistook it for artillery fire; as they retreated, the French advanced to capture the bridge and win the battle.

(After photo by J.-P. Aerts)

The drummer boy.

D 943 goes south to cross the Durance; turn left into N 561 and, after 2.7 km - 1 1/2 miles, right towards the power station.

St-Estève-Janson Power Station (EDF St-Estève). – Balcony and explanatory panel *(in French)* at the base of the building. Annual production: 680 million kWh.

Reservoir St-Christophe (Bassin de St-Christophe) – *To visit first apply to the Société des Eaux de Marseille, Service Adduction, 25 Rue Edouard-Delanglade, Marseilles; then with the authorization apply to the caretaker who lives in the administrative buildings along the D 543 and the reservoir.* The reservoir waters, reflecting rocks and pines in a surface 22 ha - 54 acres in extent at the foot of the Côtes Chain, derive from the Durance and tributary EDF Canal, and are destined, finally, as supplies for Marseilles.

Rognes. – Pop 2 216. The village, which is known for the masonry stone quarried to the west, has an early 17C church *(visit by appointment only)* which contains a series of **altarpieces**★, (17 and 18C), remarkable for their quality – note especially those at the high altar and along the north side of the chancel.

Return to the reservoir: skirt it to the left until you come to D 561 on the left.

Silvacane Abbey★. – *Open 10 to 11.45am and 2 to 6.45pm (4.45pm 1 October to 31 March); closed Tuesdays, 1 January, 1 May, 1 and 11 November, 25 December; 8F.*

The abbey, built for the Cistercian order in 1144, enjoyed only a brief prosperity: in 1357 it was pillaged and fired; in 15C the ruins passed to Aix Cathedral, only to be forfeited at the Revolution and sold as farmland.

The main feature throughout the now restored buildings, is the high vaulting. The **church** itself is broken barrel arched above the nave and square chancel, ribbed above the crossing, and sloping above the aisles – note how the south aisle is raised to accommodate the angle of the hillside. The **cloisters,** dating from late 13C, are beamed and barrel vaulted with wide, round, arches overlooking the garth. The early 13C **conventual buildings** have pointed arches descending on plainly foliated capitals and consoles, except in the chapterhouse where the ribs drop directly on to the spirally fluted centre pillar. In the large refectory, rebuilt in 15C, the vault is ribbed, the capitals are intricately ornamented and the windows straight and tall except for one in the form of a rose.

La Roque-D'Anthéron. – Pop 3 759. *Facilities p 8.* At the centre of the town stands 17C Florans Château flanked by round towers (now a convalescent home).

Continue along D 561 to D 23c on the right. (**Mallemort Power Station** – EDF Mallemort – production 420 million kWh – on the left). *Beyond Mallemort town turn into D 32 to cross the river; turn left into D 973. Continue for 2 km - 1 mile and just before a bridge, bear right into a small road which skirts a quarry.*

Régalon Gorges★. – *1 1/4 hours on foot Rtn. 200m further on bear right, ignoring the uphill road on the left. Leave the car in the parking-area; take the path opposite which skirts the stream; cross the olive grove on your left and go through a narrow gap to enter the gorge. Note (a) it will be colder, (b) the rocks are often wet and slippery – go suitably clad and shod therefore; (c) on showery-rainy days the stream becomes a rushing torrent and the expedition should not be attempted.*

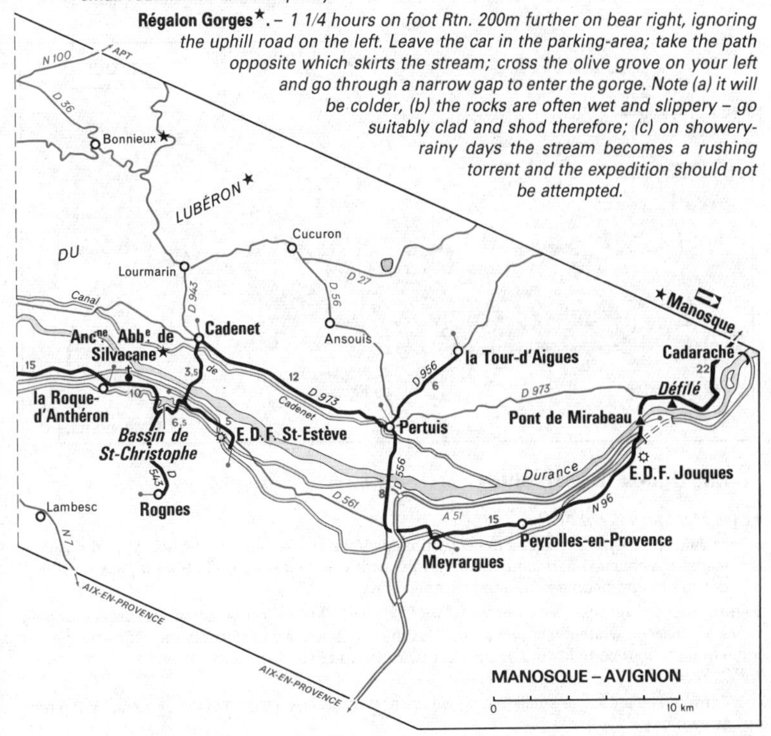

The route follows the bed of the stream, beneath a huge rock caught fast between the sides of the gorge, and over a rocky and sometimes slippery section, before coming to a cave. The tunnel bends sharply into a passage 100m long and 30m - 95ft high but only 80cm - 30ins wide in places. The cave and passage are the most remarquable part of the gorge. *At the end retrace your steps.*

Continue once more along D 973 as it skirts the Lubéron Range (p 78).

Cavaillon. – *Description p 67.*

Orgon. – *Description p 33.*

Leave Cavaillon by D 938 going N; turn left into D 973.

Chartreuse de Bonpas. – *Courtyards, the Romanesque chapel and formal gardens are open 10am to 5pm; 5F.* The charterhouse entrance is through a fortified gateway – porter's lodge on the right. The church and conventual buildings erected by the Templars in 13C beside a small Romanesque chapel, enjoyed a period of prosperity in 17C, when the chapterhouse was constructed. All was abandoned in 18C at the Revolution. The house, named Bonpas by the Knights and recently restored to include a dwelling house, provides a clear view, from the terrace, of the Alpilles and the Durance spanned by 500m - 1/3 mile long bridge.

Pass under the motorway and turn right into N 7 and right again into D 28.

Noves. – Pop 3 693. Noves is an old town with a network of narrow winding streets, two medieval gateways and 12C stone roofed church covered by a disproportionately large dome on squinches.

Châteaurenard. – Pop 11 072. *Facilities p 8.* The town at the foot of a hill beneath medieval twin towers has become a national market, with a designated site of 140 000m^2 - 35 acres, handling the produce (360 000 tons in 1983) harvested from the market gardens and fruit farms in the neighbouring plain.
The Griffon Tower *(guided tour – time: 20 minutes – 10am to noon and 2 to 7pm; 2F)* which, with its twin, is all that is left of the feudal castle after the Revolution, commands a **panorama**★ of the town and surrounding countryside, the Montagnette (WSW), Avignon and Villeneuve-lès-Avignon (NW), the Dentelles de Montmirail and Mount Ventoux (NE), the Lubéron (SE) and the Alpilles (S).

D 571 and N 570 bring you to Avignon (p 44).

The ESTAQUE Mountains★

Michelin map 246 fold 14

The Estaque Mountains, which divide the Berre Lagoon from the Mediterranean, are an unusual limestone formation, arid in appearance and almost uninhabited. Deep inlets *(calanques – p 66)* in the steep coastline shelter a few small fishing villages which scrape a meagre living from the exhausted Mediterranean but now hope to profit from the expansion of the port of Marseilles, the increasing industrialization of the area and the tourist trade.

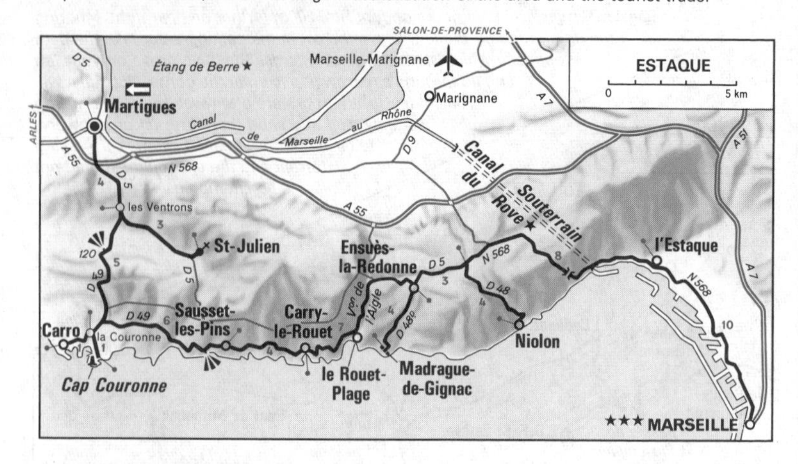

Martigues to Marseilles – *67 km - 41 1/2 miles – about 3 hours*

Leave Martigues (p 88) by D 5.

St-Julien. – *3 km - 2 miles by the D 5 from Les Ventrons.* A path *(on the left)* from the village leads to a chapel where embedded in the north wall there is a Gallo-Roman relief (1C) of a group of eight people in a funeral scene.

Return to Les Ventrons, turn right into D 49. The road climbs through an arid landscape of dark pines against the white limestone and, at 120m - 395ft, looks back (observation tower) over the industrial harbour complex of Lavéra, Port-de-Bouc and Fos. *4 km - 2 miles further on, bear right for Carro.*

Carro. – The attractive small fishing village and resort lies well protected at the back of a rock strewn bay.

Make for La Couronne by way of D 49^B; turn right before the church.

Cape Couronne. – From the lighthouse on the point there is a view right round to Marseilles, with the Estaques in the foreground, the Étoile Range (NE) and the Marseilleveyre (S).

On leaving the headland, turn right into D 49. The road winds through the hills before dropping down to follow the coastline.

Sausset-les-Pins. – Pop 3 876. *Facilities p 8.* The fishing village, seaside resort has a fine amenity in its promenade from which one can look across the sea to Marseilles.

Carry-le-Rouet. – Pop 4 570. *Facilities p 8.* The onetime fishing village is now a seaside resort. Summer residences can be seen in the woods which line the bay.

Le Rouet-Plage. – An attractive inlet with a good beach and small harbour, and, half-hidden among the pinetrees, some elegant houses.

The road up the **Aigle Valley** is bordered by pines and holm oaks.

Ensuès-la-Redonne. – Pop 2 204. A village at the centre of vineyards and olive groves.

On leaving Ensuès, turn right into D 48^D which drops down through a pinewood.

Madrague-de-Gignac. – The village lines a creek which faces Marseilles across the roads.

Return to D 5 and turn right and right again into D 48 for Niolon. The road crosses an arid, treeless stretch of countryside, before reaching a few wind-blown pines.

Niolon. – The village clings to the hillside above an inlet of the same name.

From D 5 there is a clear view of the Étoile and Estaque Mountain Chains. *Turn right into N 568.* As you emerge from the tunnel there is a glimpse of Marseilles before the road goes under the railway bridge and over the entrance to the Rove Canal.

Rove Underground Canal★ (Canal Souterrain du Rove). – *Access: take the Chagnaud Quarry road – pass under the railway before turning down the slope to the entrance.*
The tunnel was cut in 1920s beneath the Estaque Mountains to link the Marseilles docks and the Berre Lagoon, and was used regularly by 1 200 ton barges until obstructed by a rock fall in 1963. It is more than 7 km - 4 miles long and dead straight – one can still see daylight at the far end. Height, width and water depth respectively are 15.4, 22 and 4.5m (50, 69 and 15ft).

L'Estaque. – The Marseilles fishing fleet and private yachts now fill the harbour.

The road continues through the industrial suburbs to the tunnel beneath the Old Port into the heart of Marseilles *(p 82).*

Numerous camping sites have:
shops, licensed premises, laundries,
games rooms, mini-golf,
playgrounds, paddling and swimming pools.

Consult the Michelin Guide,
Camping Caravaning France.

The FOS Complex ★

Michelin map 246 folds 13, 14, 27 and 28

The development of the new complex, which complements the port of Marseilles, was begun in 1965 on Fos Bay. The advantages of the site, some 10 000ha - 24 700 acres, are a deep water channel, no tides and the stoney surface of the Crau Plain *(p 69)* which makes an ideal foundation on which to build an industrial estate.

The port. – With its approximately 90 million tonnes of traffic per year, of which Fos handles two thirds, the combined Marseilles-Fos complex is the largest port in France and second only to Rotterdam in Europe.

Fos is equipped to handle two types of traffic: Dock 1 with its two basins can accommodate vessels up to 400 000 tonnes carrying bulk cargoes such as oil, gas and minerals; Docks 2 and 3 (Gloria Basin) handle commercial traffic such as containers, vehicles and wood. The South Dock is reserved for steel and petrol exports.

In 1983 Dock 1 was linked to the Rhône and the Berre Lagoon by a canal built to European standards and capable of carrying 4 400 ton barge convoys.

The industrial zone. – More than half the available land is given over to factories, some with their own quays, accommodating basic processing and first stage industries such as steel (Solmer – sheet and laminates: 4 million tons p.a., Ugine Aciers – production and lamination of special steels: 200 000 tonnes); metal construction; petrol (Esso: 8 million tonnes); chemicals (ATOCHEM: 150 000 tonnes of chloride, MCV Fos Company 200 000 tonnes of MVC); petrochemicals (ICI: 100 000 tonnes of polyethylene). Approximately 3 000 milliard cubic metres of liquid natural gas are treated each year by Gaz de France and distributed after conversion. Crude oil and refined products supply the South European Oil Pipeline *(p 58)* and the Mediterranean-Rhône Oil Pipeline respectively.

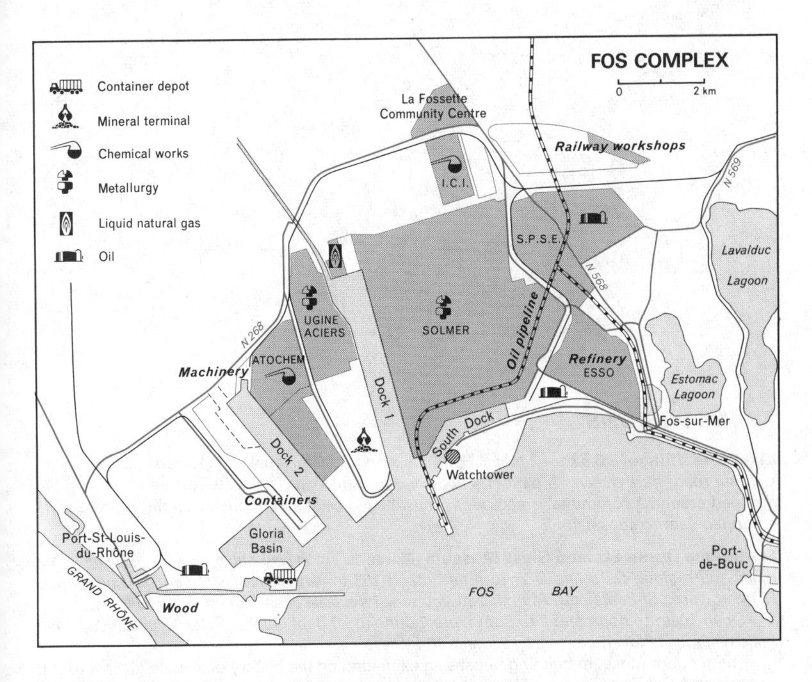

Fos Community Information Centre (Le Centre de Vie). – *Open 9am to noon and 1 to 5pm; closed Saturdays, Sundays and holidays* ☎ *42 05 03 10.*

On the spot known as La Fossette, an exhibition and information centre displays a model of the area, shows films *(Mondays to Fridays)* etc. The adjoining arboretum contains specimens of the trees and flowers in the numerous public gardens.

Tour of the docks. – *For information on the guided tours apply to the Services des Relations Publiques du Port Autonome de Marseille, 23 Place de la Joliette, 13000 Marseille,* ☎ *91 91 90 66.*

Boat trips start from the watch tower, which gives a good overall view of the harbour, and include tours of the major basins.

EXCURSIONS

Fos-sur-Mer. – Pop 9 446. NE. The town, which stands on a rock to the northwest, is named after the Fosses Mariennes, a canal dug at the mouth of the Rhône by Marius' legions in 102 BC (*fosse:* hole, pit, canal). Medieval rather than Roman remains are evident in sections of 14C ramparts and castle ruins. The chief attraction, however, is the **view** from the terrace and rampart garden of the new town of Fos, the harbour, Port-de-Bouc (SE), Lavalduc Lagoon (NNE) and the St-Blaise heights (E).

Port-St-Louis-du-Rhône. – Pop 10 378. *15 km - 10 miles SW.* A town and port have developed around the St-Louis Tower built to defend the mouth of the Grand Rhône in 18C.

The dock, constructed in 1863 and now part of the Marseilles complex, is used both by seagoing ships and Rhône barges, and handles products as diverse as hydrocarbons, liquid chemicals, timber and wine.

Port-de-Bouc. – *Description p 88.*

GORDES ★

Michelin map 246 fold 11 – *Local map p 127* – Pop 1 607 – *Facilities p 8*

The houses of Gordes rise in picturesque tiers above the Imergue Valley on the edge of the Vaucluse Plateau. The **site**★ can be best seen from a rock platform belvedere (no barrier) about 1/2 mile short of the village on the Cavaillon road, D 15.

Château. – *Open 10am to noon and 2 to 6pm; closed Tuesdays and 25 December; 9.50F.*

The Renaissance château on the site of 12C fortress, stands at one end of the village. The north face flanked by round machicolated towers, is austere, the south monumental, relieved by mullioned windows and small end turrets.

Inside, in the great hall on the first floor, two flanking doorways show off a splendid **chimney-piece**★ ornate with pediments and pilasters, shells and flowers.

Five rooms and the stair well have been remodelled as a **Vasarély Museum**★; the artist's geometrically influenced work includes both painting (figurative and self-portraits) and sculpture.

Gordes.

EXCURSIONS

The Borie Village. – *3.5 km - 2 miles. Continue along D 15; just beyond D 2 fork, turn right into a tarred road; park the car.* A path *(1/4 hour on foot Rtn)* leads to twenty restored *bories (p 78)* grouped around a communal bread oven. The village has been arranged as a museum of rural life *(open 9am to sunset 10F).*

Frédérique Duran Stained Glass Museum (Musée du Vitrail Frédérique Duran). – *3.5 km - 2 1/2 miles south along D 15 and D 2; turn left into D 103 towards Beaumettes and left again into D 148 towards St-Pantaléon. After 100 m you reach a place called Moulin des Bouillons.*

Open 10am to noon and 2 to 5pm (7pm 1 June to 30 September); Saturdays, Sundays and holidays only 1 November to 31 January; 10 F.

The modern museum building houses an exhibition on the history of stained glass making, and the works of Frédérique Duran, contemporary painter, glassmaker, with her own distinctive technique for obtaining jewelled results.

In the nearby 16 to 18C *bastide* (mineral display) is an antique oil mill *(open 1 June to 30 September, same times and ticket as the museum)*; note the **press**★ made of a whole oak tree trunk weighing 7 tons.

Sénanque Abbey★. – *Round tour of 15 km - 8 miles. Leave Gordes by D 15; turn right into D 177.* The arid Senancole Valley closes in as the narrow road *(passing places)* descends into the canyon to disclose the beautiful east end of the abbey church.

Open 1 June to 31 August, 10am to 7pm; the rest of the year 10am to noon and 2 to 6pm; 16F, children 5F. Ticket includes «The Deserts of Man» Exhibition. The cultural centre organizes artistic and cultural events. In summer concerts of ancient music are performed; for information ☏ 90 72 02 05.

The abbey was founded on its desolate **site**★ in 1148 by the Cistercians who remained until the Revolution. They returned in 1854 only to leave again in late 19C returning yet again in 1928 and staying until 1969. Restoration of the abbey has been going on ever since.

Abbey buildings★. – The church with its well proportioned but plain interior, the monks' dormitory lit by small windows beneath a fine Romanesque broken barrel vault, the calefactory and the chapterhouse with its view of the cloister all date from 12C and make Sénanque together with its restored refectory one of the few Cistercian houses to possess a full complement of buildings of the same early period.

«The Deserts of Man» Exhibition. – *Same times and charges as the abbey, except in winter when open on application only.* The aspects of life of a group of Tuareg people in the desert is displayed.

Continue N up the Senancole Valley (D 177) for a couple of miles before turning right into D 15 for the return to Gordes.

GRIGNAN ★

Michelin map 246 fold 8 and 22 – Pop 1 147

The old town owes its fame to the delightful letters written in the last years of 17C by **Mme de Sévigné** to her daughter, Mme de Grignan, wherein she recounts with a keen eye and nice turn of phrase, life at the court of Louis XIV and Paris society, visits to the country and day-to day domestic matters. Typical was Mme de Sévigné's comment when in 1669 her daughter married as his third wife, the Count de Grignan, Lieutenant-General of Provence: « The prettiest girl in France », she wrote to her cousin, « is marrying not the most handsome of young men – the count was very ugly! – but one of the most honest in the kingdom ».

(After photo by Arch. Phot., Paris)

Madame de Sévigné.

The Good Provençal Life. – Madame de Sévigné made several long stays at the castle, which stands on an outcrop of rock at the centre of the old town. She enjoyed her visits and described the castle as « very fine and magnificent », adding characteristically « one eats well and there are masses of visitors ».

She gives a mouth-watering description of how the partridges were fed on thyme, marjoram and herbs to give them flavour, how the quail had fat and tender legs, the doves were succulent and the melons, figs and muscat grapes perfect...; she enjoyed it all most infectiously.

Although she admired the view from the terrace, she preferred the cool fragance of the nearby grotto to write in; her only hate, and that a perpetual one, was the *mistral,* which she described as « that bitter, freezing wind which cuts one's being to the quick ».

The misplaced curiosity of 18C phrenologists. – Mme de Sévigné died at the castle in 1696 aged 69 from over fatigue after nursing her daughter. She was buried in the chapel, but during the Revolution her coffin was stripped of its lead lining and her head dispatched to Paris for examination by avid phrenologists. It has since disappeared.

The literary pilgrims. – « I am so proud to be here that I feel inclined to sit up all night and write letters if for no other reason than that they might bear the castle address. My imagination is so filled with Mme de Sévigné that at every moment I expect to see her before me! ». So wrote a late 18C traveller, nicely expressing a sentiment felt by those who still relish the letters and come on literary pilgrimage.

Château★★ – *Guided tour (time: 1 hour) 9.30 to 11.30am and 2.30 to 5.30pm (6pm July and August); closed Tuesdays, Wednesday mornings, all November, 1 January and 25 December; 8.50F.*

The south façade is Renaissance and looks onto Mount Ventoux; the courtyard opens onto a terrace which is enclosed on the left by a transitional Gothic pavilion and on the right by a Renaissance building.

To be visited are: the grand staircase, saloons, audience chamber, Gothic staircase, the lovely panelled Adhémar gallery (Adhémar was the family name), the Count de Grignan's apartments, Mme de Sévigné's bedroom and the state room.

The **furnishings**★ evoke an atmosphere of the past: Louis XIII furniture, Italian writing desk in the audience chamber; Régence style and Louis XV period furnishings in the Grignan's apartments where the parquets are lovely. The walls are hung with Aubusson tapestries (17C mythological scenes).

From the terrace, constructed over St-Sauveur Church *(see below)*, there is a vast **panorama**★ including Mount Rachas and the long ridge of the Lance (NE), Mount Ventoux and the Dentelles de Montmirail (SE), the Comtat Venaissin Plain, the Alpilles, Suze-la-Rousse and the Chamaret belfry (SW), Grignan Woods and the Vivarais Mountains (NW).

St-Sauveur. – 16C with a Flamboyant Gothic rose window in the west front.

Inside the features of interest are the small gallery beneath the roof which communicated directly with the castle until the Revolution when the door was bricked up; 17C **organ loft** *(organ recitals in summer)*, 17C altarpiece and the chancel panelling, and on the north side the marble funerary stone to Mme de Sévigné.

Belfry. – The belfry, 12C town gateway, was heightened and transformed in 17C.

Rochecourbière Cave. – *1 km - 1/2 mile. Take D 541 S out of Grignan; branch off to the right by the Calvary. After about 1 km - 1/2 mile park the car and walk back to the stone steps on the right.* The grotto was one of Mme de Sévigné's favourite places to sit and write.

LARGENTIÈRE

Michelin map 80 N of fold 8 – *Local map p 36* – Pop 2 625

The town owes its name to old silver mines worked, from 10-15C, by the Counts of Toulouse and Bishops of Viviers. Overlooking the old quarter which lies in a bend of the River Ligne, a tributary of the Ardèche, is 15C castle, now the hospital, and on the opposite bank of the river, a Greek Temple built in 18C to house the law courts.

The Recollets Gate was once the main entrance to the old town, a network of narrow streets, at the south end of which stand a sober 15C mansion (now the town hall) flanked by a corner turret and, on a raised terrace, a Gothic church built in 13C with a triple-sided apse. Spire restored in 19C.

EXCURSIONS

Chassiers. – Pop 1 025. *1.5 km - 1 mile NE along D 103.* The old Vivarais town, stepped up a hillside above the Lower Ardèche Plateau, is dominated by its **fortified church,** *(open in summer; in winter apply to Town Hall);* the east end overlooks the main square. From here the 14C building is seen to best advantage. A tower, once part of the town's defences, supports the crocket ribbed spire which rises above the flat apsidal wall. A stairway *(south side)* leads down to the west front which boasts a fortified and emblazoned projecting bay.

St-Benoît Chapel (below the main street; *to visit apply to the Town Hall)* is a plain Romanesque building with twin adjoining aisles but separate apses – note the lanterns and processional monstrances in the north aisle and the taper stands in the pews. **La Mothe-Chalendar Castle,** a low 14-16C construction, stands at the south end of the town and, with its flanking towers and turrets pierced only by loopholes, looks like a military outpost.

Montréal. – *1.5 km - 1 mile S by D 5, D 212 and D 312.* The still impressive square towers of the 13C fortress, built to protect the Largentière silver mines, overlook the particularly attractive village with its many town houses built of dressed sandstone.

Tauriers. – Pop 147. *2 km - 1 mile NW by D 305, a small road starting from the Place Mazon by the church in Largentière.* The once fortified village is perched on a rock spur commanding the Ligne Valley.

Vinezac. – Pop 571. *8 km - 5 miles E along D 103 and D 423.* The old town's Romanesque church has an unusually high polygonal apse and a belfry decked with a grin of gargoyles. Inside *(to visit apply at the presbytery or to Mme Deguilhem),* the nave vaulting is supported on massive beams which rest on archaic style capitals; on the right, as you enter, is a rough bas-relief of the story of Daniel.

Joyeuse. – Pop 1 410. *Round tour 40 km - 25 miles – about 2 hours. Leave Largentière by S, D 5 and D 212.* The town retains a few dignified, old houses in a terrace facing north towards the Tanargue Massif.

In 16-17C the town was the cradle of an illustrious family of the same name; the viscount who founded the dynasty became a marshal of France; the second generation included one son who married the sister of Henri III's queen, a second, who from archbishop was elevated to cardinal, presided over the States General of 1614 and crowned Louis XIII in Rheims in 1610, and a third who alternated between the military and the monastic life, leading a detachment of the Catholic League against Henri IV and serving a term as governor of Languedoc before resuming his Capuchin habit and returning to his monastery.

D 203 goes from Joyeuse to Deux-Aygues and then follows the line of the Upper Beaume Gorges of schist rock needles and granite boulders.

Return to Largentière along D 24 and D 5.

The LUBÉRON Range ★

Michelin map 81 folds 12, 13 14 and 15

The Lubéron, an anticlinal fold of calcareous rock of the tertiary era, which runs eastwest between the Coulon and Durance Rivers, is the southernmost of the three great mountain ranges in eastern Provence - Mount Ventoux, the Vaucluse Plateau and the Lubéron.

The mountain is divided from north to south by the Lourmarin Coomb into the Grand and Petit Lubéron. The steep northern face, scarred by ravines and densely wooded, contrasts with the gentle southern slope and its lusher Mediterranean vegetation.

In 1977 a Regional Park **(Parc naturel régional du Lubéron)** of 100 000ha - 247 000 acres was established which is served by the road along the mountain ridge, now worn smooth by erosion.

A 'borie .

Bories. – Scattered over the Lubéron and the Vaucluse Plateau are drystone huts *(bories),* rectangular or round in shape, one or two storeys high with pointed stone roofs.

The Vaudois. – In 1545 Francis I sent a punitive expedition to the Lubéron against a sect known as the Vaudois after their founder in 13C, Pierre Valdo, who based his faith exclusively on the Gospels. During his lifetime, the greater part of the Bible was translated into Provençal. The sect, which had remained obdurate against reform by the Church and had even pillaged and set fire to many local churches, suffered cruelly at the hands of the royal force; Lourmarin, Cadenet, Ménerbes, Mérindol and twenty other villages were sacked, nearly 2 000 men and women were hanged, stoned, beheaded or put to the sword, 600 were sent to the galleys. Thousands fled accross the Italian border and settled in what are now known as the Vaud Alps (Switzerland) *(see Michelin Green Guide to Switzerland).*

The GRAND LUBÉRON★★

Round tour starting from Apt

119 km - 74 miles - allow 1/2 day - Local map p 81

Leave Apt (p 34) by D 48 going SE. As the road climbs, the perched site of Saignon, the Apt Basin, the Vaucluse Plateau and Mount Ventoux come into view.

Saignon. – Pop 967. The village on a promontory, close to a tall rock, contains a Romanesque church with a west front rebuilt in 16C to include beautiful, trilobed blind arcading. Inside a pair of Roman columns marks the opening of the blind arcaded, heptagonal apse.

Continue along D 48.

After crossing a cultivated mountain shoulder, the road skirts the Claparèdes Plateau and the occasional *borie.*

Just before Auribeau bear right on the unsurfaced forest road towards Mourre Nègre. At the intersection of the forest road and the GR 92 is an open area where you can park the car.

Mourre Nègre★★★. – *1 1/4 hour on foot Rtn.* The Mourre Nègre at 1 125m – 3 690ft is the highest point in the Lubéron Chain and the site of the Paris-Nice television relay mast. The **panorama**★★★ embraces four points of the compass: the Lure Mountain and Digne Pre-Alps (NE), the Durance Valley with Mount Ste-Victoire in the back-ground (SE), the Berre Lagoon and the Alpilles (SW), the Apt Basin, Vaucluse Plateau and Mount Ventoux (NW).

Lavender distillery.

Return to the D 48 and continue through Auribeau.

Castellet. – Pop 72. The minute, stepped hamlet, is today a lavender distillery centre.

The road crosses a *garrigue (p 14)* landscape before reaching the Calavon Valley.

Turn right along N 100.

Céreste. – Pop 862. Ramparts can still be seen here and there surrounding the village.

Leave Céreste by the Forcalquier road, N 100, but turn left almost immediately into Avenue du Pont Romain.

On the right is a Roman bridge spanning the Encrème.
Continue, bearing right over the first foothills of the Vaucluse Plateau.

After 3.5 km - 2 miles turn left downhill.

Prieuré de Carluc. – At the far end of a small and tranquil valley stand the ruins of a 12C priory. The modest church *(to visit, apply to town hall in Céreste)* has a pentagonal apse decorated with small columns and a billet frieze and, flanking the north wall, a gallery hewn out of the living rock, formerly roofed in part with ribbed vaulting. Tombs can be seen embedded in the floor and benches. The gallery led to a second church of which a part was built into the rock.

Return to N 100, direction Fourcalquier, and take D 214 on the left.

Reillanne. – Pop 892. The picturesque village houses climb the hillside to 18C St-Denis Chapel, erected on the old castle site, and to the apse of an earlier 12C church. Avenue Long-Barri leads up to the viewing table past the Forges gateway, all that remains of the castle. The terrace looks down over the village and surrounding countryside.

Return to Céreste and turn left into D 31.

The road runs the length of a small valley before winding up the north slope of the Grand Lubéron from where one can see over the Calavon Valley to the Vaucluse Plateau. The road then descends the southern slope passing through Vitrolles down into the plain; turn right into D 42; continue along D 27, which skirts the Bonde Lagoon (leisure centre).

Cucuron. – Pop 1 409. Inside the church which has a Romanesque nave and Gothic apse and chapels, are an early 18C marble altarpiece, a multicoloured marble pulpit and a 16C painted wood *Christ Seated and Chained.*
Opposite the church, in 17C Bouliers House is a small Lubéron Museum: prehistory, Gallo-Roman period, and later local traditions *(open 10am to noon and 3 to 6pm; closed mornings out of season).*
From the pavement below the medieval keep you can see how the belfry was once a gateway in the old walls and a look-out over the Cucuron Basin to Mount Ste-Victoire on the horizon.

Ansouis. – *4.5 km - 3 miles SE by D 56.* Pop 612. **Sabran Castle**★ *(guided tour - time: 40 minutes - 2.30 to 6pm; closed Tuesdays, 25 December and 1 January; 15F),* half castle, half country house, it has been in the same family for centuries, each generation leaving its own mark of improvement. From the north it looks like a fortress, but go up the stone steps and a ramp leading into a chestnut walk and one is greeted by a welcoming Louis XIII façade. The terrace affords a beautiful view of the Durance Gap and the Trévaresse Range. In the grounds hanging gardens contrast with the elegant design of the broader lower terraces. Inside the house are a late 16C grand staircase, a notable display of 17-19C arms in the guardroom, 17C Flemish tapestries in the dining noom, a tester bed and credence table in the so-called François I room, a kitchen with bright copper pans, the prison and the chapel. The village possesses a so-called **Extraordinary Museum** *(guided tour - time: 1/2 hour - 2 to 7pm - 6pm 1 October to 31 March; closed Tuesdays; 10F)* of underwater life and Provençal furniture.

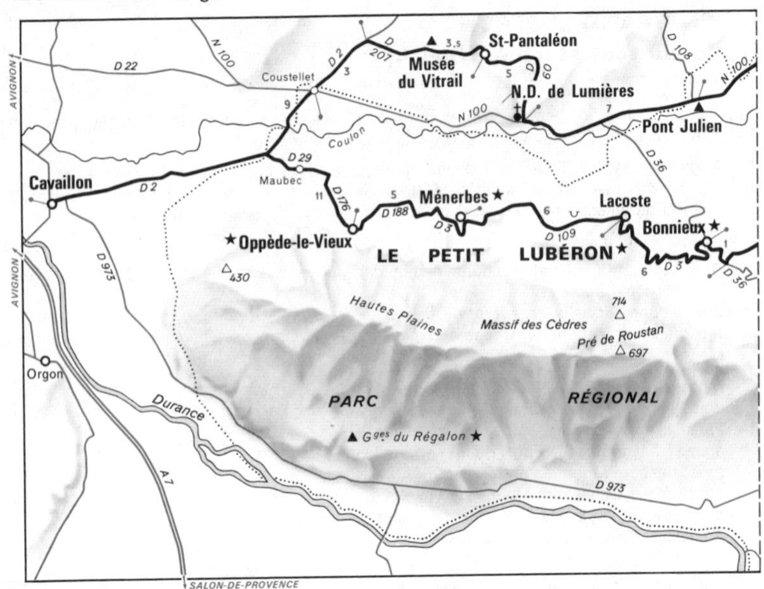

Lourmarin. – Pop 858. The village at the south end of the coomb of the same name, is dominated by its château built high on a rock bluff.
The **château**★ *(guided tour - time 3/4 hour - 9 to 11.45am and 2.30 to 6.15pm (5.45pm 1 October to 30 June); closed Tuesdays 1 November to 31 March; 12F; – now the Aix-en-Provence Academy)* is in two parts, 15C wing, now the library and students' rooms, overlooking wood and stone arcaded courtyards, and a Renaissance wing of remarkable stylistic unity containing large chimney-pieces ornamented with caryatids or Corinthian columns. The grand staircase ends dramatically with a slender pillar supporting a stone cupola.
Fifty-six steps in the hexagonal turret lead to a platform which commands a **view** of the combe, the Lubéron, the Durance and Mount Ste-Victoire.

D 943 travels NW up the Lourmarin Coomb. The River Aigue Brun has cut through the rock so steeply that only a rare bush manages to survive on the cliff face.

Prieuré de St-Symphorien. – A beautiful square Romanesque tower rising out of the greenery is all that remains of the ancient priory.

The road continues along a picturesque gorge, overlooked by scrub covered limestone slopes, and through a children's holiday camp, before crossing a bridge. *Turn right before some houses to reach a car park.*

Fort de Buoux. – *1/2 hour on foot Rtn, plus 3/4 hour tour. Go through the iron gate and follow the path beneath a vertical rock wall to the porter's lodge. Open 8am to 7pm (5pm out of season); 6F.* The rock spur on which the fort stands is a natural defence which has, in consequence, been occupied by Ligurians, Romans, Catholics and Protestants. Richelieu ordered its demolition in 1660 – there nevertheless remain three defensive walls, a Romanesque chapel, houses, silos hewn out of the rock, a keep, a Ligurian sacrificial altar and a concealed staircase.
From the rock spur there is a fine view up the valley of the River Aigue Brun.

Return to the holiday camp and turn right into D 113. Beyond Buoux village the road returns to Apt by a picturesque route.

The PETIT LUBÉRON★

Round tour starting from Apt – *77 km - 48 miles – allow 1/2 day*

Leave Apt (p 34) by D 943 going SW. After the Pointu Pass, turn right into D 232. The road crosses the Claparèdes Plateau, studded with *bories* among vineyards and truffle beds *(p 16)*. *Bear right into the D 36.*

Bonnieux★. – Pop 1 385. The village, its ramparts still visible, rises steeply in picturesque tiers of houses. Make for the **Upper Village.** From the **terrace** of the 12C parish **church** (to visit apply to the tourist information centre) surrounded by ancient cedars the **view**★ extends from the hill village of Lacoste (W), across the Coulon Valley (NW) to the Vaucluse Plateau and the villages of Gordes (NW) and Roussillon (N). Mount Ventoux rises in the background. In the **new church,** a vast edifice dating from the second half of the 19C, behind the high altar *(time-switch: 1F)* are four 15C **paintings**★ in bright colours on wood panels, after the German school: *St Veronica wiping Jesus' face, Ecce Homo, The Crown of Thorns* and *The Scourging.*

Leave Bonnieux by D 3 S then bear right into D 109. The road winds along the slope of the Petit Lubéron, behind you Bonnieux appears picturesquely.

Lacoste. – Pop 309. This hill village has an elegant 17C belfry and is dominated by the imposing ruins *(partially rebuilt)* of a château which belonged to the Sade family. The Marquis de Sade (1740-1814), author of erotic works *(The Adversities of Virtue and Justine, or the Misfortunes of Virtue)*, was the lord of Lacoste for some 30 years, yet he lived there but 4 years (1774-78) before being imprisoned.

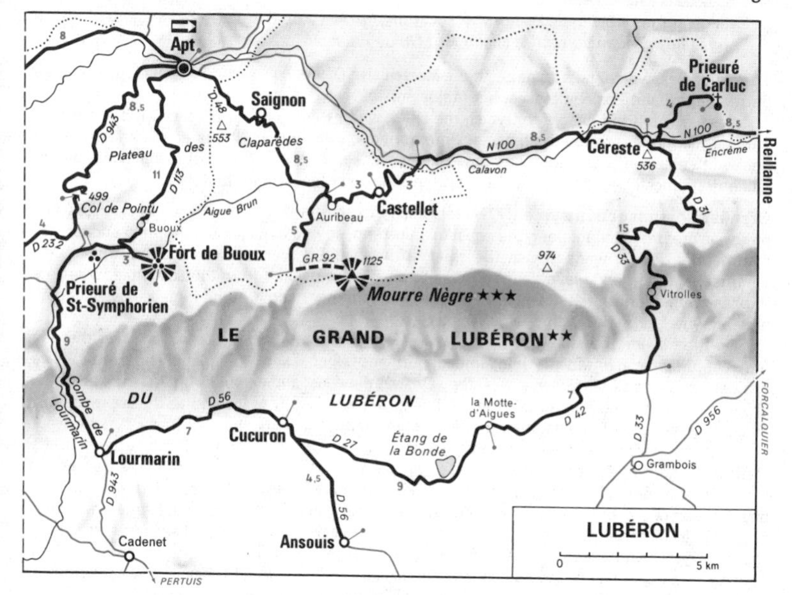

Continue to Ménerbes via D 109; note the quarries which extract freestone in the area near Lacoste.

Ménerbes★. – Pop 1 027. The old village, jutting from the north face of the Lubéron, was the Calvinist's final stronghold in the Wars of Religion and capitulated only after a 15 month siege. The **citadel** *(not open)*, still impressive with flanking towers and machicolations, dates back to 13C, the **church** to 14C. From the east end there is a **view★** (N) of the Coulon Valley, and, beyond, of the villages of Gordes and Roussillon, the latter, in front of ochre coloured cliffs, Mount Ventoux, the Vaucluse Plateau and (S) the Lubéron.

Go S along D 3 and then take D 188. The route offers attractive views of the Vaucluse Plateau and Mount Ventoux.

Oppède-le-Vieux★. – Pop 1 015. *Tour: 1/2 hour.* The village, on its picturesque rock **site★**, once partially abandoned, has come to life again through the restoration of its authentic character by artists and writers taking up residence in the old houses.
Park the car in the new car park. A gateway in the walls leads to the upper village with its 11-13C church *(not open)* and ruined castle. The **view★** from the church terrace is of the Coulon Valley and Vaucluse Plateau (N), Ménerbes village (ENE) and, from the rear of the castle, of the ravined north face of the Lubéron.

Cross the Maubec wine region (via D 176 and D 29) and bear left.

Cavaillon. – *Description p 67.*

Leave the town by D 2 NE. The road climbs the lush Coulon Valley covered with market gardens and melon fields.
3 km - 2 miles after Coustellet bear right into D 207 to Moulin des Bouillons.

Frédérique Duran Stained Glass Museum (Musée du Vitrail). – *Description p 76.*

St-Pantaléon. – Pop 91. In the village is a fascinating small Romanesque church with 3 naves. It is built out of the rock and its central part dates from the 5C. The church is surrounded by tombs, also carved out of the rock.
The tombs are almost all of children's size. Perhaps the site is one of those «sanctuaries of respite» several examples of which have been found in Provence: children who died before being baptized were brought by their parents and – according to the beliefs of the time – restored to life long enough to be baptized; they died right after the baptismal mass and were buried on the spot.

Leave the village by D 104, then bear right into D 60 which takes you to N.-D.-de-Lumières.

N.-D.-de-Lumières. – The statue of Our Lady in the crypt of this 17C sanctuary is the object of a popular Provençal pilgrimage; in the chapel above, on the third south altar is 17C Pietà in carved and gilded wood. The park is open.

The N 100 climbs the Coulon Valley. On the left is ochre country *(pp 14 and 34-35)*.

Julien Bridge. – *Description p 34.*

The N 100 returns to Apt.

MARSEILLES ★★★

Michelin map 245 folds L and M – *Local map p 74* – Pop 878 689 – *For additional plan of Marseilles see the current Michelin Red Guide France*

Marseilles, which gave its name to the **Marseillaise,** is France's second city and, including the Berre Lagoon and Fos complexes, her major port.

It has a very long history for which the city itself has little time or respect – it has not, with minor exceptions, preserved its ancient monuments, in every age it has erected new ones; it does not celebrate past traditions but, whatever its situation – and its fortunes have risen and fallen dramatically – it has kept its eye on the future and new opportunities.

Greeks, Romans, countrymen. – History recounts that in 600 BC Phocean Greeks from Asia Minor, came prospecting along the coast in ships and, spying a deep inlet, dropped anchor. The commander, Protis, went to visit the chief of the local Ligurian tribe and found himself at a banquet at which the chief's daughter was to choose a husband from the assembled warriors. Princess Gyptis presented the cup to the handsome stranger and brought him, as dowry, the hill now crowned by the Church of N.-D.-de-la-Garde.

On the hillside the **Phoceans** built a village which they named **Massalia** and, over the next four centuries, converted the inlet into a port and established trading posts at Arles, Nice, Antibes, Agde, La Ciotat. Further west they cleared the coast and planted fruit orchards and olive groves; finally they opened up trade with seaports ranging from Iceland to the west coast of Africa. Massalia itself developed into a flourishing republican city state.

Such prosperity aroused the envy of the native Ligurians and recently arrived Celts. Massalia called on **Rome** to defend it; in three years of bitter warfare, the Romans cleared the region of insurgents to establish, in 122 BC, Trans-Alpine Gaul with Aix and Narbonne as local provincial capitals and Massalia as an autonomous republic. The city state became embroiled, however, in imperial politics and had to choose between the warring Caesar and Pompey; it chose wrongly and was soon besieged by Caesar who stripped the city of its merchant and fighting ships and distributed its riches to Arles, Narbonne and other towns. The excavations of the old quarters have uncovered the wharfs of this period.

For several hundred years, first under the Romans, then through barbarian and Saracen invasion and outbreaks of plague, Marseilles continued in the depths of misfortune, until the end of 11C and the advent of the **Crusades.** The commercial opportunity was recognized and quickly seized: ships were built, crusaders provisioned, transported and, eventually, even accommodated in Marseilles' own acquired quarter in the City of Jerusalem. Once revitalized, the city's old seaboard trade with ports all round the Mediterranean was also rapidly re-established.

Fortune changed again, however, when the city and Provence were united to the Kingdom of France in 1481 – from then on Marseilles became permanently involved in the nation's politics, usually in voluble dissent!

The Marseillaise, 19 and 20C. – The town welcomed the Revolution. In 1792, at a farewell banquet for 500 supporters about to march to Paris, the battle song of the Army on the Rhine, composed in Strasbourg by a young sapper officier, Rouget de Lisle, was sung and immediately adopted by the volunteers who sang it all the way to the capital, by which time it had become famous as the *Marseillaise,* the French national anthem.

The city itself, however, Federalist at heart, found the Convention's strict rule unbearable; it revolted but unsuccessfully, so that it became a « city without a name »; a guillotine was permanently installed on the Canebière.

By the early 19C the city had recovered once more and, under the Empire, declared itself to be Royalist – trade had been hard-hit by the British fleet and the continental blockade! Under the restored Louis XVIII, once more in opposition, it preferred the exiled Emperor!

The port. – The old port (Vieux Port), the inlet which attracted the Phoceans in 600 BC, even enlarged, dredged and supplemented by additional quaysides had, by 18-19C, become totally inadequate. In mid-19C, therefore, construction began on the **Grande Joliette,** the first of the new basins which now extend north, half way round the great anchorage.

This 19C dock development coincided with the coming of the railway, which in itself transformed the situation, and also with the construction under Ferdinand de Lesseps of the **Suez Canal,** which from the time of its opening afforded the port a potential undreamed of, even by its early traders. A century later history was in part repeated as expansion and redevelopment after wartime stagnation and destruction were paralleled by the post-war reconstruction of the French railway system, the transformation of road transport and the discovery of natural gas and oil in North Africa.

The Port of Marseilles is now an umbrella term for what is a vast dock and industrial complex, including the city docks proper, the east and south shores of the Berre Lagoon from Port-de-la-Pointe via Marseilles-Marignane Airport to Martigues, the length of the Caronte Canal and the shore of Fos Bay, from the oil port of Lavéra via Port-de-Bouc and Port de Fos to Port St. Louis.

Behind the docks an industrial zone is developing – a vast area comprising oil storage tanks, tall chimneys and factory buildings – which looks dramatically different when lit up at night.

In terms of turnover the port of Marseilles today has an annual total of nearly 86 620 000 tons in 1983 of which nearly 75 million is represented by crude oil and petroleum products. In addition more than 1 million passengers pass through the port annually.

■ MAIN SIGHTS *time: 4 hours*

The Canebière★★ (CV). – Marseilles' most famous street, which runs east from the Old Port to the **Church of St-Vincent-de-Paul** (DUV), (Neo-Gothic built on the site of a chapel of a reformed Augustinian monastery; the area between the church and Boulevard Dugommier is the site of a Santons Fair) is lined along its short half mile by hotels and restaurants, shops and pavement cafés and presents a ceaseless hum of vitality.

The street's name may come from the hempfields *(chènevières)* once cultivated on the marshes round the harbour to provide ships' cordage.

Marseilles' Maritime Museum (BV). – *Open 10am to noon and 2 to 6.30pm; closed Tuesdays and holidays.* The museum, in the former stock exchange overlooking the Place Général de Gaulle (BV), concentrates principally on the period from 17C to the present.

The Old Port★★ (Vieux Port) (ABVX). – The inlet into which the Phoceans sailed in 600 BC is now almost exclusively a closely packed pleasure boat harbour. It is still lined by quays, constructed by Louis XII and XIII in 15 and 17C and guarded by the forts of St John to the north and St Nicholas to the south – the latter built by Vauban, the great military engineer-architect of Louis XIV.

Corniche Président-J.-F.-Kennedy★★. – The road *(on plan in Michelin Red Guide France)*, which follows the coast for more than 5 km - 3 miles, looks out across the bay to the offshore island and the Marseilleveyre Massif *(p 87)*. Just beyond the **Memorial to the Dead** in the Orient *(S off map)* below a bridge, lies the picturesque fishing village, **Vallon des Auffes.**

Continue skirting the beaches to a T junction marked by a statue of David. Turn left up the Avenue du Prado and right at the roundabout into the Boulevard Michelet.

Le Corbusier's Tower Block. – *About 1 500m - 1 mile down on the right.* The controversial and much imitated prototype for vertical living, designed by **Le Corbusier** in 1952, is a single block of reinforced concrete cellular structure, raised on a double row of squat tapered stilts. It contains 16 stories of 23 different types of flat – 337 apartments in all – with characteristic two storey living rooms. Half-way up a « shopping street » provides a restaurant, laundry, post office, nursery school; on the roof is a community centre. Most of the service machinery is placed underneath the building, but whatever emerges above the roof line, such as the exhaust funnel, is disguised as abstract sculpture.

The original project **(Cité Radieuse)** was for six such multiple dwellings **(Unité d'Habitation)** but only one was completed.

Return to the centre by the Boul. Michelet, the roundabout, Ave du Prado and Rue de Rome.

N.-D.-de-la-Garde Basilica (BY). – *12% and 15% gradients (1 in 8 and 1 in 7) and slippery surfaces in wet weather. From the Rue de Rome turn up the Rue Dragon, then left into the Rue Breteuil, right into the Boulevard Vauban and, finally, right into the Rue Fort-du-Sanctuaire which comes out on the Plateau de la Croix (car parks).*

The present church, on a site on which a chapel with the same dedication stood in 13C, dates from 19C and is in the, then fashionable, Roman-Byzantine style. Surmounting the belfry is a huge gilded statue of the Virgin. A popular pilgrimage to Notre-Dame takes place on 15 August each year.

The interior, faced with multi-coloured marbles, is notable for the ex-votos which cover the walls and a moving *Mater Dolorosa* carved in marble by Carpeaux, in the crypt.

The **panorama★★★** is, however, the principal reason for most visitors' climb to the top of the 162m - 530ft high bluff on which the church stands. Out to sea, are the Ratonneau and Pomègues Islands, and closer inshore, the Château d'If *(p 87)*; inland, the Marseilleveyre Massif (S); the Étoile Mountain Chain (NE); across the anchorage (NW), the Estaque Mountains and, in the foreground, the Pharo Park and the Old Port.

■ ADDITIONAL SIGHTS

Old Port Quarter

St Victor's Basilica★ (AX). – *Open 10am to noon and 3 to 6pm; closed Sunday mornings and certain holidays; 5F.*

The church is the last relic of the abbey founded in 5C by St John Cassian, a monk from Egypt, in honour of St Victor, patron of sailors and millers, who suffered martyrdom in 3C by being slowly ground between two millstones. The sanctuary, destroyed in a Saracen raid, was rebuilt *c*1040 and subsequently remodelled and so strongly fortified that it became known as the « key to Marseilles' harbour ».

(After photo by Ed. de France, Marseille)

The Old Port and N-D-de-la-Garde, Marseilles.

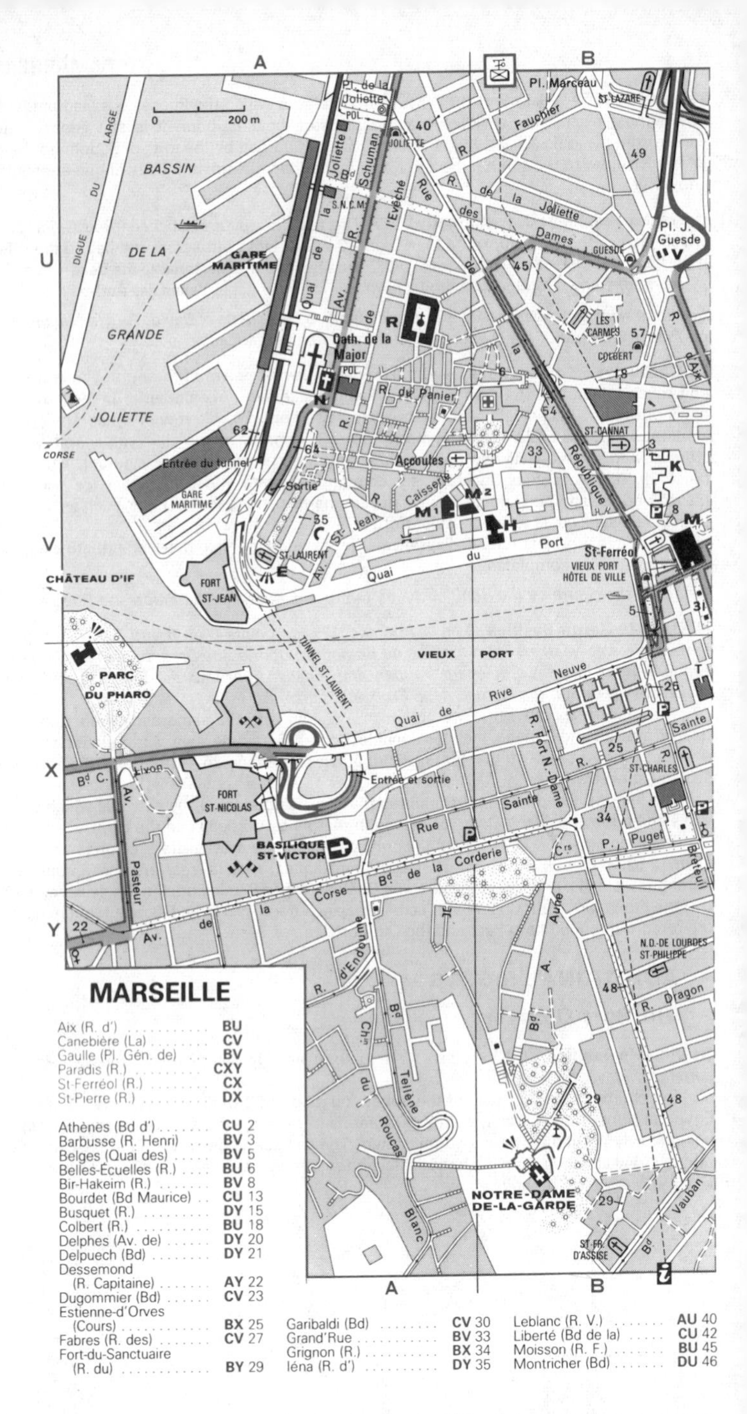

From outside, with its battlemented towers, it still resembles a fortress. Inside three periods of Gothic vaulting are evident: in the heavy ribs of 1140 in the porch, in the finer moulding of 13C over the nave, and the aisles of 14C above the chancel and transept.

The most interesting part of the building, however, is the basilica constructed by St John Cassian in 5C and buried when the church was rebuilt in 11C so that it now serves as a vast **crypt**★★ to the edifice above. In the crypt are catacombs, a chapel to St Victor and, in the central chapel, a 3C martyrium.

Pharo Park (AX). – The Pharo Park, which is situated on the promontory commanding the harbour entrance, was originally laid out as the garden to the residence of the Empress Eugénie, wife of Napoleon III. It commands a unique **view**★ of the Old Port *(telescope)*, St John's Fort and the Major Cathedral.

St Laurent Belvedere (AV E). – The complementary **view**★ looking south from in front of the church *(92 steps)*, above the road tunnel, covers the Old Port with its forts at the entrance, N.-D.-de-la-Garde and the beginning of the Canebière.

Roman Docks Museum★ (AV M[1]). – *Open 10am to noon and 2 to 6.30pm; closed Tuesdays, Wednesday mornings and holidays; 3F.* The docks included warehouses opening on to the quayside and an upper storey with access to the main street.

The museum describes the port and traces the town's history as a trading centre. There are displays of storage jars, ships' stays and timbers and maritime industries.

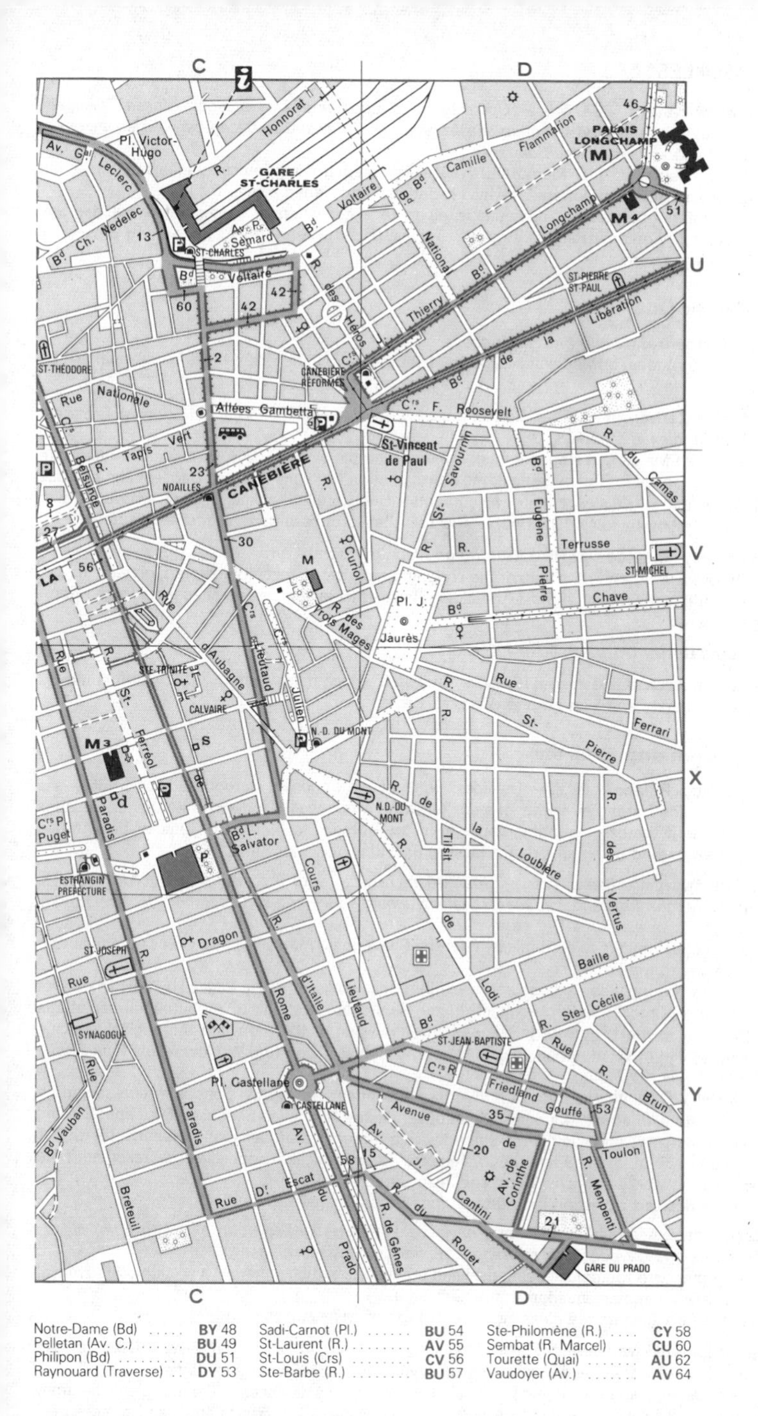

Notre-Dame (Bd)	BY 48	Sadi-Carnot (Pl.)	BU 54	Ste-Philomène (R.)	CY 58
Pelletan (Av. C.)	BU 49	St-Laurent (R.)	AV 55	Sembat (R. Marcel)	CU 60
Philipon (Bd)	DU 51	St-Louis (Crs)	CV 56	Tourette (Quai)	AU 62
Raynouard (Traverse)	DY 53	Ste-Barbe (R.)	BU 57	Vaudoyer (Av.)	AV 64

Museum of Old Marseilles★ (ABV M²). – *Open 10am to noon and 2.30 to 6.30pm; closed Tuesdays, Wednesday mornings and holidays; 3F, free Sunday mornings.*

The museum is in the 16C Maison Diamantée, so-called because of the faceted stones used in its construction.

Inside is a grand staircase beneath a coffered ceiling.

In the various rooms Provençal life is reflected in arrangements of 18C furniture, domestic utensils in copper and pottery, 18C cribs and 19 early 20C *santons (p 24).*

On the top floor are a relief map and prints of 19C Marseilles and the Camoin Gift which displays the moulds and techniques used in making playing cards by 18-20C Marseilles firm of Camoin.

Town Hôtel (Hôtel de ville) (BV H). – 17C façade.

St-Ferréol (BV). – The Church's Renaissance style front dates from 1804.

The ramparts of ancient Marseilles (BV K). – 3 and 2C BC fortifications, 1C AD wharfs of the ancient port and a 4C AD road giving access to the city were discovered behind the Chamber of Commerce.

At the end of the garden (Jardin des vestiges) on the ground floor of the Centre-Bourse shopping centre is a **Historical Museum of Marseilles** *(open 10am to 7pm; closed Sundays, Mondays and certain holidays; 3F)* which displays finds from recent excavations (wreck of a Roman merchant vessel - 19m long and 8m wide - 62 × 26ft).

Cantini Museum★ (**CX M**[3]). – *Open 10am to noon and 2 to 6.30pm; closed Tuesdays, Wednesday mornings and 1 January, Easter Sunday, 1 May and 25 December; 3F (fee increased if there is an exhibition), free Sundays.*

The museum, in 17C Montgrand House, is noted for its collection (nearly 600) of old **Marseilles and Moustiers pottery**★★ which includes many signed pieces.

The greater part of the museum is given to a collection of **contemporary painting and sculpture;** 400 works by Balthus, Hartung, Tapiès, Bacon, César and Adami among others are exhibited in rotation.

Panier Quarter

Major Cathedral (AU). – *Closed Mondays.*

The sumptuous, domed edifice, 140m - 459ft long and 70m - 230ft high, is in Romanesque-Byzantine style.

Old Major Cathedral★ (AU). – *Guided tour 9am to noon and 2.30 to 6pm (2 to 5pm 1 October to 30 April); closed Mondays; 3F.*

The « Old Major », in stout contrast, is a fine example of mid-11C Romanesque, truncated in 19C to make space for the building of the new cathedral. Only the chancel, transept and one bay of the nave and side aisles remain. The contents include a reliquary altar of 1073, a ceramic relief of the Deposition by Luca della Robbia and 15C altar to St Lazurus by Francesco Laurana.

Old Charity Hospice (**AU R**). – *Restoration work in progress.*

The west wing and rose tints of the crowning stonework, recently restored, give an idea of the once fine appearance of the 17C building. Inside this ensemble is a chapel built after Pierre Puget's plans.

Accoules Belfry (AV). – Relic of 12C church.

Triumphal Arch (Aix Gateway) (**BU V**). – This arch, which dates from the 19C, commemorates the Revolutionary and First Empire Wars.

Longchamp Quarter

Longchamp Palace★ (DU). – The focal point of the imposing Baroque edifice (*c*1860) is a central cascade framed by flights of steps leading up to a well disguised water-tower, which is the outflow of the canal bringing water from the Durance to Marseilles. Circular balustraded colonnades extend on either side to classical pavilions now museums.

Fine Arts Museum★ **(Beaux Arts)**. – *Open 10am to noon and 2 to 6.30pm; closed Tuesdays, Wednesday mornings and 1 January, Easter Sunday, 1 May and 25 December; 3F, free Sunday mornings.*

In the stair well are two murals by Puvis de Chavannes: Marseilles as a Greek Colony and as the Gateway to the Levant.

On the ground floor a large room exhibits the works of **Pierre Puget** (1620-94) native of Marseilles, sculptor, painter, architect. In the centre are castings of monumental sculptures found either in the Louvre or in Genoa. On either side of the room are the **original works**★: drawings, paintings – of remarkable imagination, statues *(The Faun)* and low reliefs *(The Plague at Milan, Louis XIV Riding).*

16 and 17C painting is housed in two large galleries. The French School is represented by Vouet *(Virgin with a rose),* Le Sueur, Rigaud, Largillière; the Italian School by Perugino, Cariani, Carraci, Guercino; the Flemish School by Jan Bruegel, Jordaens and Rubens (Portrait - presumed to be of - Hélène Fourment), Teniers. The Provençal School is well represented; note especially the works of Michel Serre and Jean Daret.

The **African art** collection includes carvings from Senegal and Zaïre.

Natural History Museum★ *(right hand pavilion). – Open 10am to noon and 2 to 6pm; closed Tuesdays all day, Wednesday mornings; 3F, free Sunday mornings.*

Together with zoological, geological and prehistoric exhibits, there is a section on Provençal flora and fauna and an **aquarium** in the basement.

In the park beyond the palace is a *zoo* (U) *(open daily 9am to 6pm; 5F).*

Grobet-Labadié Museum★★ (**DU M**[4]). – *Open 10am to noon and 2 to 6.30pm; closed Tuesdays all day, Wednesday mornings and holidays; 3F, 10F during exhibitions.*

The 19C mansion bequeathed by Louis Grobet remains as it was in the musician's lifetime: a still life of the richer bourgeois life style, complete with 16-18C French and Flemish tapestries, paintings by well known artists, furniture, 18C porcelain, ecclesiastical plate, ironwork and the owner's own collection of old musical instruments.

Borély Quarter south of the city map 93 fold M

Borély Château and Park. – *Open 9.30am to noon and 1 to 5.30pm; closed Tuesdays all day, Wednesday mornings and holidays; 3F, fee increased during exhibitions; free Sunday mornings.*

The château of 1767-78, which stands in its own extensive grounds *(cars prohibited),* is named after the family of wealthy city merchants who built and furnished it.

The mansion, in addition to 18C rooms, now houses the **Museum of Mediterranean Archaeology**★ rich in **Egyptian antiquities**★★, Greek and Roman pottery, antique glass, and Etruscan, Greek and Roman bronzes. A collection of 18C French master drawings on the upper floor includes works by Boucher, Fragonard, Ingres, Lemoine, Greuze, Watteau... Italian, Flemish and Dutch paintings include works by Tiepolo, Titian, Bruegel, Willem Mieris.

The château's outbuildings shelter a **lapidary museum** (Roman remains, Christian sarcophagi and other objects found in the region).

Amable-Chanot Park. – The city conference centre (Palais des Congrès) in the park (Parc Chanot) is the setting for the annual Spring and Great International Marseilles Fairs *(late March-early April and last fortnight in September).*

Near the park, Marseilles' Radio and Television House can be seen.

■ The DOCKS★★

From the Outer Breakwater *(Digue du Large)* one can walk along and look at the Grande Joliette Basins and those of the modern port. *Enter by Gate no 1 (Joliette). Open Sundays and holidays only, 7am to 9pm (6pm 1 October to 31 March). For guided tours of the port on weekdays apply at least a week before hand to: Direction du Port Autonome, Service des Relations Publiques, 23 place de la Joliette, 13002 Marseille, ☏ : 91 91.90.66.*

EXCURSIONS

Château d'If★★. – *About 1 1/2 hours including boat trip and a tour of the castle. Embarkation: Quai des Belges, Old Port* (**CX**)*; regular boat service in summer 9am to 5pm; in winter schedule varies but basically 9.30am to 4pm; round trip: 24F, children 2F. ☏ : 91 90.47.33.*

The round towered, medieval castle *(open according to boat timetable)* on the rock projecting from the sea is best known as a prison both in history and in fiction: in 16 and 17C Protestants were held there before being sent to the galleys, in 1848 the political opponents of Napoleon III, and in 18C, probably in well organized ease, **Mirabeau** for non-payment of his debts *(p 29)*. Most famous of all, however, is the legendary **Count of Monte Cristo** in Dumas' novel.

The **panorama**★★★ from the old chapel terrace is remarkable. Note the causeway which now links the Ratonneau and Pomègues Islands creating a new harbour, the Port du Frioul.

Étoile Chain★. – *Round tour of 93 km - 58 miles – allow 1 day. Leave Marseilles by N 8. At La Malle turn right into D 6 to Gardanne.*

Gardanne. – Pop 15 374. The industrial town with its bauxite and cement works and coal mining lies in the valley between the Etoile Chain and Mount Ste-Victoire.

Leave by D 58 going south which becomes D 8. After 7 km - 4 miles turn right to Mimet.

Mimet. – Pop 2 531. From the terrace in the old hill village there is a fine **view**★ of the Luynes' Valley, Gardanne and its furnaces.

Take the narrow road which climbs through a landscape of cork oak, evergreen oak and pine trees up Baou Traouqua Mountain to Ste Anne Pass (Col Ste Anne).

Ste-Anne Pass. – Alt 600m - 1 970ft. The pass is dominated by the Pilon du Roi (W). Park the car *(at the pass)* and take the well-kept path to the right *(1 1/2 hours on foot Rtn)* which skirts the north face of the three peaks of the Etoile Chain: Pilon du Roi (alt 670m - 2 200ft), Etoile Peak (alt 652m - 2 139ft) and Grande Etoile (alt 590m - 1 935ft). There is a splendid **panorama**★★ over the Gardanne Basin (N) and the south face of the Etoile Chain.

The road descends by steep hairpin bends with views of Marseilles before plunging into a pine forest. *Turn right at Logis-Neuf into N 8 bis and in Plan-de-Cuques right again along D 44^{F}.*

Château-Gombert. – The plane tree shaded main square is overlooked on one side by 17C church and opposite by the mansion, now housing a **Museum of Popular Art and Traditions** *(open Mondays, Saturdays, Sundays, 3 to 7pm; out of season 2 to 6pm; 10F)*. The rooms have been arranged to display Marseilles, Moustiers and Montpellier pottery, pewter and glass, furniture, also a *radassié* or vast country couch from a bastide. Local costumes and the dress harnesses used in St Eligius' feast day processions are also on view.

Leave by the Marseilles road; turn right into Chemin de la Baumo Loubière.

Loubière Caves. – *Guided tours in summer, 9am to noon and 2 to 5.30pm (10am to noon and 2.30 to 5.30pm Sundays and holidays); the rest of the year, 9.30 to 11.30am and 2 to 5pm (10.30 to 11.30am and 2.30 to 5pm Sundays and holidays); closed Tuesdays, 1 January and 25 December; 15F.* The five caves extend for some 1 500m - 3/4 mile and are filled with multicoloured stalactites and stalagmites, columns, translucent curtains and eccentrics.

Take D 44^{F} to D 4^{B}, bear left then right to Allauch.

Allauch. – Pop 13 528. The suburb of Allauch (pronounced Allau) rises in tiers up the most westerly of the Estaque foothills as did the old village which preceded it *(museum: open Wednesday, Saturday and Sunday afternoons 3 to 6pm and Sunday mornings 10am to noon; 4F.)* A good **view**★ of Marseilles and its harbour is visible from either the Esplanade des Moulins or the terrace of the chapel of the now ruined 11-12C castle *(1/2 hour on foot Rtn)*.

Continue southwards; at Les 4-Saisons bear left, and left again.

Camoins-les-Bains. – This small spa enjoys a picturesque greenery.

La Treille. – **Marcel Pagnol** (1895-1974) writer and film director who was born in Aubagne *(see below)* is buried in La Treille cemetery.

Return to Camoins-les-Bains and take D 44^{A} to Aubagne.

Aubagne. – Pop 38 571. The town, which dates back to the early Middle Ages, has since 1962 become widely known as the home of the **French Foreign Legion.** The regiment, raised by Louis-Philippe in 1831, was based in Algeria until the country gained its independence in 1962. It was then posted, together with its **Sacred Way** (formerly in Sidi-Bel-Abbès) and battle honours won throughout the world, to metropolitan France. **Museum**★ *(open 1 June to 30 September daily except Mondays 10am to noon and 3 to 7pm; the rest of the year, Wednesdays, Saturdays and Sundays 10am to noon and 2 to 6pm; closed Saturday mornings and 25 December).*

Return to Marseilles by D 2, N 8 or the motorway A 52.

Callelongue; Marseilleveyre Massif. – *13 km - 8 miles south. Leave Marseilles by Promenade de la Plage (the continuation of Corniche Président-J.-F.-Kennedy).* The **road**★★ skirts Prado Beach, crosses Pointe Rouge (small pleasure boat harbour); after La Madrague-de-Montredon the road climbs into the Marseillveyre Massif past Mont Rose (alt 81m - 266ft); good views of Cape Croisette and Ile Maire. The road then drops down to sea level where, at the end of a creek of the same name, is the fishing village and pleasure boat harbour of **Callelongue.** From the terrace of the old **lookout post** *(Ancien poste de vigie: 3/4 hour on foot Rtn; bear right into the path between two houses, continue to a retaining wall and then bear right again)* there is a **view**★ of Pomègues Island and the Estaque Chain (NW), Ile Maire, the villages of Les Gourdes and Callelongue (W), the Jarre and Riou Islands (SE) and Cape Aigle (E).

MARTIGUES

Michelin map 246 folds 13 and 14 – *Local maps pp 59 and 74* – Pop 42 039 – *Facilities p 8* – *See town plan in the current Michelin Red Guide France*

Martigues, like its twin town Lavéra, is being transformed and extended as a result of the expansion of the oil industry and its subsidiaries around the Berre Lagoon.

It took its name in 1581 on the amalgamation of the three fishing villages whose names are retained as town quarters: Ferrières to the north, the Ile in the centre and Jouquières to the south.

At the turn of the century, when it was still a small Provençal fishing village, Martigues attracted writers and painters, notably Corot and Ziem *(see below)*, and gradually became popular as a holiday resort.

Pont St-Sébastien. – The bridge at the centre of the Ile Brescon, is a vantage point from which to **view★** the brightly coloured pleasure craft moored along the St-Sébastien Canal and Brescon quayside. This has long been a favourite spot with painters and is known as the Birds' Looking Glass.

Caronte Road Viaduct★. – Since 1972 the Caronte Canal, which connects the lagoon with the sea, has been spanned by a spectacular 300m long road bridge comprising a metal deck suspended 50m above the water between inclined supports. It affords a good, bird's-eye **view** of the town.

The Birds' Looking Glass, Martigues.

Ste-Madeleine-de-l'Ile. – The church beside the St-Sébastien Canal on Ile Brescon, has a Corinthian style west front and pilasters, cornices and an imposing organ loft inside.

Ziem Museum. – *Open 10am to noon and 2.30 to 6.30pm (afternoons only 1 September to 30 June); closed Mondays, Tuesdays, 1 January, 1 May, 14 July, 15 August, 1 November and 25 December; 5F, free Sundays.*

Grouped around the works of Felix Ziem (1821-1911), painter of landscapes and oriental scenes, are works by Provençal artists from 19C (Guigou, Manguin, Monficelli, Hurard, Loubon) and 20C (Seyssaud).

Also exhibited in the museum are collections of local archaeology and ethnology, and contemporary art.

EXCURSIONS

Berre Lagoon★ and St-Blaise archaeological site. – *Round tour of 113 km - 78 miles. Description p 58.*

N.-D.-des-Marins. – *3.5 km - 2 miles N – Local map p 59. Leave Martigues by N 568; after 1.5 km - 2/3 mile bear right at the main crossroads into D 50^C^ (towards the hospital); 1.2 km - 1/2 mile further on, just before the top of the hill, turn right.* The **panorama★** sweeps round from Martigues and the Caronte road and railway bridges (S), to Port-de-Bouc and Lavéra (W), and beyond to Fos and Port-St-Louis. To the east are the Berre Lagoon, the Étoile and Vitrolles Mountains and, further away, Mount St-Victoire (ENE) and, on clear days, Mount Ventoux (NE). On the lagoon are Berre town (NE), the Marseille-Marignane Airport (E) and the line of the Marseille-Rhône Canal breakwater (SE). St-Mitre-des-Ramparts lies between two hills to the northwest.

Lavéra. – *5 km - 3 miles W along D 49^E^.* The road skirts the Caronte Canal spanned by the 1972 road bridge described above and a railway bridge 943m - 3 192ft long, including a 114m - 374ft mobile section.

The Société Française des Pétroles BP allows visitors into the refinery on prior application to the Information Service, S.F.BP. Boîte postale n° 1, 13117 Lavéra.

On coming out of the refinery continue along D 49^E^ to a narrow road on the left leading to a viewing table overlooking Port-de-Bouc, Lavéra and the Berre Lagoon.

Port-de-Bouc; Fos Complex★. – *9 km - 5 miles by N 568.*

Port-de-Bouc. – Pop 20 106. The lighthouse, built in 12C as a harbour defence, was incorporated by Vauban, the military architect, in the far-reaching defences he constructed in 1664. When these became obsolete, it was converted to its present purpose. The town, like Martigues and Lavéra, is developing rapidly.

Continue along N 568.

Fos Complex★. – *Description p 75.*

The MONTAGNETTE

Michelin map 246 fold 25

The Montagnette is a range of hills, none of which tops 200m - 600ft, which parallels the Rhône as it flows southwest below Avignon. On a small scale it offers a typical Provençal landscape of rock escarpments, hillsides fragrant with wild flowers and aromatic herbs, quiet hollows sheltering olive, almond and apricot trees, pines, poplars and cypresses.

Round tour starting from Barbentane – *39 km - 24 miles – about 3 hours*

Barbentane. – Pop 3 249. *Facilities p 8.* The small town, built against the north slope of the Montagnette, looks down on the plain which provides its livelihood as a market for fresh fruit and vegetables dispatched to all parts of France.

The past is visible in two **medieval gateways** – the Calendale, opening on to the Cours, and the Séguier at the upper end of the town – respectively in the Renaissance fronted **Maison des Chevaliers** *(not open)* and the **Anglica Tower,** the keep of 14C castle which still commands the plain and river confluence from the height above. More recent is 17C **château** which belongs to the Duke of Barbentane *(guided tour – time: 1/2 hour – Easter Sunday to 31 October 10am to noon and 2 to 6pm; the rest of the year Sundays and holidays, same times; closed Wednesdays except in July August and September; 14F). Walk up the Rue du Château (left of the post office).* Behind the ordered façades and balustraded terraces, decorated with stone lions and flower filled urns, are an 18C **interior★**, rich with Louis XV and XVI furniture, painted ceilings and wall medallions, Chinese porcelain, Moustiers china...

Leave Barbentane by D 35^E^. As the road rises the Rhône comes into view and, on the left, through the pines, Brétoul Windmill (18C), the last of many which once served the region.

St-Michel-de-Frigolet Abbey. – *Apply to the shop near the entrance on the right after the arch; guided tour 9 to 10am and 2 (2.15 Sundays and holidays) to 6pm; weekdays: mass 11am, vespers 8.10pm; Sundays: mass 8am and 6pm; special feast and holiday masses.* The abbey, nestling in a hollow, fragrant with rosemary, lavender and thyme, and sheltered by cypresses, pines and olives, was founded in 10C by monks from Montmajour *(p 44),* who came to this idyllic spot to recover from the fevers they contracted while draining the marshes around their mother house. They dedicated the chapel to Our Lady of Goodly Remedy.

Religious of different orders inhabited the conventual buildings before all was confiscated at the Revolution and later converted into a boarding school attended for a time by Frédéric Mistral *(see below).* In mid-19C, once more a monastery, St Frigolet was medievalized by the construction of a towered perimeter complete with curtain walls, machicolations and crenelations; in addition large pilgrim hostels were built and a lavishly ornate church, enclosing as the apse to the north aisle, the monks' original 11C Chapel to Our Lady. The **gilded panelling★** was the gift of Anne of Austria, who had come in pilgrimage and in 1638, bore the king a son, Louis XIV. The abbey cloister is 12C, the stalls in the chapterhouse 16C and St Michael's Church, behind 19C west front is a dignified 11C structure with a stone roof and openwork crest. The **museum** contains Provençal furniture and 18-19C pharmacy jars.

Turn round and take D 81 on the left. The road circles W to Boulbon.

Boulbon. – Pop 1 042. An impressive fort marks the site of the town on the Montagnette hillside. The local, Romanesque chapel *(apply to M. Betton, 10 Rue de l'Enclos)* contains a number of statues, particularly 14C recessed tomb with a recumbent figure and weepers. On 1 June each year a picturesque Bottle Procession makes its way to the chapel for the blessing of the local wine.

Drive S along D 35. The road skirts the mountainside, where the strata are clearly visible.

Tarascon★ and Beaucaire★. – *Description p 56.*

Leave Tarascon by N 570 going NE. The road drops to the densely cultivated Petite Crau.

Graveson. – Pop 2 276. The church of this modest town standing amidst fruit orchards, has an oven vaulted apse decorated with a low-level, delicately carved, blind arcade.

Maillane. – Pop 1 430. *3 km - 2 miles from Graveson along D 5.* The town at the centre of the Petite Crau is typical, with shaded squares and streets of brown tiled, white houses. It is famous for the birth and burial of the great Provençal poet, **Frédéric Mistral** (1830-1914). His funeral monument, which he himself copied from Queen Jeanne's pavilion *(p 56)* at Les Baux, stands in the cemetery.

The **house,** which he built and lived in from 1876 until his death, is now a **museum** (Mueson Mistral) *(open 10am to noon and 2 to 5pm (4pm 1 November to 31 March); 1 June to 30 September 9am to noon and 2 to 6pm; closed Mondays and holidays; 4F).* Opposite is the Lézard House *(not open)* where he lived previously with his mother and where he completed the work which won him early renown, *Mireio* (1859).

Return to N 570 towards Avignon; at the entrance to Rognonas turn off left into D 34 for Barbentane.

(After photo by Arch. Phot., Paris)

Frédéric Mistral.

The times indicated in this guide
when given with the distance allow one to enjoy the scenery
when given for sightseeing are intended to give an idea of the possible length or brevity of a visit.

Michelin map 246 fold 21 or 22 – *Local map p 102* – Pop 30 213. *See town plan in the Michelin Red Guide France.*

Montélimar owes its name to a medieval fortress, Mont-Adhémar, built in 12C by the powerful Adhémar family, ancestors of Mme de Sévigné's son-in-law *(p 77).*

The Montélimar **hydro-electric undertaking,** following that of Donzère-Mondragon both in time and design, was a major part of the Rhône undertakings of 1960-70 *(p 101).* The deviation of the Montélimar feeds the **Châteauneuf power station.**

Nougat. – The nougat industry, as such, is relatively new: production was originally home-based, starting in 16C with the introduction of almond trees from the Orient. Cultivation of the trees spread rapidly from the experimental orchard, planted by Olivier de Serres at Le Pradel *(p 131),* to the Gras Plateau; cooks and confectioners combined the harvested almonds with local honey in secret recipes. In early 20C mechanization displaced the private confectioner.

Castle. – *Open 10am to noon and 2 to 7pm; closed Tuesdays, Wednesday mornings, 25 December and 1 January; 8.50F.* 12C fortress, the first to be built on the site, was enlarged under papal jurisdiction in 14C. It served as a prison from 1790 to 1929. There is an extensive **panorama** to be seen from the rampart walk. Also worthy of attention are nine Romanesque windows on the castle west front and the absidal wall paintings in 11C Ste-Guitte Chapel.

EXCURSIONS

Rochemaure Castle★. – *7 km - 4 miles by D 11 going NW – about 3/4 hour.*

Facing Montélimar across the Rhône, crowning the ridge marking the most eastward point of the volcanic Coiron Plateau, stand the ruins of Rochemaure Castle. The **setting★★** is striking for, in contrast to the white limestone cliffs of the region, the old fortress is built on an outcrop of black basalt (Rochemaure: *roche noire*). It and the feudal village within its walls, were constructed between 13 and 16C and, after centuries of strife, abandoned in 18C.

Rochemaure

Castle ruins. – *In Rochemaure village, take the narrow road between the Monument aux Morts and the town hall* (mairie)*, which passes twice through the fortress walls on the way up. Park the car at the foot of the inner defence and continue on foot by the first path on the left (1/4 hour Rtn).* The summit commands a good **view★** of the Montélimar Plain.

Chenavari Peak★★. – *4.5 km - 3 miles from the castle. From the St-Laurent Chapel take the right hand road through Les Videaux. Leave to the right a path which leads to a farm (ferme) and take an unsurfaced road to the left. From the electricity pylons, walk up to the summit (3/4 hour on foot Rtn).* From the summit (alt 507m - 1 063ft) there is a **view★★** of the Rhône with Rochemaure Castle in the foreground, the Lower Ardèche Hills (S) and, on the horizon (ESE), the Vercors Range and the Baronnies. From below, a basalt flow extends south to end in a columnar formation on the Rhône.

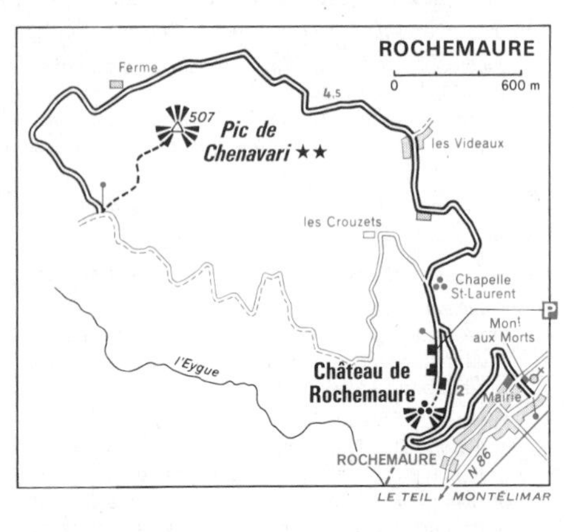

Round tour of the medieval towns★. – *78 km - 50 miles – about 3 1/2 hours. Leave Montélimar by D 540 going E; turn right into D 327 for Puygiron.*

On your way you pass typical Valdaine Plain houses of bare limestone, occasionally protected on the north side from the *mistral* by blind curtain walls and lines of cypresses.

Puygiron. – Pop 293. The village, dominated by its old 13-16C castle, is interesting mainly for its **site★** which overlooks Trois Becs, Marsanne and the Coiron Plateau.

Return to D 540 and turn right.

La Bégude-de-Mazenc★. – Pop 1 024. *At the central crossroads in the modern town, turn left into D 9 and then into the narrow, surfaced road up to the old perched village; park the car.* Walk through the fortified gateway abutting the apse of the partly Romanesque church, to enter a mass of alleys lined by old houses gradually being restored and re-inhabited. A steep path leads to the pinewood which crowns the rock bluff. In the old cemetery stands the triple apsed Chapel of Notre-Dame which dates from 12C.

The D 540 climbs, towards Dieulefit, the Jabron Valley.

Le Poët-Laval. – Pop 565. The village is overlooked from its cliff **site★** by the ruins of a commandery of the Knights Hospitallers of Malta (only the belfry and Romanesque apse of a former church remain). The onetime Protestant church now houses a museum of Protestantism in the Dauphiné *(open 15 June to 30 September, 3.30 to 6.30pm; Easter to 14 June Sundays only; the rest of the year on application only, ☎ 75 46 42 54).*

Return to the D 538. Scattered throught the Jabron Valley are potters workshops.

Dieulefit. – Pop 2 990. *Facilities p 8.* The small, largely Protestant, town, attractively sited where the Jabron Valley opens out, thrives on tourism and its decorated chinaware.

D 538 descends the Lez Valley, commanded from above by the ruins of the feudal Castle of Béconne and 14C Blacon Keep. *Turn right into D 14 which goes to Grignan.*

Grignan★. – *Description p 77.*

Return to Montélimar along D 4. The road offers good views of the Vercors and Roubion Basin. After Le Fraysse, straight ahead in the distance, are the imposing ruins of the Rochefort-en-Valdaine Castle overlooking the wooded Citelles Valley.

Le Teil. – *6 km - 3 miles W by N 102.* Pop 8 352. This industrial town on the west bank of the Rhône, is still overlooked by the ruins of 13C Castle of Adhémar de Monteil. It lives by the lime and cement quarries, first exploited in the early 19C for the construction of the railways and, from 1859-69, for the Suez Canal which cause the great scars on the countryside and the dense layer of white powder which covers everything within range.

Mélas Church. – *Enter by side door; if closed apply at the presbitery near the church or to Mme Rieu in the house opposite the church.* The modest **church** has 12C broken barrel vaulted nave, an 11C north aisle and a deep cupola on squinches over the chancel; two 12C decorated capitals *(nave north)* depict the *Sacrifice of Isaac* and the *Weighing of Souls.*

Opening off the north aisle is a **baptistry★**, built in 10C on the site of an early necropolis.

The NESQUE Gorges ★★

Michelin map 246 folds 10 and 11

The Nesque River rises on the east face of Mount Ventoux and after some 70 km - 45 miles flows into a tributary of the Sorgue, west of Pernes-les-Fontaines *(p 127)*. In its upper reaches the river has cut a spectacular gorge through the calcareous rock of the Vaucluse Plateau.

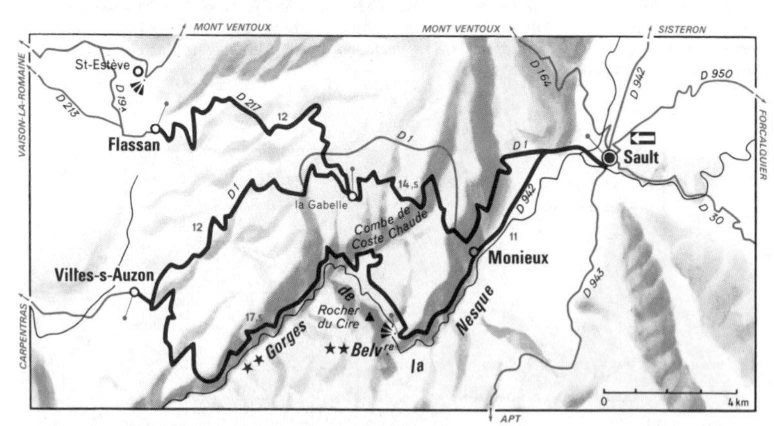

Round tour starting from Sault – *55 km - 36 miles – about 2 hours*

The road has been widened in places to allow parking and good views of the gorges.

Sault. – Pop 1 231. *Facilities p 8.* The town is built in a semicircle, 765m - 2 510ft up on a rock promontory at the west end of the Vaucluse Plateau above the Nesque Gorges (best view from a **terrace** at the north end of the town). It is at the centre of the lavender country and is known for its honey and nougat. The 12-14C **church** has a fine elevation and a gabled transept; the **nave★** is remarkable for the arches of its broken barrel vaulting which descend on to tall engaged columns. The chancel is lined with 17C panelling. A drystone *borie (p 78)* in the north transept contains a crib *(p 24)*. The **local museum** *(open 15 June to 15 September and 2.30 to 5pm; closed Wednesdays; 2F)*, located on the 1st floor of the library, contains coins, arms, archaeological and geological finds.

Leave Sault SW along D 942. A corniche road follows the right riverbank through the gorge.

Monieux. – Pop 171. A now almost deserted perched village overlooked by a tower.

Belvedere★★. – Alt 734m - 2 408ft. The viewpoint *(left of the road)*, signalled by a stele bearing verses from Mistral's *Calendal*, overlooks the gorges and the jagged Cire Rocks.

The descent begins with a passage through three tunnels. At this point the Nesque runs in a cleft so deep that it is invisible although clearly audible.

D 942 moves out of the gorge to cross the Coste Chaude Coomb. At the exit to the fourth tunnel there is a good view back along the gorge to the **Cire Rock** (872m - 2 860ft high). Suddenly the landscape changes as the river emerges into the Comtat Venaissin Plain, and the horizon expands to include Mount Ventoux to the east and Carpentras and its countryside straight ahead. The beautiful Hermitage Coomb precedes the next village.

Villes-sur-Auzon. – Pop 767. A street of plane trees and splashing fountains rings the village which is centred on a large square overlooked by old houses.

Return to the entrance to Villes-sur-Auzon and turn left along D 1 towards La Gabelle. As the road crosses the plateau, Mount Ventoux (N), the Dentelles de Montmirail (NW) and Carpentras Basin (W) fill the horizon. At the entrance to La Gabelle the view extends to the opposite slope, with the Nesque Gorge in the foreground and the Lubéron in the background (S)

Flassan. – Pop 295. *12 km - 7 miles from La Gabelle by D 217.* The minute village has ochre walled houses and a typically picturesque Provençal square.

Beyond La Gabelle the road drops gently to the floor of the Coste Chaude Coomb from which there is a view of the Sault Basin. *D 942, on the left, leads back to Sault.*

NÎMES ★★★

Michelin maps 240 fold 25 and 83 fold 8 – Pop 129 924 – *Facilities p 8*
For plan of built up area see the current Michelin Red Guide France

Nîmes makes the most of the Roman buildings and 18C gardens for which it is famous, floodlighting them in summer, staging bullfights in the arena where once gladiators fought, and festival concerts in the Temple of Diana and Jardins de la Fontaine... Gastronomic pleasures range from pickled olives to almond cakes (caladons).

The crocodile in chains. – The Nîmes city arms incorporate a crocodile in chains. It commemorates the defeat of Antony on the Nile by the Emperor Augustus, who rewarded his legionaries with grants of land in the flourishing colony of Provence. The town, called Nemausus after the spirit of a local Vauclusian spring, prospered until the end of 2C AD.

The Dark Ages. – The eclipse of the Romans, the overunning of the town by the Vandals, the Visigoths, the Saracens and finally the French themselves in the Wars of Religion, left few traces of a once civilized society. The town was Protestant and supported first the Albigensian then the Huguenot cause, in the times of war and persecution which occurred sporadically until the Revolution; in addition, in 15C, the city suffered plague, famine and earth tremors; in 16C, after riches had been heaped upon it by Francis I, it was devastated by war in 17C, then Louis XIV conferred privileges on the Nîmes' Academy; in 18C prosperity reigned and the town was embellished by fine houses and beautiful gardens. 19C saw the opening of a new age with the arrival of the railway, the second half of 20C, there were even further developments with new industries such as textiles, clothing, footwear and canning, an increase in local wine and the advent of mass tourism.

■ MAIN SIGHTS *time: 1 hour*

The Roman Monuments (Amphitheatre, Maison Carrée, Diana's Temple, Tour Magne) are open 9am to noon and 2 to 7pm (5pm in winter); the Amphitheatre is open 9am to 7pm in summer – except during performances; closed 1 May; inclusive ticket 20F available at any of the four monuments and museums.

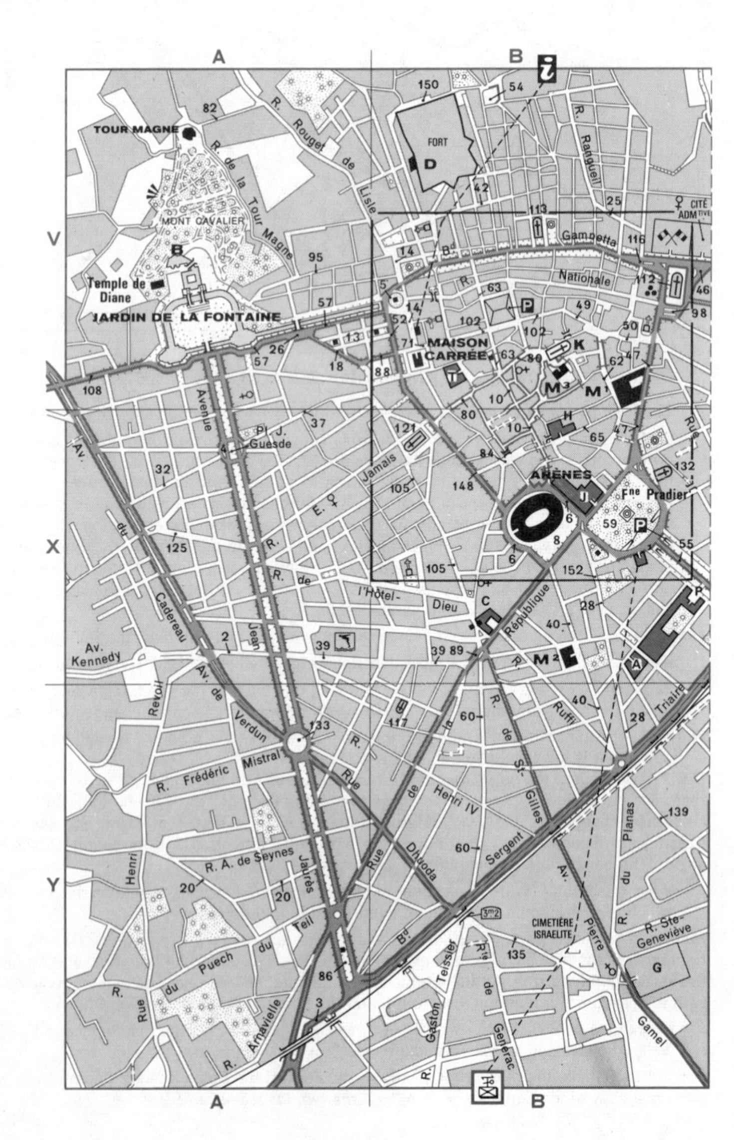

Amphitheatre★★★ **(Arènes)** (BX). – Although the Nîmes arena ranks twentieth in size among the 70 known to have existed, it is the best preserved. Dating from 50AD it is slightly smaller (131 × 100m - 430 × 329ft) than its contemporary at Arles and by the same architect, T. Crispius Reburrus. Its 21 000 spectators could vacate the stadium in five minutes by means of the many internal stairways and galleries, which are barrel vaulted in the Roman style. The attic storey where the slaves sat can be seen as well as the sockets that held the awning poles. The arena could be flooded to provide aquatic spectacles.

Between the eras of Roman and modern performances, the amphitheatre suffered many vicissitudes: the Visigoths turned it into a fortress, blocking arches, building towers, surrounding it with a deep moat; an independent society, the Knights of the Arena, held it for a period; it became a village, occupied by 2 000 poor people who built houses and a chapel within the oval perimeter, using stones from the theatre itself. Rehabilitation in 19C began with the removal of a 6m - 25ft layer of accumulated rubble.

Today, in summer the tiers fill again, as colourful crowds come to watch and cheer Spanish and Provençal style bullfights.

Continue the tour of the city along the Boulevard Victor Hugo.

Maison Carrée★★★ (BV). – The temple, which has been known as the Square House since 16C, despite its obvious rectangular shape, was built in 1C BC probably overlooking the Forum. The dedication is uncertain; it may have been to Jupiter, Juno and Minerva, since the building was known as the Capitol until 16C, or else to Rome and Augustus. It is the best preserved of all Roman temples still standing and shows strong Greek influence. The building's length is twice its width; the podium and pediment are each one fifth of the overall height. The sanctum, two thirds of the length, is surrounded by semi-engaged columns which extend to form a peripteral portico above a flight of 15 steps. The capitals are Corinthian, beneath an architrave decorated on three sides with carved rosettes and acanthus leaves.

(After photo by Ed. Estel, Blois)

The Nîmes Venus.

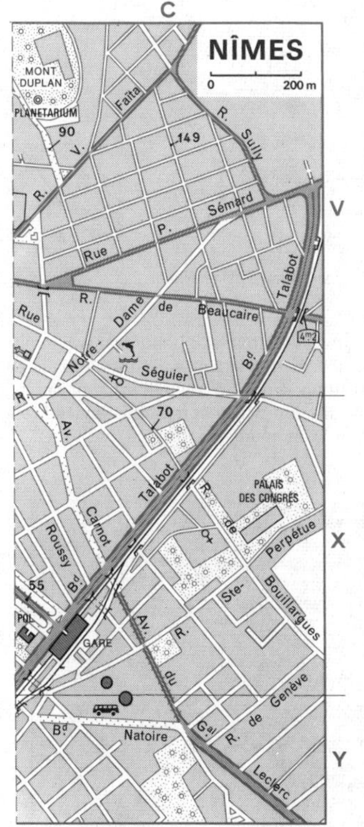

Aspic (R. de l') .... BVX 10
Courbet (Bd Amiral) ..... BV 47
Crémieux (R.) .... BV 49
Curaterie (R.) .... BV 50
Daudet (Bd Alphonse) ... BV 52
Gambetta (Bd) .... BV
Grand'Rue .... BV 62
Guizot (R.) .... BV 63
Madeleine (R.) .... BV 80
Nationale (R.) .... BV
Perrier (R. Général) ..... BV 102
République (R. de la) .... BXY
Victor-Hugo (Bd) .... BX 148

Abattoir (R.) .... AX 2
Ancienne-Gare (R. de l') .... AY 3
Antonin (Sq.) .... BV 5
Arènes (Bd) .... BX 6
Arènes (Pl.) .... BX 8
Arnavielle (R.) .... AY
Assas (Pl. d') .... AV 13
Auguste (R.) .... BV 14
Beaucaire (R.) CV
Boissier (R.G.) .... AV 18
Bosc (R. A.) .... AY 20
Bouillargues (R.) CX
Bourgogne (R.) .... BV 25
Briand (Pl. Aristide) ..... AV 26
Briçonnet (R.) .... BX 28
Cadereau (Av) .... AX
Cadereau (R.) .... AX 32
Carnot (Av.) CX
Chassaintes (R.) .... AX 37
Cirque-Romain (R. du) .... BX 39
Cité-Foulc (R.) .... BX 40
Clérisseau (R.) .... BV 42
Condé (R. de) .... BV 46
Dhuoda (R.) .... BY
Dr-Cantaloube (Pl.) ..... BV 54
Faïta (R. V.) CV
Feuchères (Av.) .... BX 55
Fontaine (Q. de la) ...... AV 57
Gamel (Av. P.) .... BY
Gaulle (Espl. de) .... BX 59
Générac (Rte) .... BY
Générac (R.) .... BY 60
Genève (R. de) .... CY
Greffes (R. des) .... BX 65
Guesde (Pl. J.) .... AX
Henri IV (R.) .... BY
Hôtel-Dieu (R.) .... BX
Jamais (R. E.) .... AX
Jardins (R. des) .... CX 70
Jaurès (R. J.) .... AY
Leclerc (Av. Gén.) .... CY
Mallarmé (R. Stéphane) .. AV 82
Marché (Pl. du) .... BX 84
Martyrs-de la R. (Pl.) .... AY 86
Mistral (R.) .... AY
Molière (R.) .... BV 88
Montcalm (Pl.) .... BX 89
Mont-Duplan (Av.) ...... CV 90
Natoire (Bd) .... CY
Notre-Dame (R.) CV
Notre-Dame et St-Castor (Égl.) .... BV K
Pasteur (R.) .... AV 95
Péri (Pl. G.) .... BV 98
Planas (R. du) .... BY
Porte-de-France (R. de la) .... BX 105
Puech-du-Teil (R.) .... AY
Rangueil (R.) .... BV
Revoir (R. H.) .... AY
Roosevelt (Av. Franklin) .... AV 108
Rouget-de-Lisle (R.) ..... AV
Roussy (R.) CX
Ruffi (R.) .... BY
St-Baudille (Égl.) .... BV 112
St-Charles (Égl.) .... BV 113
Saintenac (Bd Étienne) .. BV 116
St-François-de-Sales (Égl.) .... BY 117
St-Gilles (Rte de) .... BY
St-Gilles (R.) .... BY
St-Paul (Égl.) .... BX 121
Ste-Anne (R.) .... AX 125
Ste-Geneviève (R.) ...... BY
Ste-Perpétue (Égl.) ...... BX 132
Ste-Perpétue (R.) CX
Séguier (R.) CV
Sémard (R. Pierre) CV
Séverine (Pl.) .... AY 33
Seynes (R. A. de) .... AY
Simon (R. A.) .... BY 35
Sully (R.) CV
Talabot (Bd) CX
Teissier (R. Gaston) ..... BY
Tour-de-l'Évêque (R. de la) .... BY 139
Tour Magne (R.) .... AV
Triaire (Bd Sergent) ..... BY
Verdun (Av. de) .... AY
Villars (R.) .... CV 149
Vincent (R.) .... BV 150

The main shopping streets are indicated at the beginning of the list of streets, which accompany town plans.

For a pleasant stroll in a town look for the pedestrian streets indicated on the town plans.

(After photo by Ciccione, Rapho)

The Maison Carrée, Nîmes.

Like the amphitheatre, the Maison Carrée's fortunes have been varied: it has served as a town hall, a private residence, a stable, and Augustinian monastery church... Colbert, Louis XIV's minister, suggested dismantling it stone by stone and re-erecting it at Versailles.

At long last it was bought by the town and the exterior restored and ultimately, after further vicissitudes, the interior adapted to serve, most appropriately, as a setting for the **Museum of Antiquities**★. Among the exhibits are a bronze head of Apollo, a colossal statue of the same god, mosaics, a statue of Venus, discovered in fragments and reassembled, a white marble head of Venus, friezes and funerary columns.

Turn left into the Quai de la Fontaine (**AV** 57) *which parallels the canal.*

Jardin de la Fontaine★★ (**AV**). – *Floodlit in summer until 11.30pm.* The garden is the unexpected creation of an 18C army engineer.

Planted with tall densely foliated trees, pines and cedars, shading lawns, terraces and stone balustraded paths, and filled with flowers, the gardens extend from the famous Nemausus spring (**B**) up the slopes of Mount Cavalier to the white octagonal form of the Tour Magne *(see below)*.

The Jardin de la Fontaine, Nîmes.

In Roman times the area was almost a quarter on its own with the spring, a theatre, a temple and baths; of these remain a *piscina,* a double flight of stairs, and the **Temple of Diana** now largely in ruins, which provides a romantic setting for summer festival recitals.

Since the creation of the gardens in 18C, the spring water was collected in a mirror-like pool surrounded by balustraded walks, before flowing through a water garden to the canal.

Tour Magne★. – The great octagonal tower, composed of three diminishing storeys, was built around the end of 1C BC as one of the 19 towers in the town's circuit wall, probably as a watchtower but possibly as a victory memorial. The top storey is now missing. It is a long climb even to the base of the tower and another 140 steps to the top which commands a **view**★ of Mount Ventoux (NE), the Alpilles (ESE), Nîmes, the Vistre Plain and the Garrigues (N).

NÎMES

Antonin (Square) . . . . **BV** 5
Arènes (Bd des) . . . **BX** 6
Arènes (Pl. des) . . . **BX** 8
Auguste (R.) . . . . . . **BV** 14
Bernis (R. de) . . . . **BVX** 16
Bouquerie (Square de la) . . . **BV** 24
Bourgogne (R. de la) **BV** 25
Bruxelles (Bd de) . . . . **BX** 30
Calade (Pl. de la) . . . . **BV** 33
Chapitre (R. du) . . . . **BV** 35
Château (Pl. du) . . . **BV** 38
Comédie (Pl. de la) . . . . **BV** 44
Condé (R. de) . . . . . **BV** 46
Couronne (Square de la) . . . **BX** 48
Crémieux (R.) . . . . . . **BV** 49
Curaterie (R. de la) . . **BV** 50
Daudet (Bd Alphonse) . . . **BV** 52
Feuchères (Av.) . . . . **BX** 55
Fort (R. du) . . . . **BV** 58
Grand'Rue . . . . **BV** 62
Guizot (R.) . . . . **BV** 63
Halles (R. des) . . . . **BV** 66
Herbes (Pl. aux) . . . **BV** 68
Libération (Bd de la) . . . . . . **BX** 73
Lombards (R. des) . **BV** 77
Madeleine (Pl. de la) **BX** 78
Madeleine (R. de la) **BV** 80
Marchands (R. des) **BV** 83
Marché (Pl. du) . . . . **BX** 84
Pragues (Bd de) . . . **BX** 106
Saintenac (Bd Étienne) . . . . **BV** 116

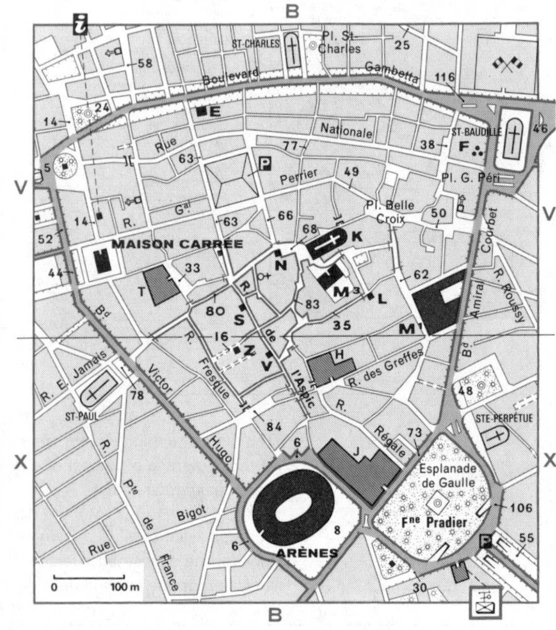

■ ADDITIONAL SIGHTS

Castellum (BV **D**). – The basin was the Roman collecting point from which water brought by the Pont du Gard aqueduct *(p 99)* was distributed in the town by means of 10 canal ducts.

Make for the tree shaded Boulevard Gambetta (no 20: birthplace of Alphonse Daudet, BV **E**).

Augustus Gate (BV **F**). – The gate, more properly called the Arles' Gate, is a relic of an entrance through the 1C BC perimeter. It comprised two roads for wheeled traffic flanked by pedestrian paths beneath narrow arches. The bronze now at the centre is of Augustus.

Museums of Archaeology★ and Natural History (BV **M**[1]). – *Open 9am to noon and 2 to 6pm; closed Sunday mornings, Tuesdays in winter, 1 and 2 January, 1 May, 1 and 11 November, 24, 25 and 31 December; 6F combined ticket for all the museums.* Displays of statuary, Roman glass, Greek pottery (8C BC-6C AD) and **coins.**

On the Ist floor the ethnographic section includes masks, costumes and arms from Africa, Asia, Oceania and Madagascar; the natural history section includes regional exhibits.

Pradier Fountain (BX). – The fountain executed in 1848 by the sculptor Pradier depicts Nîmes surrounded by allegorical fluvial figures. His model was his mistress, Juliette Drouot, who later became Victor Hugo's mistress.

Fine Arts Museum★ (Beaux-Arts) (BX **M**[2]). – *Same times and charges as the museums of Archaelogy and Natural History.* On the ground floor is a huge mosaic depicting the proposal of Admetus' hand in marriage. The collection comprises paintings of 17-18C French School and contemporary artists as well as the major European schools of 16-19C.

Old Nîmes. – The old city lies around the cathedral with interesting houses in the following streets: **Regis House** (**L**), **no 14 Rue du Chapitre** where the façade is 18C, the paved courtyard 16C; **no 1 Rue de la Madeleine** (BV **80**), where there is a carved Romanesque street front (**N**); **no 8 rue de l'Aspic** (BVX) where three palaeochristian sarcophagi and a small funerary column have been embedded in the porch walls and there is also a Renaissance staircase (**S**), and **no 14** (**V**) has a 17C double spiral grand staircase; **no 3 Rue de Bernis** (**Z**) has a 15C front complete with mullioned windows and an inner court with an antique style well.

Notre-Dame and St-Castor (BV **K**). – The cathedral, which was originally erected in 1096, has been remodelled many times and in 19C underwent almost total reconstruction.

The west front, surmounted by a classical pediment, is decorated by a partly old, partly new, frieze of scenes from the Old Testament (Adam and Eve, Cain and Abel).

Museum of Old Nîmes (BV **M**[3]). – *Same times and charges as the Museums of Archaeology and Natural History (see above).* The museum is in the former episcopal palace which dates from 17C and affords a perfect setting for a collection of 17 and 18C furniture, notably six magnificent cupboards, massive in size and richly carved with Biblical and bucolic scenes.

In addition there are displays of handsomely embroidered 18C waistcoats, materials and textile printing blocks, a small stocking weaving loom... Two rooms are devoted to tauromachie (bullfighting) – one in the Spanish style, the other Provençal.

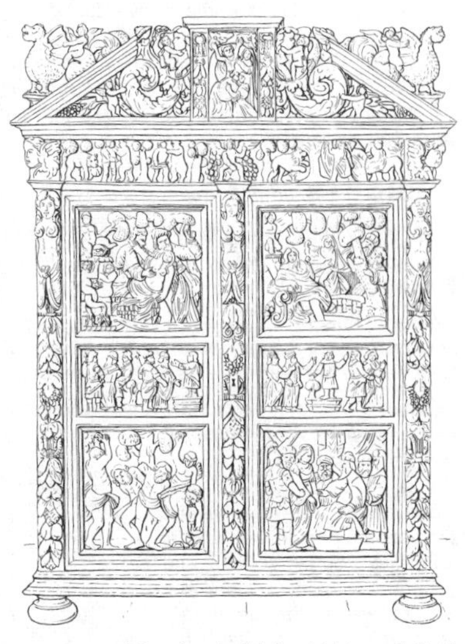

(After photo by Ed. Gaud, Moisenav-le-Petit)

Cupboard from Museum of Old Nîmes.

EXCURSIONS

The Garrigues. – *11 km - 7 miles along D 979 to the junction with D 135 where you join the drive described on p 118.*

Nages Oppidum; Perrier Spring. – Michelin map 83 folds 8 and 9. *Round tour of 42 km - 26 miles – about 2 1/2 hours. Leave Nîmes by D 40 going west.*

Caveirac. – Pop 1 879. In the centre of the village stands an impressive 17C horseshoe shaped château. The carriage porch is so big that it bestrides the road (D 103).

Continue along D 40 for 5 km - 3 miles, turn left into D 737.

Nages Oppidum. – *3/4 hour on foot Rtn. Park the car in Nages and follow the marked, stoney path up the hill.* Excavations *(in progress, no entry)* show that the settlement was inhabited in pre-history, surrounded by a perimeter wall with gateways and three towers. View of Mount Ventoux (NE), the Lubéron Range (E), the Alpilles (ESE), the Camargue (SE) and, on the coast, the Grande Motte (SSW) and Sète Mountain (SW).

Just before entering Nages on the return, walk along the first street on the left to see the Roman cistern which still provides water for the village's small fountains.

Take D 345 through Boissières (overlooked by a much restored medieval castle) *and D 107 on the left. Turn right into N 113 and left into D 139.*

Perrier Spring. – *Guided tour (time: 50 minutes) 9 and 10am and 1.30, 2.30 and 3.30pm; closed weekends and holidays and 24 December to 2 January.* The spring forms an underground lake (15°C-58°F). The abundant natural gas is captured and reinserted in the water under pressure. The visitor tours bottling, labelling and packing plants. Annual consumption in the Common Market, Switzerland and the USA exceeds 700 million bottles.

The N 113 brings you back to Nîmes.

ORANGE ★★

Michelin map 246 fold 24 – Pop 27 502 – *See town plan in the current Michelin Red Guide France*

Two monuments, a theatre and a commemorative arch, are all that now stand of the proud Roman city of Arausio. The other buildings have to be imagined from excavated foundations and incomplete remains, the town having been overrun by the Alamans and Visigoths in the Dark Ages and the stone quarried in succeeding centuries to construct ramparts and other fortifications, municipal buildings and private houses.

HISTORICAL NOTES

Roman Orange. – The Romans captured the Celtic market town at their second assault in 102 BC when the famous General Marius avenged the death of 100 000 legionaries, killed three years earlier by the town's ferocious Cimbrian and Teuton defenders.

Once in possession, the Romans built a theatre, arena, circus, gymnasium, temples, baths and a commemorative arch.

Dutch Orange. – In the 12C the town had become the capital of a minor principality whose rulers were heir to the German duchy of Nassau, subsequently increased by extensive territorial grants in the Netherlands.

In 16C, the then prince of Orange and Nassau, William the Silent, transformed his fief into the United Provinces with himself as first stadtholder; his great grandson lost the French holding to Louis XIV *(see below)* but in 1689 gained a kingdom when he and his wife were invited to become joint sovereigns of England, as William and Mary of the House of Orange. A separate branch remains to this day, the ruling house of the Netherlands.

French Orange. – The city was fortified in 1622 by Maurice of Nassau with a castle and surrounding wall built of stone taken from the remaining Roman monuments; the Roman arch was transformed into an outlying fort and the theatre incorporated in the ramparts. The town soon fell, however, when it was attacked in 1672 by French forces under the Count de Grignan *(p 77)*, and gave Louis XIV an early victory in his war against the Netherlands, concluded only in 1713 with the Treaty of Utrecht.

Today Orange is a peaceful provincial town with one unique sight, the theatre, and numerous small squares and shaded streets lined by 19 and 20C houses. For the first time in 2 000 years, it is no longer on France's main road: the N 7 has been relieved by the A 7, the **Autoroute du Soleil.**

■ SIGHTS *time: 2 hours*

Visitors approaching Orange from Montélimar along the road N 7 will see the Commemorative Arch first, but we suggest that anyone arriving from elsewhere should begin with the Roman Theatre.

Roman Theatre★★★(Théâtre Antique). – *Open 1 April to 30 September 9am to 6.30pm; the rest of the year 9am to noon and 2 to 5pm; closed 1 January, 1 May and 25 December; 10F combined ticket with the Municipal Museum (p 97).*

Exterior. – The theatre is known as the most beautiful and best preserved Roman Theatre in existence. It was constructed in the last decade BC in Augustus' reign, to the same dimensions as the one at Arles but the tiers are built into a hillside, affording both speed and economy in construction. The « finest wall in the Kingdom » as Louis XIV described the front overlooking the square, is 103m - 338ft long, 36m - 118ft high. In Roman times, the square was probably a garden, surrounded on all sides by a colonnade which, at the foot of the theatre wall, measured 8m - 25ft across. The row of projecting stones at the top originally supported awning poles.

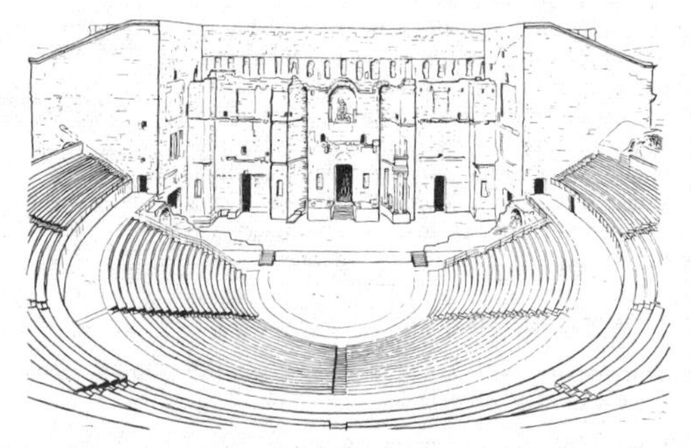

The Roman Theatre, Orange.

Interior. – Inside, the stage has lost its decorated ceiling, columns and statues but can still be imagined as the setting for dramatic presentations; the perfection of the accoustics may be checked by climbing to the top tier and listening to someone speaking on the stage.

The Roman Theatre of Orange is also unique in still possessing its imperial statue: Augustus, discovered in fragments but now reassembled, stands 3.55m - 10ft 2ins tall in the central alcove.

Gymnasium and Capitol. – Go through the theatre to the excavations of a former temple and the gymnasium 400m - 1 312ft long by 80m - 262ft wide. Only two other Roman gymnasiums are known.

It is believed that the Orange one comprised a colonnade encircled courtyard, complete with baths, and an athletics track enclosed by a two storey portico. The track was divided into three lanes, one open, one covered, one enclosed, all 180m - 591ft long and all straight. Combats were staged at the far end on a raised stone platform at the centre of a majestically colonnaded dais on which there once stood, probably in Hadrian's time, a grand central temple of which the foundations and podium can still be seen.

A second, small temple 28m - 92ft away on the site of the town reservoir, was approached by a double staircase. Dominating all, was a grandiose capitol of three temples on a rectangular east-west podium 60m - 197ft wide, and heavily buttressed to north and south.

Commemorative Arch★★. – The Orange Arch is in the later triple-arched style and was built between 21 and 26 AD. It is the third largest in existence and the best preserved, particularly the north face (the west has been restored).

It celebrates Roman military and naval prowess, in particular the exploits of the II legion which colonized Orange in 36 BC. Note especially (north face, top central relief) the vanquishing of the Gauls, middle ranges, left and right) a naval battle – prows, anchors, ropes, etc.; (lower east face) prisoners in chains; coffered vaulting.

(After photo by Arch. Phot., Paris)

The Commemorative Arch, Orange.

St-Eutrope Hill. – *Take Montée des Princes-d'Orange-Nassau; at the top of the hill bear left. After skirting a wall you will see the car park on the right. Walk along the path which crosses the moat of the former princely palace to Square Reine-Juliana; on the left excavations of the former palace; (viewing table beside the statue of the Virgin).*

The **view★** includes in the foreground, the Roman theatre; in the middle distance, the town; in the far distance, the Marcoule atomic energy centre, the Rhône plain and surrounding mountains. To the left are the ruins of the capitol and gymnasium.

Former Cathedral of Notre-Dame. – Antique inspired carvings still decorate the southern porch of the cathedral. The interior is Provençal Romanesque.

Municipal Museum. – *Open 9am to noon and 2 to 6.30pm (5pm 1 October to 31 March); closed 1 January, 1 May, 25 December. Combined ticket with Roman Theatre.*

The museum's lapidary department contains relics of a unique land survey, inscribed on marble, of the area round Orange made in 77 AD; the local history department has illustrations of the manufacture of printed cloth for which the town was known in 18C.

EXCURSION

The Princes of Orange Road. – *101 km - 63 miles NE – allow one full day. Leave Orange by D 975.*

The road *(109 km - 67 1/2 miles long)*, which links the Rhône Valley and the High Alps by way of the north face of Mount Ventoux, Vaison-la-Romaine, the Perty Pass (alt 1 303m - 4 210ft), was probably travelled by Hannibal when he crossed the Alps in 218 BC with an army of 60 000 and the famous elephants. It was certainly and with considerable frequency ridden from 14 to 18C by members of the House of Orange-Nassau as they journeyed between their domains which, at one time, included territory in the Netherlands, in the Lahn Valley (east of Koblenz) in Germany and, of course, Orange.

The road goes through Camaret, where two gates of the medieval city walls remain, past mile upon mile of vineyards (Rasteau, just off the road is a wine centre) and along the Ouvèze. There is a view to the right (SE) of the Dentelles de Montmirail.

Vaison-la-Romaine★★. – *Description p 119.*

Leave Vaison by D 938 going SE; after 3.5 km - 2 miles turn left into D 54.

Entrechaux. – Pop 724. The village is overlooked by the ruins of a medieval castle.

Continue along D 13 going NE.

Mollans-sur-Ouvèze. – Pop 690. The small village, on the banks of the Ouvèze, is the proud possessor of a square, decorated with a typical, local style fountain, and a bridge which spans the river in a single arch. On either side of the latter is a square belfry, erected on the foundations of a round tower once part of the perimeter wall, and an attractive corbelled chapel.

Pierrelongue. – Pop 84. The village church is strangely perched upon a high rock.

Buis-les-Baronnies. – *Description p 53.*

D 546 goes up the Ubrieux Gorges, deeply hollowed by the Ouvèze River, before continuing up the valley proper.

St-Auban-sur-l'Ouvèze. – *Description p 54.*

The road (D 65) from St-Auban to Labouret is described, in the reverse direction, on p 53.

Orpierre. – *Description p 54.*

Make up your own itineraries

- ***The map on pages 4 to 6 gives a general view of tourist regions, the main towns, individual sights and recommended routes in the guide.***
- ***The above are described under their own name in alphabetical order (p 27) or are incorpored in the excursions radiating from a nearby town or tourist centre.***
- ***In addition the Michelin Maps nos 80, 81, 83, 84 and 93 show scenic routes, places of interest, viewpoints, rivers, forests...***

The ORGNAC Aven ★★★

Michelin map 240 fold 23 – *Local map p 52*

The great hole in the ground was ignored until 1935 when the speleologist **Robert de Joly** (1887-1968) descended into it and discovered a series of chambers so extensive that even now the system has not been fully explored. (Tourist caves: 1/5 explored area.)

The caves *(avens)* are especially interesting because the natural development of underground streams, fed by infiltration and through fissures in the calcareous rock. It was tumultuously interrupted at the end of the tertiary era some 50 million years ago by a major earthquake;

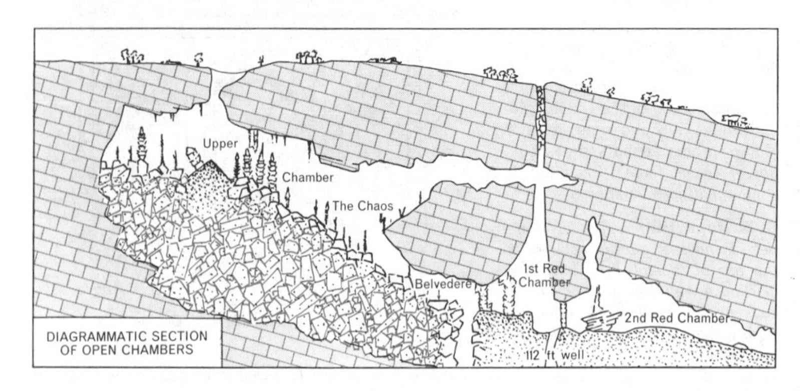

as a result new faults appeared, old fissures broke in different directions, boulders fell from the cave roofs. Afterwards the streams filtered along new courses, bored new passages. Stalagmites and columns made of joined stalagmites and stalactites were toppled and broken, but new ones have grown on the debris as slim spikes formed drop by drop on what had been ancient columns, or rose from former stalagmites which had fallen at an angle, thus creating forked shapes like antlers or tree branches. Climatic variations following the quake, altered the water flow: warm and humid periods would add 2" to a stalactite in 100 years, ice ages halted growth until the thaw brought a rush of water, often along new channels and possibly, therefore, including new salts which affected the formations' colouring.

(After photo by Alix Bagnères-de-Bigorre)

The Orgnac Aven.

TOUR *about 1 hour*

Guided tour 1 March to 15 November, 9am to noon and 2 to 6pm (5pm in March, October and November); 23F; temperature: 13 °C - 55 °F; 788 steps.

The upper chamber is vast: 250m - 820ft long, 125m - 410ft wide and between 17 and 40m - 200 and 450ft high. A pale blue light, filtering through the hole increases the « other world » aspect of massed boulders supporting magnificent stalagmites.

The **Chaos Chamber** is outstanding for the many hued « curtain » which falls from a fissure in the roof. A steep staircase *(393 steps)* leads to the belvedere of the First **Red Chamber:** the scene is like a science fiction film set with all red concretions in a setting of deep red rock walls and floors, coloured by carbonate of lime in the water and a stratum of ferruginous clay. Nearby is a well, the deepest in the aven, 34m - 112ft; beyond are a second Red Chamber and a cave 180m - 600ft below ground level.

■ The ORGNAC PLATEAU

(South or right bank of the Ardèche) – Local map pp 38-39

Aiguèze. – Pop 182. The old fort's ramparts command a good **view**★ of the river.

Les Crottes. – A village deserted since 3 March 1944, when the villagers were all shot.

The Forestière Aven★. – *Open 1 June to 31 August, 10am to 7pm; in April, May and September, 10am to noon and 2 to 6pm; time: 1 hour; 21F.*

The cave is not far below ground and is easily accessible. The dramatically lit chambers are rich in attenuated concretions such as the macaroni-like strips which hang from the roof, variegated stalactite curtains, phantasmagoric and eccentric formations and floors bristling with stalagmites. A small zoo has a variety of crustaceans, fish, batrachia and insects.

Gaud Bend Belvedere★★. – It commands a good **view**★★ of the river at the foot of the Gaud Rock Cirque.

The Orgnac Aven★★★. – *See above.*

The PONT DU GARD ★★★

Michelin map 246 fold 25 – *Local map p 118*

The vigour of the construction, the perfect proportions, the creamy gold stone against the green river valley have made the Pont du Gard an impressive and majestic sight since it was built nearly 2 000 years ago.

The aqueduct. – The Gard aqueduct was constructed by Agrippa in about 19 BC to carry the water of the Eure near Uzès *(p 116)* to Nîmes some 25 miles away. A covered canal was constructed entirely of stone, with openings only for ventilation and maintenance, and an incline of 34cm per km or 1:300 falling more steeply just before the valley to reduce the height of the bridge. The maximum daily flow was 20 000 cubic m - 44 million gallons which provided 400 litres of water per person *(p 19)*.

Whenever Nîmes was besieged, as often happened, the aqueduct was breached. From 4C it ceased to be maintained, so that lime deposits built up, until finally by 9C the course had become blocked and it had fallen into disuse. Land holders along the course thereupon began to remove the dressed stones for their own use. In 19C, after 1 000 years of neglect, it was restored by Napoleon III.

The bridge★★★. – The water channel *(specus)* is carried 130ft high over the river valley by the topmost of three tiers of arches which form the bridge. It is composed of dressed blocks of masonry, some weighing as much as 6 tons, which were laid without mortar, the courses being held together with iron clamps. The stone was lifted into position by block and tackle with goats as auxiliaries and a winch worked by a massive human treadmill.

The Pont du Gard.

The three stages are recessed, the piers in line one above another. Statistical details are: height above the Gardon at low water: 49m - 160ft; lowest level: 6 arches, 142m long, piers 6m thick, arches 22m high (465ft, 20ft, 72ft); middle level; 11 arches, 242m long, piers 4m thick, arches 20m high (792ft, 13ft, 65ft); top level, the one carrying the canal, 35 arches, 275m long, piers 3m thick, arches 7m high (900ft, 10ft, 23ft). The figures tell only part of the story: to avoid the monotony often seen in later constructions the architect varied the span of the arches very slightly within each range; each arch was constructed independantly to give flexibility in the event of subsidence. The stones obtruding from the face were scaffolding supports, and were left not only to facilitate maintenance work but to add interest to the surface, as do the ridges on the piers which held the semicircular wooden frames on which the arches were constructed.

TOUR

Leave the car in the car park beside the D 981 downstream from the bridge (during the summer the bridge is one-way).

Walk. – *Time: 1 hour. On the south bank of the Gardon off the D 981 is a small road which passes underneath the aqueduct.* Continue on the road to St-Privat Château and the banks of the Gardon from where the view of the aqueduct is superb.

Return towards the aqueduct, 50m before passing underneath it, bear right onto a winding path up through the undergrowth.

When you reach the third bend a path on the right leads to a **viewpoint** from which there is a good view of the aqueduct and the village of Castillon framed by one of the arches.

Continue up the winding path to the top level of the aqueduct (those who do not want to cross the bridge can take the path on the left, which passes under the last span of the bridge ending downstream from the bridge on the D 981. Walk across the bridge, either in the canal trough (impeded in places by chalk deposits), a safe but dull path because it has no outlook, or, if you have a good head for heights, along the canal's stone roof from which, of course, there are views on all sides. At the end descend the spiral staircase and turn right.

By the river. – *Hire of canoe or kayak for the Pont du Gard (time: 1/2 or 1 hour) or the Gardon Gorges (time: 1/2 or 1 day – p 118). It is essential to be able to swim.*

The RHÔNE Valley ★★★

Michelin map 246

The Rhône is France's biggest river: more water flows down it more swiftly than down any other. It may also be the most varied scenically, running from the High Alps on the Swiss border to the wide delta, marked by the Berre Lagoon and the Camargue, on the Mediterranean.

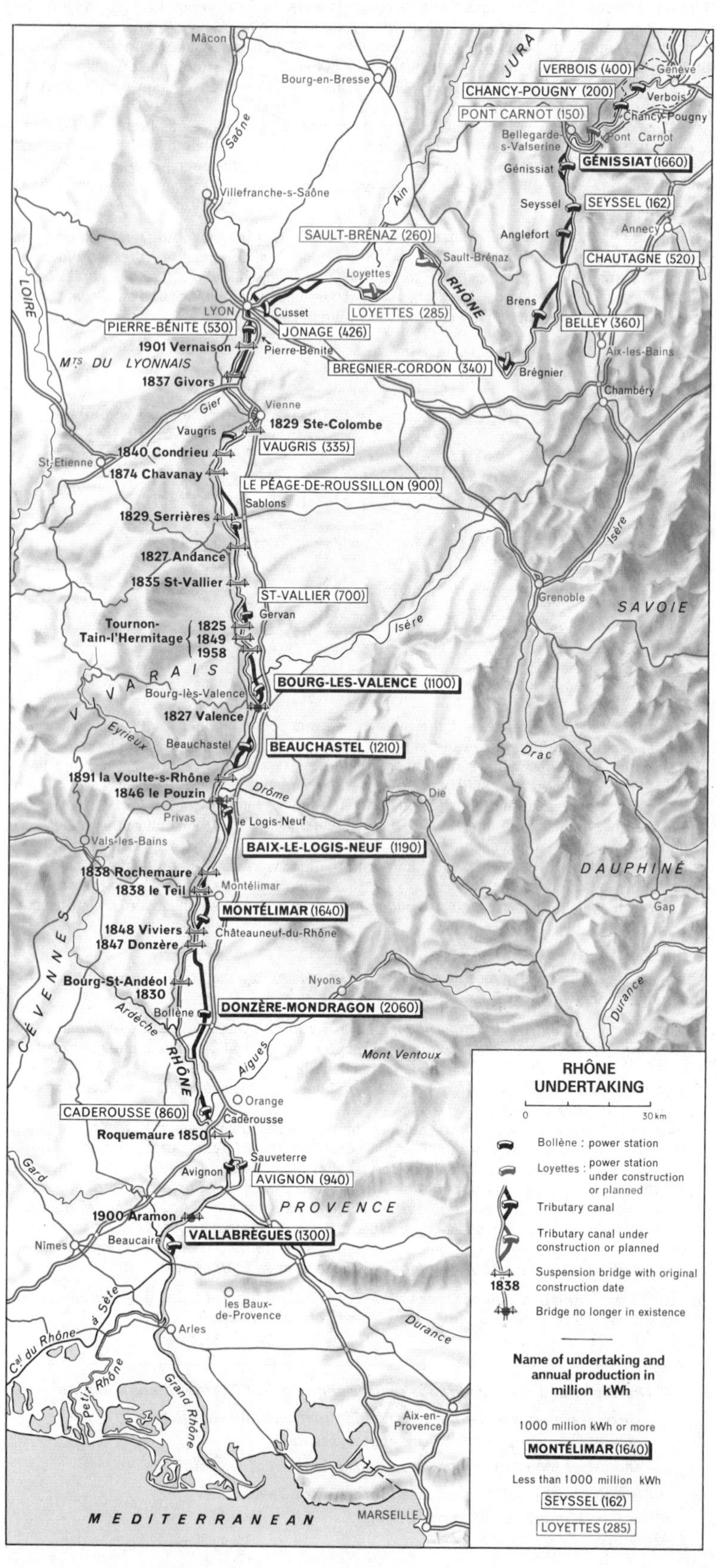

Its course is spanned by innumerable bridges, the flow diverted into tributary canals constructed to supply hydro-electric power stations; sometimes the banks are lined by factories, quarries and other industrial undertakings; sometimes by vineyards and orchards, by vast fields of fruit and early vegetables, and by the quaysides of large and small towns which have lived by their river trade for centuries. Elsewhere the banks give place to towering rock walls where the stream has carved a gorge.

The Mistral. – The wind dominates the valley below Valence on certain days, particularly in winter. Atmospherically it is a strong, dry, cold north-northwest draught which sweeps down when the pressure is high over the mountains, from the Massif Central to the Mediterranean, funnelling through the narrow Rhône Valley to everyone's discomfort and depression.

The waterflow. – South of Lyons, the river resembles a gigantic gash cleaving apart the Massif Central and the Pre-Alps. The course widens where the stream has been able to erode the permeable ground to the east or has brought down pebbles from the mountains and spread them around; elsewhere the water has bored downwards, through calcareous rock or soft limestone, to create spectacular defiles.

The origin of the tributaries accentuates the contrast between the east and west banks: from the west the rivers tumble headlong from the mountains and high plateaux and are subject to seasonal spates, whereas those from the east, though rising in the mountains, cross wide, temporizing, alluvial plains before joining the main stream.

The bridges. – The Romans built two bridges across the river, a wooden one at Arles and a stone one at Vienne.

Medieval builders constructed three more: the St-Bénézet *(p 45)* at Avignon in 12C and those at Lyons and Pont-St-Esprit *(p 105)* in 13C.

With 19C came the suspension bridge, but the 1939-45 War led to the destruction of nearly every one of the 17 which had been built, as traffic increased. Reconstruction has provided reinforced concrete structures or larger suspension bridges with central spans sometimes exceeding 200m (Le Teil: 235m, Vernaison: 231m).

The river as a thoroughfare. – The river has been an important thoroughfare for 2 000 years; landmarks in its history can be traced in the Roman remains in the towns along its banks, the ruins of medieval castles commanding the valley against invaders and marauding neighbours, the Romanesque and later churches, the walled or perched villages, the castles converted into Renaissance châteaux, all within sight of the river.

The Phocean Greeks of Marseilles are said to have sailed up the river on their way to Cornwall to get supplies of tin; in Roman and medieval times the chief commerce was wine, the shippers becoming the strongest and most prosperous guild in the region. Gradually there developed regular goods and passenger services between the towns, most of which had their own quays and warehouses.

In 1829 the first steam driven vessel appeared on the river and traffic increased still more. Then the railway arrived and river traffic diminished.

Only recently has it revived, owing to the creation by the state in 1934 of the **Compagnie Nationale du Rhône, (CNR).** The company's brief could be summed up as: to produce electricity, to make the waterway navigable to modern river traffic and to irrigate the countryside on a scale never contemplated before.

Today the traffic takes the form of flotillas of 1500 ton river barges carrying hydrocarbons, phosphates, metal products, cement and masonry stone from the valley itself, chemicals and salt from the Camargue – an annual total of 3 1/2 million tons.

The River Rhône undertaking. – The post-war CNR determined to transform the Rhône, from Lake Geneva to the Mediterranean, into a giant water staircase capable of producing 16 000 million kWh (total French production: 310 000 million kWh in 1984). 23 stations were planned of which 19 were to be constructed by the company. The section between Lyons and the sea was completed in 1980.

The hydro-electric stations and the river. – Each – and 23 have been constructed *(see map)*, comprises a dam across the river and a tributary supply canal to the station which stands at water level.

The canal ensures a constant supply sufficient for the necessary fall, after which the water returns to the river. Locks make the river navigable at all times.

Industrial expansion. – The large scale production of electricity has facilitated local industrial expansion so that now long stretches of the banks below Lyons are lined with refineries, metal and chemical works, textile mills, foundries, lime and cement works, an atomic plant at Marcoule and Le Tricastin and a uranium enrichment establishment at Pierrelatte.

Irrigation. – The final advantage of harnessing the river has been irrigation: water is now supplied to some 200 000ha - 1/2 million acres transforming vast areas, which until twenty years ago were arid plains, into fertile market gardens, orchards and vineyards.

Descent of the river by boat. – Passenger steam yachts with ample seating – some including full dining saloons, others milk and snack bars – sail up and down the Rhône between Lyons and Arles from April to October. For further details apply to S.N.C.M. Lyon, 3, rue du Président Carnot 69002, ☎ 78.42.22.70.

For boat trips on the Petit Rhône passing through the Camargue, see p 63.

MONTÉLIMAR TO AVIGNON★★ *– 60 km - 38 miles - allow 1 day*

Come out of Montélimar (p 90) by Avenue J Kennedy, N 102, going W; after the bridge across the canalized river, turn left into D 237. This small road runs between the Châteauneuf hydro-electric station canal and the natural riverbed.

The willow-lined road appears to lie at the very centre of the valley; to the right the Lafarge Cement works have bitten deeply into the Vivarais hillside; to the left the huge bulk of the Châteauneuf power station looms over you as you pass by at the foot of the wall, overlooking the out-fall; straight ahead are the ruins of the castle above Châteauneuf-du-Rhône. Beyond, the cliffs on either bank close in and you are at the entrance to the Donzère Defile.

At the entrance to Châteauneuf-du-Rhône, turn right towards Viviers.

N.-D.-de-Montcham. – *5.5 km - 3 miles from Châteauneuf. Turn left into D 126 and right into a steep uphill road at the entrance to Malataverne.* From a point to the right of the chapel there is a **view*** southeast of Mount Ventoux and in the foreground, the gap through which N 7, A 7 and D 169 all pass.

The two forts, **Châteauneuf** and **Châteauvieux,** both once in the hands of the bishops of Viviers, commanded the entrance to the defile. To the right, on its rock pedestal, rises the Flamboyant Gothic Viviers' Cathedral.

Donzère Defile**. – The Rhône has forced a narrow and beautiful passage through the rock; the sheer walls rising vertically on the east side contrast with the jagged spikes jutting out of the water to the west. A statue of St-Michael looks down on those who risk the hazardous passage through the defile.

The bridges at either end of the ravine are, obviously, excellent places from which to look along it. *(Park off the bridges. To reach the river, walk down a path on the west bank near Viviers to the municipal camping site – 1/4 hour on foot Rtn).* The upstream bridge spans the river where the tributary canal rejoins the main stream in a boiling, bubbling, confluence.

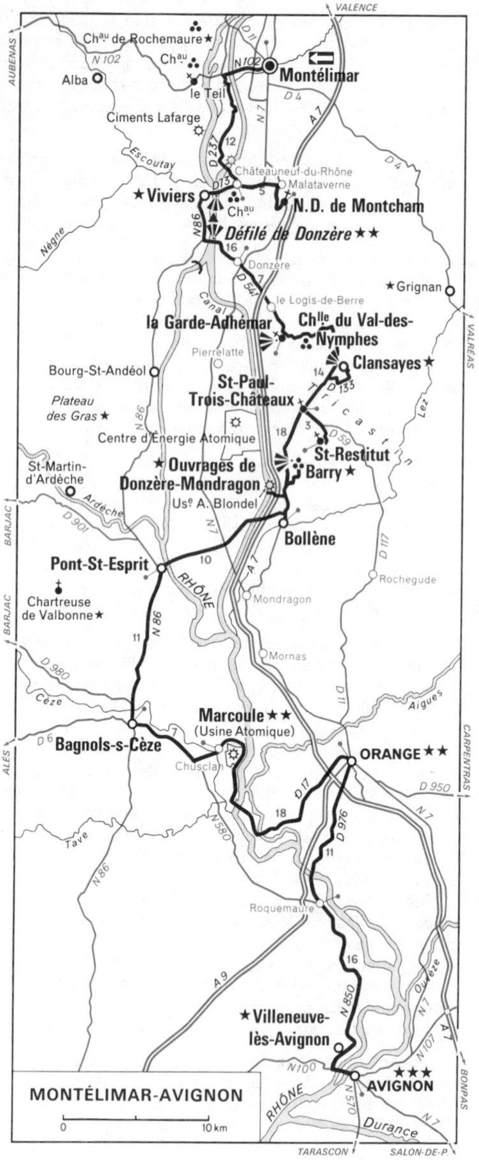

Viviers*. – Pop 3 287. *Facilities p 8.* The city is an old episcopal seat which dates back to 5C and gave its name to the Vivarais province of which it is the capital.

The bishops, who moved to Viviers in 4C after the destruction of Alba by the barbarians, began by building a stronghold to command the defile but finally accumulated a vast domain to the west of the Rhône – the east bank and hinterland were under the Holy Roman Empire.

By late 13C, however, after centuries of independence, when they minted their own coinage and acted as hosts to St Louis when he was travelling south to set out on the Seventh Crusade (1248), the bishops were finally compelled to recognize the royal suzerainty (1308).

In the Middle Ages the townspeople in true Midi or southern French style, used to celebrate the bishop and the church on Boxing Day (not a usual holiday in France) with a riotous Fools' Carnival. Ecclesiastical customs and personalities were parodied, a « mad » bishop was elected who ruled

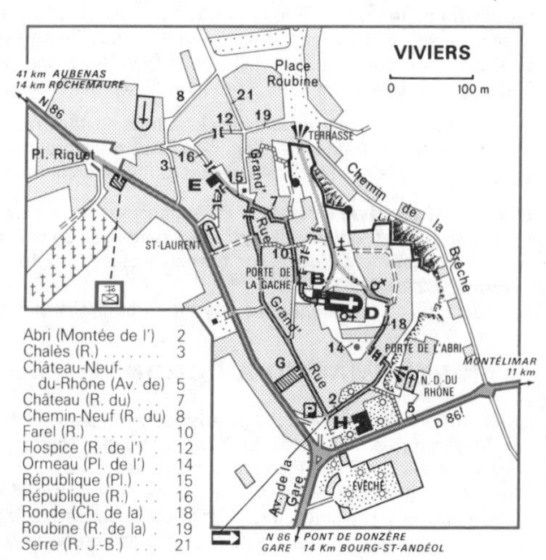

the city for three days while carnival reigned. After many decades, the bishops ceased to see the humour of the by then somewhat orgiastic event and put an end to it; although revived in subdued form, it finally ceased in 18C.
The ecclesiastical **old town**★ stands on the hill above the modern centre which extends down to the riverbank. The most interesting old houses are to be found between the Grand' Rue and the Place Riquet and lining the streets on the following walk.

Park the car in the small shaded square at the junction of D 86[i] and N 86. On one side is 18C bishopric, on the other, 18C Roqueplane House, now the town hall (**H**), each in its own garden.

Walk up the narrow Montée de l'Abri, from which there is a good view of the mouth of the defile, and turn left to pass through a gateway into the Place de l'Ormeau.

After looking at the Flamboyant decoration at the east end of **St Vincent's Cathedral** (**D**), go round to the north side, cross the open space and, by way of an alley, make for the far edge of the large terrace.
The view extends from right to left across the Rhône to the Lafarge quarries, the Montélimar Plain, the Châteauneuf power station and the old town roofs.

Return and continue round the cathedral and down the steps. The **tower,** (**B**) was originally part of the defences of the long gone Château-Vieux, where St Louis stayed on his way to the Crusade. The tower, which now serves as a belfry, is linked to the cathedral by a square portico; on the first floor is a Romanesque Chapel, higher still a 14C octagonal paved platform with a look-out turret, known as the Bramardière. Of 12C building of St Vincent's, there remain the porch and west front and the foundations of the nave. The chancel is notable for its finely ribbed vaulting and its stained glass fenestration.

On leaving, go down the steps and through the **Gache Gate** (Porte de La Gache – once the only communication between the old and new towns). Turn right into an alley leading down to the Place de la République. Standing on the corner of the square is the **Knights' House** (Maison des Chevaliers) (**E**) with a fine front of 1546 which includes richly framed windows and the two reliefs after which the house is named, a knightly tournament on the right and on the left a knightly cavalcade. *Return to the car by the Grand' Rue.*

(After photo by Trincano, Ed. Arthaud)

The Knights' House, Viviers.

Leave Viviers by N 86 going S; after 3 km - 2 miles bear left on to a bridge over the Rhône and D 86 to Donzère. Continue along D 541 which crosses over N 7 underneath the motorway to reach Le Logis-de-Berre, turn right in the direction of St-Paul-Trois-Châteaux. Almost immediately, however, turn off left up a small road to a perched church.

La Garde-Adhémar. – Pop 1 077. The perched church has long been a famous local landmark. The medieval village was a stronghold held by the Adhémar family who, in 16C, were replaced as the local overlord by the Baron de la Garde, a shepherd turned soldier who ended his career as an ambassador and commanding officer of all France's galleys. The Renaissance château he built has vanished but there remain, from earlier times, two **fortified gateways** on the north side of the town and the Romanesque **church**★ which has a two stage octagonal belfry, surmounted by a small spire (added later) and apses at either end – note the frieze encircling the west apse and the dependant chapels.
On 24 December each year the plain interior is the setting for the characteristic Provençal midnight mass complete with a « live crib » *(p 24).*
The **view**★ from the terrace embraces the Rhône Plain around Pierrelatte with the Dent de Rès rising above the Vivarais foothills.

Leave La Garde-Adhémar towards Pierrelatte and bear left on the narrow road (572 A) leading to Val-des-Nymphes.

Val-des-Nymphes. – In a small valley, alive with waterfalls, which may have been a pagan place of worship, as its name suggests, stand the ruins of 12C Romanesque Chapel: an apse with two tiers of arcading beneath a fine oven vault and an elegant Romanesque west front.

2 km - 1 mile beyond the chapel turn right into D 133 and 3 km - 2 miles further on, left into D 571, which climbs up to the once fortified village of Clansayes.

Val-des-Nymphes Chapel.

Clansayes★. – Pop 287. *Park the car on the esplanade and make for the end of the bluff on which stands a monumental statue of the Virgin.* The **view**★★ extends across the jagged Tricastin heights, deeply indented by erosion; rock falls have revealed a patchwork of coloured scars; enormous boulders are poised precariously on cliff edges awaiting their turn to fall. From this distance, the valley panorama is more extensive, reaching from La Garde-Adhémar (NW), across the Rhône-Pierrelatte Plain with uranium and industrial buildings clearly distinguishable, to the Lower Vivarais Mountains and the Dent de Rès.

(After photo by Lescuyer)

St-Paul-Trois-Châteaux Church.

St-Paul-Trois-Châteaux. – Pop 6 455. The old town is encircled by ramparts but it never possessed three castles *(trois châteaux)* – it may have acquired its name literally through a medieval clerical error! St-Paul does, however, possess a rare **cathedral**★ *(to visit apply at the presbytery 12 Place de l'Esplan or to Mme Ernet 6 Rue de l'Église)* begun in 11C and completed in 12C and a remarkable example, because it is so early, of pure style Provençal Romanesque.

The most striking exterior features are the height of the transepts and the mass of the nave; the austere aspect is relieved by the finely sculptured west doorway.

Enter through the north door. The cradle vaulted nave is 24m - 79ft high. The decoration includes a false triforium above the bay before the transept, recesses between pilasters, small columns surmounting a finely carved frieze and a remarkably planned apse. The organ loft is 18C, the unusual low relief on the second pillar on the left and mosaics behind the altar 12 and 13C respectively. Masons' marks and devices are visible both inside and out.

Take D 59 SE out of St-Paul, then turn right into D 59^A to St-Restitut.

St-Restitut Church.

St-Restitut. – Pop 630. The old perched village possesses a Provençal Romanesque **church** and an unusual funerary tower. The church has a carved Classical and Gallo-Roman inspired **decoration**★ visible at the east end, in the south porch and in the elegant cornice which runs above the capitals in the nave; note also the Corinthian capitals in the apsidal arcading. The funerary **tower** flanks the west wall and is said to have been built over the tomb of St Restitut, the external frieze appears to be 11C.

Return to St-Paul and take the road going south towards Bollène via D 71 and D 26 and then bear left on a road to Barry.

Barry★. – The village built into the hillside, with parts of some of the houses hollowed out of the rock, has been abandoned and overgrown. The approach road is rough but it leads to a bird's-eye **view**★★ of the Donzère-Mondragon power station, the Tricastin nuclear site, the Drôme Plain (NNE), the Vaucluse Plateau (SE), Lower Vivarais (NW) and the Donzère Defile to beyond Pont-St-Esprit (SSW).

The ruins of a 12C castle can be seen on the top of the hill.

Return to the main road and turn left.

Donzère-Mondragon Undertaking★ (Ouvrages de Donzère-Mondragon). – Donzère, a small market town built in tiers up a hillside below a 15C castle, came to fame as the site for the construction of the CNR's major hydro-electric installation between 1948-52. Although it is now over 25 years old, the station remains a giant among the Rhône projects and even among international hydro-electric undertakings. The feeder **canal,** the largest to be constructed to serve a hydro-electric station, is 28 km - 20 miles long, 145m - 476ft wide and some 10m - 33ft deep and had to be spanned by two rail and eight road bridges.

Controlling the waterflow on the Rhône River and the Canal are a river dam 1 500m - 4 921ft below Donzère, and two breakwater dams before the power station entrance and the canal's navigable course; these constructions enable the flow to be kept above 2 000m^3 - 440 000 gallons per second along the 17 km - 10 miles stretch to the station, where it is further controlled by the highest dam on the Rhône, a 375yds long complex combining a 26m - 85ft fall, the station outflow and a navigation lock 215yds long by 13yds wide – the lock uses the power station outflow as a supply source. Below the dam 25m^3 - 5 720 gallons of the current is diverted for irrigation purposes.

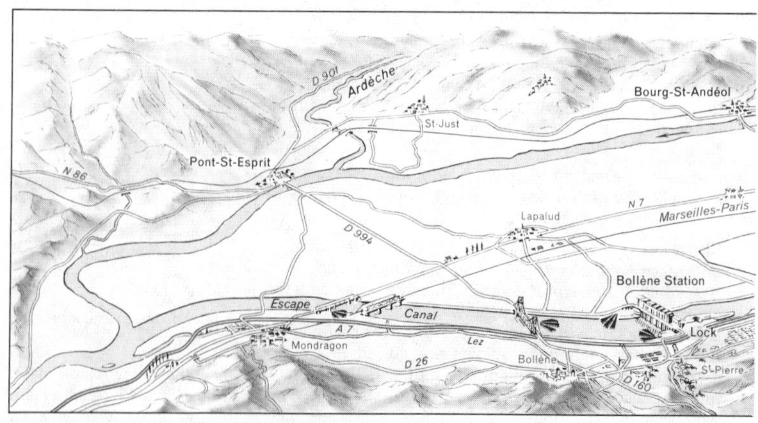

Donzère-Mondragon

Another benefit conferred by the construction is that one of the most difficult 40 km - 25 miles stretches of the Rhône is now by-passed by a canal enabling even the vast international barges to go all the way from the Mediterranean to Lyons.

Pierrelatte Atomic Energy Centre. – Upstream from the great **Bollène hydro-electric station** (capacity 2.1 milliard kWh *not open*) on the far bank between the canal and N 7, the French Atomic Energy Commission has built an isotope separation complex *(not open)*.
The centre, virtually a uranium refinery, spreads over 700ha - 1 730 acres and comprises four enrichment factories, the first and second treating the original substance to 2 and 8%, the third to 25% and the final one to more than 90%.
In 1979 on the same site a European uranium enrichment undertaking (EURODIF) came into service which should have reached full production in 1982 (covering 25% of the world's needs in enriched uranium). There is a carworthy road on the downstream side of the Bollène works and a terrace area on either bank affording comprehensive **views** of the entire Donzère-Mondragon undertaking.

Tricastin Nuclear Power Station. – *Guided tour daily except weekends and public holidays, 9am to noon and 2 to 5pm; apply in advance ☏ : 75 50 37 10, Service des Relations Publiques CPN de Tricastin, BP 9, 26130 St-Paul-Trois-Châteaux; time: 2 1/2 hours; passport required.* On the right bank of the Donzère-Mondragon canal, this nuclear power station includes 4 reactors with a total annual production of 24 000 million kWh. The station provides the electricity for the nearby uranium enrichment plant (EURODIF). The annual production of the latter supplies 100 reactors similar to Tricastin.

Continue along the small road going S to Bollène.

Bollène. – Pop 2 690. *Facilities p 8.* The town, which stands on a hillside, has been an agricultural marketing centre since the days of the Avignon popes. A few houses and fine doorways remain as mementoes of the past in what is now a typical Provençal town with wide shaded boulevards marking the line of the ancient ramparts and a web of narrow streets at the centre. From both the **Pasteur Garden** (Belvédère Pasteur) – the scientist was staying in the town in 1882 when he discovered an inoculation against swine fever – and **St Martin Collegiate Church** (**B**) *(open 1 July to 1 September 9am to noon and 3 to 7pm)*, a 12-16C former parish church which stands beneath its solidly built belfry on a hillock to the east of the town, there are good views of the surrounding countryside.
The **municipal museum** (**M**) – *open 1 April to 30 September 9am to noon and 2 to 7pm; closed Mondays and Tuesdays)*, located in a former Romanesque Chapel, possesses an interesting collection of **Picasso** and **Chagall** drawings besides a selection of local artists' paintings and sculpture.

BOLLÈNE

Chabrières (R. des) 5
Fabre (R. Henri) 7
Gambetta (Bd) 9
Giono (Av. Jean) 10
Hôtel-de-Ville (Pl. de l') 12
Louis (R. Auguste) 13
Paroisse (Montée de la) 14
Puy (R. du) 15
Récollets (Pl des) 16
République (Cours de la) 17
Tour (R. de la) 19
Zola (R. Émile) 21

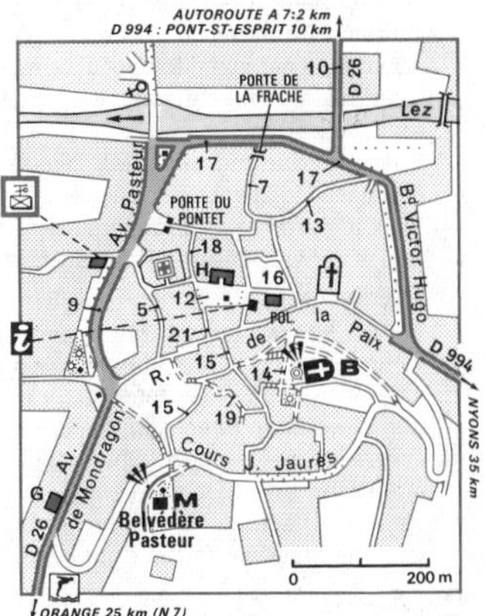

South of Bollène you may follow the east bank taking D 26 to Mondragon and N 7 to Orange or you may cross to the west bank taking D 994 to Pont-St-Esprit.

Pont-St-Esprit. – Pop 8 135. *Facilities p 8.* The town owes its name (in translation Holy Spirit Bridge) to the bridge over the Rhone constructed by the Brotherhood of the Holy Spirit Bridgebuilders between 1265 and 1309. Despite numerous subsequent bridges, the town has remained a major crossing and important halfway halt on the Rhône.
Park the car at the end of the Allées Jean-Jaurès and walk up the Rue St-Jacques. The street is lined by old town houses – notably 17C Roubin House (no 10 - **B**) and 12-16C Chevaliers or Knights' Mansion (no 2 - **D**) with a Romanesque window – and opens out into Place de l'Hôtel de Ville with 12C Roch House (**E**) and an old style mansion (**F**).

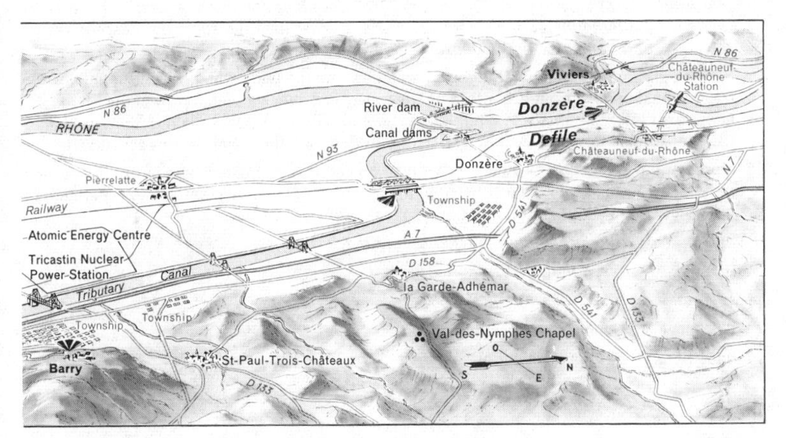

Undertaking

Paul Raymond Museum (M[1]). – *Open 1 June to 30 September, 10am to noon and 3 to 7pm; the rest of the year, only Wednesdays, Thursdays and Sundays 9am to noon and 2 to 5pm; closed Tuesdays, 1 January, 1 May, 14 July, 1 November and 25 December; 5F.*

This museum in the former town hall, contains collections pertaining to local prehistory and religious art (silver-gilt chalice and patera from the Languedoc area, 1650, and a canvas by the Provençal primitive Raymond Boterie portraying the Fall of the Angels, 1510). Of particular interest is the pharmacy, from the former hospital, with its splendid array of about 220 jars from the early 18C pottery workshops of Montpellier. Note also the fine selection of medieval Hispano-Moorish pieces. In the basement is the town's former ice house (1780). *To visit apply to the reception desk.*

Take Rue Haut-Mazeau to reach Place St-Pierre, a square bounded on three sides by 15C Parish Church of St-Saturnin, the Baroque façade of the Penitents' chapel, and 17C domed Church of St-Peter. The square's east side forms a **terrace** overlooking the Rhône, the quay and the bridge.

PONT-ST-ESPRIT

Haut-Mazeau (R.)	8	Couvent (R. du)	5
Joliot-Curie (R.)		Doumergue (Av. G.)	6
Minimes (R. des)		Gaulle (Av. du Gén.-de)	7
Mistral (Allées F.)	15	Hôtel-de-Ville (Pl. de l')	9
République (Pl. de la)	21	Jaurès (Allées J.)	10
St-Jacques (R.)	25	Jemmapes (R.)	12
		Paroisse (R. de la)	17
Allègre-Chemin (Bd)	2	Plan (Pl. du)	18
Bas-Mazeau (R.)	3	St-Pierre (Pl.)	26
Bruguier-Roure (R. L.)	4	19 Mars 1962 (R. du)	28

Descend the monumental, circular staircase to Quai de Luynes and walk towards the bridge. Just before you reach it glance to your left at the old public wash-house *(lavoir)* and the Renaissance windowed Maison du Roy (**K**).

The **bridge** *(pont)* is nearly 3 281ft long (London Bridge: 1 000ft); like a dam, it is slightly curved against the current.

In appearance it has suffered two major alterations: it has lost all trace of the medieval bastions which once defended it at either end and, although 19 of its 25 arches are ancient, two piers have been demolished to provide wider spans for modern shipping. *Walk to the centre of the bridge.* Downstream the Rhône flows past the town towards Avignon; upstream, a 15C Flamboyant Gothic doorway which was once the entrance to the collegiate church (N) stands near the site of the town citadel. To obtain a closer view of the doorway, take the stairway to the right of the Tourist Information Centre.

Head S along N 86.

Bagnols-sur-Cèze. – *Description p 51.*

An interesting short detour *(9 km - 6 miles)* can be made southeast of Bagnols off N 580 along D 865 through Chusclan to Marcoule.

Marcoule Atomic Energy Centre★. – The centre, which can be identified from afar by its two 80 and 100m tall chimneys (250 and 315ft), is surrounded by vineyards and retreating scrubland. It produces by transmutation, elements for industry, medicine and research and contributes energy to the national network.

(The EDF site to the north – between the Rhône and D 138 – in operation since 1973 and known as the **Phoenix Station,** is a prototype fast breeder reactor.)

Belvedere-museum★★. – *Access: via the D 138 E of Chusclan. The viewing platform: open daily 8am - 7pm; The museum: the galleries are open daily mornings and afternoons in July and August; April - June and September - October afternoons only except Tuesdays and Thursdays; afternoons during all school holidays, other than the summer ones; the rest of the year afternoons only on Wednesdays and weekends.*

Viewing platform: a panel on the raised area between the two exhibition halls identifies the main installations. From the platform there is also an extensive scenic view of the Rhône (E), Orange and its Roman Theatre (E), Mount Ventoux (E), the Comtat Plain (ESE), the Alpilles (S), the Ardoise iron and metalworks (S foreground) and the Lower Gard Valley (SW).

Museum: the first gallery presents the world of the atom, fission, nuclear energy and fuel and radio-activity; the second illustrates the function of the Marcoule plant, in the separation of plutonium 239 from uranium and the resultant energy.

Drive south along the Rhône, turn left across it to reach Orange.

Orange★★. – *Description p 96.*

Leave Orange by D 976; turn left into N 580.

Villeneuve-lès-Avignon★. – *Description p 132.*

Continue along the N 580 to Avignon (p 44).

Avoid visiting a church during a service.

The STE-BAUME Massif ★★

Michelin map 84 fold 14

Ste-Baume is the name of a forest and of a cave – *baoumo* is Provençal for cave – where, according to local tradition, Mary Magdalene spent her last 33 years; it is now a place of pilgrimage. The **forest**★★, some 138 hectares - 340 acres, sheltering at the foot of the steep northern face of Ste-Baume Massif, has an unexpectedly northern character owing to the huge beeches, limes and maples which thrive in an undergrowth of holly, ivy and yew. The brilliant white cliff of the massif, which contains the cave, rises as high as 250m - 820ft in places and provides excellent sport for mountaineers.

The Provençal Legend. – For 13 years after the crucifixion, Mary Magdalene lived with Jesus' mother until, together with her brother, Lazarus, her sister, Martha, and other saintly people, including St-Maximinus *(p 112)*, she was set adrift by the Jews of Jerusalem in a boat which came ashore at Stes-Maries-de-la-Mer *(p 108)*. The party split up, Mary retiring to the solitude of her cave at Ste-Baume until, anticipating death, she came down into the plain to receive the last communion from St-Maximinus at a spot, on N 560, a few hundred yards from the entrance to St-Maximin Abbey marked by the Petit Pilon Monument.

Since the early Middle Ages, on the feast of Ste-Mary Magdalene (22 July), midnight mass is celebrated in the cave which has become a popular place of pilgrimage; cairns were set up along the path by engaged couples who went to pray for a family – one stone per child.

Round tour starting from Gémenos

69 km - 43 miles - about 3 hours, excluding the ascent of St-Pilon

Gémenos. – Pop 4 548. *Facilities p 8.* The small town, where 17C château now serves as the town hall, stands where the small green St-Pons Valley opens into the larger Huveaune.

Drive 3 km - 2 miles up the D 2 along the St-Pons Valley.

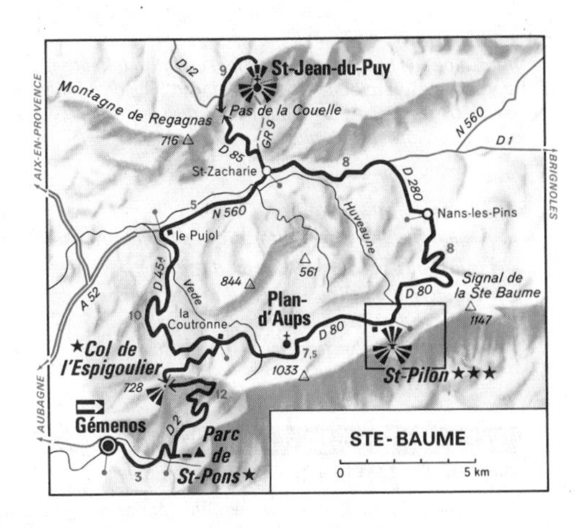

St-Pons Park★. – *Park the car before the bridge and walk along the path beside the stream. Open 1 April to 30 September, 9am to 8pm; the rest of the year 10am to 6pm; closed Mondays.* An old watermill fed by the St-Pons stream, a Vauclusian spring, and the extensive ruins of 13C Cistercian abbey, abandoned in 15C *(not open)*, are set in a well-wooded park of beech, spruce, hornbeam, ash and maple, uncommon trees for so southerly a latitude. In spring there are Judas trees in flower.

The road climbs the steep bare southern slope by a succession of hairpin bends.

Espigoulier Pass★ (Col de l'Espigoulier). – Alt 728m - 2 390ft. The views from the pass extend over the Ste-Baume Range itself (SW-SE), the Aubagne Plain (SW), St-Cyr Chain (SW), Marseilles (W) and the Étoile Chain (NW).

The descent down the north face offers further views of the Étoile and of Mount Ste-Victoire (N) beyond the Fuveau Basin. *Turn right into D 80 at La Coutronne.*

Plan-d'Aups. – The small health resort is distinguished by a correspondingly small Romanesque church.

The pilgrim hostel (Hôtellerie).– The hostellery 675m - 2 215ft up on the plateau in the lee of the forest, was rebuilt in mid-19C when the Dominicans eventually returned after the Revolution. It became a cultural and spiritual centre in its own right in 1968; in 1972 a chapel was created in the vaulted hall, the original pilgrim shelter.

To the left of the hostel is the austere cemetery of the former community of Dominicans.

Access to the cave. – *1 hour on foot Rtn. There are two alternative starts to the route: the first is along a path left of the hostel and through the Canapé, a group of moss-covered rocks; the second, which is easier, is from D 80-D 95 or the Oak Tree crossroads (Carrefour des Chênes), along the « Kings' Way ».* The paths meet at the Oratory crossroads *(Carrefour de l'Oratoire)* where a wide path on the right leads to a flight of steps *(150)* cut into the rock face; halfway up there is a decorated gate and a bronze Calvary in a niche to the left.

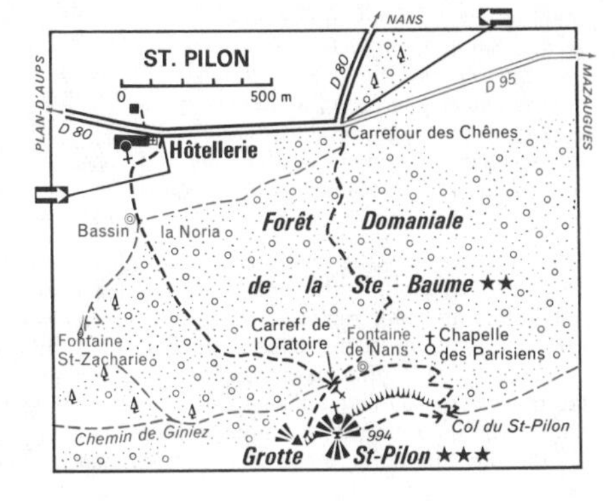

Terrace. – The stairway ends at a terrace on which a stone Cross and bronze *Pietà* have been set up as 13th Station of the Cross. The terrace itself commands a **view**★ of Mount Ste-Victoire and in the foreground, Plan d'Aups, the hostellery and dense woodland.

The Cave (Grotte) – The semicircular cave lies north of the terrace at an altitude of 946m - 3 105ft. Inside, to the right of the high altar, is a shrine with relics of the Magdalene brought from St-Maximin-la-Ste-Baume Abbey *(p 112)*; behind the altar, 3m - 10ft up the wall, is an irregular cavity, the only dry place in the cave, known as the Place of Penance, which contains a recumbent statue of the saint.

St-Pilon★★★. – *1 1/4 hour on foot Rtn starting at the Oratory cross roads. Pass in front of the oratory and follow the right hand path (red and white GR9 signs) which climbs to the abandoned Parisians' Chapel and continues by a zigzag route and a turn to the right to the St-Pilon Pass* (Col du St-Pilon). A column, since replaced by the small chapel, formerly marked the summit – hence the name. According to legend, angels bore Mary Magdalene to this spot seven times a day so that she might listen to the music of paradise.

From the St-Pilon (alt 994m - 3 260ft) there is a magnificent **panorama**★★★ *(viewing table)*: to the north, the hostel in the foreground, Mt Aurelien, Mt Regagnas and Mt Ste-Victoire with the Lubéron behind them, and Mt Ventoux in the far distance; to the south, the Maures Massif, the Ste-Baume Hills and La Ciotat Bay.

Return to the car and make for Nans-les-Pins along D 80. The road as it descends in hairpin bends through the woods affords views of Mount Regagnas. *In Nans-les-Pins turn left into D 280 which crosses a pinewood before meeting N 560 where you turn left to travel the Upper Huveaune Valley to St-Zacharie.*

St-Jean-du-Puy Oratory. – *9 km - 6 miles from St-Zacharie, plus 1/4 hour on foot Rtn.* Turn right into D 85 from which, as it climbs by means of hairpin bends, there are views of the St-Zacharie Basin and, in the distance the Ste-Baume Range. Shortly after the Pas-de-la-Couelle, a narrow track on the right leads up a short sharp slope to a military radar post. Park the car and continue on foot up an easy marked path to the oratory. From the site there is a good **view**★ of Mount Ste-Victoire and the St-Maximin Plain (N), the Maures and Ste-Baume Massifs (SE) and Mount Regagnas in the foreground, and the Étoile Chain and Aix countryside far away (W).

Continue along N 560 to Le Pujol where you turn left into D 45^A^. The road first ascends the Valley of the Vede, a stream at the foot of terraced hillsides, before turning aside to overlook the bare, rock walled gorges. *At La Coutronne, turn right for Gémenos along the road taken in the opposite direction at the outset.*

STES-MARIES-DE-LA-MER ★

Michelin map 246 fold 27 – *Local map p 63* – Pop 2 045 – *Facilities p 8*

At the heart of the Camargue lies Stes-Maries-de-la-Mer, a place of legendary origin and a pilgrimage for gypsies. Its fortified church is visible for miles across the marshlands. A new pleasure boat harbour lies to the west.

The saintly ship. – According to the Provençal legend, in *c*40, in the boat, abandoned to the waves by the Jews of Jerusalem, which, without the aid of sail or oar, fetched up safely on the shore where Stes-Maries is now situated, had Mary Magdalene and Martha, aboard, as well as their brother Lazarus, St Maximinus, Mary, the mother of James Minor, Mary Salome, the mother of James Major and John, and Suedonius, the man born blind. Sarah, the black servant of the two Marys, left behind on the shore, wept aloud until Mary Salome threw her mantle on the water so that Sarah could walk over it to join the others. The legend continues that after erecting a simple oratory to the Virgin on the shore, the disciples separated: Martha went to Tarascon *(p 56)*, Mary Magdalene to the Ste-Baume *(p 107)*, Lazarus to Marseilles *(p 82)*, Maximinus and Suedonius to Aix *(p 29)*. The two Marys and Sarah remained in the Camargue and were buried in the oratory.

The St Marys in their boat.

The pilgrimage. – The saints' tomb rapidly became the object of a cult attracting pilgrims from afar while gipsies and other nomads developed a particular veneration for Sarah. By the mid-9C the oratory had been replaced by a fortified church which, in 869, was being incorporated in the town ramparts under the personal supervision of the Archbishop of Arles, when suddenly the Saracens made a lightning raid and carried off the archbishop. In the short time it took to collect the ransom of 150 livres of silver, 150 mantles, 150 swords and 150 slaves, the prelate died; unperturbed, the Saracens returned with the corpse, set apart on a throne, and departed with the ransom before the Arlesians discovered their double loss.

In 12C, the church was replaced by the present Romanesque construction, still strongly fortified; in 1448, King René *(p 29)* ordered the exhumation of the saints whose relics were then enshrined with great ceremony and have remained ever since the object of a deep and widespread veneration. Two vast celebratory **pilgrimages** are still held each year: 24 and 25 May, the **Gipsy Celebration**★★; the weekend in October closest to the 22nd. The ceremony, dating back to the Middle Ages, is always the same: on the afternoon of the first day the saints' shrines are lowered by rope and pulley from the upper chapel on to an altar, which is their exact combined size, in the chancel; the next day, following an all night vigil and mass, they and the carved and painted wood figures of the saints in their boat and the figure of Sarah are marched in procession to a blessing of the sea, attended by Arlesians in costume, Camargue *gardians* on horseback, gipsies and a vast concourse. Finally, after vespers, the shrines are returned to their chapel on high.

The shrine.

Festivals and fairs, *farandoles* and *ferrades,* horse races and bullfights, accompany the celebrations of the pilgrimage.

■ SIGHTS *time: 1 hour*

The church★. – The massive crenellated exterior walls, surmounted by the keep-like structure of the upper chapel, which carries a triple gabled belfry, are decorated with Lombard bands at the east end, pierced by a few lancet windows, and with two lions devouring their prey supporting the south porch.

(After : carte postale Iris)

The fortified church.

Interior. – Enter through the small door on the Place de l'Église. *Time switches – 1F each – light the nave, chancel, and vault.*

Along the north wall, where the bays are all hollowed out of the thickness of the walls, are the carved boat with the Marys standing in the prow, a worn block of marble incorporated in a column discovered with the saints' relics in 15C and known as the Saints' Pillow, a finely carved 17C wood Crucifix *(high up),* and a pagan altar. In the nave pavement, protected by a wrought iron railing, is a well of fresh water for use in time of siege.

The chancel, raised when the crypt was constructed, contains the altar, on to which the reliquaries descend from the upper chapel *(see below)* for the pilgrimage celebrations, and at the east end, there is blind arcading supported on eight marble columns with splendid, vigorously carved capitals: a monster devouring its prey, the *Sacrifice of Isaac,* the *Annunciation,* men's heads, gloomy and gleeful, a satyr...

The **upper chapel** *(closed for restoration),* which is unusually situated above the steps descending to the crypt, was richly panelled in green and gold in 18C. It now houses the reliquary shrine of the two Marys, which is exposed in the window overlooking the nave, except during pilgrimages.

Mistral *(p 43)* set the final scene of his romance, *Mireio,* in the chapel where his heroine came to pray for help from the « queens of heaven ». Mireio herself, as pictured by the sculptor Mercié, may be seen in the main square.

Crypt. – *Open 15 May to 15 September 7.30am to noon and 2 to 7.30pm; the rest of the year 7.30am to 7pm.*

In the low crypt, bright and warm with lighted candles, are the ancient altar and reliquary, the cross carried in 24 May procession and **Sarah,** patron saint of the gipsies, a dark figure with glinting eyes, clad in white.

Rampart walk. – *53 steps. Open 1 April to 31 October 10am to noon and 2 to 7pm (5pm April, May and October) the rest of the year Saturdays 2 to 5pm and Sundays 10am to noon and 2 to 5pm; 8F.* Climb to the paved sentinel walk which circles the church roof, commanding a **view** of the sea, the town, the Camargue – sunset seen from Stes-Maries is unforgettable.

Baroncelli Museum. – *Open 9am to noon and 2 to 5pm (7pm 1 June to 30 September); closed Wednesdays October to May, 1 May and December; 6F.*

The museum owns the collection of books and other literature on the Camargue amassed by the **Marquess' Folco de Baroncelli** who brought the Camargue and its customs back to life. It also displays local fauna, furniture, landscape paintings and cowboys' kit.

A narrow spiral staircase *(44 steps)* leads to a terrace with a **view** of the church and town, the Vaccarès Lagoon (NE), Petit Rhône (W) and the Camargue around Aigues-Mortes.

The layout diagram on page 3 shows the Michelin Maps covering the region. In the text, reference is made to the map which is the most suitable from a point of view of scale and practicality.

Mount STE-VICTOIRE ★★

Michelin map 84 folds 3 and 4

The mountain, immortalized by Cézanne, is, in fact, a range extending from the east of Aix some 20 miles further east with the Pic des Mouches at 1 011m - 3 315ft, the highest point. The north face of the calcareous rock ridge slopes gradually down in a series of limestone plateaux to the Durance Plain; the south drops steeply to the Arc Basin.

In 102 BC the mountain was the site of the battle in which Marius' legions overcame the Teutons as they were about to start an advance on Rome.

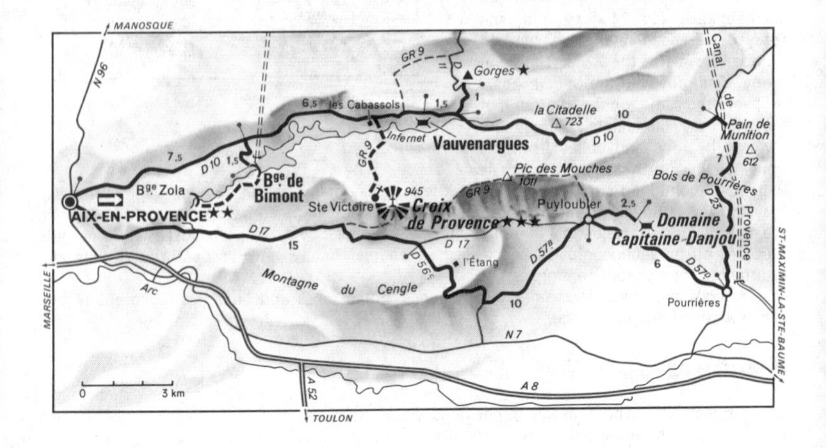

Round tour starting from Aix – *74 km - 46 miles – allow a full day*

Leave Aix (p 29) by D 10 going E; turn right towards the Bimont Dam.

Bimont Dam. – The arched dam across the Infernet River, is the principal undertaking in the Verdon Canal *(p 71)* extensions. It stands in a beautiful, wooded site at the foot of Mount Ste-Victoire; downstream, steep gorges descend *(1 hour on foot Rtn)* to the Zola Dam, the second undertaking in the scheme which supplies water to local towns and villages and irrigation to some 60 local communes.

Return to D 10 and turn right. The road skirts the reservoir.

Croix de Provence★★★. – *3 1/2 hours on foot Rtn. Park the car to the right of the road at Les Cabassols Farm and walk along the Venturiers path, a muletrack which rises rapidly through a pinewood before easing off into a winding path up the hillside.* The first staging post is at 900m - 2 950ft, the N.-D.-de Ste-Victoire Priory, built in 1656 and occupied until 1879. It comprises a chapel, a conventual building and parts of a cloister; a terrace laid in a breach in the wall gives a **view** of the Arc Basin and Étoile Chain (SW).

Bear left of the cloister to make the short climb to the 945m - 3 100ft high summit marked by 17m Cross upon an 11m base 56 and 36ft high respectively. The **panorama**★★★ of Provençal mountains and plains includes the Pic des Mouches (E) in the foreground, the Lubéron and Durance Valley (N), the Crau Plain (W), the Vitrolles (WSW), the Étoile Range (SSW) and the Ste-Baume Massif (SSE).

Vauvenargues Château. – *Not open.* The 17C château stands on a rock spur overlooking the Infernet Valley.

Pablo Picasso *(p 44)*, who lived in the mansion at the end of his life (1881-1973), is buried in the park.

Beyond Vauvenargues turn left into D 11 towards Jouques, continuing for about 1 km - 1/2 mile. The road follows the narrow **gorge**★. *Return to D 10.* The road goes up the wooded Infernet Gorge, overlooked on the left by the 723m - 2 370ft high Citadelle.

The Alpine foothills can be seen in the distance as you descend from the low pass at the gorge's end to D 23 where you turn right to circle the far east end of Ste-Victoire; to your left is the Pain de Munition (alt 612m - 2 005ft). *The road goes through Pourrières Wood to the town of the same name where you turn right for Puyloubier.* The region is a grape growing area.

Domaine Capitaine Danjou. – *Open 9am to noon and 2 to 5pm; closed Saturdays and Sundays.* A path to the right in Puyloubier leads to Le Général Château, now the Domaine, which houses the Pensioners' Hospital of the **Foreign Legion** *(p 87)*. The tour visits the workshops (pottery, bookbinding, ironworks) only.

Return to Puyloubier and take D 57B and then turn right into D 56C. Good views continue of Mount Ste-Victoire, also of the Trets Basin and Ste-Baume Range before the road climbs the slopes of Mount Cengle. D 17, on the left, winds between the Ste-Victoire and the Cengle Plateau to reach Aix.

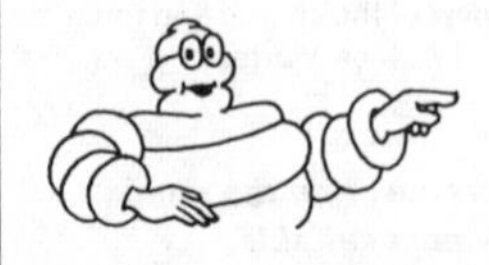

You will find a selection of touring programmes on pp 9-11.

Plan your route with the help of the map of principal sights on pp 4-6.

ST-GILLES ★

Michelin map 246 fold 26 – Pop 10 845 – *Facilities p 8*

The claim to fame of the town, which is the eastern gateway to the Camargue, is the west front of its ancient abbey.

St Giles and the hind. – Legend has it that in 8C St Giles gave all his money to the poor and set out from Greece aboard a raft which was borne by the sea to Provence. The hermit was befriended by a hind which he later saved from a huntsman, miraculously snatching the arrow in mid-flight and so amazing the bowman that he, being of a rich and noble family, founded an abbey on the site in commemoration of the event. St Giles journeyed to Rome to obtain recognition for the new foundation and was presented, by the Pope, with two doors for the abbey which he promptly launched on the Tiber and which after being carried out to sea, landed on the Provençal shore at the same time and place as the saint on his return.

On his death Giles was buried in the church, but it was replaced in 12C by a larger abbey church which rapidly became a popular place of pilgrimage; the Benedictine monastery was enriched by the papacy and Kings of France; the village prospered and became a merchant port from which pilgrims embarked for the Holy Land.

Decline. – In 1208 the Papal Legate, sent by Innocent III to persuade the Count of Toulouse to act against the heretics in his territory, was murdered at the door of St-Gilles by one of the Count's men. On being excommunicated, the Count submitted and did penance in St-Gilles on 12 June 1209. He soon revolted again, however, and was killed at Muret (1213) during the ensuing **Albigensian Crusade,** led by Simon de Montfort (father of the Simon de Montfort of English fame), which resulted in half a century of local strife, the burning and pillaging of hundreds of villages and towns in the south and the slaughter of thousands of the population.

16C brought the Reformation followed by the Wars of Religion. In St-Gilles in 1562 the monks were thrown down the well and the church was burned; in 1622 the great belfry was destroyed. The Revolution left only the west front to recall the glory of the medieval abbey.

(After photo by Arch. Phot., Paris)

The west doorway, St-Gilles.

■ ST-GILLES CHURCH *time: 3/4 hour*

Originally a small church was erected over St Giles' tomb. In 12C this was replaced by an abbey which was ruined during the Wars of Religion and has been largely rebuilt since 17C.

The West Front★★. – The three doorways occupy the full width to form a magnificent sculptured panorama of the Life of Christ. All the carving was done between 1180 and 1240: the centre door, the oldest, by sculptors from the Toulouse school, the lateral doors, with some of the most accomplished figures, by men from the Ile-de-France. The Apostles, added last in the embrasures and advanced areas, are by a local, less skilled school. The scenes actually depicted include *Christ in Majesty* on the central tympanum, with the *Last Supper* on the lintel; to the right, Judas and Christ in the Garden of Gethsemane; in the doorways, the *Adoration of the Magi,* the *Entry into Jerusalem* and on the right, on the tympanum, lintel and side panel, respectively, the *Crucifixion,* the *Holy Women* buying perfumed oils and at the tomb, and *Christ appearing to the Disciples.*

The Church. – The 17-19C rib vaulted church occupies only the nave area of the former abbey church. Below is the 12C **crypt★** (50 × 25m - 164 × 82ft) which shelters St-Giles' tomb. *(Open July to September, 9am to noon and 2 to 6pm; Sundays 9.30am to noon; fortnight around Easter, 14 July and 15 August 9.30am to noon and 3 to 6pm. Guided tours the rest of the year (apply to the Tourist Information Centre), 9am to noon and 2 to 5pm, excluding Sundays and holidays. Closed 5 January to 5 February; 8F for the crypt and the spiral staircase).* Together with Jerusalem, Rome and Santiago de Compostela, it was one of the four great Christian pilgrimages. The ogival vaulting is the earliest of its kind in France; the decoration reflects Burgundian influence. The monks ascended to the upper church by a staircase and ramp.

Spiral staircase★ (Vis de St-Gilles). – *Same opening times as the crypt.*

The spiral staircase, known as St-Gilles' screw, is famous among stonemasons for its perfection. It serves the northern of two belfries which flanked the five ambulatory chapels to the east of the **choir** of the 12C abbey church.

EXCURSIONS

Arles★★★. – *16km - 10 miles E along N 572. Description p 40.*

The Camargue★★. – *Alternative routes, pp 62-4.*

ST-MAXIMIN-LA-STE-BAUME ★★

Michelin map 84 folds 4 and 5 – Pop 5 552

St-Maximin, which lies at the centre of a small basin, once the bottom of a lake, is known for the basilica built, so the legend goes, where **Mary Magdalene** *(p 107)* and, later, **St Maximinus** *(p 107)* were both buried.

Legend become history. – The small Gallo-Roman town of Villa-Latta, which on St Maximinus' death took his name, became famous throughout the south of France in 13C when the saint's and Mary Magdalene's graves were discovered. According to legend both had been buried in the church crypt, but in 716, when the Saracens were devastating the region, the relics had been hidden and then lost; they were re-discovered in 1279 by Charles of Anjou, brother of St Louis, who built a church on the crypt foundations and a vast U-shaped, three storey monastery for the Dominicans he charged to guard the relics, and supervise what soon became a major pilgrimage.

The Revolution and since. – At the Revolution the Dominicans were expelled but by great good fortune the basilica and monastery were taken over by **Lucien Bonaparte,** Napoleon's youngest brother, then officer in charge of military store. He turned the cathedral into a food depôt and saved the organ from harm by having the *Marseillaise* played regularly upon it. The young officer, with an intelligence second only to Napoleon's, became a well known figure in the town, as he developed into a rousing speaker and was elected president of the local Jacobin club.

In 1966 the monastery became a cultural centre, Collège d'Échanges Contemporains *(for details concerning their programmes: ☏ (94) 78.01.93).*

■ The BASILICA★★ *time: 3/4 hour*

Organ concerts Sundays 4.30pm May to October. The basilica's construction on the foundations of 6C Merovingian church began in 1295 by command of Charles II, Prince of Salerno, future King of Sicily and Count of Provence. Work continued until 1316, by which time the apse and chancel were complete. After nearly a century, in 1404, the old crypt was reduced to ground level to allow for the construction of the new basilica floor. Again there was a break until between 1508-32 the building progressed to its present state.

Exterior. – Devoid of belfry, transepts and ambulatory, the basilica has a squat appearance reinforced by the incomplete west front and the massive buttresses reaching high up the nave walls. It is nonetheless the most important example of the Gothic style in Provence.

Interior. – The building comprises a nave, two aisles and the chancel. The nave, in two stages, and with ogive vaulting, is 29m - 95ft high, the aisles 18m - 62ft, to allow for a clerestory, and the side chapels lower still to enable more light to penetrate. The grand chancel ends in a pentagonal apse, the aisles in quadrangular apsidal chapels. A touch of colour appears in the nave roof bosses, emblasoned with the arms of the Counts of Provence and Kings of France; the stained glass has been almost entirely lost.

The restraint of the architecture acts as a perfect foil to the richness of the works of art.

1) The organ, which has a double case and still has the pipes saved by Lucien Bonaparte, was made by the lay Dominican, Isnard of Tarascon and is known, with the one in Poitiers Cathedral, as one of the finest 18C instruments in France;

2) Gilded wood statue of John the Baptist;

3) 15C altarpiece of the Four Saints: Lawrence, Anthony, Sebastian and Thomas Aquinas;

4) Reliquary containing the sumptuous cope of St Louis of Anjou, Bishop of Toulouse who died in 1297; 30 silk embroidered medallions illustrating the lifes of Christ and the Virgin encircled by four winged cherubim *(electric switch on the pillar);*

5) Rosary altar adorned with 18C gilded wood statue of the Virgin; 16C altar front carved with four low reliefs of the life of Mary Magdalene;

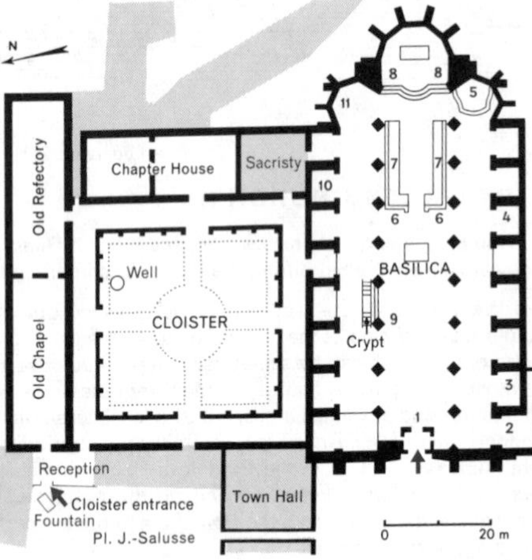

6) 17C choir screen carved in wood with wrought iron inlets emblasoned with the arms of France.

7) choir stall panelling enclosing 94 stalls, decorated with 22 medallions of men and women saints of the Dominican Order, carved in 17C by the lay brother, Vincent Funel;

8) 17C stucco decoration by J. Lombard before which stand, to the right, a terra-cotta of the Magdelene's communion, to the left, a marble of the saint's ecstasy and, at the centre, the altar surmounted by a glory;

9) Pulpit carved in 1756 by the Dominican, Louis Gaudet, with representations on the sounding board, in great size, of the ecstasy of the Magdalene, and on the staircase panels of her life. The rail is cut from a single piece of wood and is a masterpiece in itself;

10) 15C Provençal school predella (lower part of the altarpiece) illustrating the beheading of John the Baptist, St Martha taming the Tarasque *(p 56)* on Tarascon Bridge and Christ appearing to Mary Magdalene;

11) 16C painted wood **retable★** by Ronzen of the Crucifixion, surrounded by 18 medallions.

Crypt. – *Time-switch: 1F.* The crypt, the funeral vault of a late 4-early 5C Gallo-Roman villa, before becoming first the Merovingian and later a 13-14C church, contains four sarcophagi which are among the oldest Christian tombs in Gaul.

At the back, in a 19C gilded bronze reliquary, is a cranium, long venerated as that of Mary Magdalene, also four *c*500 AD marble or stone tablets with still distinguishable engravings of the Virgin, Abraham, and Daniel.

■ ADDITIONAL SIGHTS

Former Royal Monastery★. – *Open 1 April to 31 October 10am to noon and 2 to 6pm; closed 1 May; 5F.*

The monastery, begun like the basilica in 13C, was finally completed in 15C with the erection of the **cloister★**. The pure lines of its 32 bays frame an unexpectedly luxuriant garden of box-wood, yew, lime and cedar, where festival concerts are held. An old chapel with surbased vaulting, the refectory complete with lectern, and the **chapter house** with rib vaulting above slender columns, ending in foliated capitals, entered through a door flanked by windows, comprise the conventual buildings.

The pilgrim hostellery, a large 17C building, is now the town hall.

Rue des Arcades. – The 14C arcaded street in the town, stands on the site of the old Jewish ghetto.

ST-RÉMY-DE-PROVENCE ★

Michelin map 246 fold 26 – *Local map p 32* – Pop 8 439 – *Facilities p 8* – *See town plan in the current Michelin Red Guide France*

The citizens of the small town, close to France's greatest fruit and market gardening area, have specialized in the commercial production of flower and vegetable seeds for private gardeners and allotment holders.

The town's attraction as a tourist sight, however, lies in the Roman monuments half a mile to the south.

■ GLANUM★ and ROMAN MONUMENTS (Les Antiques)★★ *tour: 1 1/2 hours*

On a plateau in the northern foothills of the Alpilles, beside a spring sacred to a native healing spirit, Phoeceans enlarged an alreading existing trading post in 6C BC for their dealings with the merchants of Marseilles; by 2C BC it had developed into a town of Greek style houses built of massive blocks of stone, complete with temple, forum and council chamber.

This town was devastated in 2C BC by invading Teutons before Marius beat them back in 102 BC at Ste-Victoire *(p 110)*. A new town was then erected on the site using existing and new materials but with less craftsmanship in the matching of the stone in the drystone walling. After Caesar's capture of Marseilles in 49 BC, Glanum with the rest of the province, was Romanized, buildings being restored with mortar and evenly dressed, smaller, stones. In 3C AD Barbarians invaded Provence and all was again destroyed except for the mausoleum and arch, known locally as Les Antiques.

Roman Monuments, St Rémy-de-Provence.

The Mausoleum★★. – The monument dates from the early years of 1C AD and is one of the best preserved and most outstanding of its type. It is built of white stone in three stages, comprising a four-way arch, standing on a square sculptured podium on a stepped base and surmounted by a circular colonnade beneath a conical roof. Only the crowning pine cone finial is missing. The sculptures of men in combat around the podium are drawn from mythology.

It is, in fact, a cenotaph erected, according to the inscription on the frieze above the arcade, to Caius and Lucius Caesar, sons of Julia and Agrippa, grandsons of Octavia and the Emperor Augustus, who had named the young men as his heirs. They died prematurely, however, the first of a wound, the second of a fever.

Their statues are just visible inside the colonnade on the second floor.

The Commemorative Arch★. – The Commemorative or Municipal Arch, which dates from the early years of Augustus' reign (31 BC-14 AD) is, therefore, slightly earlier than the mausoleum.

Although in a ruined state, the monument displays traces, particularly in its proportions and such carved decoration as remain, of the Greek influence evident elsewhere in Glanum. The single arch is decorated with garlands of fruit and leaves, the vault with deeply incised *paterae.*

On either side of the opening are the remains of sculptured groups of prisoners chained to a tree, of a captured woman sitting mournfully awaiting her fate and of the victorious combattants.

Glanum excavations★. – *Open 9am to noon and 2 to 6pm, (5pm 1 October to 31 March); closed 1 January, 1 May, 1 and 11 November and 25 December; 11F weekdays; 5.50F Sundays and holidays.*

After the 3C devastation *(see above)* the water courses became blocked, alluvium descended from the nearby Alpilles, and the site gradually disappeared. Excavation began in 1921 and has continued intermittently ever since, the sculptural and mosaic finds being displayed at Sade House in the town *(p 114)*.

The excavations have produced evidence of three periods of occupation – Gaulish, Greek and Roman – as archaelogists have uncovered level after level of superimposed buildings, discarded artefacts of unexpected periods, coins, mortared and drystone walls, new and obviously re-used building materials, water ducts and drains, mosaics and statuary, including the probably unique portrait head of Julia, Augustus's daughter and mother of the two young men commemorated in the mausoleum.

Make for the viewing table for an overall view of the excavations then follow the route on the plan.

Cybele's Temple. – The temple to the mother-goddess stands on the site of a former market.

Atys' House. – There are traces of interior decoration in the fragmentary reliefs and mosaics in the house named after Atys, Phrygian god and Cybele's lover.

The House of the Square Pilasters or Antes. – This mansion, erected in the Greek style favoured in Glanum in 2C BC, was built surrounding a central peristyled courtyard which contained the water cistern. Unusually, as can be seen from the shortness of the columns and the end staircase, it also had an upper storey. (Building materials show that it was modified in the Gallo-Roman Period).

Fountain basin. – 2C BC.

Baths. – Typical late 1C BC, small provincial town baths with a boiler-room (**2**) and cold (**3**) and warm chambers (**4**), a hot bath (**5**), an open, once colonnaded, courtyard for exercise and the cold pool, possibly fed by the stream. Mosaics (**6** and **7**).

Covered canal. – This remarkable work, probably a drain, was so constructed that the stone covering doubled as the main street pavement. It skirts an apsed building near which altars to the forest god Silvanus have been found.

Forum. – The open square on older foundations, is outlined to the east and west by the bases of old columns and to the south, by a wall with a rounded recess. To the north, beneath the roof, are two primitive mosaics (**8**), discovered on a lower level and possibly the oldest in Gaul.

Fortified gate. – The gate in the temple defence wall was a solid, Greek style construction of well matched stones, comprising a carriage-way and zig-zag wicket gate.

The Nymphaeum spring. – The source round which Glanum developed is marked by a basin, with masonry walls of large, Greek style stones, restored by Agrippa in 20 BC, from which steps lead to a swimming pool still filled with water from the spring; there are votive altars to Hercules.

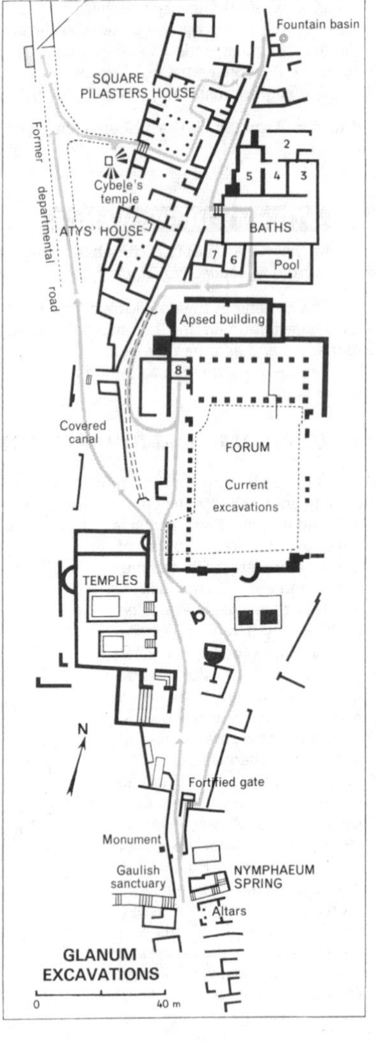

The temples. – To the west are several temples: those facing east and tiered are 6C BC and Gaulish; the others, late 1C BC and Roman, were dedicated to Caius and Lucius Caesar. Portrait sculptures of Octavia and Julia, once in the temple, are now in the Sade Museum *(see below)*.

Old St-Paul-de-Mausole Monastery. – The former monastery, now a convalescent home, situated near the plateau, can be distinguished in the wooded landscape by the attractive belfry which crowns its Romanesque church. Its foundation dates back to the early Middle Ages, its delightful small **cloister**★, with circular arches in groups of three, divided by slender paired columns with richly carved capitals, to 12, early 13C *(open 8am to 7pm - 6pm in winter)*. Van Gogh, whose bust stands (left) beside the path to the church, passed the last year of his life (1889-90), in the convalescent home.

■ ST-RÉMY

The small town boasts two museums which stand close together, north of the church, at the corner of Favier Square:

Sade House. – *Guided tour (time: 1 hour) 10 and 11am and 3, 4 and 5pm everyday in April and June to September; Saturday and Sunday March and October; Saturday, Sunday, Monday and Ascension Day in May; additional tours at 9am and 6pm June to September; 6F.*

This 15-16C house contains lapidary **exhibits**★, in particular the finds excavated at Glanum, including *(1st floor)* the white marble busts of Octavia and Julia *(see above)*.

Pierre de Brun Alpilles Museum. – *Open April to October 10am to noon and 2 to 6pm (7pm July and August); March and November Saturdays and Sundays 10am to noon and 2 to 4pm; closed Tuesdays; 6F.* Mistral de Mondragon House, a vast 16C mansion built round a courtyard with a circular staircase turret and overlooked by covered balconies, contains collections of traditional popular art, furniture, costume, *santons (p 24)* and bibliographical material on **Nostradamus** *(p 115)* who was born in the house with a mullioned window on Avenue Hoche.

SALON-DE-PROVENCE ★

Michelin map 246 fold 12 – Pop 35 845 – *Facilities p 8 – See town plan in the current Michelin Red Guide France*

The town at the heart of France's olive growing country, which was already a major production centre by 15C, today not only produces olive oil but also refines mineral or hydrocarbon oils.

The agricultural produce market has expanded rapidly in the last few years and in 1936 the officers training school for the French Air Force was established in Salon.

The town, which was badly shaken by a severe earth tremor in 1909, is in two parts: the old city climbing up the hill to the castle *(see below)*, and the new *quarter* which lies at its feet, divided by a broad belt of tree shaded avenues.

Two 16C visionaries. – Salon knew two famous men of science in 16C: the civil engineer, **Adam de Craponne** (1527-76), the physician and astrologer, **Nostradamus** (Michel de Notredame, 1503-66).

De Craponne brought fertility to the region through the construction of the irrigation canal *(p 71)* bearing his name which takes water from the Durance along the original river course through the Lamanon Gap to the Berre Lagoon and the sea.

Nostradamus first studied medicine, travelled in France and Italy and went on to discover successful remedies against the plague epidemics which recurred in Aix and Lyons, but he kept his cure secret and so roused the jealousy of his colleagues that they expelled him from the profession. He went into retirement and took up astrology, eventually producing (1555), in the form of verse quatrains, a book of predictions on the future of the world which he entitled *Centuries*. The publication was fantastically successful and the author attracted the attention of Catherine de Medici; Charles IX made him his Physician in Ordinary. Four centuries later his predictions still excite interest.

The sage's house is now a **museum** *(open 10am to noon and 2.30 to 6.30pm; closed Tuesdays and in winter sometimes closed Sundays and holidays).*

(After photo by Bibliothèque Nationale)

Michael Nostradamus.

St-Laurent and St-Michel. – The town's two principal churches are both medieval: the first 14-15C, a good example of southern French Gothic, contains Nostradamus' tomb and his portrait painted by his son (3rd north chapel), also 16C Virgin in alabaster and a massive 15C *Descent from the Cross* (1st north chapel); the second, dating from 13C is original in that it possesses two belfries, one built at the time of the church's construction and ornamented with a five bay arcade, the second a 15C addition. The tympanum of St Michael's, carved with the Paschal Lamb and encircling snakes, pre-dates the church, being 12C.

Empéri Castle. – *Open 10am to noon and 2.30 to 6.30pm (2 to 6pm 1 October to 31 March); closed Tuesdays, 1 January, 1 May and 25 December; 8F.*

The massive castle on top of the Puech Rock, begun in 10C, rebuilt in 13C and remodelled in 15C, was once the residence of the archbishops of Arles, Lords of Salon. The covered entrance leads to the main courtyard with a Renaissance gallery, 12C chapel and, in the state apartments, a finely sculptured chimneypiece.

(After photo by Musée de l'Empéri)

The Empéri Castle.

Museum★★. – The castle's main interest, however, now lies in the military museum of some 10 000 exhibits on the history of the French Army from the time of Louis XIV to 1918, with special reference to the Napoleonic years. The once private collection, now an annex of the Military Museum in Paris, includes uniforms, insignia, arms, documents...

Salon and Crau Museum. – *Avenue de Pisavi (Pélissanne road, D 17). Open Wednesdays, Thursdays and Fridays 10am to noon and 2 to 5pm; closed holidays; 3F.*

The museum, in a huge 19C mansion known in the town as the Pavilion, contains displays of the regional fauna, local landscape paintings and Provencal furniture.

EXCURSIONS

La Barben Castle★; Lambesc; Vernègues. – *Round tour of 51 km - 31 miles – about 2 1/2 hours. Leave Salon by N 538 going S; turn left into D 572 towards Aix and then at Pélissanne turn left into D 22^A.*

La Barben Castle★. – *Guided tour (time: 35 minutes) 10am to noon and 2 to 6pm; closed Tuesdays, 15 September to Easter; 15F.* The mediaeval castle, rebuilt and enlarged in 14 and 17C, includes a Henri IV or late 16C staircase to a terrace, from which there is a view of the formal gardens designed by Le Nôtre. Inside are painted ceilings, a Second Empire Aubusson tapestry in the Grand Saloon and the reception hall is covered with Cordovan leather★ made near Avignon in 1680. On the second floor, the Empire style apartments of Napoleon's sister, Pauline Borghese, in which the boudoir is decorated with a hand painted wallpaper of the Four Seasons, is worth admiring. The castle annexes have been converted into a **vivarium** with tropical and European fresh water fish and reptiles and an aviary, 30ha - 74 acres *(Open 10am to noon and 1.30 to 6.30pm (5pm in winter); open all day on Sundays; 20F, children 12F)* and **zoo** *(open same times; 30F, children 15F).* A stairway *(112 steps)* brings you to the central enclosure inhabited by elephants, giraffes, wild boar, bison, zebra, carnivores and monkeys.

Continue along D 22^A and left into D 572. The road follows the fertile Touloubre Valley and passes beneath the Marseilles Canal *(p 71).*

St-Cannat. – Pop 2 384. The town was the birthplace of **Admiral Suffren** (1726-88), who was in constant, and usually successful, action against the Royal Navy throughout a career which spanned the Seven Years' War and the American War of Independence. The house in which Suffren was born is now the town hall. Glance inside the church at the stoup converted from an antique reliquary crowded with small carved figures.

Lambesc. – Pop 5 353. The small town, now by-passed by N 7, has a large 18C church which incorporates 14C belfry of an earlier sanctuary; the spire collapsed in the 1909 earth tremor. Note 16C gateway supporting a clock with jacks.

Continue along N 7. In Cazan turn left into D 22 and follow the signs.

Château-Bas. – At the far end of the castle park are the ruins of a Roman temple probably of late 1C BC, contemporary with the St-Rémy arch *(p 113)* or Maison Carrée in Nîmes *(p 93).* The remains include a wall ending in a square pilaster, surmounted by a Corinthian capital and a 7m - 23ft fluted column still standing intact. Among the surrounding fragments – a second temple and semicircular precinct – is a chapel, abutting the left wall of the temple, with barrel vaulting, an oven vaulted apse, 16C doorway and niche.

Continue along D 22 to D 22^C on the right. As the road rises the view extends to include besides the Lubéron and Durance, the Côtes Hills, and Aix countryside.

Vernègues. – Pop 377. The post - 1909 village was built after an earth tremor had destroyed the original perched settlement.

Vieux-Vernègues. – The uphill road circles the ruins *(not open)* left by the 1909 earthquake. From the small tower there is a remarkable **panorama**★ *(viewing table)* of a large area of Provence.

Return to Vernègues; turn right into D 22^B then left into D 68. The road goes into the small, deep Cuech Valley. *At the entrance to Pélissanne turn right into D 17 for Salon.*

Calès Caves (Grottes de Calès). – *10 km - 6 miles N along N 538 and D 72^E on the left to Lamanon.* The caves in Mount Défends lie below a rock bearing a statue of N.-D.-de-la-Garde.

Access. – *3/4 hour on foot Rtn. Take the uphill road right of the church which continues as a footpath and finally a paved way. 400m - 1/4 mile after, turn right into a stone path.* On either side of the arch are caves believed to have been hollowed out by the Ligurians and occupied subsequently by the Saracens and later invaders up to the Middle Ages. Exploration reveals enclosures, steps, cave shelters, defences and even storage silos.
Continue along the path which circles the spur and leads to the statue. The **view** between the pine trees, extends north across the Durance Valley to Mount Lubéron, east over the troglodyte caves and south to the Lamanon Gap, the Salon Plain, the far distant Berre Lagoon and Estaque Mountain Chain. The Crau Plain lies away to the southeast.

UZÈS ★

Michelin map 80 fold 19 – *Local map p 118* – Pop 7 826 – *Facilities p 8*

Uzès, living medieval town, was prosperous in the 17 and 18C owing to its fabrication of linen, serge and silk. It has interests other than tourism from which it has, nevertheless, benefited, having received grants towards the restoration of the main square, Place aux Herbes, and to several old streets enabling the quarter to be brought to life again.

It is a town of towers: the Bermonde, Vicomté, Évêques, Du Roi and the distinctive Fenestrelle, which looks like a small scale Leaning Tower of Pisa.

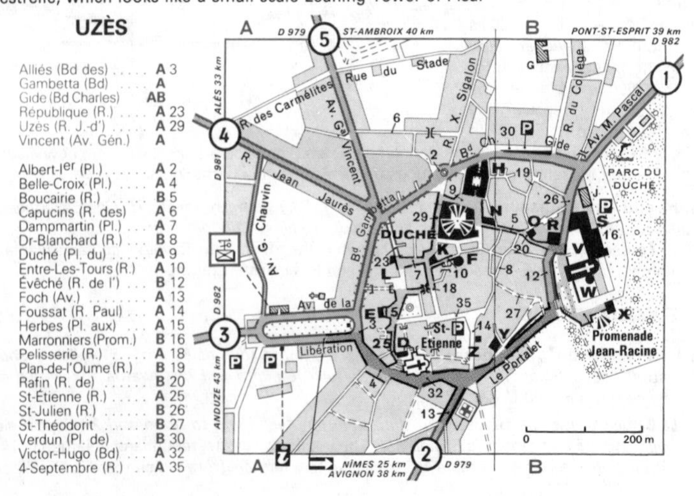

■ SIGHTS *time: 1 1/2 hours*

Start from the Avenue de la Libération; turn right into the Boulevard des Alliés.

St-Étienne (A). – *To visit apply to the tourist information centre.* The church with a curved west front decorated with flaming urns is 18C; the square tower flanking the north wall, five centuries older.

The economist Charles Gide (1847-1932) was born in the house (**A D**) which stands on the church square.

Rue St-Étienne (**A 25**). – No 1, the faceted stone doorway is 17C; a little further along on the left at the end of a blind alley is a Renaissance façade.

Place aux Herbes (**A 15**). – The old square named after the medieval herb market is arcaded; among the old houses note the house standing back – Aigaliers House (**A E**).

(After photo by M. Thierry Vincent)

The Place aux Herbes, Uzès.

Walk through an alley off the far right (NE) corner into the narrow Rue Pélisserie and from there into the Rue Entre-les-Tours. The towers in question are 12C **Tour de l'Évêque** (now the **Clock Tower** – **A F**), the **Bermonde,** the 14C **Vicomté** in the Ducal Palace and the **Tour du Roi** – all symbols of power when king, local duke and church were rivals in the Middle Ages.

Dampmartin House (**A K**). – *No 1 Rue Jacques-d'Uzès.* The Renaissance façade is flanked by a round tower, the Renaissance inner court embellished by a fine staircase. Note the frieze surrounding the first floor window overlooking the street.

Cross Dampmartin Square to look at 16C front of **Joubert et d'Avéjan House** (**A L**) at no 12 Rue de la République. *Return to the Rue Jacques-d'Uzès and turn left.*

Ducal Palace* **(Duché)** (A). – *Guided tour (time: 20 minutes) 9.30am to noon and 2.30 to 6.30pm; the rest of the year, 10am to noon and 2 to 5pm; 17F, children 8F.*

From outside the palace appears as a massive feudal pile, with buildings of various periods exemplifying the rise of the Uzès family.

Courtyard. – The courtyard *cum* walled garden is distinguished by two towers, a 16C Gothic chapel (Vicomté 19C restored) and the 14C Tower, with its octagonal turret, commemorating the lords of Uzès' elevation to a viscounty in 1328; the square **Bermonde,** named after the manorial lord of the time, was built for defence in 11C and still commands a **view*** from the summit *(148 steps)*, far and wide over the *garrigue* countryside.

The palace **façade*** is Renaissance and was erected by the first duke in *c*1550 to plans by Philibert Delorme, royal architect of the Tuileries and of several châteaux of the Loire. Although it is an early example of the superimposition of the Classical orders, Doric, Ionic and Corinthian, in domestic architecture, any severity is modified by the perfect proportions, and the decorative framing of the windows with alternate triangular and segmental pediments and intervening carved panels.

Interior. – The apartments include a large Louis XV saloon, richly decorated with stucco and contemporary furniture and furnishings; the furniture in the dining room is Renaissance and Louis XIII. To the left as you leave is the 12C Vigie Tower.

Town Hall (**AB H**). – The well styled courtyard is 18C.

Crypt (**AB N**). – *Guided tour (time: 1/2 hour) 1 June to 31 August 9.30 to noon and 2.30 to 7pm; 5F.*

In one of the low reliefs in the baptistry, the figures have been given glass eyes; the wall niches in 4C, early Christian sanctuary, were intended to hold liturgical vessels.

Follow the Rue Boucairie. At the Rue Rafin corner stands the **Old Mint** (**B O**), a reminder that medieval bishops of Uzès were permitted to strike their own coins.

The Baron of Castille's Mansion (**B R**). – The late 18C front is preceded by a colonnade – a particular predilection it would seem, since the baron's other château, Castille Château *(see below)* is similarly adorned.

Former Bishop's Palace (**B S**). – *Under restoration.* Late 17C residence which houses in its right wing the library and museum.

Museum. – *Open 1 July to 31 August 9am to noon and 2 to 6pm; the rest of the year Saturdays and Sundays 2 to 6pm; 3.50F.*

Devoted to folklore, local crafts (ceramics, painting, sculpture) and **Charles and André Gide.** Paul Gide (1832-80), lawyer and Charles Gide (1847-1932), professor and economist were both born in Uzès. They were respectively father and uncle to André Gide (1869-1951) writer (Nobel Prize for Literature in 1947) who spent his holidays with his grandmother in Uzès and recounts his sojourns in *If It Die... (Si le grain ne meurt).*

St-Théodorit Cathedral (**B V**). – 17C cathedral behind 19C remodelled west front, contains a very fine gilded 17C **organ★**, which has preserved many of its 18C pipes; it has since been restored. The painted shutters on either side used, long ago, to be closed over the instrument in Lent. *(To light the organ, insert 1F in the time-switch on 3rd south pillar.)* Note the 17C lectern and, a most interesting feature, the continuous balconies with wrought iron rails, midway up the walls.

Fenestrelle Tower★ (**B W**). – *Not open to the public.* The tower, which abuts the cathedral south wall, is 12C and the only relic of the former Romanesque cathedral destroyed during the Wars of Religion, when the town suffered through some citizens being Protestant, others Catholic.

The Fenestrelle is unique in its style in France; it rises 42m - 138ft from a square base through six diminishing circular stages to a low pyramidal roof behind a parapet.

Jean-Racine Promenade (**B**). – The avenue, which runs into the wide, chestnut shaded, Promenade des Marronniers, overlooks the ducal park, the *garrigue,* and the Alzon Valley where the River Eure was collected at its source by the Romans and diverted along the Pont du Gard aqueduct *(p 99)* to provide water for Nîmes. To the left is an old advanced tower, once part of the fortifications, restored in late 18C and now named the **Racine Pavilion** (**B X**). Jean Racine, the would-be writer was sent as a young man (22 years old) in 1661 to stay with his uncle, vicar-general of the town, in the hope that he would enter the church and give up, to the family's way of thinking, his outrageous idea of becoming a playwright. Racine enjoyed the town and local countryside but at the end of a year returned to Paris, to become France's greatest classical dramatist.

Continue past the Renaissance **Portalet House** (**AB Y**). At no 3 Rue Paul-Foussat, note the beautiful Renaissance door (**A Z**).

EXCURSION

The Guarrigues. – *51 km - 31 miles – about 4 hours. Leave Uzès by ② D 979 going S.*

The Guarrigues are a limestone formation which sweep like sea surf along the foot of the more ancient Massif Central. The peaks rise (200-300m – 656-1 000ft in the area which is covered by the guide) above arid, eroded slopes which support only gorse, scrub, lavender, thyme and rosemary. Rivers have cut through the stone, hollowing out deep and sometimes picturesque gorges. The road winds through the countryside offering views of Uzès and its environs.

Pont St-Nicolas. – The seven arch bridge, built in 13C by the Bridge Brotherhood *(p 45),* spans the River Gardon in a particularly beautiful spot. D 979 climbs by way of hairpin bends affording good views as it does so; in the right bend at the top, park the car and look at the spectacular **view★** along the course of the Gardon Gorge.

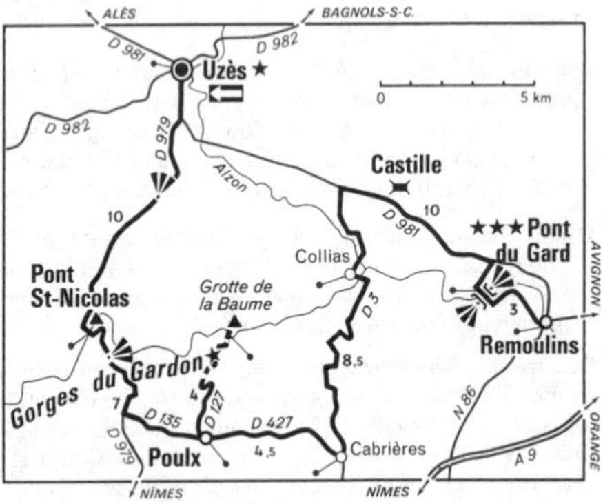

Turn left into D 135 and, just before Poulx, left again into D 127.

Gardon Gorges★. – *Poor surfaced road, passing difficult, sometimes impossible except in lay-byes hewn out of the rock: at the final bend, park the car (all motor vehicules are forbidden beyond the car park).*

A path *(1 hour on foot Rtn)* ends at the bottom of the gorge in a picturesque spot, facing the opening of the Baume Cave in the cliff on the far bank of the river.

Poulx. – Pop 725. Village with a small, single aisled, Romanesque church.

Continue along D 427 to Cabrières where you turn left into D 3. The road rises to the plateau (views of the Rhône Plain and the Alpilles), before descending into the Gardon Valley. *Bear right into D 981.*

Castille Château. – *Not open to the public.* An avenue of yew leads to the château, which was built in 16C and remodelled in 18C by the Count of Castille to present an interplay of columns and balustrades at the centre, and two low wings on either side. The whole is surrounded by a colonnade preceded by a vast balustered, horseshoe shaped, peristyle.

Continue along D 981.

Pont du Gard★★★. – *Description p 99.*

Remoulins. – Pop 1 866. *Facilities p 8.* The village set amidst cherry and other fruit orchards, is protected in places by its medieval wall.

VAISON-LA-ROMAINE ★★

Michelin map 245 fold 9 – *Local maps pp 70 and 128* – Pop 5 864 – *Facilities p 8*

Vaison-la-Romaine has the attraction of being a town of three cultures in a beautifully wooded mountain setting, glorious in spring and early summer with roses, irises and fruit blossom against the tall dark cypresses... A visit is an integral part of the discovery and understanding of Roman civilization in Provence, since it shows a wealthy settlement away from the famous, main city centres.

The site. – The town site, which occupies only 5ha - 12 acres is divided by the green waters of the River Ouvèze, spanned since Roman times by a high, 17m - 56ft wide, single arched stone bridge, unaltered except for repairs to the parapet in 19C.

HISTORICAL NOTES

Vaison's earliest inhabitants were the Ligurians in the Bronze Age; by the end of 4C BC, the Iron Age, it had become the capital of a Celtic tribe. The Romans came first in 12 BC but consolidated their rule only half a century later when they conferred on the settlement the title of Federated City. The colonizers, who included men of considerable wealth, writers, merchants and former legionary officers, built spacious houses and the civic amenities common to Roman towns, such as a market, temples and a theatre: the city, in fact, became so wealthy that a writer described it as the very richest – Urbs Opulentissima. It prospered for 400 years, until the late 5C when it was destroyed by Frankish invaders from the east.

In 12C, Count Raymond of Toulouse built a castle on the hill on the opposite bank, part of his general defences in the ceaseless campaigns he waged against his peers. In the Middle Ages the people who still lived in the locality decided to revive the town, but finding the site on the right bank too open and vulnerable to the marauding bands of the time, they migrated across the river and built a perched village, known as the Upper Town, on the hillside below the castle.

By 18C, the population had grown and times become quieter, so the townsfolk returned once more across the river, and began to build a modern town beside and on top of the largely buried Roman ruins.

Expansion in 19C encroached on the Roman remains still further until in 1907 the excavations were started which continue to this day.

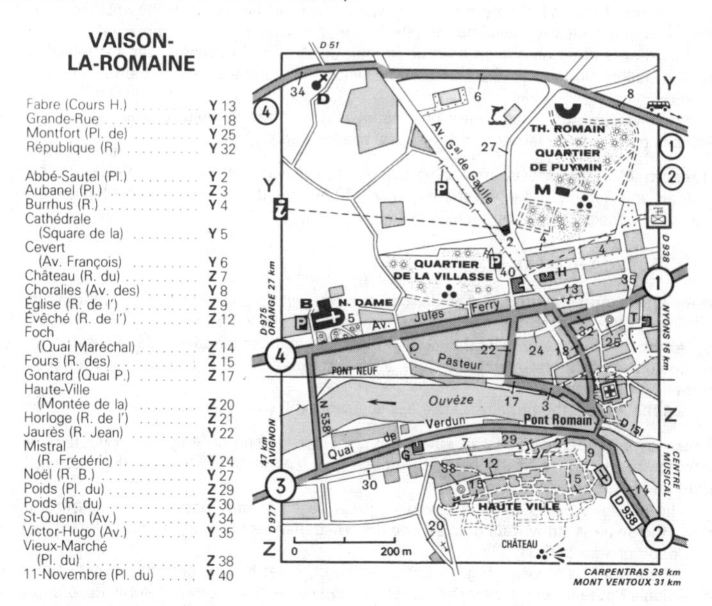

■ The ROMAN RUINS★★ *time: 1 1/2 hours*

Open 1 June to 30 September 9am to 7pm (6pm 1 March to 31 May and 1 October to 30 November; 5pm 1 December to 28 February); closed 1 January and 25 December; all inclusive ticket (obtainable: Puymin entrance or cathedral cloister): 13.70F.

Puymin Quarter

Messius' House. – The villa illustrates the spacious living of a wealthy family even though some rooms remain buried below the buildings of the modern town. Clearly to be seen are the street entrance, the partially covered inner court *(atrium*-**1***)* with its central water cistern *(impluvium)*, the master of the household's rooms *(tablinum)*, the large room (**2**) in which the head of Venus was discovered, the reception room *(oecus*-**3***)*, the peristyle or colonnaded court with its basin, the kitchen (**4**) with ovens and sink, the lavatories and the bath suite (**5**).

Pompey's Portico. – The elegant, walled public promenade, 51m - 167ft square, excavated along its north and part of its west sides, was paved, columned and richly decorated with murals.

Statues stood in the central garden and in the wall recesses as does now **Diadumenos,** the athlete crowning himself (cast – the original Roman marble discovered at Vaison, after the lost Greek bronze by Polyclitus, is in the British Museum).

Rented Houses. – The houses' rarity lies in their having been purpose built for lease. The massive urn *(dolium)* held communal provisions.

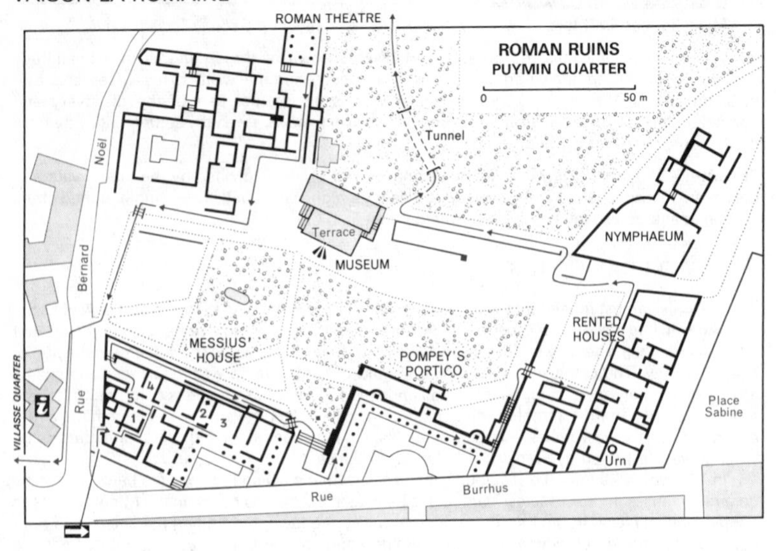

Nymphaeum. – The so-called nymphaeum or fountain, was the central water cistern from which spring water was distributed by underground canal and lead pipes to all parts of the town. A variety of buildings were erected around it.

Roman Theatre★. – The theatre, dating from 1C AD and 96m - 305ft in diameter or 10m - 33ft smaller than those of Arles and Orange, was built against the hillside – it is entered by way of a tunnel through the hill. The entire stage was cut out of the rock and the shell has, therefore, remained intact, clearly revealing the pits for stage machinery, curtain holes, etc.

Another feature, unique among the Roman theatres in Provence, is the partial existence of the top gallery portico. Statues, discovered when the stage was excavated in 1912, are in the museum.

After visiting the theatre return to the west side of the Puymin quarter where remains of Romans houses (with latrines and frescoes) are located.

Museum (M). – The most outstanding among the excavation finds are the **Emperor in Armour★**, Hadrian and Sabine, the white marble head of Venus with a circlet of laurel leaves, the silver bust of a patrician and a complete set of imperial coins.

Villasse Quarter

Main street and basilica. – A wide, paved street with a pedestrian side walk runs from the entrance to the excavations, towards the river and the modern town.

At the end, on the right, is the parallel Shop Street, lined by an arcade to provide shade for the customers going from store to store, each store being the front room of the terrace houses bordering the street.

On the left are the remains of the basilica. Note the covered road gutter.

House of the patrician of the silver bust. – Near the end of Shop Street is the pillared (1) entrance to the house of the patrician whose bust, cast in silver (now in the museum), once adorned his property.

The house is complete: the paved entrance leads to the Tuscan pillared *atrium* with its basin, the owner's study *(tablinum-2)*, and the two peristyles (colonnaded private gardens) – one with pool, private bath (3)...

To the north is a hanging garden, further south other houses and mosaics (4), to the west the **Dolphin House** of which the main entrance, marked by an important colonnade and five steps leading to the atrium (5) and other rooms, is on the far west side, in a street parallel to the main street. There is a peristyle (6) with pool and to the north are the latrines and private bath (7) To the south is another peristyle with its pool.

Opposite the Dolphin House, the **Colonnade Street** is 43m – 142ft long.

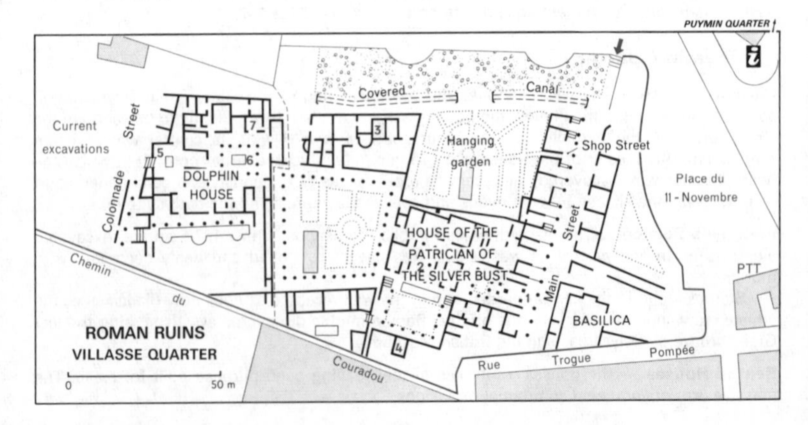

■ The MEDIEVAL BUILDINGS

Old Notre-Dame Cathedral (Y) – *Same times and charges as Roman ruins (p 119) but closed between noon and 2pm from October to April.*

The first church, which dated from Merovingian times, 6 or 7C, and fell into ruin during the Frankish invasions, was rebuilt in 12 and 13C.

Outside, note the off-centre, square belfry decorated with a foliated frieze, cornice and crenellated crest, the window surrounds, the buttresses, the square end to the apse, which is semicircular inside, and, finally, how the apse and apsidal chapel foundations were built with column shafts and capitals quarried from the Roman buildings.

The interior combines many periods: there are 15C tombs in the chancel and, beyond the high **altar**★, an oven vault above the old Romanesque bishop's throne. St Quenin, bishop of his native Vaison from 556-575, lies buried in a gabled sarcophagus before the throne. Circling the apse is arcading which descends on Corinthian capitalled Roman columns...

The square, barrel vaulted **cloister**★ (Y B) *(open: see Roman ruins p 119),* which adjoins the north wall, was built in the 11 and rebuilt in the 12C and presents a fine interplay of semicircles: each gallery of four rounded bays is subdivided into three slim bays resting respectively on fluted or chevroned piers, or slim, paired columns with foliated capitals. The long inscription in Latin to be seen from the cloister, on the cathedral north wall, ending in « Peace be on this house », is an imprecation to the 12 canons of the time to be mindful of the monastic rule.

(After photo by V. Ulrich)

The bishop's throne.

St-Quenin★. (Y D) – The chapel is, in several respects, an archaeological riddle: the strange, triangular apse of skilfully dressed stone with fluted full length and short pilasters and capitals, and a frieze decorated with inexplicable but often cheerful carvings, most of which are not Biblical, is now explained as being 12C Romanesque chapel embellished with original carvings. In the 17C the nave was rebuilt.

■ The UPPER TOWN (Haute ville) (Z)

Cross the **Roman River bridge** (Pont Romain) and start walking uphill through the maze of narrow alleys and minute squares, decorated with street fountains and overlooked by creeper covered houses, dating from any time between 14 and 18C. Of the alternately shaded and sunlit alleys, bright with flowers in hanging baskets or visible through wrought iron gates, the most attractive are Rue de l'Horloge, through the town gate beneath the lopsided belfry, with the characteristic open wrought iron bell cage, Rues de l'Église, de l'Évêché and des Fours and Place du Vieux Marché. The late 12C castle *(steep, overgrown path)* rebuilt in 15C and now a ruin commands a **view** of the new town, the Ouvèze Valley, the Baronnies and Mount Ventoux.

EXCURSIONS

Mount Ventoux★★★. – *Two round tours starting from Vaison-la-Romaine: p 128*

Dentelles de Montmirail★. – *Round tour of 63 km - 39 miles. Description p 70.*

Nyons; Valréas; Grignan★**; Chamaret; Richerenches.** – *Round tour of 85 km - 53 miles. Leave Vaison by ①, D 938 which cuts between W foothills of the Baronnies to skirt the Eygues River.*

Nyons. – Pop 6 293. *Facilities p 8.* Situated within a protective ring of mountains astride the River Eygues, where it emerges from a gorge into the Tricastin Plain, Nyons enjoys a gentle climate where exotic plants bloom in the open and old people live long. Local enterprises include a truffle market, preserved fruit, and above all olive oil production. *Oil mills in full time operation 15 November or 1 December to end of February –* **Ramade Mill,** *4th turning left off Avenue Paul Laurens going west; guided tour – time: 20 minutes – 9am to noon and 2 to 7pm; Sundays 9am to noon; closed holidays –* **Autrand Mill,** *Avenue de la Digue, open 9am to noon and 2 to 7pm; closed Sundays in July and August –* **Oil Co-operative,** *Place Olivier de Serres; guided tours Mondays to Saturdays 10am to noon; 10F).* Nyons' unique feature is the so-called **Forts Quarter** built in the Middle Ages on the northern outskirts. Starting from the arcaded Place du Dr-Bourdongle (east of the main Place de la Libération), go past the church and town hall and continue up the Rue des Petits-Forts, a narrow alley bordered by low-roofed old houses and 13C Tour Randonne containing the minute N.-D.-de-Bon-Secours Chapel. Turn left to enter the **Rue des Grands Forts**★, an extraordinary covered way leading to a gateway, once the castle entrance.

The town still possesses its **Old Bridge**★, 14 and 15C humped back with a single 40m - 131ft wide span which makes it one of the most daring undertakings of its time.

VAISON-LA-ROMAINE**

Take D 538 NW out of Nyons and after 7 km - 4 miles turn left into D 541.

Valréas. – Pop 8 796. *Facilities p 8.* The town, an important centre for agriculture and light industry in the fertile Coronne Valley, is situated in the Valréas Enclave, a canton of the Vaucluse Département entirely surrounded by the Drome Département. The enclave was formed in 15C when Charles VII forbade further sales of land to the popes at Avignon, who were trying to link their recent northern acquisitions – Valréas, Visan, Richerenches and Grillon – to the Comtat Venaissin *(p 69).* The town lies within plain tree shaded boulevards planted on the site of former ramparts of which only the Tivoli Tower, on south side, remains. Within the bounds are the **Town Hall** *(guided tour 10am to noon and 3 to 7pm),* 18C, and in parts 15C, house of the granddaughter of Mme de Sévigné *(p 77),* the **Church of N.-D.-de-Nazareth,** in which 12C south doorway, has four decorative covings descending on to small columns, and 17C **White Penitents' Chapel** *(open 1 June to 31 August 10am to noon and 3 to 7pm),* with contemporary woodwork and a finely wrought iron gate entrance. There are also a number of **old houses** scattered in the town (36 Grande-Rue, corner of Rue de l'Échelle, Place Gutenberg).

Continue W along D 941.

Grignan*. – *Description p 77.*

Take D 541 and turn left into D 71.

Chamaret. – Pop 349. A clock tower converted from a fine belfry, relic of the massive castle perched high on a rock, dominates the landscape.

Continue along D 71. The road is bordered by fields of lavender separated by clumps of oak trees, beneath which truffles are found, and by lines of cypresses.

Montségur-sur-Lauzon. – Pop 925. The modern village stands at a crossroads. *In front of the town hall, take the street on the left, turn right and then take the uphill path.* The original village was built on the hilltop with a network of streets coming out by the half-underground church. From the ramparts there is a **panoramic view** of the Tricastin countryside, Baronnies and Mount Ventoux.

Take D 71B going E. There are views of the Lance Mountain and the Nyons countryside.

Richerenches. – Pop 590. The town, a truffle market, was founded as a commandery by the Templars in 12C. The plan is rectangular with the walls still flanked at the corners by round towers; the gate is beneath the belfry, a square machicolated tower with a heavy, nailed door. The remains of the temple stand to the left of the church.

D 20 goes SE through Visan.

N.-D.-des-Vignes Chapel. – *Guided tour 1 April to 1 December 2 to 5pm, closed Tuesdays; the rest of the year Saturdays and Sundays only 2 to 5pm.* The 13C chapel is decorated in the nave with 15C panelling, in the chancel is a 13C polychrome wood statue of the Virgin, the object of a popular pilgrimage on 8 September.

D 20 continues across D 94 to join D 975 where you turn left for Vaison.

VALS-LES-BAINS

Michelin map 246 fold 21 – *Local map p 36* – Pop 3 976 – *Facilities p 8*

The spa town of Vals-les-Bains, barely 300m wide, extends for over a mile up the valley of the Volane, from its confluence with the Ardèche at the foot of volcanic mountains.

The 150 cold mineral springs were first discovered to be impregnated with bicarbonate of soda (the most well known Source St Jean) and, in one case (Source Dominique), with traces of iron and arsenic, in 17C; by mid-19C when « taking the waters » was as much a fashionable as medicinal occupation, Vals received as many as 55 000 visitors in the season *(1 May to 30 September).* Today more water than ever is consumed owing to the bottling plant (**D**) *(open)* in the centre of the town, which each year dispatches some 4 million bottles to all parts of France. Among the well kept **parks,** two favouiites are the Casino and the **Intermittent** (**B**); the latter is named after a spring, surrounded by a basalt lined basin, which sends up a 8m - 26ft jet of water every six hours *(11.30am and 5.30pm in summer; 10am to 4.30pm in winter).*

Combes Rock (Rocher des Combes). – *2 km - 1 mile – plus 1/4 hour on foot Rtn.* The summit (alt 480m - 1 575ft) commands a view of the Ardèche Gap (SE), the Tanargue Massif (WSW), Ste-Marguerite Chapel on its hill (NW), the low Mézilhac Range (N), the Gourdon Rock and the Coiron Plateau (E).

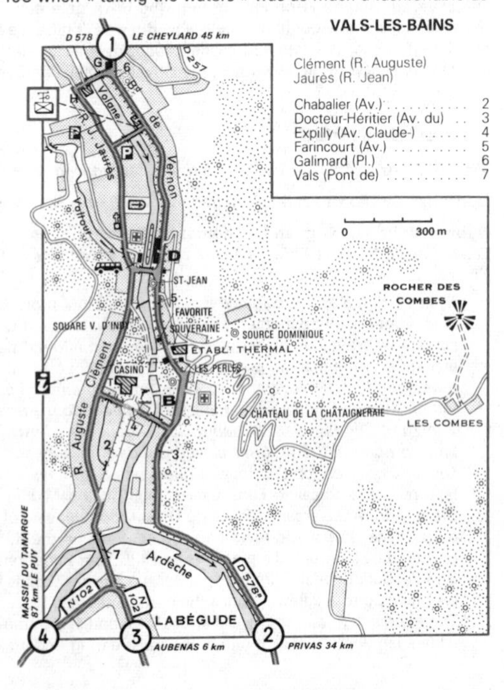

EXCURSIONS

Tanargue Massif★★: from Vals-les-Bains to Valgorge – *62 km - 38 1/2 miles – about 3 hours – Local map below*

The Tanargue, a crystalline range of granite, gneiss and micaschist at the southern tip of the high volcanic masses of south central France, is one of the wildest mountain areas in the locality.

Much of its attraction lies in the jagged outline of its peaks, formed by the upheavals in the Tertiary and Quaternary Eras when the old part of the Hercynean chain, which had been smoothed by erosion to a plateau by the end of the Secondary Era, was forced up in the Tertiary Era by the Alpine folding, exposing the micaschist layers to erosion.

Intense volcanic activity in the Quaternary Era caused rock flows on the periphery of the region, such as the one at Jaujac which filled the Lignon Valley and has now been partially worn away by the river.

The Tanargue is well known for the violence of its autumn storms: thunder echoes awsomely; streams suddenly become raging torrents, as water pours from the sky down the steep mountainsides, and just as suddenly abate.

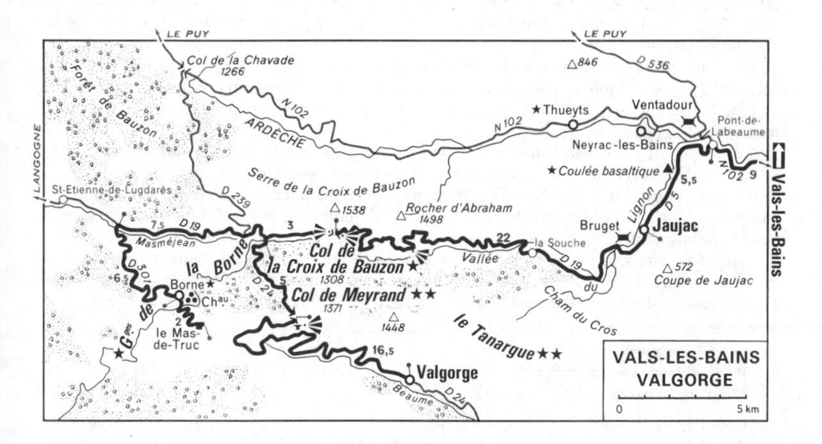

Leave Vals-les-Bains by ④, N 102 towards Le Puy. Bear left at Pont-de-Labeaume into D 5 towards Jaujac.

The road follows the Lignon Valley, still partially blocked by basalt rocks which flowed down it in the Quaternary period during the eruption of the Jaujac Coupe, a volcano which lies southeast of the town of the same name *(see below)*. Halfway up the valley, park the car *(signboard)* and walk to the edge of the rock ledge along which the road has been laid, to look at the **flow★** (coulée basaltique) which is remarkable for its composition of vertical black rock columns, relieved by an occasional grey-blue riser.

Jaujac. – Pop 1 085. The Chastelas quarter, on the left bank, distinguished by 15 and 16C houses and the ruins of the medieval fortress, is the most attractive part of the town.

On leaving you can see the small 15C Bruget Castle immediately on the right, and to the left Jaujac Coupe where there are mineral water springs.

Beyond La Souche the landscape becomes truly mountainous: ahead rises the summit of the Rock of Abraham (alt 1 498m - 4 915ft); pine trees cover the north facing slopes to the left of the winding road.

After 10km - 8 miles there is a **view★** back down the Lignon Valley to the Coiron Plateau on the horizon.

Croix de Bauzon Pass★. – The **view★** from the 1 308m - 4 290ft high pass takes in the line of the Borne and Masméjean Valleys, with the Margeride Mountains on the horizon to the west.

For a detour to Borne Gorges follow D 19.

Borne Gorges★. – *Detour of 14 km - 9 miles from the junction of D 19 and D 24. Follow D 19 going towards St-Étienne de Lugdarès; turn left into D 301 (narrow road).* Broom covered moors give way to a bird's-eye view of the gorge as the road descends to **Borne★**, poised on its secluded site above the constricted channel of the River Borne, which is dominated by castle ruins framed by a rock cirque. The mountain to the south west is the Goulet.

The detour can be extended *(4 km - 3 miles)* to **Mas-de-Truc,** a hamlet deep in the mountains. *Return to D 24.*

Take D 24 going south.

Meyrand Pass★★. – Alt 1 371m - 4 500ft. Suddenly a splendid corniche road opens up. Below the pass, to the left of a single, upstanding boulder, there is a balcony viewpoint from which an immense **panorama★★** extends from left to right to include the Tanargue Summit (E), the Valgorge Valley and range (ESE), with the Ardèche Valley dominated by the Dent de Rès in the background (SE) and dominating everything to the southwest is the 1 699m - 5 575ft, high, Mount Lozère.

Beyond the small village of Loubaresse the road is sheltered by chestnut trees with successive views of Valgorge Gap. Below the bare slopes of the Tanargue Heights the road winds down into the Baume Valley.

Valgorge. – Pop 433. This modest village stands in a verdant setting of orchards and vineyards.

Montpezat-sous-Bauzon. – Pop 831. *10 km - 6 miles – Local map p 36. Leave Vals by ③, N 102; at Pont-de-Labeaume bear right into D 536.* Immediately to your left at the road fork are the commanding medieval ruins of Ventadour Castle. Montpezat is known for its 20C prototype hydro-electric station. The village stands on a basalt flow of rock which spilled out of a neighbouring volcano (Gravenne de Montpezat) in the early Quaternary period and thus spans a million years in geological and scientific interest.

The **hydro-electric complex** *(visit for groups on written application to EDF-GRPH Loire BP 54, 42005 St-Étienne Cedex),* which came into operation in 1954, is sited at the Atlantic/Mediterranean watershed: the Loire River rises nearby at an altitude of approximately 1 000m - 3 250ft, and 17 km - 9 miles away on the southeast slope of the Mézenc Range, is the Fontolière, beginning its course south at an altitude of 350m - 1 000ft. A tunnel was bored between the two rivers resulting in a waterfall of approximately 650m - 2 250ft; a power station, built 60m - 200ft below the water course, now produces, on average, 300 million kWh a year. To control the waters of the Upper Loire a number of dams have been constructed and a mountain reservoir created at Lake Issarlès. (For the part played by the hydro-electric stations in the overall production of electricity in France, *see pp 14, 100 and 101*).

300m beyond the road to the power station and still some 500m - 1/3 mile before the village, turn right. Park the car at the end of the brief surfaced track and walk (1/4 hour Rtn) towards the concrete remains.

A promontory, the **Éperon de Pourcheyrolles★,** about 100m - 300ft, below the last pylon, commands a view of the basalt spur crowned by the ruins of the medieval Pourcheyrolles Castle, and the basalt stream (right) which ends in an impressive cirque of dense black rock, over which tumbles the sparkling Pourseille Cascade.

Return to the main road and cross the bridge. Turn right into Route des Chaudouards.

At the end of the narrow road stands, **N.-D.-de-Prévenchère,** *(to visit out of season, apply at the house nearby)* a sober 12-13C church whose appearance belies its interior interest. It comprises four short aisles, roofed with a variety of Romanesque and Gothic vaulting which is even compartmented above the polygonal apses.

The **main street** is marked by squat old granite houses typical of mountain settlements; many of the front walls are bowed, most are pierced at the centre with a low round arched porch. Note the house *(right)* built of black volcanic rock and decorated with 17C carving.

Les VANS

Michelin map 80 fold 8 – Pop 2 582

Bounded on the west by the jagged silhouette of the Barre Range, Les Vans lies at the centre of a fertile basin watered by the Chassezac. Approached from the Mas de l'Air, the site offers a vivid contrast between the harsh character of the schist ranges, and the white limestone of the southern landscape with its spring covering of golden broom and wild flowers.

The **church** has had a turbulent history. In 16C, on the conversion of the town to Protestantism, the existing parish church was demolished and a new one built; in 17C, with the return of Catholicism, the building was demolished and rebuilt. Later a new Protestant church, with a classical west front, was erected; a 15C Catholic church (restored) also stands.

EXCURSIONS

Naves. – Pop 286. *2.5 km - 1 1/2 mile W from Les Vans, D 901, and D 408 to the left.* The old village overlooking the Vans basin, remains medieval in character with narrow, arch spanned alleys, houses built of both schist and limestone, and, at the far end of the main street, a small Romanesque church *(temporarily closed, under restoration).*

Gravières; Les Salelles; Thines★★. – *Round tour of 43 km - 25 miles. Leave Les Vans by D 901 going W and turn right into D 113.*

Gravières. – Pop 445. The 12-15C church *(open Fridays 5.30 to 6pm in summer, 4.30 to 5pm in winter; daily before services),* recognizable from a distance by its solid belfry, contains, on the chancel wall, an interesting but mutilated Tree of Jesse carved in 14C.

Continue along D 113 to the bridge over the Chassezac; turn right into D 413.

Les Salelles. – Pop 181. The village, which overlooks a bend in the river, has a Gothic church (St-Sauveur) *(open Sundays 8.30 to 9am and 9.30 to 10.45am)* of beautiful pinkish sandstone. The fortified tower, which had been struck by lightning, was reconstructed early this century.

Return to D 113 and turn right; after 7 km - 4 miles, turn right again into D 513 and after a further 4 km - 2 1/2 miles right, into a small winding road.

Thines★★. – Pop 87. The minute village at the end of the road which climbs the Thines ravine, is surrounded by harsh, schist rock. Traditional crafts are sold at a house near the entrance to the village.

The Romanesque church is of exceptional interest.

The doorway, built of variously coloured stone, incorporates no less than four statue columns and a lintel carved with the *Entry into Jerusalem, The Last Supper,* and *Judas' Betrayal Kiss.* The decoration of the upper part of the building, particularly the **east end★** is amazing in so remote a district: below an imaginatively decorated cornice, the columns of the miniature blind arcading descend on to carved consoles, four of which continue as engaged columns to ground level.

To emphasize the architectural decoration the arches are outlined in alternate blocks of red sandstone and grey granite while the capitals are carved out of white limestone. Inside *(if closed, apply at the presbytery nearby)* note the extra large capital at the chancel opening.

Thines Church: the east end.

Return to Les Vans by the same route.

The Vivarais Cévennes villages★. – *Round tour of 34 km - 21 miles - allow 2 1/2 hours. Leave Les Vans by D 10 going N, turn right into D 250.*

Chambonas. – Pop 520. The village is still approached across an old bridge. The church, in part Romanesque, is a stout work ornamented with a sculptured frieze. Close by stands 12-17C castle flanked by towers with glazed tile roofs, at the centre of formal gardens attributed to Le Nôtre *(not open).*

Continue along D 250. The road crosses the Chassezac tributary, the Sure, before climbing up the boulder strewn hillside through vineyards and pinetrees to Payzac.

The Berre Range comes clearly into view as the road rises; there is also a glimpse, to the west, of the St-Pierre-le-Déchausselat belfry *(below).*

Payzac. – Pop 424. The village, firmly planted on the stoney upland, possesses a delightful small 12-15C country church *(open 2nd and 4th Saturdays each month, 5 to 8pm; 1st and 3nd Sundays each month 10am to noon).*

Take D 207 going north towards St-Jean-de-Pourcharesse.

Grey sandstone gives way to red; St Peter's Church and the Barre Range come into view. Beyond the village of Brès, built of red sandstone, another change of landscape occurs as the sandstone is replaced by schist and the road winds downhill through clumps of chestnut trees.

St-Jean-de-Pourcharesse. – Pop 55. The church is typical of the region with a stone roof and open gable belfry. From the terrace to the south the beak-like Bannelle and Guidon-du-Bouquet promontories are clearly visible beyond Les Vans *(p 52).*

Return to D 207 and bear right and then left into D 350. The unsurfaced road is bordered by chestnuts as it passes through a landscape of schist ravines where occasional impoverished villages perch on the steep rock walls. The houses, built of large blocks of stone, often copper coloured with age, usually have stone slab roofs with tiled later additions.

St-Pierre-le-Déchausselat. – The village rises in tiers up a hillside. Park the car by the church and walk down to the vineyards below the lowest row of houses to look west at the landscape.

D 350 continues down the hillside to the Chassezac River and Chambonas where D 10 returns to Les Vans.

Païolive Plateau★. – *19 km - 12 miles. Leave Les Vans by D 901 going SE and turn into D 216 by the Protestant church; turn left into D 251 going towards Banne.* Just before the village the road goes through a landscape of eerily eroded rocks.

Banne. – Pop 505. *Park the car in the square and walk up the slope behind the calvary.* The path leads to a grass plot overlooking the Jalès depression; climb to the top, the site of Banne's former citadel, for a **panorama★** extending from the Gard River (SSE) to the Lower Ardèche (E).

Make for D 901; turn left; after 3 km - 2 miles, bear right into D 252 to enter the woods.

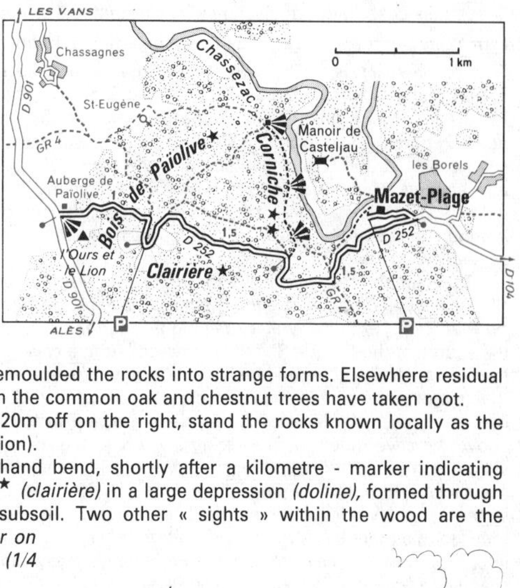

Païolive Woods★. – The woods extend for some 16 km² - just over 6 sq m on either side of the Chassezac; the ground consists of a grey jurassic schist which is both hard and permeable, making it resistant to wind and weather erosion, but susceptible to waterborne chemicals which have enlarged the fissures into deep defiles and remoulded the rocks into strange forms. Elsewhere residual rock has turned to clay on which the common oak and chestnut trees have taken root.

About 200m from D 901, some 20m off on the right, stand the rocks known locally as the Bear and the Lion (l'Ours et le Lion).

Further along D 252 in a left hand bend, shortly after a kilometre - marker indicating « Casteljau 4 km », is a **clearing★** *(clairière)* in a large depression *(doline),* formed through chemical erosion of the rock subsoil. Two other « sights » within the wood are the **Chassezac Corniche★★** *(3/4 hour on foot Rtn)* and the **Mazet-Plage** *(1/4 hour on foot Rtn).*

To get to the corniche, park the car at the second major bend (see map) by a heap of gravel and walk along the second of the two paths bearing left (beneath the telephone wires). The castle flanked by two towers is **Casteljau Manor.** The path bears to the left, still in sight of the manor, and brings you to the edge of the gorge, 150m - 450ft, above the green water winding past below at the foot of the cave pitted cliffs. The corniche path continues to the left for a further 175m, passing in front of the manor to reach a belvedere from which you can return either by the way you came or through the woods by the path marked on the map.

The Chassezac from Païolive Woods.

Cocalière Caves★. – *16km - 10 miles. Leave Les Vans by S, D 216; at St-Paul-le-Jeune turn right into D 104; turn left 100m after the right turn to Courry.*

The caves comprise an explored system of some 38km - 24 miles. *Open Spring school holidays to All Saints school holidays, 9am to noon and 2 to 6.30pm; 1 1/4 hours; 24F.*

A half mile long gallery at the foot of the entrance shaft leads to a series of chambers, rich and varied in colouring, and concreted formations, casting their reflections in still pools or rippling cascades; mysterious great disks, still unexplained by the specialists, sprout from the overhanging walls; roofs are covered with stalactites of pure white calcite or coloured by metal oxydes; a small dammed lake conceals precious cavities still being formed. Beyond the speleologists' base another dammed lake overflows into a scintillating **cascade,** and underground rivers plunge through shafts to lower levels. A rock chaos and the contorted roofs of a second group of caves illustrate the effects of chemical erosion.

The VAUCLUSE Plateau

Michelin map 81 folds 13 and 14

The Vaucluse Plateau, or heights, is an area of very considerable size, bordered by the Ventoux Massif (N), by cliffs which drop steeply to the Comtadin or Comtat Venaissin Plain (W) and by the wide Coulon Valley (S). To the northeast it is extended by the even higher **Albion Plateau** which ends in the lower slopes of Mount Lure.

The Albion Plateau, partially enclosed as a military missile base, is gently undulating country, served by wide roads and riddled with potholes *(avens)* – narrow fissures or gaping mouths – leading to a network of underground caves in the calcareous rock. Rainwater filters down into underground rivers at the impermeable rock base and emerges in resurgent springs, the most famous of which is the **Vaucluse Fountain** (Fontaine de Vaucluse) *(see below).*

Among the deeper caves in the system on the plateau are the **Aurel Aven** at 130m - 426ft; **Jean Nouveau,** 350m - 1 150ft which has an inner vertical face of 163m - 535ft; and further E, near Montsalier, in Mount Lure, the **Caladière** where speleologists have descended 487m - 1 598ft and discovered a fossilised hydrographic canal system. The **Cèdre Cave** has been penetrated to a depth of 210m - 690ft without any trace of water being discovered.

D 4 climbs the northern slope of the Vaucluse Plateau between Carpentras and Apt by means of a deep valley to the Col de Murs, from which the view opens out to the south over the Coulon Valley. The D 942 from Carpentras to Sault follows the line of the Nesque Gorges.

TOWNS AND SIGHTS

Banon. – Pop 973. The old fortified town stands on a rock spike dominating the new town with its tiled ridge roofs (view from behind the church apse). Banon has given its name to a well known goat's milk cheese, distinguished by its chestnut leaf wrapping.

Ferrassières. – Pop 124. Each July the village seems to float on a sea of purple lavender fields.

Fontaine-de-Vaucluse. – Pop 606. The village overlooked by a ruined **castle** *(1/2 hour on foot Rtn),* is famous on two counts: for the resurgent stream and as the place where the Italian poet, **Petrarch,** lived from 1337-53. During those years, he composed, in the Provençal-Sicilian style, the 366 poems and sonnets of the *Canzonière,* which were inspired by the unknown « Laura » whom the poet first saw in a church in Avignon on 6 April 1327 (d 1348). **Museum** *(temporarily closed).*

(After doc. of Bibliothèque Nationale)

Petrarch.

The fountain★★★ *(leave the car in the car park - 6F - from the Place de la Colonne take the chemin de la Fontaine 1/2 hour on foot Rtn),* fed by rainwater draining through the plateau, is the source of the Sorgue River and emerges from a cave at the foot of a rock cirque formed by high cliffs. In winter and spring the flow of water can rise to 150 cubic m a second - 32 985 gallons, and reach the level of the fig trees growing in the rock above the cave mouth before racing away over the rocks in a vivid green fury of tumbling foaming water. It is a magnificent spectacle and ranks among the most powerful resurgent streams in the world. In summer and autumn when the flow is reduced to a mere 8 cubic m - 1 760 gallons, the spring bubbles into a pool at the cave mouth before slipping away almost silently to join the nearby Sorgue River. *(Son et Lumière: 15 June to 15 September 9.30pm.)*

Between the fountain and the village is the **Underground world of Norbert Casteret** *(Chemin de la Fontaine. Guided tour 10am to noon and 2 to 7pm; closed Mondays and Tuesdays, except in July and August, and 1 November to 1 February; 12F)* which contains the **Casteret collection★** of limestone concretions collected by the speleogist during his 30 years of cave exploration. Next to the museum is a paper mill (Vallis Clausa) where paper can be seen being made according to the traditional methods. In the village stands a small Romanesque church, **St-Véran,** *(light switch at the church's entrance),* with barrel vaulting, an oven vaulted apse flanked by antique fluted columns and, in the crypt, the coffin of the saint, 6C bishop of Cavaillon, credited with having dispatched a local monster, known as the Coulobre.

Gordes★. – *Description p 76.*

L'Isle-sur-la-Sorgue. – Pop 13 205. The small town stands on an island in the River Sorgue at the foot of the Vaucluse Plateau. The site, the plane trees and general calm are enhanced by the town's two official sights: the church and the old hospital.

The **church,** which was rebuilt in 17C when it was given a west front of two superimposed classical orders, is of interest chiefly for its rich 17C interior **decoration★** after the Italian style. The **hospital** *(apply at the main gate, guided tour - time: 20 minutes - daily 1 June to 30 September; closed Sundays and holidays),* beside the Sorgue, boasts a great hall (gilded wood

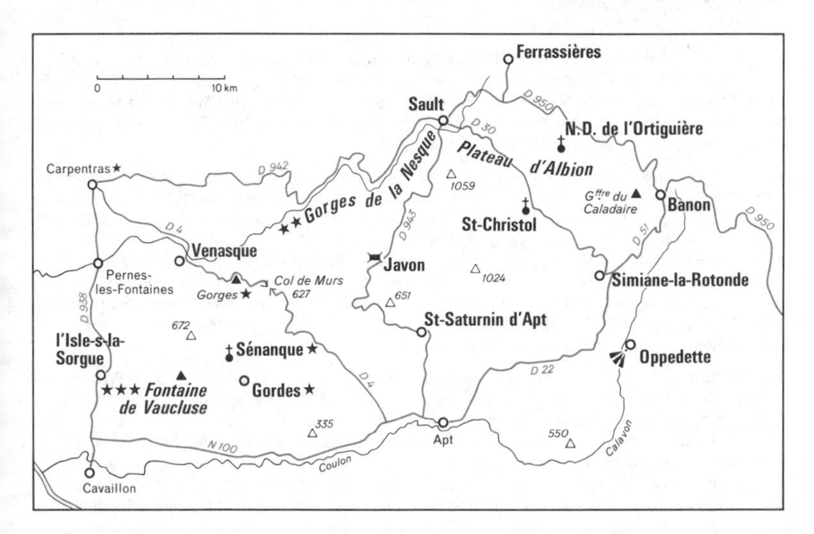

Madonna) and grand staircase, embellished by 18C wrought iron banister, a chapel with 18C woodwork, and pharmacy with Moustiers pottery jars and a huge 17C mortar. An additional attraction is the peaceful garden, ornamented by 18C fountain.

Javon Castle. – Four round towers flank the vast 16C, mullion windowed castle.

Nesque Gorges★★. – *Description p 91.*

N.-D.-de-l'Ortiguière. – The small 13C chapel, partly rebuilt in 19C, stands on a slight rise at the centre of the Albion Plateau. Inside are a table altar and four small geometrical pendants, ending in atlantes' heads. The adjoining hermitage is 17C.

Oppedette. – Pop 62. The hamlet perched on a spur, affords a good **view**★ *(belvedere near the cemetery)* of the deep gorge hollowed out by the Calavon and the site of the village itself.

Pernes-les-Fontaines. – Pop 6 961. The former capital of the Comtat Venaissin (968-1320) earns its living by preserving the cherries, strawberries, melons and grapes, grown in the locality.

The point of greatest interest is the old bridge over the Nesque. The bridge itself is a corbelled structure on which, over one of the piles, a minute chapel was built in 16C; at one end stands the contemporary 16C **Notre-Dame Gateway**★, to the right, the keep of the former castle of the Counts of Toulouse, now known as the **Clock Tower**, and slightly back, the unusual 18C **Cormorant Fountain.** On the far bank is the Church of **N.-D.-de-Nazareth** which is late 11C in parts.

The strange **Ferrande Tower** *(guided tours: apply at the tourist information centre in season, out of season Saturdays 10am - 12 noon; 6F)*, a quadrangular, crenellated building, on a little square but now hemmed in by houses, contains curious, unrelated, 13C frescoes.

St-Christol. – Pop 1 832. The church in this small town on the edge of the Albion Plateau, was built by Benedictines from the abbey in Villeneuve-lès-Avignon *(p 132)* in 12C, and enlarged by the addition of an aisle in 17C. *Door difficult to open.* The most interesting feature is the carving in the oven vaulted apse: the blind arcading is supported on six fluted columns, chiselled with reliefs of leaves, fruit and birds; above are foliated capitals; below are bases decorated with masks and fantastic animals. The Carolingian altar is carved on three sides.

St-Saturnin-d'Apt. – *Description p 35.*

Sault. – *Description p 91.*

Sénanque Abbey★. – *Description p 76.*

Simiane-la-Rotonde. – Pop 369. Tall houses form the ramparts of this minute fortified town crowned by a 12-13C tower, the former castle keep. Nice view of the countryside.

Venasque. – Pop 656. The village which was once capital of the Comtat Venaissin *(p 69)* and gave its name to the grant of land, stands on a foothill overlooking the Carpentras Plain. There are two buildings of interest and of ancient date in Venasque, and one nearby : respectively the baptistry, Notre-Dame Church and N.-D.-de-Vie Chapel.

The **baptistry**★ *(entrance, right of the presbytery; closed noon to 2pm; guide)*, dating from 6C or Merovingian period and remodelled in 11C, is one of France's oldest religious buildings. The Greek cross plan, with rib vaulting over the centre square, has arms of unequal length ending in apsidal chapels, each oven vaulted and decorated with blind arcading on slender marble columns with antique or, in the case of the east apsidal, Merovingian capitals. The hollow in the floor was for the font.

The **Church of Our Lady** which is 12 and 13C with considerable 15-18C alterations, contains, in the chancel, a 17C carved retable and a tabernacle door of the Resurrected Christ appearing to the disciples at Emmaus. In 2nd north chapel is a 15C Avignon school Crucifixion.

The **N.-D.-de-Vie Chapel** *(2.5 km - 1 1/2 mile N along D 28 and D 4 on the left)* which is 17C on 6C site, possesses a remarkable specimen of Merovingian sculpture in the tomb of Bohetius, Bishop of Carpentras and Venasque, who died in 604.

(After photo by Guillet-Lescuyer, Lyon)

N-D-de-Vie-Chapel: Bohetius' tombstone.

Mount VENTOUX ★★★

Michelin map 245 folds 9 and 10

Mount Ventoux is the dominant feature in the Provençal landscape. The lonely majesty of its white pyramid asserts its presence, commanding attention, although it is only 1 909m - 6 262ft high. The approach to the summit can be made from several directions and is one of the best excursions in Provence; the reward is an immense panorama over the Rhône Valley (W), the Vaucluse Plateau (S) and the Baronnies Plateau (N).

Weather. – There is nearly always a wind on Mount Ventoux, as its name suggests, particularly when the *mistral (p 101)* is blowing. The temperature at the top is on average 11°C - 20°F lower than at the foot; rainfall is twice as heavy and drains down the southern slopes to feed the Vauclusian springs. In winter the temperature may drop to -27°C (-17°F); the mountain is usually snow-capped above 1 300m - 4 265ft from December to April, and the slopes at Mont Serein on the north side and Chalet-Reynard on the south provide good skiing. *For information on driving conditions (mountain roads may be blocked between November and May) phone Mont Serein 36.03.20 or Carpentras 67.20.88. Note also that the D 974 is closed to traffic 15 November to 15 April between Chalet-Reynard and Mont Serein.*

Vegetation. – The lower slopes are covered with the trees and flowers typical of Provence - cypress, broom, aromatics and wild iris; polar species such as the Spitzbergen saxifrage and Icelandic poppy flourish near the summit *(first fortnight of July).*

The forests which once covered the mountainside were felled in 16C for ship building. Replanting, which has been going on since mid-19C, has now produced mature woods of Aleppo pine, oak, cedar, beech, pitch pine, fir and larch – at their most attractive in autumn. Above 1 600m - 5 250ft the terrain alters to become a vast field of dazzling white shingle.

The « conquest » of the summit. – From 1902-73 the road between Bédoin and the summit was used for motor car hill trials: the pre 1914-18 record, established by Boillot in 1913 in a Peugeot was 17′ 38″ (73 kmph - 45mph); in 1973, Mieusset in a March trial took 9′ 03.6 (142.278 kmph - 90 mph). The summit is sometimes included in the Tour de France cycle race.

1 ASCENT BY THE NORTH FACE★★

Round tour starting from Vaison-la-Romaine – *73 km - 45 miles – 1 day*

As in summer the summit may be shrouded in cloud or midday mist, it is advisable to set out early or remain at the top until sunset. In winter the atmosphere tends to be clearer but the last stage of the ascent has to be made on skis.

Road subject to restrictions: see above.

Leave Vaison-la-Romaine (p 119) SE by D 938. The road goes up the smiling Grozeau Valley, overlooked from W by the Dentelles de Montmirail (p 70).

Crestet. – *2.5 km - 1 1/2 miles along D 76. Description p 70.*

Malaucène. – *Description p 70.*

Leave Malaucène by D 974. The road was laid in 1933 as a tourist route and, although as steep as the south face road, is more open and airy in hot weather; after high winds and storms the last 3 km - 2 miles may be slow, owing to stones and boulders on the road, but it is seldom completely blocked. Drivers are advised to go up by this road and down through Bédoin to spare their cars.

N.-D.-du-Grozeau. – The old square chapel stands probably on the site of a pagan temple, sheltered by trees and the surrounding cliffs. It was built by Benedictines as part of a monastery, where Clement V, first of the dynasty of French popes at Avignon, came to stay on several occasions.

Le Grozeau Vauclusian Spring (Source Vauclusienne). – The spring forms a pool of clear water as it emerges from a rock beneath trees to the left of the road.

The road continues up the northern slope, revealing a view of the Vaucluse Plateau; it climbs through pastures and pinewoods past the Mont Serein refuge to reach the steepest and most *ravined* face of the mountain.

The **belvedere★** to the left of the road, beyond the Ramayettes hut, overlooks the Ouvèze (NW) and Grozeau Valleys (WNW), the Baronnies Massif (NE) and the Plate Summit (N).

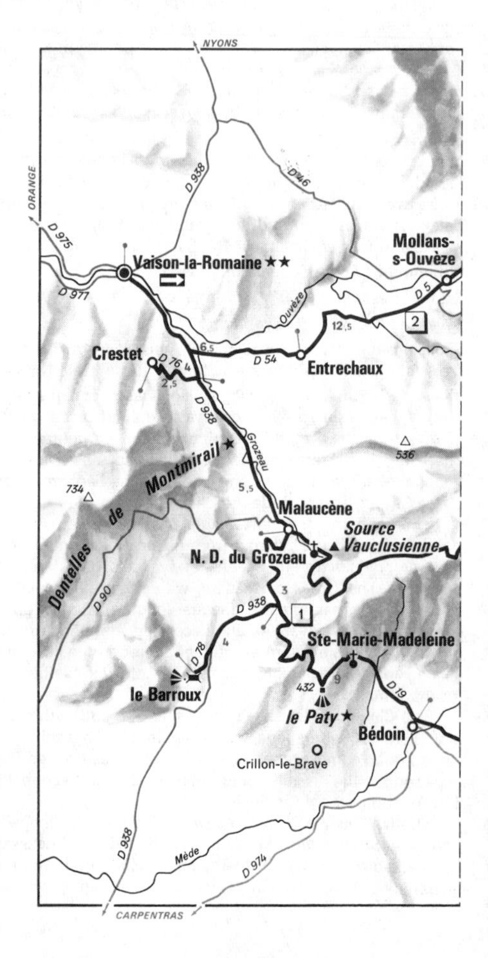

Mont Serein. – Alt 1 445m - 4 740ft. Winter sports resort.

The panorama widens to include the Dentelles de Montmirail (W) and the heights along the Rhône west bank. Two more long hairpin bends bring the road to the top.

Mount Ventoux Summit★★★. – The 1 909m - 6 260ft summit is spiked with scientific equipment: a weather observatory, an air force radar station and a television mast. The view from the car park looks east-northeast towards the Alps with the Vercors Range due north, but it is the platform on the south side that reveals the almost circular **panorama★★★** *(viewing table):* it swings from the Pelvoux Massif (NE) to the Cévennes (W) by way of the Lubéron (SSE), Ste Victoire (SE), Marseilles, the Berre Lagoon and the Estaque Hills (S), the Alpilles (WSW) and the Rhône Valley (W). On very clear days the Canigou (alt 2 786m - 8 140ft) is visible way over to the southwest in the Pyrenees.

At night the Provençal plain is transformed into a dark carpet studded with clusters of glittering lights. On the coast the lighthouses probe the darkness in a regular pattern.

The road which winds down the south face through the white shingle to the woods, is the oldest road, built in 1885 to serve the observatory. In 22 km - 14 miles of hairpin bends to Bédoin, it descends 1 600m - 5 200ft.

Le Chalet-Reynard. – Excellent local slopes have made Chalet-Reynard a popular resort for skiers from Avignon, Carpentras and other nearby towns.

Below the belts of pinetrees, beeches, oaks and cedars, the slopes have been planted with vines, peaches, cherries and a few small groves of olives. The view extends across the Comtadin Plain (SW) and the Vaucluse Plateau (S) to the Lubéron.

St-Estève. – From the sharp bend just before the village there is a good **view★**, towards the Dentelles de Montmirail and the Comtat Venaissin Plain (W) and to the Vaucluse Plateau (E).

Bédoin. – Pop 1 842. *Facilities* *p 8.* Picturesque small streets lead to the Jesuit-style church which possesses several elegant altars.

Take the D 19.

Ste-Marie-Madeleine Monastery. – *Not open to the public.* The modest 11C chapel is pure Provençal Romanesque in style, with three small, rounded, apsidal chapels covered with stone tiles and a disproportionately massive square belfry with twin bays above the chancel.

Le Paty★. – The panoramic **view★** with the picturesque stepped village of Crillon-le-Brave in the foreground, extends from the Alpilles (SW), across the Comtat Venaissin and more distant Vaucluse Plateau (S) to Mount Ventoux (E).

Le Barroux. – Pop 437. *5 km - 3 miles off D 19 along D 938 and D 78.* The restored Renaissance **château** *(open 1 July to 31 August)* above the village has a terrace *(open 10am to 7pm)* which commands an almost circular **view★** from the Dentelles de Montmirail (NW), across the Carpentras Plain to the Vaucluse Plateau and Mount Ventoux (NE)

Return to Vaison-la-Romaine along D 938.

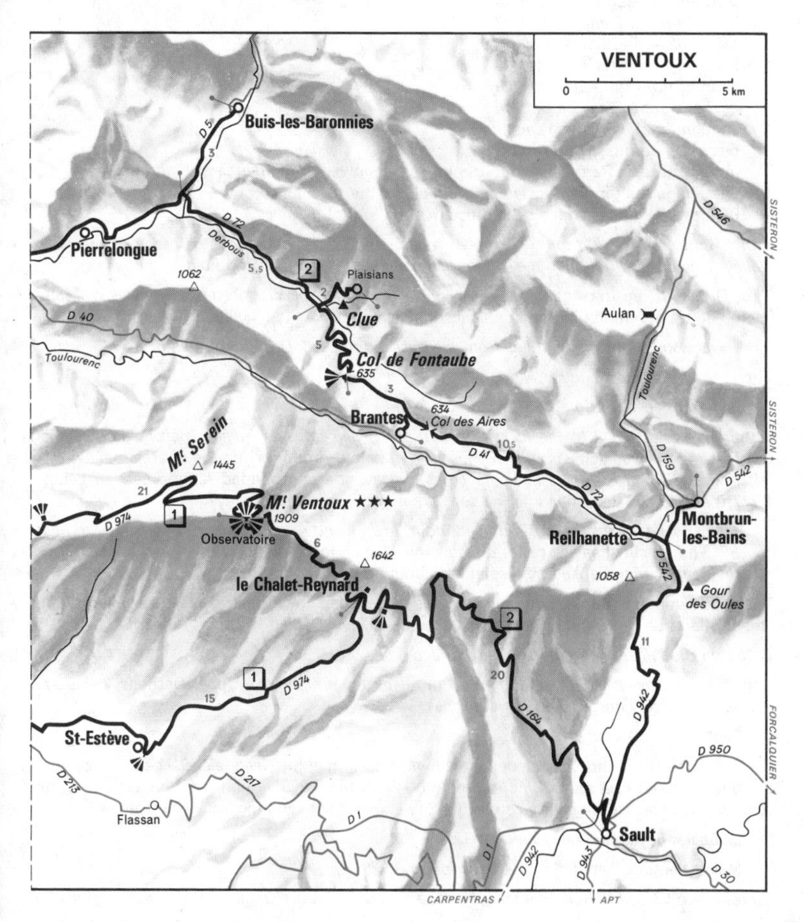

2 ASCENT BY THE EAST FACE★★

Round tour starting from Vaison-la-Romaine

113 km - 70 miles – 1 day - Local map p 128.

Road subject to restrictions: p 128.

Leave Vaison-la-Romaine (p 119) SE, by D 938; turn left into D 54.

Entrechaux. – *Description p 97.*

Shortly before Mollans-sur-Ouvèze, D 40 turns right along the Toulourenc Valley to join up with D 72 between Col-des-Aires and Reilhanette described below.

Mollans-sur-Ouvèze. – *Description p 97.*

Pierrelongue. – *Description p 97.*

D 5 goes through the southern section of the closely ravined Baronnies range *(p 53).*

Buis-les-Baronnies. – *3 km - 2 miles from D 5-D 72 T junction. Description p 53.*

Turn right into D 72 to go up the Derbous Valley.

Plaisians Clue. – The road plunges into this most unusual gorge: small, short and narrow.

Fontaube Pass. – Alt 635m - 2 083ft. View of the Baronnies (NNW).

Brantes. – Pop 85. The picturesquely built village on the steep north side of the Toulourenc Valley, looks straight across from its spectacular **site**★ to the summit of Mount Ventoux.

(After photo by Léo Pélissier)

Brantes.

As D 41 climbs to the Col-des-Aires (alt 634m - 2 080ft) it overlooks the Toulourenc Valley, Brantes village and the ravined north face of the Ventoux.

Reilhanette. – Pop 114. This small village stands on a knoll.

Montbrun-les-Bains. – Pop 523. *1 km - 1/2 mile off D 72 by D 542.* A 14C belfry or clock tower in the main street, a church *(to visit apply at the barber's shop Place de Beffroi)* containing 17C carved altarpiece by Bernus *(p 66),* framing a picture by Parrocel, and four round castle towers *(not open),* testify to the great age of the village built in tiers up the hillside, above the confluence of the Anary and Toulourenc Rivers. New houses have been erected at the foot of the hill.

From Montbrun a round tour (37 km - 23 miles - allow 1 1/2 hours) can be made up the Anary Valley to Séderon and down the Toulourenc Valley. Michelin map **81** *Fold 4*

Take D 542 NE up the Anary Valley, spiked with needle rocks and affording views of Mount Albion and the Ventoux, before it reaches the **Macuègne Pass** (alt 1 068m - 3 503ft).

Ferrassières. – *10 km - 6 miles from the pass along D 63. Description p 126.*

The road continues along the Méouge Valley.

Séderon. – *Description p 53.*

Continue along D 542 to the fork; turn left into D 546 towards Buis-les-Baronnies. The road climbs to the **Mévouillon Pass** (alt 889m - 2 917ft) before dropping into the Charuis Valley; bear left into D 359, which rises again to cross the lavender surrounded Aulan Pass (alt 845m - 2 772ft) and finally descends into the somewhat arid Toulourenc Valley.

Aulan Castle. – *Guided tour (time: 1/2 hour) in July and August 10am to noon and 2 to 6pm; 8F.* The castle (heavily restored) built on a spur to command the valley, consists of a residential wing flanked by a solid keep abutted by a round tower.

The road overlooks the Toulourenc Valley as it cascades down deep **gorges**★ between Mount Ubac (S) and Le Buc (N) before entering a fertile valley carpeted with fruit orchards.

D 159 on the left returns you to Montbrun-les-Bains.

Continue by way of D 542 going south out of the town along the Upper Derbous Valley and across the narrow gorge, the **Gour des Oules.**

Sault. – *Description p 91.*

Go NW along D 164 through the upper, cultivated section of the Nesque *(p 91)* before ascending the pine covered east face of Mount Ventoux. From the belvedere on the lefthand side of the road there is an extensive **view** across the Sault countryside and the Vaucluse Plateau.

Le Chalet-Reynard. – *Description p 129.*

Mount Ventoux Summit★★★. – *Description p 128.*

To return to Vaison-la-Romaine take the road described on p 129, but in the opposite direction.

VILLENEUVE-DE-BERG

Michelin map 246 fold 22 – Pop 2 083 – *Facilities p 8*

Villeneuve was created from political expediency as far back as 13C; the King, Philip the Bold, wished to extend the royal prerogative in Vivarais, and the abbots of Mazan, established to the northwest close to the source of the Ardèche, were in search of a protector. A treaty was duly signed between monarch and monastery in 1284, providing for the construction of a fortified town and granting a charter of privileges to the citizens. The town, once conceived, was built in six years, prospered, and remained the legal centre of the Lower Vivarais until the Revolution.

Old town. – Despite the ravages of the Wars of Religion, several of the 14C rampart towers still stand. Almost as old is 14C doorway to the hospital, over which can be seen the combined arms of the town's protectors: *the fleur-de-lys* and the abbey cross. In the area south of N 102, the 17C character of the old town comes fully into its own with entire streets lined with the carriage doorways of stately mansions whose façades are flanked by ornamental turrets, and possess courtyards dignified by grand staircases, by Renaissance house fronts decorated with wrought iron balconies and fanlights...

St-Louis. – The exterior of the church shows the influence of Mazan Abbey in the sobriety of its Cistercian lines; inside are two Baroque 17 and 18C altarpieces and a carved wood pulpit with a magnificent 17C eagle at the foot.

Viewing table. – Walk round to the rear of the statue of **Olivier de Serres** (1539-1619), Huguenot, native of the village and Father of French Agriculture, who put his ideas into practice and then wrote them down in a book which became a classic, not only for its contents but also as French literature – *The Changing Scene in Agriculture and Management of the Fields.*

The panorama extends from Mount Lozère (WSW) to the Coiron Plateau (NE). The Mirabel Tower *(opposite)* stands out in the foreground to the right (N).

EXCURSIONS

Upper Valley of the Ibie. – *12 km - 8 miles S by D 558 which follows the river's course along the western edge of the Gras Plateau (p 60).*

St-Maurice-d'Ibie. – *Description p 61.*

Les Salelles. – *Description p 61.*

Montbrun Caves. – *13 km - 8 miles – plus 3/4 hour on foot Rtn. Leave Villeneuve (NE) by N 102 towards Viviers; turn left into D 7 at St-Jean-Le-Centenier; after approximately 6 km - 3 miles on the plateau turn right into a road to « Les Balmes ». Park the car by the farm (signposted).*

The walls of the narrow ravine are pitted with caves (balmes), which at one time served as troglodyte houses. To get the best view, go down the left wall; the path is difficult but you will see rare two storey dwellings, the largest of which opens on to a small, grassed terrace, complete with benches carved from the living rock.

Le Pradel; Mirabel★. – *12 km - 8 miles by N 102 and D 458.*

Le Pradel. – Turn off, left, to visit the onetime estate of Olivier de Serres *(see above)*, now an Agricultural School.

Return to D 458 and turn right into D 258.

Mirabel★. – Pop 313. Mirabel was a strategically situated strongpoint commanding the main highway between the Cévennes and the Rhône and as such played an important part in the Wars of Religion and subsequent unrest, until it was dismantled in 1628. All that remains on the basalt rock platform is the square keep *(private property)*, built of dark basalt stone strikingly relieved by white limestone quoins.

From the edge of the basalt plateau above the village *(take the uphill path on the left just beyond the war memorial)*, there is a **panorama★★** of the Auzon Depression, the Lower Vivarais countryside (SW), the Ardèche breach (S) and the sawtoothed crests of the Tanargue Massif (W).

A second feature is the **drive★ to Le Baumier** *(2,5 km - 2 miles)* - Drive 200 yards beyond the keep before turning right and continue for a further 1 1/2 miles. This short itinerary, following the cliff edge, affords wide views of the Lower Vivarais countryside.

Alba; La Roche. – *14 km - 9 miles by N 102.*

Alba. – Pop 824. 12-16C Alba castle *(open end of June to early September, 10am to noon and 3 to 7pm; in May, September and October Sunday afternoons only; 7F)*, a massive southern fortress, stands in a commanding position above the Escoutay River *(painting exhibitions are held)*. In the valley below lie the remains of Alba Augusta Helvorium, capital of the Helvii, a thriving Gallo-Roman town, to which Augustus granted many privileges. It was destroyed by Barbarians in 4C when the bishop fled to Viviers *(p 102)*. Recent excavations have uncovered traces of a house, theatre, forum and baths on either side of D 107 going south.

Beside the river in the shadow of a volcanic chimney, exposed by erosion, stands the medieval village of **La Roche,** where casemate houses have been built into the remains of the ramparts.

VILLENEUVE-LES-AVIGNON ★

Michelin map 246 fold 25 – *Local maps pp 72 and 102* – Pop 9 535 - *Plan of built up area in the current Michelin Red Guide France under Avignon.*

Villeneuve-lès-Avignon, the City of the Cardinals, shared in the prosperity of its majestic neighbour, the City of the Popes, during the 100 years of papal residence in Avignon. Sunset is the best time for admiring the view of the Popes' Palace from the ramparts of Villeneuve.

HISTORICAL NOTES

The name means « new town by Avignon » and the town owes its origins to the rivalry between the rulers of France and the Holy Roman Empire, who became neighbours on the Rhône in 1271 after the Albigensian Crusade. Whenever the river, which belonged to the French crown, flooded parts of Avignon, the French king claimed them as his territory and demanded taxes from the inundated citizens. In 13C Philip the Fair fortified his end of St-Bénézet Bridge and in 14C John the Good and Charles V built a massive fortress, the St-André Fort, on Mount Andaon, then an island in midstream.

The Cardinals, arriving at the papal court in 14C and finding no suitable accommodation in Avignon, began to build magnificent residences *(livrées)* across the river in Villeneuve until at one time there were 15. The prosperity, which the Cardinals' patronage of churches and monastic houses brought to the town, remained long after the papal court had returned to Rome. In 17 and 18C fine houses lined the Grande-Rue; in the convents, which became veritable museums, an active and brilliant life flourished until the Revolution swept away the aristocratic and ecclesiastical regimes.

■ VAL DE BÉNÉDICTION CHARTERHOUSE★ *time: 1 hour*

Open 1 April to 30 September 9am to noon and 2 to 6.30pm (all day in July); the rest of the year 10am to noon and 2 to 5pm; closed 1 January, 1 May 1 and 11 November and 25 December; 9F, 4.50F Sundays.

In 1352 the papal conclave met in Avignon and elected the General of the Carthusian Order as Pope, but he refused the throne out of humility. To commemorate this gesture Innocent VI, who became Pope instead, founded a Charterhouse on his own land *(livrée)* in Val de Bénédiction. The house became the most important in France.

The Carthusian Order was founded in 1084 by St Bruno. It consisted of Fathers, who used the title Dom, and Brothers, who lived a communal life like monks in other orders. The Fathers, however, lived singly in cells spending their time in prayer, study and manual work. Three times a day the monks met in chapel to sing the offices. They took their meals alone except on Sundays when brief periods of conversation were also allowed.

The Charterhouse is now a cultural centre (C.I.R.C.A.) organizing artistic and cultural events. In July and August International Summer Meetings, for programme information ☏ (90) 25.05.46.

Enter by the great door, no 60 Rue de la République. A plaque on the right of the door marks the highest flood level reached by the Rhône on 1st May 1856.

Cloister door. – It separates Place des Chartreux from Allée des Muriers. The proportions and ornamentation of the 17C door can be admired from inside: fluted consoles supporting the balconies, lions' heads, fir cones decorating the pediment, noble draperies crowning the central section.

Pass through the reception bureau (bureau d'acceuil) and skirt the church's south side.

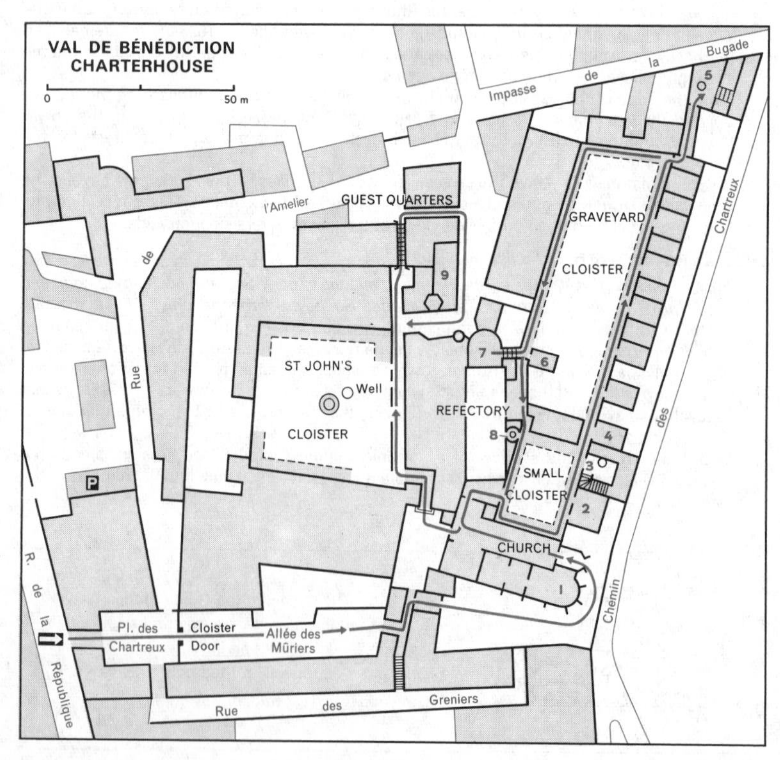

Church. – Go through the nave, the apse opens out with a view on to St-André Fort *(below).* On the north side, the apse of the other nave contains the tomb of Innocent VI (1): the white marble figure lies on a high plinth of Pernes stone decorated with arcading; the Flamboyant Gothic canopy has been restored. The two chapels that follow, dedicated to St Michael and St Bruno are open only during exhibitions.

Small Cloister. – The east gallery opens into the chapter house (2) and the Sacristans' yard (3) with its well and picturesque staircase.

Graveyard Cloister. – The great 12C cloister, 80m - 262ft × 20m - 66ft, with its warm Provençal colouring, is lined with cells for the Fathers, each cell consisting of a small open court and two rooms, one of which communicates with the cloister by a hatch. The first cell (4) can be visited.

At the northeast end of the cloister a corridor leads to the *bugade* (5), the wash-room, which has preserved its well and chimney for drying clothes.

Opening off the west gallery is a little chapel (6) corresponding to the apse (7) of the Fathers' refectory. This chapel is decorated with lovely frescoes attributed to Matteo Giovanetti (14C) *(p 46).* They illustrate scenes from the life of John the Baptist and the life of Christ. Particularly fine are the Presentation in the Temple and the Entombment.

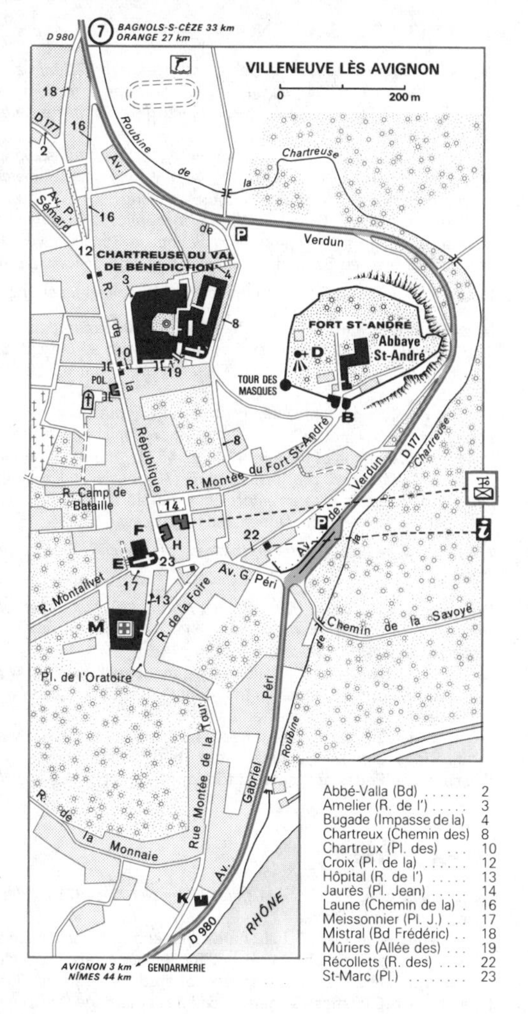

Refectory. – *Not open to the public.* It is the former Tinel (18C) now a concert hall. Between it and the northwest corner of the small cloister is the lavabo (8), a small circular building beneath a beautiful 18C cupola.

St John's Cloister. – The galleries are no more, but several of the Fathers' cells remain. At the centre stands the huge 18C St John's fountain with its well and handsome basin.

At the end of a court (northeast of St John's Cloister) a staircase descends under the guest quarters, altered in the 18C (lovely north façade). Come back towards St John's Cloister, skirting the crenellated east end of the Tinel; note the bakery (9) with its hexagonal tower.

■ ADDITIONAL SIGHTS

St-André Fort★. – *Open 1 April to 30 September 9am to noon and 2 to 6.30pm; the rest of the year 10am to noon and 2 to 3pm; closed 1 January, 1 May, 1 and 11 November and 25 December; 5.50F. Doors close 1/2 hour before closing time.*

The fortification, erected by John the Good and Charles V in the last half of the 14C *(see above),* consists of giant twin towers (**B**) guarding a **gateway★**, one of the finest examples of medieval fortifications still to be seen. Within the ramparts were a Benedictine monastery, a 12C Romanesque chapel, N.-D.-de-Belzévet (**D**) *(not open to the public)* and the village of St-André all of which are in ruins.

The platform *(85 steps)* at the summit of the twin towers commands a beautiful **view★★**: *(foreground)* the town, Philip the Fair's Tower, the Rhône Valley, Avignon and the Palace of the Popes; *(distance)* Mount Ventoux (NE), the Lubéron Range (ESE) and the Alpilles (SSE).

St-André Abbey. – *Terraces and gardens are open 10am to noon and 2 to 5pm; 4F.*

The entrance gate, left wing, – with a good **view★** of the Rhône Valley, Avignon and Roquemouret – and well shaded gardens are all that remain of the Benedictine abbey founded in 10C on the ancient pilgrims' way to Ste-Casarie (6C).

Church (**E**). – Closed Tuesdays. The former collegiate church, when founded in 1333 by Cardinal Arnaud de Via, nephew of Pope John XXII, was built with a separate belfry at the east end which straddled the public footpath. Later on the monks obtained permission to re-direct the path. They blocked off the belfry arcade, converted it to a chancel and linked it to the existing church by adding an extra bay to the nave.

It contains paintings by Philippe de Champaigne (*Visitation* – 1st north chapel), Simon Vonet (*The Healing of Tobias* – 6th chapel), Nicolas Mignard (*St Bruno* – right of the chancel), Pierre Mignard (*Mystical Marriage* and *Virgin with Lamb* – 3rd south chapel).

The 18C high altar is ornamented with a low relief depicting Christ Laid in the Tomb, from the Charterhouse. On the right is an abbot's chair (18C) from St-André Abbey.

Sacristy. – *Open 1 April to 30 September, 10am to 12.30pm and 3 to 7.30pm; the rest of the year, 10am to noon and 2 to 5pm; closed Tuesdays and February; 8.40F; combined ticket with the Municipal Museum 15.80F.*

The 15C sacristy houses a **Virgin**★★, a beautiful sculpture in polychrome ivory carved in the 14C with Mary's back following the curved line of the tusk and both figures smiling.

Note also the 15C marble Virgin, in duplicate with the figures back to back, from the Nuremberg School, a Renaissance halberd and an 18C Blessed Sacrament veil adorned with delicate pearls.

(After photo by Arch. Phot. Paris)

The Ivory Virgin.

Cloister (F). – The cloister belongs to the 14C collegiate church.

Municipal Museum (M). – *Open 1 April to 30 September, 10am to 12.30pm and 3 to 7.30pm (2 to 5pm 1 October to 31 March); closed Tuesdays, February, 1 January, Easter, 1 May and 25 December; 8.40F.*

The exhibits come, for the most part, from the charterhouse, the abbey or other establishments long since vanished. The pictures include a **Coronation of the Virgin**★★ of 1453 by the Avignon painter, Enguerrand Quarton, the furniture, 15-17C chests and a Louis XIII cupboard. There is also an interesting marble death mask (15C) of King René's second wife, Queen Jeanne of Laval.

Owing to a possible transfer the rest of the collection is not on display.

Philippe-le-Bel Tower (K). – *Open 1 April to 30 September, 9am to 12.30pm and 3 to 7.30pm; the rest of the year 10am to noon and 2 to 5pm, closed Tuesdays, 1 January, all February, Easter, 1 May and 25 December; 5.50F.*

The tower with its foundations deep in the rock, was the key structure in the defence work at the west end of the bridge. As first built (1293-1307), it was two stages high, then in 14C it was increased by a further storey and a watch tower.

The **view**★★ from the terrace *(176 steps)* extends over Villeneuve and the St-André fortifications, along the course of the Rhône, across the St-Bénézet Bridge to Avignon and the Palace of the Popes and beyond to Mount Ventoux (NE), the Montagnette (S) and, further still, the Alpilles (SE).

EXCURSION

N.-D.-de-Grâce. – *18 km - 11 miles W by N 100, D 976 on the right and, after 5 km - 3 miles, a narrow turning to the left.*

The unspectacular 12-19C charity chapel on a hillock at the edge of the Rochefort Forest is of interest not for its architecture but for its remarkable collection of ex votos (more than 100 dating from 17-20C), including one offered by Anne of Austria for the birth of the future Louis XIV in 1638 after 23 years of childless marriage (ex voto dated 1666 on the south pillar of the chancel). Off the cloisters is an echo-chamber where two people standing in opposite corners facing the wall, and speaking quietly, can hear each other distinctly. It was used for hearing the confessions of lepers.

Go round the entrance building to the right to the Stations of the Cross; from the terrace there is a **view**★ of the Lance Mountain (NE), Mount Ventoux (NE), the Vaucluse Plateau (E), the Montagnette and the Alpilles (SSE) and the Rhône Plain.

Abbreviations used on maps and town plans

Abb^{e}	abbaye	**abbey**
Anc^{ne}	ancienne	**old, former**
Av.	avenue	**avenue**
B^{d}	boulevard	**boulevard**
Belv^{re}	belvédère	**viewpoint**
B^{ge}	barrage	**dam**
C^{ade}	cascade	**waterfall**
C^{al}	canal	**canal**
Carr^{es}	carrières	**quarries**
Cath.	cathédrale	**cathedral**
Ch.	chemin	**path, track**
Ch^{au}	château	**castle, château**
Ch^{lle}	chapelle	**chapel**
C^{que}	cirque	**circus**
D^{r}	docteur	**doctor**
Égl.	église	**church**
Établ^{t}	établissement	**institution**
Ét^{g}	étang	**pool, lake, lagoon**
F^{ne}	fontaine	**fountain**
G^{al}	général	**general**
G^{ffre}	gouffre	**abyss, hole**
G^{ges}	gorges	**gorges**
Gr^{de}	grande	**large, big**
M^{al}	maréchal	**marshal**
MF, M^{on} F^{re}	maison forestière	**forester's lodge, hut**
M^{gne}	montagne	**mountain**
Mon^{t}	monument	**monument**
M^{t}	mont	**mount, hill, mountain**
Nat.	national	**national**
N.-D.	Notre-Dame	**Our Lady**
Pl.	place	**square**
Pl^{au}	plateau	**plateau**
Prés^{t}	président	**president**
P^{te}	porte	**gate, gateway, door**
Q.	quai	**quay**
R.	rue	**street**
Rd-Pt	rond-point	**roundabout**
R^{er}	rocher	**rock**
S^{ce}	source	**spring**
S^{t}	saint	**saint**
S^{te}	sainte	**saint**
Sup.	supérieure	**upper**
Th.	théâtre	**theatre**
U^{se}	usine	**factory, works**
V^{on}	vallon	**valley**

INDEX

Fontaine-de-Vaucluse .... Towns, sights and tourist regions.
Claparèdes Plateau .... Other places referred to in the text.
Sévigné, Mme de .... Historic personnages described, titles of works and local terms
Manades explained in the text.

Where there is more than one reference, main articles are in bold type; amphitheatres are under A, canals and caves under C, excavations (Roman) under E, museums under M, Nature reserves under N and Roman theatres under T.

The Department is given in brackets after the town; where names have had to be abbreviated Alpes-de-H.-Pr.: Alpes-de-Haute-Provence, B.-du-R.: Bouches-du-Rhône

MANUFACTURE FRANÇAISE DES PNEUMATIQUES MICHELIN
Société en commandite par actions au capital de 700 000 000 de F.
Place des Carmes-Déchaux – 63 Clermont-Ferrand (France)
R.C.S. Clermont-Fd B 855 200 507

Dépot légal 10-85 – ISBN 2 06 013 642-3 – ISSN 0763-1383

Printed in France 7-85-30
Photocomposition : Coupé S.A., Sautron – Impression : Lazare-Ferry à Paris n° 8164